NATIONAL GEOGRAPHIC KiDS

ALMANAC 2026

An emperor penguin in Antarctica goes airborne at the edge of an ice floe.

NATIONAL GEOGRAPHIC KiDS

ALMANAC 2026

NATIONAL GEOGRAPHIC
WASHINGTON, D.C.

National Geographic Kids Books
gratefully acknowledges the following people for their help
with the *National Geographic Kids Almanac*.

Stacey McClain of the
National Geographic Explorer Programs

Amazing Animals

Suzanne Braden, Director, Pandas International

Dr. Rodolfo Coria, Paleontologist,
Plaza Huincul, Argentina

Dr. Sylvia Earle, National Geographic
Explorer in Residence

Dr. Thomas R. Holtz, Jr., Senior Lecturer,
Vertebrate Paleontology,
Department of Geology, University of Maryland

Dr. Luke Hunter, Executive Director, Panthera

Nizar Ibrahim, National Geographic Explorer

Dereck and Beverly Joubert,
National Geographic Explorers in Residence

"Dino" Don Lessem, President, Exhibits Rex

Kathy B. Maher, Research Editor (former),
National Geographic magazine

Kathleen Martin, Canadian Sea Turtle Network

Barbara Nielsen, Polar Bears International

Andy Prince, Austin Zoo

Julia Thorson, Translator, Zurich, Switzerland

Dennis vanEngelsdorp, Senior Extension Associate,
Pennsylvania Department of Agriculture

Space and Earth
Science and Technology

Tim Appenzeller, Chief Magazine Editor, *Nature*

Dr. Rick Fienberg, Press Officer and Director of Communications,
American Astronomical Society

Dr. José de Ondarza, Associate Professor,
Department of Biological Sciences, State University
of New York, College at Plattsburgh

Lesley B. Rogers, Managing Editor (former),
National Geographic magazine

Dr. Enric Sala, National Geographic Explorer in Residence

Abigail A. Tipton, Director of Research (former),
National Geographic magazine

Erin Vintinner, Biodiversity Specialist,
Center for Biodiversity and Conservation at the
American Museum of Natural History

Barbara L. Wyckoff, Research Editor (former),
National Geographic magazine

Culture Connection

Dr. Wade Davis, National Geographic
Explorer in Residence

Deirdre Mullervy, Managing Editor,
Gallaudet University Press

Wonders of Nature

Anatta, NOAA Public Affairs Officer

Dr. Robert Ballard,
National Geographic Explorer in Residence

Douglas H. Chadwick, Wildlife Biologist and Contributor
to *National Geographic* magazine

Susan K. Pell, Ph.D., Science and Public Programs Manager,
United States Botanic Garden

History Happens

Dr. Sylvie Beaudreau, Associate Professor,
Department of History, State University of New York

Elspeth Deir, Assistant Professor, Faculty of Education,
Queens University, Kingston, Ontario, Canada

Dr. Gregory Geddes, Professor, Global Studies,
State University of New York–Orange,
Middletown-Newburgh, New York

Dr. Fredrik Hiebert, National Geographic Visiting Fellow

Micheline Joanisse, Media Relations Officer,
Natural Resources Canada

Dr. Robert D. Johnston,
Associate Professor and Director of the
Teaching of History Program, University of Illinois at Chicago

Dickson Mansfield, Geography Instructor (retired),
Faculty of Education, Queens University,
Kingston, Ontario, Canada

Tina Norris, U.S. Census Bureau

Parliamentary Information and Research Service,
Library of Parliament, Ottawa, Canada

Karyn Pugliese, Acting Director, Communications,
Assembly of First Nations

Geography Rocks

Dr. Kristin Bietsch, Research Associate,
Population Reference Bureau

Carl Haub, Senior Demographer,
Conrad Taeuber Chair of Public Information,
Population Reference Bureau

Dr. Toshiko Kaneda, Senior Research Associate,
Population Reference Bureau

Dr. Walt Meier, National Snow and Ice Data Center

Dr. Richard W. Reynolds, NOAA's National Climatic Data Center

United States Census Bureau, Public Help Desk

Experts cited here formed the foundation of research and consultation during the creation of earlier editions of the *National Geographic Kids Almanac*. Subsequent editions have been published every year. Each edition is thoroughly reviewed and updated using additional sources and in collaboration with current experts and National Geographic Explorers.

Contents

YOUR WORLD 2026 — 8

- TALKING PLANTS **10**
- SHEEP "LAMB-SCAPING" **10**
- AMAZING SPOTLESS GIRAFFE **11**
- INCREDIBLE 3D-PRINTED HOUSE **11**
- SERIAL BURGLAR BEAR **12**
- TEENAGE TYRANNOSAUR'S LAST MEAL **12**
- HOW ANIMALS SEE COLOR **13**
- CAT FACIAL EXPRESSIONS **14**
- FLOATING SOLAR PANELS **15**
- WORMS IN A DEEP FREEZE **15**
- COOL EVENTS 2026 **16**
- EARTH-SIZE EXOPLANET **17**
- CAR-CHARGING ROAD! **17**
- CARTWHEELING SNAKES **17**

GREATEST BREAKTHROUGHS — 18

- DISCOVERIES **20**
- RESEARCHING OUR WORLD **26**
- MORE FOR YOU **32** 
  - Greatest Breakthroughs Quiz
  - Write a Letter That Gets Results

AMAZING ANIMALS — 34

- ANIMAL FUN **36**
- CLASSIFICATION **44**
- ANIMALS IN PERIL **46**
- INTO THE WATER **50**
- STANDOUT SPECIES **54**
- ANIMAL FRIENDS **58**
- INTO THE WILD **60**
- INSECTS **64**
- WILD CATS **68**
- ANIMALS IN ACTION **74**
- DINOSAURS **76**
- MORE FOR YOU **84**
  - Amazing Animals Quiz
  - Wildly Good Animal Reports

SPACE AND EARTH — 86

- SPACE **88**
- EARTH **96**
- MORE FOR YOU **106**
  - Space and Earth Quiz
  - Ace Your Science Fair

AWESOME EXPLORATION 108

EXPLORERS 110
PLANET PROTECTION 116
PHOTOGRAPHY 118
NO LIMITS 122
IN THE KNOW 124
MORE FOR YOU 126
   Awesome Exploration Quiz
   How to Write a Perfect Essay

FUN AND GAMES 128

BOREDOM-BUSTING GAMES, PUZZLES, AND MORE FUN STUFF 130

LAUGH OUT LOUD 148

JOKES AND RIDDLES TO TICKLE YOUR FUNNY BONE 150

CULTURE CONNECTION 164

HOLIDAYS 166
AROUND THE WORLD 174
FOOD 176
MONEY 178
LANGUAGE 180
ANCIENT BELIEFS 182
RELIGION 184
MORE FOR YOU 186
   Culture Connection Quiz
   Explore a New Culture

CONTENTS

SCIENCE AND TECHNOLOGY 188

INVENTIONS AND TECHNOLOGY 190
BIOLOGY 194
PLANTS 196
HUMAN BODY 198
FUTURE TECHNOLOGY 206 
MORE FOR YOU 210
  Science and Technology Quiz
  This Is How It's Done!

WONDERS OF NATURE 212

BIOMES 214
OCEANS 218
AWESOME NATURE 220
WEATHER 222
TURBULENT EARTH 230
MORE FOR YOU 234
  Wonders of Nature Quiz
  Oral Reports Made Easy

HISTORY HAPPENS 236

LIFE IN THE PAST 238
INTERNATIONAL CONFLICTS 250
WORLD LEADERS 252
MORE FOR YOU 266
  History Happens Quiz
  Brilliant Biographies

GEOGRAPHY ROCKS 268

MAPS 270
GEOGRAPHIC FEATURES 276
CONTINENTS 278
COUNTRIES 306
TRAVEL 332
MORE FOR YOU 352
  Geography Rocks Quiz
  Finding Your Way Around

GAME ANSWERS 354 | MORE RESOURCES 355 | TEXT CREDITS 356
ILLUSTRATION CREDITS 357 | INDEX 360

YOUR WORLD 2026

In 2026, the Winter Olympics will take place in Italy, in the cities of Milan and Cortina d'Ampezzo.

TALKING PLANTS

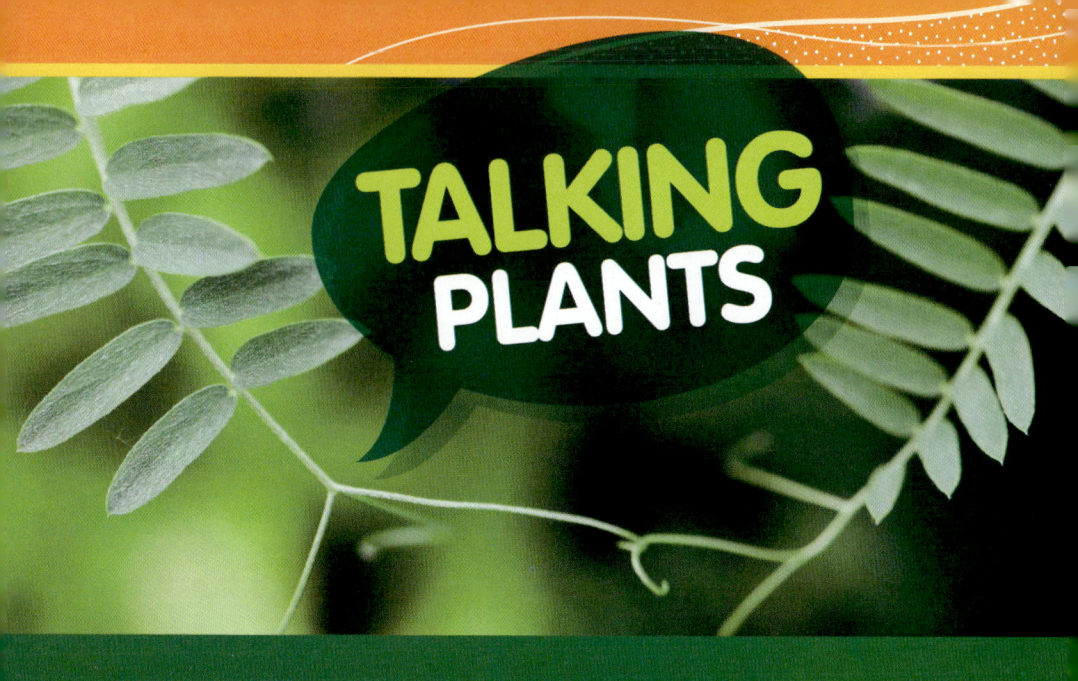

Do plants talk to each other? You better be-leaf it, say scientists in Japan, who have recorded communication between neighboring plants. But it's not like the plants are having an actual conversation; rather, one will release certain molecules into the air as a warning sign when it's facing potential harm from threats like insects. The neighboring plant then "sniffs out" those molecules through cells lining the tiny holes in its leaves, which act like a nose to sense the surrounding conditions. When the healthy plant picks up on potential danger, it knows to defend itself from those incoming insects so they'll, well, bug off.

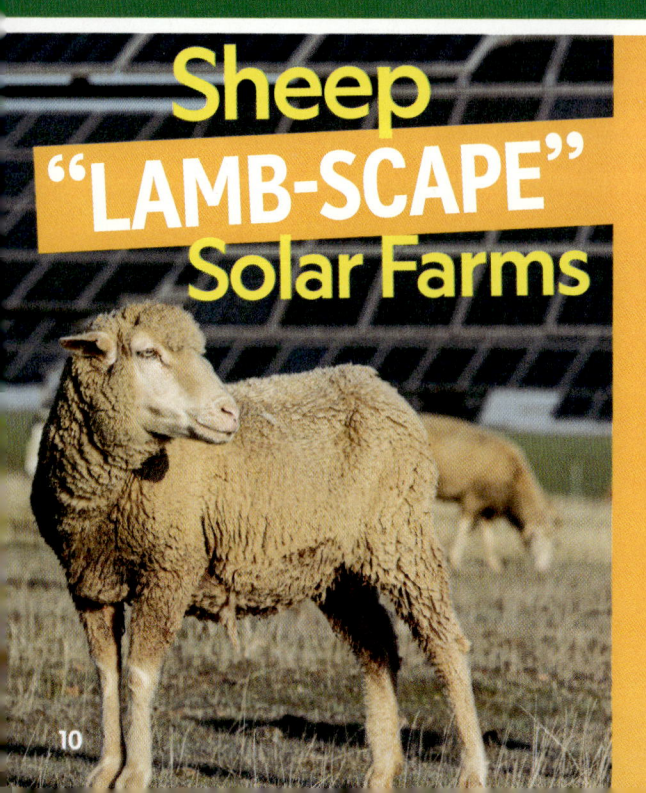

Sheep "LAMB-SCAPE" Solar Farms

Why mow the grass when you can just have sheep munch it?
That's the idea behind solar-farm grazing. Herds of sheep snack on the wildflowers, weeds, clover, and other plants that pop up on solar farms, where fields are filled with panels that collect the sun's energy. Instead of farmers having to hire a human to mow with a machine—which is more expensive and can cause pollution—the hungry herds take care of business by keeping the farm's vegetation short in an eco-friendly way. "Lamb-scaping" away the pesky plants ensures that the solar panels are absorbing enough sunlight and reduces the risk of fire. In turn, the sheep stay happy and healthy. Now that's what you call a win-win.

YOUR WORLD

Spotless Giraffe
BORN IN TENNESSEE

Baby giraffes are amazing to begin with: They're the size of an adult human at birth, and they can run within 10 hours of being born. But one giraffe calf in a Tennessee, U.S.A., zoo was extra special, as it was born without spots! Said to be one of the only patternless giraffes in the world, Kipekee—a name that means "unique" in Swahili—likely got its rare appearance from a genetic mutation or a rare condition that, so far, doesn't seem to be impacting its health. And while a giraffe's iconic pattern does help keep it camouflaged in the wild, Kipekee, who was immediately accepted by the rest of the giraffes at the zoo, should stay safe and sound living in captivity.

FIRST TWO-STORY 3D-PRINTED HOUSE IN THE U.S.

You can 3D print just about anything these days—even a two-story house! That's what the design studio HANNAH did in Texas, U.S.A., by creating a three-bedroom home using layers of concrete. The spacious house, which is sturdy enough to withstand hurricanes and heavy storms, took 330 total hours to print, using a machine that weighs more than two elephants. Could 3D printing be the wave of the future when it comes to construction? Experts say it's a strong possibility, because printing requires less time—and money— than traditional building techniques, allowing for more affordable housing options.

THIS BEAR WAS A SERIAL BURGLAR

Captured! After a run of 21 home invasions, one bandit of a black bear was finally (and safely) apprehended by wildlife biologists in South Lake Tahoe, California, U.S.A. Before she was caught in the act, the burgling bear known as "Hank the Tank" went viral for lurking around local homes, where she'd tear off screen doors, rummage through garbage bins, and scratch up cars. But did authorities catch the correct bear? Originally, it was thought that Hank was a single male bear, but the animal they apprehended was actually female. So while one Hank is off the streets—and living in an animal sanctuary—other brazen bears may still be at large.

TEENAGE TYRANNOSAUR'S LAST MEAL

DINO DRUMSTICKS: It's what's for dinner. At least it was for one teenage *Gorgosaurus*, which scarfed down the hind legs of two small, birdlike dinosaurs before it died some 75 million years ago. Paleontologists were able to determine the meal's details by inspecting the fossilized contents in the stomach of the *Gorgosaurus* individual—a close cousin of *T. rex*—whose remains were unearthed in Alberta, Canada. By removing some rock from its rib cage, they revealed the complete back legs of two baby dinosaurs, indicating that it wasn't long after the young predator had eaten that it died. This meal reveal marked the first time a tyrannosaur skeleton was found with its stomach contents preserved inside, offering experts their fill of insight about the giant carnivore's diet.

YOUR WORLD

HOW ANIMALS SEE COLOR

Is the sky blue? Not if you ask many species of birds, which actually see a violet sky above. Why? Because of the unique structure of their eyes, birds can see ultraviolet light, allowing them to take in a broader and bolder array of colors than humans can. So while the sky may appear to be a periwinkle blue to us, birds peer up and see purple.

Birds aren't the only animals that see colors differently from how humans see them. It's all about the number and types of cone cells in the eyes, which are sensitive to different wavelengths of light. For example, humans have three types of cone cells, which allow us to see blue, green, and red light. These cone cells in the eye work together with the brain to help us perceive millions of colors. Birds, on the other hand, have up to five types of cone cells, enabling them to see an even wider rainbow than we do. A honeybee, which is equipped to pick up ultraviolet (UV), green, and blue wavelengths, is most attracted to purple, violet, and blue flowers, since they're easiest to detect.

And then there are species that see a much less colorful world: With two types of cones, dogs only see blue, yellow, and shades of gray. A mouse also has two types of cones, and sees the world in blues and greens.

But despite the differences, no one animal is at a huge disadvantage when it comes to how they take in the world around them. Over time, each species has developed unique adaptations that help them navigate through life, no matter the color.

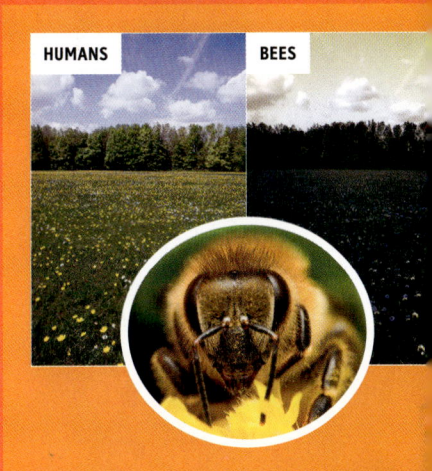

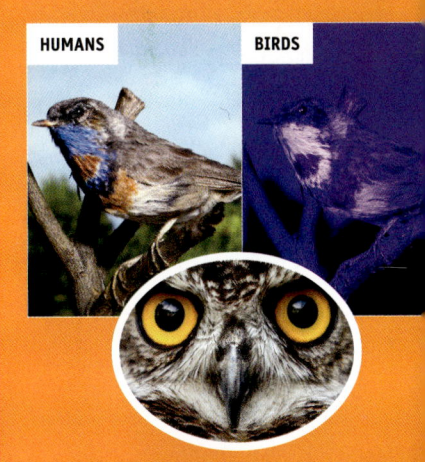

Cats have nearly 300 facial expressions

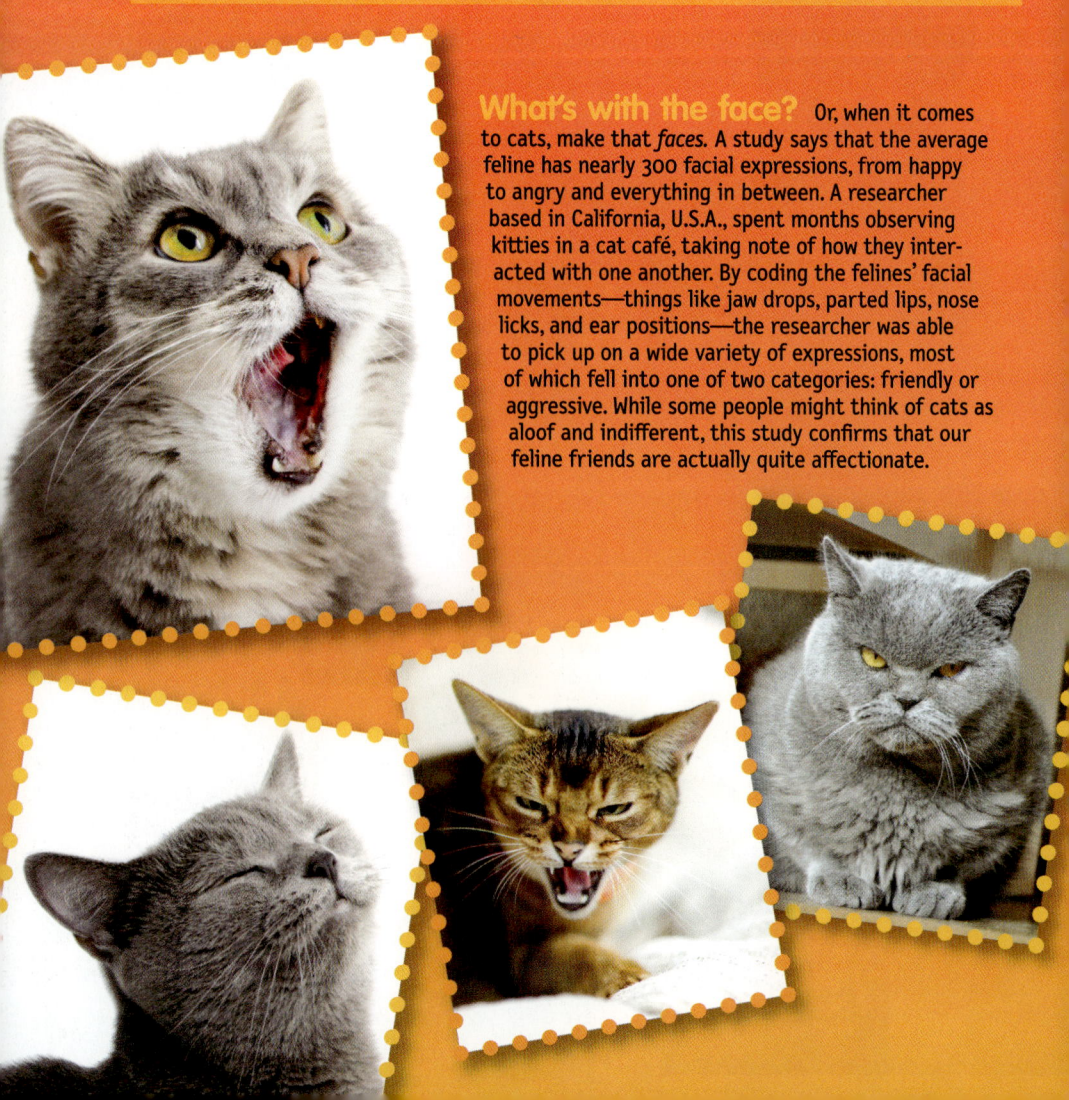

What's with the face? Or, when it comes to cats, make that *faces*. A study says that the average feline has nearly 300 facial expressions, from happy to angry and everything in between. A researcher based in California, U.S.A., spent months observing kitties in a cat café, taking note of how they interacted with one another. By coding the felines' facial movements—things like jaw drops, parted lips, nose licks, and ear positions—the researcher was able to pick up on a wide variety of expressions, most of which fell into one of two categories: friendly or aggressive. While some people might think of cats as aloof and indifferent, this study confirms that our feline friends are actually quite affectionate.

YOUR WORLD

FLOATING SOLAR PANELS

Here's an idea to float on: What happens if you attach solar panels to rafts in a lake or reservoir? The answer is a surprising new method of creating renewable energy—let's call it a wave of the future. Floating solar panels are being used around the world as a way to produce electricity from the sun in a safe and eco-friendly way. They're space savers, too: Instead of solar panels taking up real estate on land that could be used for agriculture or buildings, they're free to float around in lakes and reservoirs. One more perk of floating panels? Thanks to light reflecting off the water, some are able to absorb light from both sides, which can produce 10 to 20 percent more power than land-based panels.

Worms STILL ALIVE After 46,000 Years in a Deep Freeze

At least one species of worm has a superpower: the ability to live through thousands of years trapped in ice! Found in a chunk of 46,000-year-old Siberian permafrost, a roundworm was revived when the ice thawed. How did it stay alive? Experts say the worm was in a dormant state known as cryptobiosis, which put the species in a slumber that straddles the line between life and death. When in cryptobiosis, the worm can get by without water or oxygen and endure extreme temperatures—and ultimately emerge intact and alive. While roundworms have been known in the past to stay in cryptobiosis for a few decades, this discovery shows they can potentially stay in that state for much, much longer.

Cool Events 2026

WORLD ART DAY
Paint, craft, sculpt, or otherwise flex your creativity to honor all things art!

April 15

WORLD BRAILLE DAY
Lend your awareness to visually impaired people worldwide on this day that also celebrates the birthday of the Braille system founder, Louis Braille.

January 4

INTERNATIONAL DANCE DAY
Show off your smooth moves on this day that recognizes all types of dancing.

April 29

2026 WINTER OLYMPICS
The world's strongest winter athletes descend on Milan and Cortina d'Ampezzo, Italy, for two weeks of intense competition. 
(For more on this, see pages 348–349.)

February 6–22

INTERNATIONAL DAY OF FRIENDSHIP
Send a shout-out to all of your best buds and good friends, and hopefully they'll send the good vibes right back your way.

July 30

FRIDAY THE 13TH
Triple the 13s! This year will mark the first time there have been three Friday the 13ths since 2015.

February 13
March 13
November 13

WORLD VEGETARIAN DAY
Plant power rules on this day, intended to put the vegetarian lifestyle in the spotlight.

October 1

WORLD WILDLIFE DAY
Show some love to your favorite animal today, which doubles as a callout to act in support of endangered and threatened species worldwide.

March 3

WORLD KINDNESS DAY
A little kindness goes a long way toward making the world a happier and better place for everyone.

November 13

YOUR WORLD

EARTH-SIZE EXOPLANET
COULD GIVE CLUES ABOUT EARTH

The universe is full of surprises. Case in point? The discovery of an Earth-size planet orbiting around a sunlike star, right in our very own solar backyard. Located 73 light-years away, this exoplanet—called HD 63433 d—is similar to Earth in shape, size, and the fact that it orbits a star. But there are vast differences, too, like how HD 63433 d doesn't rotate, so one side is locked in permanent darkness and cold, while the part facing the star can reach a sizzling 2300°F (1260°C). Still, scientists can study this new young planet to get more clues about how Earth formed and has evolved.

CHARGE UP ON THE ROAD— LITERALLY!

Imagine never having to stop to charge up an electric car. Instead, you simply drive down the road, and the car charges as you go! That may be an option in the near future, thanks to a technology that can store electricity in cement. Researchers are developing a way to infuse blocks of cement with a type of carbon that conducts electricity, a method that could also power homes that have a concrete foundation. Roads made with this type of concrete could store renewable power and deliver it to electric cars as they drive, sort of like the way wireless chargers charge smartphones. Now that's powerful stuff.

CARTWHEELING SNAKES

Forget slithering: Some snakes get around by cartwheeling! Scientists in Southeast Asia observed the dwarf reed snake using a unique rolling movement by pushing its tail off the ground and launching its body forward to propel into a cartwheel motion. Researchers believe that the snake isn't just working on its acrobatic skills; it likely saves this rolling act for times when it feels threatened, perhaps as a way to confuse or distract predators. *Ssssneaky!*

GREATEST
BREAKTHROUGHS

Robots dance at a World Artificial Intelligence Conference in Shanghai, China.

DISCOVERIES

TOP 10 BREAKTHROUGHS OF THE 21ST CENTURY

While new discoveries are made almost every day, some findings are so extraordinary that their impact lasts for centuries. They create important changes around the world and open doors to new studies, technology, and cultural shifts. Here are some of the biggest breakthroughs in recent years.

HEALTH

The Year: 2001
The Breakthrough: Human Genome Mapping

It was an ambitious goal: Plot the chemical bases of some 25,000 genes that make up human DNA—also known as the human genome. But in the early 2000s, a team of scientists did just that. By determining the sequence of the bases in human DNA, researchers have gained a clearer understanding of what happens within the body and why, leading to new treatments for diseases and creating a flood of possibilities for advancement in medical research.

The project wrapped up in 2003, but mapping the human genome is a work in progress. Scientists continue to update the map and fill in gaps with the goal of creating the most complete and accurate picture of the human genome sequence. The hope? That we'll continue to learn about the human body, the origins of diseases, and how to treat them.

GREATEST BREAKTHROUGHS

COMMUNICATION

The Year: 2007
The Breakthrough: Smartphones

Can you imagine life without smartphones? Up until around 2007, that was the reality for most people. It wasn't until Apple debuted the first model of its iPhone—selling some six million units—that smartphones changed our daily lives. Other tech companies soon followed with their own versions of the devices. Suddenly, instead of having to log on to a computer at home, many people had access to the internet in their pocket or bag. Soon messaging apps, video chatting, and the ability to look up anything, anywhere, all became seamless and standard, forever changing the way people around the world communicated. Today, more than half the people in the world have a smartphone.

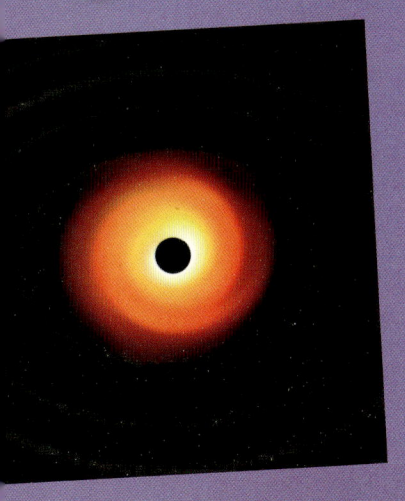

SPACE

The Year: 2015
The Breakthrough: Gravitational Waves

Detected directly for the very first time in 2015 by the super-sensitive Laser Interferometer Gravitational-Wave Observatory, gravitational waves are invisible and incredibly fast ripples in space. Traveling at the speed of light (that's 186,000 miles per second!), these waves are created when something in space moves at an extremely high rate, like when two black holes merge, or when a star explodes. The phenomenon is similar to the way a speeding boat can create a ripple effect in the water surrounding it as it moves, except these waves squeeze and stretch anything in their path. Scientists have known about gravitational waves for over a century—Albert Einstein theorized about them back in 1916—but it took until this century to detect and get a clearer image of them in real life.

PALEONTOLOGY

The Year: 2010
The Breakthrough: Dinosaurs' True Colors

Here's a bright fact: Dinosaurs weren't just green and brown! In 2010, scientists released the first full-body color reconstruction of a dinosaur. Using advanced imaging technology, researchers were able to see microscopic details inside the fossils, including the presence of melanin, the natural pigment that gives scales, skin, and feathers their color.

Scientists still have more to learn. Did dinosaurs use their coloring for camouflage, for communication, or to attract mates like animals do today? By seeing dinosaurs in this new light, researchers will get a better idea of how they behaved and interacted with one another.

CAUDIPTERYX

DISCOVERIES

TECHNOLOGY
The Year: 2010
The Breakthrough: AI in Daily Life

"Alexa, what's the weather like today?" Not too long ago, people weren't able to ask a device in their home simple questions like this one. The once far-off concept of using artificial intelligence (AI) in our daily lives became reality for many starting in the 2010s, when major companies like Apple (with Siri) and Amazon (with the Echo, which uses the voice assistant Alexa) introduced AI-based personal assistants to be used in the home. Now, AI is present all over our world, from those home devices to interacting with chatbots. While AI is super cool, it's also important to be super careful about how you use it: Not all information you get from AI is reliable or safe, so make sure you talk to a parent about how you're spending your screen time.

NATURE & ENVIRONMENT
The Year: 2023
The Breakthrough: Island Runs on 100% Renewable Power

Can you run a country entirely on renewable energy? If you look at El Hierro, the smallest of the Canary Islands off the coast of Spain, the answer may be yes. El Hierro functioned for 28 days in a row using only wind and water power. And its 11,000 residents are committed to keeping up that streak, for good reason. Because of the island's remote location, self-sufficiency is key, as it can take extra time and effort for them to receive outside help. For now, the island's main hydro-wind power station pumps out enough wind and hydro energy to drastically reduce their reliance on diesel fuel and take important steps in fighting planet-warming pollution.

ANIMALS
The Year: 2022
The Breakthrough: Insect Breaks Down Plastic

While tending to her beehive one day, a scientist removed a few wax worms—the larval stage of the wax moth—and placed them in a plastic bag. Later, she noticed the bag had holes in it! But the caterpillars didn't just eat their way through the bag. Their saliva had actually broken down the bag's plastic molecules. It turns out, the wax worm's spit contains enzymes that dissolve polyethylene, a type of plastic that can take years to break down in a landfill.

The wax worms demonstrated a neat bio-recycling trick that could one day help combat plastic pollution. While having millions of caterpillars feast on piles of plastic isn't the most sustainable (or speedy) solution, the potential to replicate their enzymes in a lab might be.

GREATEST BREAKTHROUGHS

SCIENCE
The Year: 2022
The Breakthrough: Fusion Ignition

In 2022, scientists took one step closer to tapping into near-limitless supplies of energy. How? By achieving fusion ignition, a reaction that made more energy than they put in to the process. In a special lab, researchers used lasers to heat up a tiny pellet of hydrogen atoms with enough force to fuse the atoms together to create helium—and produce excess energy. The experiment took just 20 billionths of a second to complete, but its impact will last a lifetime.

It showed that fusion ignition is possible. And because the energy that's produced doesn't rely on fossil fuels or release harmful greenhouse gases, like other types of energy do, there's a chance it could someday help fight climate change. Now that's a win-win.

Talk about a *royal* discovery: In 2022, archaeologists in the Middle East unearthed the remains of a 4,500-year-old palace in an area believed to be one of the earliest known cities in the world. An excavation in the Iraqi desert revealed the mudbrick walls of the Lord Palace of the Kings, once a grand structure in the ancient city of Girsu. The team identified exquisite carvings and tablets engraved with symbols and script as well as a temple, further fueling theories about the sophistication and innovation of this ancient Sumerian civilization. Experts hope that continued exploration of this once-lost palace will reveal even more secrets of a forgotten ancient world.

ARCHAEOLOGY
The Year: 2022
The Breakthrough: 4,500-Year-Old Palace Found

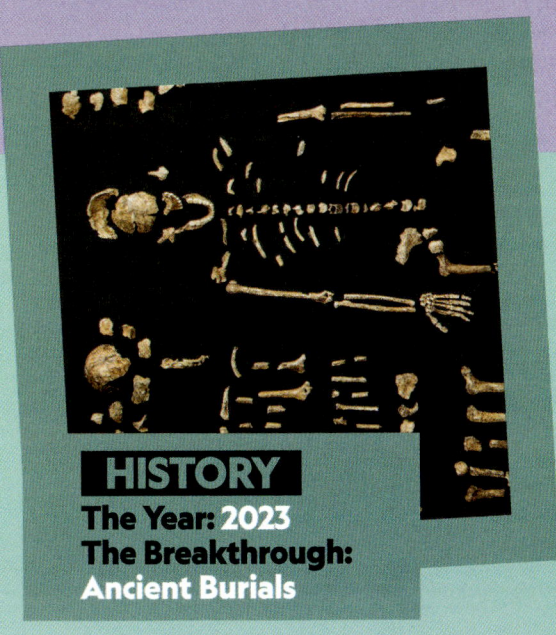

HISTORY
The Year: 2023
The Breakthrough: Ancient Burials

In 2015, Nat Geo Explorer in Residence Lee Berger reported a shocking discovery in South Africa's Rising Star cave system: the remains of a human ancestor species new to science. But the study of *Homo naledi*, as the species was named, was just beginning. In 2023, Berger and his team announced they'd found possible evidence that *Homo naledi* carefully buried their dead inside the cave system—some 100,000 years before the first known burials by human ancestors. The team's interpretation of the graves is raising new questions about how *Homo naledi* lived, and died. Berger and his team continue to examine the fossils and the site for clues about the past. (See page 24 for more information.)

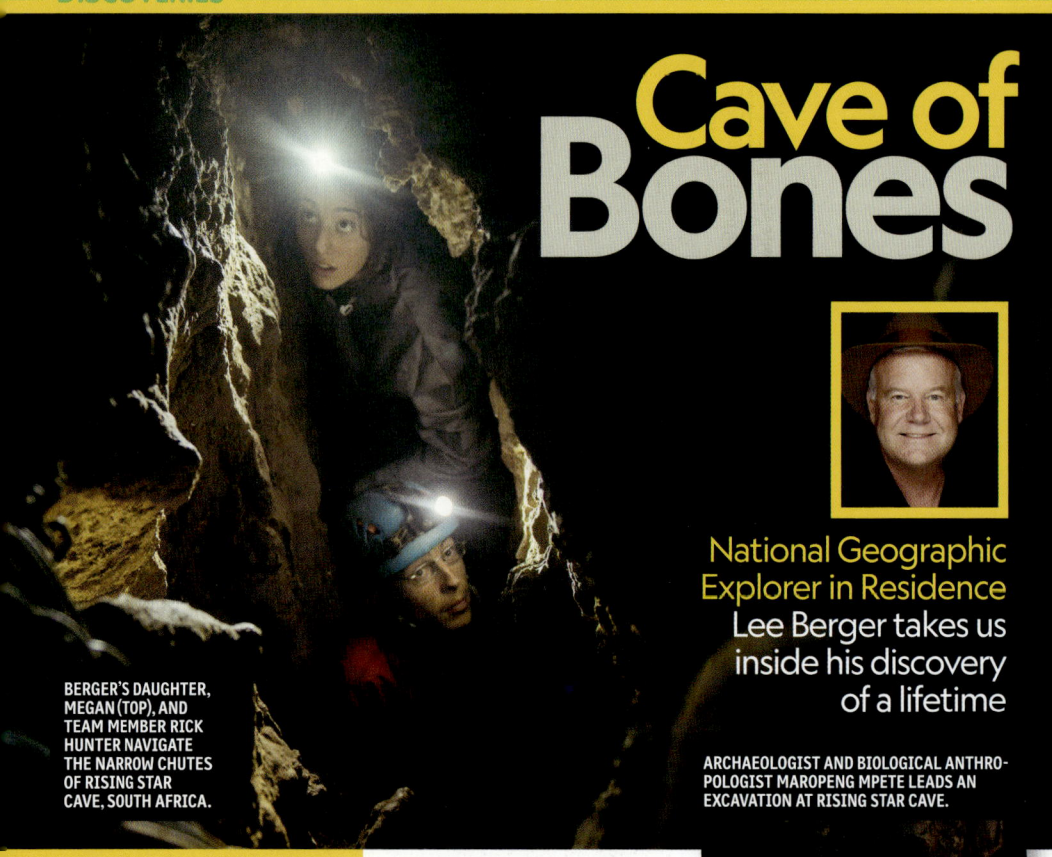

DISCOVERIES

Cave of Bones

BERGER'S DAUGHTER, MEGAN (TOP), AND TEAM MEMBER RICK HUNTER NAVIGATE THE NARROW CHUTES OF RISING STAR CAVE, SOUTH AFRICA.

National Geographic Explorer in Residence **Lee Berger takes us inside his discovery of a lifetime**

ARCHAEOLOGIST AND BIOLOGICAL ANTHROPOLOGIST MAROPENG MPETE LEADS AN EXCAVATION AT RISING STAR CAVE.

Back in 2013, a pair of spelunkers came across what looked like human remains deep within the Rising Star cave in South Africa. The cavers had shimmied their way down a narrow chute and landed in a room some 100 feet (30 m) below ground, its dirt floor littered with fossils. They snapped photos of the bones, which ultimately wound up with Dr. Lee Berger, a paleoanthropologist who then organized an expedition into the mazelike chambers and tunnels.

BELOW THE SURFACE

Berger conducted the expedition from aboveground, at first. Because of the narrowness of the passageways—no wider than a laptop in some parts—he wasn't able to safely squeeze through. "The spaces are incredibly tight and it's extremely dangerous," he explains. "So I found smaller-size, very experienced cavers and explorers who could get in there."

At first, Berger's exploration team was able to relay significant photos, artifacts, and information to him. Their first major discovery? That the bones belonged to a never-before-known species named *Homo naledi* that lived 500,000 years ago, long before humans were known to have lived. *Homo naledi* had humanlike features, but a much smaller brain— a characteristic often associated with lower intelligence.

But Berger had a hunch that *Homo naledi* may have been pretty advanced despite their brain size. The massive amounts of bones found in the room within the cave indicated that they may have used the spot as a burial ground—a behavior previously assumed was only acted out by humans. Was there any other evidence that would support this theory? Berger decided that he needed to see the room with his own eyes.

24

GREATEST BREAKTHROUGHS

BERGER REACHES OUT FROM THE LAST CHUTE INSIDE RISING STAR CAVE.

A TIGHT SQUEEZE

"There's just so much you can determine by looking through the lens of someone else's camera," he said. "To fully answer our questions, I needed to see it for myself." So he spent months carefully watching what he ate and exercising to lose 55 pounds (25 kg)—losing just enough weight to squeeze into the Rising Star cave.

"I made it in, but it was an extreme journey," he says. "It's so tight that you can't put a rope next to your body. I definitely risked my life."

NEW DISCOVERIES

Berger's difficult journey was worth it in the end: Once in the room, he was blown away by what he saw—new discoveries that included evidence of the use of fire, and primitive art carved into the cave walls, possibly to mark graves. Berger spent more than four hours in the cave, narrating everything he saw, hardly believing the words coming out of his mouth as he recorded. "To describe what I was seeing with my own eyes, in my own words, it was incredible," he said.

REWRITING HUMAN HISTORY

Once back aboveground, Berger felt confident that his discoveries debunked previous theories about human evolution. "It's an important moment for humanity," he says. "For centuries, we believed that large brains allowed us to be complex and exceptional. But it's not just about our brain. Because certain rituals were being done thousands of years before us by another species."

BRINGING THE PAST INTO THE FUTURE

Next up, Berger hopes to carefully study all of the artifacts his team has uncovered in Rising Star cave using high-tech testing and forensics to get more clues about this mysterious species. "They're still like aliens to us," he says of *Homo naledi*. "They're complex. We hope to get more of their story as we continue to study them."

However, as *Homo naledi*'s story unfolds, one thing is for sure: Berger is staying on solid ground. "I won't be going back down there. It's too risky," he says of journeying back into Rising Star. "That was a once-in-a-lifetime opportunity."

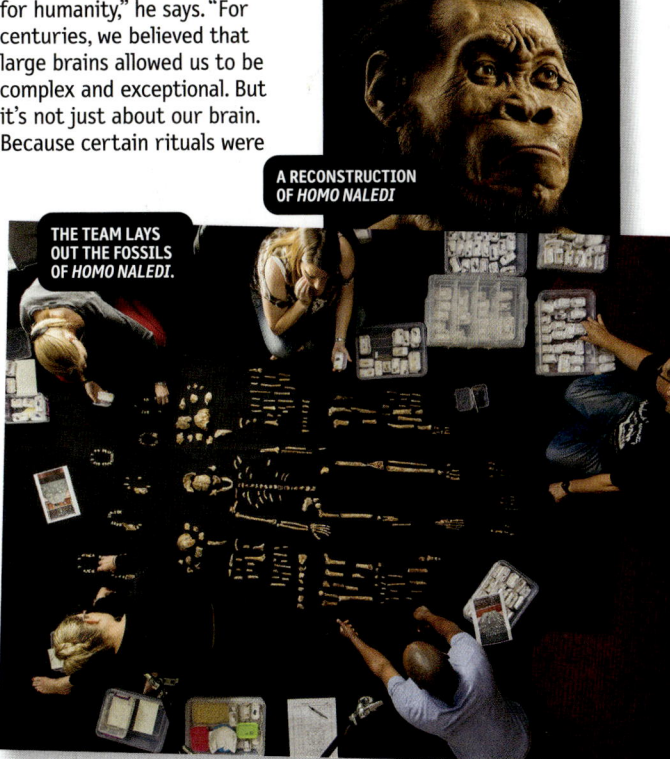

A RECONSTRUCTION OF *HOMO NALEDI*

THE TEAM LAYS OUT THE FOSSILS OF *HOMO NALEDI*.

BERGER HOLDS A SCALE NEXT TO AN ENGRAVING INSIDE THE CAVE.

25

RESEARCHING OUR WORLD

How to Find a Fossil

Lee Berger and his nine-year-old son, Matthew, were searching for fossils in Johannesburg, South Africa, when Matthew stumbled over a large brown rock and spied a thin yellow bone barely sticking out of it. He'd found a fossil—and not just any fossil. This was a fossilized bone of a prehuman ancestor, which—thanks to Matthew—would soon be known to science as *Australopithecus sediba*.

Finding a fossil is hard, but if you know what to look for, you can pick one out from all the other rocks and soil around it. Here, Berger shares the clues that led him to a fossil find in South Africa's Free State Province.

1 SCAN FOR THE RIGHT SPOT

Berger looks for an area of erosion that might reveal rocks that are older than those on the surface.

2 FOCUS IN

Next, Berger narrows his search to places where fossils might be eroding out of the surrounding soil.

GREATEST BREAKTHROUGHS

Berger looks for oddities or abnormalities—rocks or objects whose colors don't match the surrounding soil. In this case, he's spotted a white fleck.

4 TAKE A CLOSER LOOK

WHAT DOESN'T BELONG? 3

When Berger gets closer, he can see that it's part of the lower jaw, or mandible, of an ancient antelope.

EXAMINE THE DETAILS 5

Berger notices the shiny enamel of the teeth and the paler look of the bone. The mandible he's found is more than 100,000 years old.

RESEARCHING OUR WORLD

EYE IN THE SKY

Check out these stellar pictures captured by one of the world's most powerful telescopes.

The James Webb Space Telescope, the biggest, most powerful space telescope to ever exist, has been beaming images back to Earth since 2022, and these pictures are shaking up space science.

Traditional telescopes work like a more powerful version of the human eye: They sense visible light that reflects off objects, the same kind of light our brains can see. James Webb is different. It senses infrared light, a type of light we can't see. That means that in addition to capturing much more detailed images of closer objects like our planets, it can also peer way deeper into space. How? James Webb sees the infrared light from super faraway objects that regular telescopes can't see.

In fact, James Webb is so powerful that it can see the infrared light from very distant objects as they looked when light first left them. (It takes a long time for light to travel from deep space to Earth, where we can see it.) That means James Webb can detect light from the first stars, galaxies, and planets to ever form—sometimes more than 13 billion years ago.

TARANTULA NEBULA
Nebulae are star nurseries, where new stars are born. Regular telescopes showed that the Tarantula Nebula has spidery "legs" made of star dust. But the James Webb telescope also spotted tens of thousands of newborn stars here; they're the pale-blue dots in the image.

GREATEST BREAKTHROUGHS

NEPTUNE
Scientists knew that Neptune, like Saturn, has rings—they just usually can't see them very well. But James Webb captured one of the clearest images ever taken of Neptune's rings. Made of dust and rocks, the rings were probably formed from pieces of a destroyed moon.

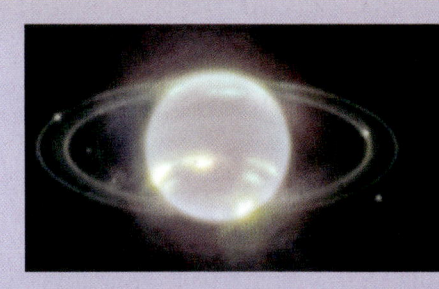

CARTWHEEL GALAXY
Scientists think the Cartwheel galaxy got its shape when a large spiral galaxy smashed into a smaller one with extreme force, creating spiral arms in between two rings that make it look like a wagon wheel. The James Webb telescope was able to spot individual stars within this galaxy.

JUPITER
In this James Webb image, Jupiter's Great Red Spot—the site of a storm wider than planet Earth—appears white because it's reflecting sunlight. The green and red haze at the top and bottom of the planet are auroras, similar to the glowing green northern lights that can be seen near Earth's Arctic region.

JAMES WEBB TELESCOPE
The James Webb Space Telescope now orbits the sun about a million miles (1.6 million km) from Earth. As tall as a two-story house, the golden mirror in the middle allows the telescope to see faraway and faint objects. The diamond-shaped, tennis-court-size sunshield protects the telescope's sensitive instruments.

RESEARCHING OUR WORLD

Make a TELESCOPE

IF YOU WANT A BETTER VIEW OF THE NIGHT SKY BUT don't own a telescope, you can build one of your own. Then take your new telescope out at night and gaze at the amazing night sky. See if you can name some of the constellations that you may spot!

GREATEST BREAKTHROUGHS

FUN FACT

Tire tracks and footprints left behind by astronauts who have visited the moon will stay there forever. Why? There is no wind on the moon to blow them away!

SUPPLY LIST

- 2 paper towel tubes
- paint (any color you like)
- paintbrushes
- scissors
- masking tape
- 2 convex lenses (You can get these from a pair of magnifying glasses, or your parent can order the lenses online.)

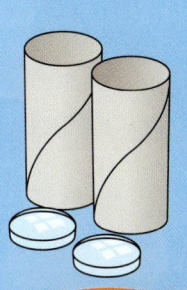

STEPS

1. Paint your paper towel tubes and let them dry.
2. Create the inner tube of the telescope. Using scissors, cut one tube lengthwise only on one side. Curl one side of the cut edge slightly over the other. Then tape the cut edge down. 
3. Insert your inner tube into the second paper towel tube. It should fit snugly into the second tube but still be able to slide in and out. If not, adjust the size of the inner tube. 
4. Tape one convex lens to the outer end of each tube, only around the rim, so you don't cover too much of the lens.
5. Hold your telescope with the inner tube facing your eye. Aim it at an object in the night sky. (Never use your telescope to look at the sun!) You can focus by sliding the inner tube in and out.

Time: about 40 minutes

HOW TO DISTINGUISH A STAR FROM A PLANET

Here's a simple trick to figure out if an object in the night sky is a star or a planet: Stars appear to "twinkle," but planets don't. Turbulence in Earth's atmosphere refracts the light from stars, making them appear to twinkle. Because planets are much closer to us than stars, they don't suffer from the turbulence the way stars do.

MORE FOR YOU

QUIZ WHIZ

What's your innovation IQ? Find out with this quiz!
Write your answers on a piece of paper. Then check them below.

1 **True or false?** The first smartphone debuted in 2017.

2 When trying to find fossils, look for _____.
a. a forest
b. an area of erosion
c. animal poop
d. a swamp

3 In 2022, archaeologists discovered a 4,500-year-old _____.
a. barber shop
b. school
c. zoo
d. palace

4 **True or false?** Jupiter has auroras like Earth's northern lights.

5 The James Webb Space Telescope orbits the sun about _____ from Earth.
a. 100 miles (160 km)
b. 1,000 miles (1,600 km)
c. 1 million miles (1.6 million km)
d. 1 billion miles (1.6 billion km)

Not **STUMPED** yet? Check out the *NATIONAL GEOGRAPHIC KIDS QUIZ WHIZ* collection for more **GROUNDBREAKING** questions!

ANSWERS: 1. False; 2. b; 3. d; 4. True; 5. c

GREATEST BREAKTHROUGHS

HOMEWORK HELP

Write a Letter That Gets Results

Knowing how to write a good letter is a useful skill. It will come in handy when you want to ask an expert for information or advice. Whether you're writing to your local park ranger or emailing a scientist in the field, a great letter will help you get your message across. Most important, a well-written letter makes a good impression.

CHECK OUT THE EXAMPLE BELOW FOR THE ELEMENTS OF A GOOD LETTER.

Your address

Date

Salutation
Always use "Dear" followed by the person's name; use Mr., Mrs., Ms., or Dr. as appropriate.

Introductory paragraph
Give the reason you're writing the letter.

Body
The longest part of the letter, which provides background and your questions. Be specific!

Closing paragraph
Explain what you will do with the answers.

Complimentary closing
Sign off with "Sincerely," or "Thank you."

Your signature

Cameron Lopez
555 Maple Street
Richmond, Virginia 23220

May 1, 2026

Dear Ranger of Richmond River Park,

I am writing to ask you for advice on how to attract local wildlife to my backyard.

Richmond River Park is my favorite place to visit. My family and I go there almost every month. Whenever I'm there, I enjoy seeing all of the different birds, frogs, chipmunks, and other animals around the park. Northern cardinals are my favorite birds!

Last time I was there, a ranger told me that many of the species I see at the park also live near my house! The ranger said that if I want northern cardinals to visit my yard, I should learn about the foods that they eat and the plants that they nest in, and ask my parents to help me add them to our yard.

I would like to know: What do cardinals like to eat? And which types of plants do they pick for building their nests? Lastly, where can my parents find the plants you recommend?

With your advice, I hope to give northern cardinals another place to find food and raise their chicks. That way, my favorite birds will have an inviting space near my house to visit whenever they want!

Thank you very much for your time.

Sincerely,

Cameron Lopez

Cameron Lopez

COMPLIMENTARY CLOSINGS

Sincerely, Thank you, Regards, Best wishes, Respectfully

AMAZING ANIMALS

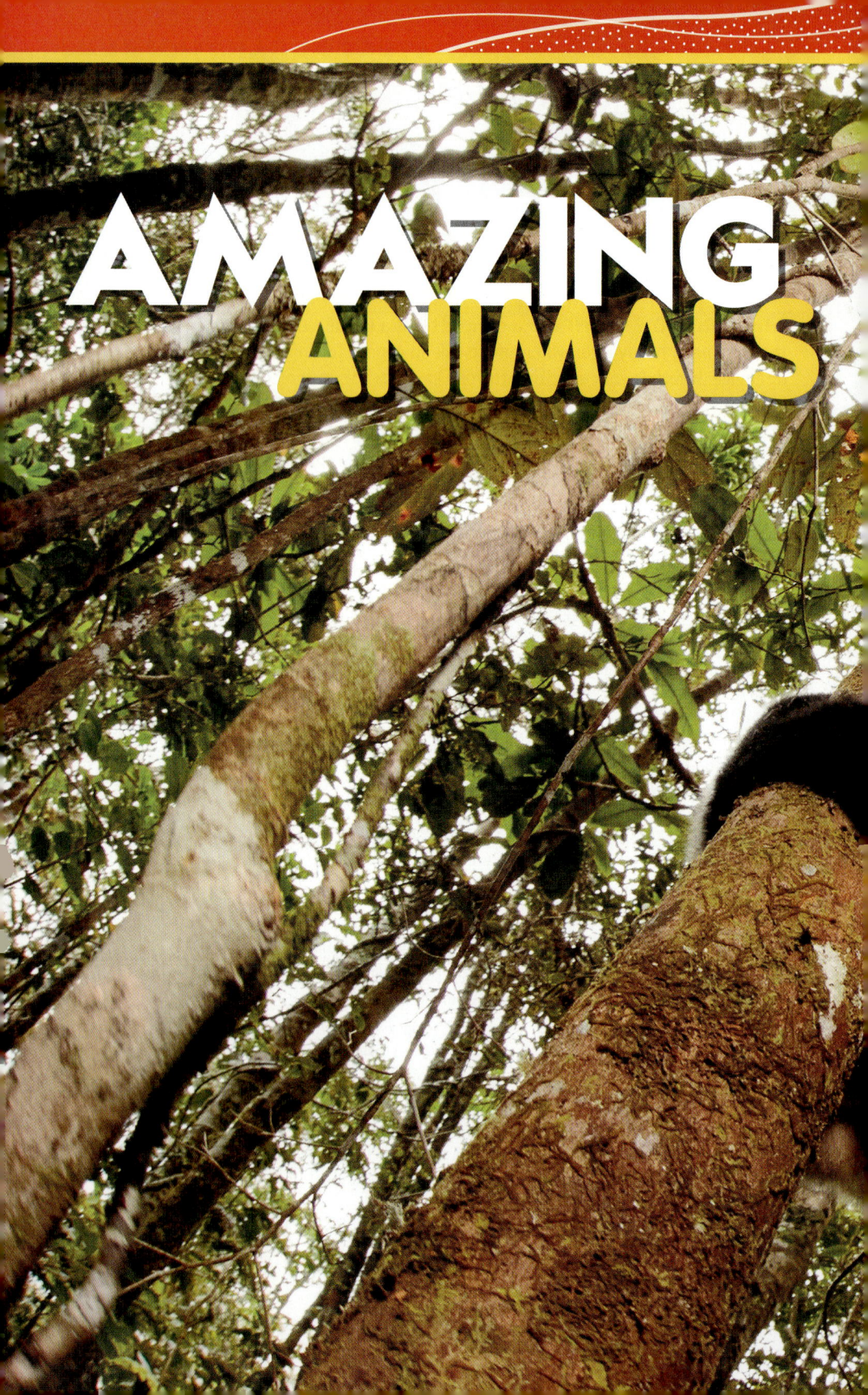

An indri, believed to be the largest lemur species, climbs a tree in Madagascar.

ANIMAL FUN

EXTRAORDINARY ANIMALS

Dog Hangs Ten

SIT? STAY? PLEASE—I CAN DO BETTER THAN THAT!

ABBIE GIRL AND OWNER MICHAEL UY HEAD BACK INTO THE WATER.

ABBIE GIRL CATCHES WAVES ALONGSIDE A HUMAN SURFER.

Pacifica, California, U.S.A.
This dog really knew how to catch ... catch waves, that is! For two years in a row, Abbie Girl the Australian kelpie took the top prize at the World Dog Surfing Championships, where she surfed the largest and longest waves. "She nailed it in every category," competition judge Charly Kayle says.

Owner Michael Uy started taking Abbie Girl to the beach after adopting her. Once the dog got used to the water, she eventually hopped on a surfboard. "Kelpies that work herd sheep by running across their backs," Uy says, noting that the breed's natural instinct might've helped Abbie balance on a surfboard. The dog also rode a custom board that was lighter, thinner, and soft on top so she could dig in her claws. And nobody minded the wet dog smell!

36

AMAZING ANIMALS

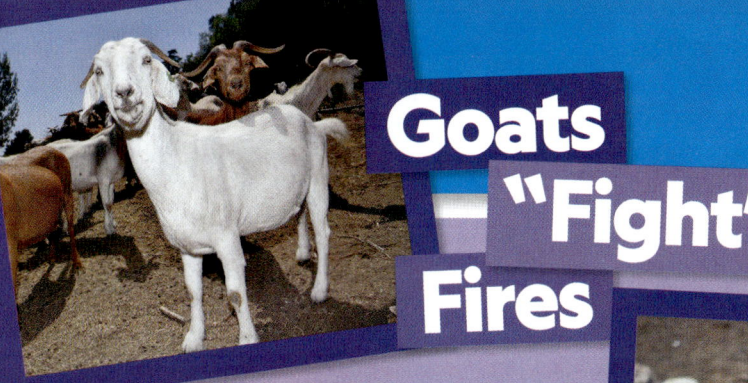

Goats "Fight" Fires

Whittier, California, U.S.A.
In California, wildfires pose serious threats to human and animal health. To control the spread of wildfires before they get started, some Californians are turning to unexpected helpers: goats! Their job? To eat invasive plants called black mustard before they can feed flames.

These weeds were brought to California from Spain in the 1700s. But black mustard overgrows native plants (the invasive plant can reach eight feet [2.4 m] tall), then releases lots of seeds before dying. The seeds sprout new plants, and the dry, dead plant matter is fuel for dangerous wildfires.

These helpful goats happily eat black mustard, even on steep hillsides that other animals and people can't reach. Even better: The seeds are no longer active once they pass through the goats' tough digestive tract.

"The seeds don't grow after they come out the other end," says Alissa Cope, who owns a company that sends out goats. These chompers are champs!

A HIRED GOAT MUNCHES ON VEGETATION IN CALIFORNIA.

PRICEY PIG PAINTING

Franschhoek, South Africa
Now that's some pig. Pigcasso holds the record for the most expensive painting by an animal, with one of her pieces selling for $26,898. (Some of the proceeds are donated to charity.) The rescued animal started painting after she picked up a stray paintbrush with her mouth and then swabbed a canvas. She even dipped her nose in beetroot ink to "sign" her work with her snout. And the South African artist created more than 400 paintings.

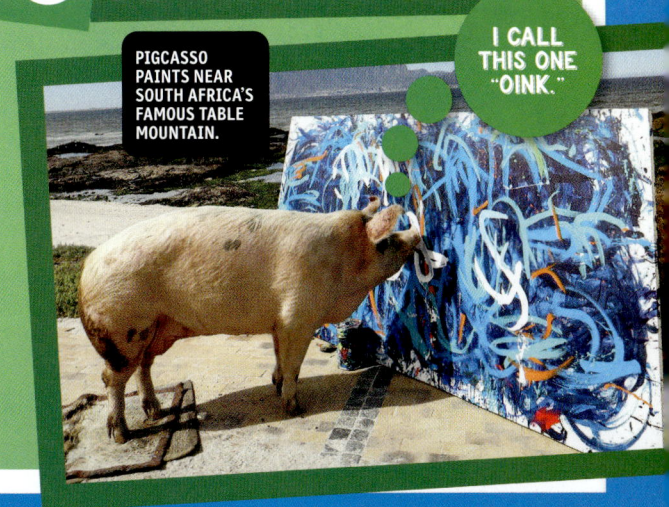

PIGCASSO PAINTS NEAR SOUTH AFRICA'S FAMOUS TABLE MOUNTAIN.

I CALL THIS ONE "OINK."

ANIMAL FUN

BIG Question

Can a groundhog predict when spring will arrive?

Groundhogs are also known as **woodchucks** and whistle pigs.

A GROUNDHOG PEEKS OUT FROM ITS BURROW.

A HANDLER HOLDS PHIL.

Groundhog Day is related to the midwinter holiday **Candlemas.** When the day is celebrated in Germany, a hedgehog predicts the **weather.**

Every February 2, people gather in Punxsutawney, Pennsylvania, U.S.A., to watch a groundhog come out of its burrow. Legend has it that if "Punxsutawney Phil" sees his shadow, the startled groundhog will go back into his burrow to wait out six more weeks of winter. If he doesn't see his shadow, an early spring is supposedly on the way. This Groundhog Day tradition goes all the way back to 1887.

Groundhogs have regular hibernation patterns, and the males always come out of their burrows in early February to claim their territory. So their annual appearance is just their natural instinct. But can that predict the weather? Data gathered showed that Punxsutawney Phil was correct only about 40 percent of the time. Sorry, Phil—that's not much better than a wild guess.

AMAZING ANIMALS

ANIMAL MYTHS BUSTED

Some people mistakenly think adult opossums hang by their tails or that porcupines shoot their quills. What other misconceptions are out there? Here are some common animal myths.

MYTH Black cats are bad luck.

HOW IT MAY HAVE STARTED As far back as the year 1200, many people believed that evil witches were real and that black cats were teaming up with them—or were even witches in disguise. This might be because cats are often active at night, a scary time for people in the past—before lightbulbs and flashlights. If a black cat was near, people thought someone nearby might be trying to cast an evil spell.

WHY IT'S NOT TRUE A cat that turns into an evil witch? Definitely not real. Cats can't cause bad luck. Black cats might even be lucky, since the gene that makes a cat's fur black may also help it fight infections.

MYTH Owls can turn their heads all the way around.

HOW IT MAY HAVE STARTED Owls can swivel their heads from a forward-facing position to look directly behind them, then keep turning until their beaks are over their other shoulder. It *seems* like the owl could keep turning its head until it's looking forward again.

WHY IT'S NOT TRUE Owls can't spin their heads in a full circle—but they get pretty close! Unlike people and other animals, these birds can't move their eyes. To see what's behind them, they turn their heads up to 270 degrees. (A full circle is 360 degrees.) If humans tried twisting that far, the motion would block the arteries in our neck that move blood to our brain—as if you bent a hose—and we'd pass out. But owls have special holes in their neck bones to keep blood flowing.

MYTH Touching toads will give you warts.

HOW IT MAY HAVE STARTED In the past, people understood that warts—growths on human skin that can sometimes be painful—can be passed from person to person. (And today, we know that's because warts are caused by a virus.) But for centuries, people incorrectly thought that the lumps and bumps on a toad's skin were warts, too, and they worried that touching a toad could spread them.

WHY IT'S NOT TRUE The bumps on a toad are organs called glands that produce a poisonous liquid. The substance tastes bad to predators and can make them sick, so these glands help keep toads safe. Even though you won't get warts from handling a toad, you might get a rash from the poison—leave these hoppers alone!

ANIMAL FUN

Cool Animal
SUPERLATIVES

Funky features. Superpowers. Sensational size.
No doubt, all animals are cool. But whether they've got cool colors, funky hair, or endless energy, some species are extra impressive. Here are 15 of the coolest creatures on Earth.

STRIPIEST HIDE

The okapi's unique look is said to help the hooved animal blend into the partial sunlight that filters through the Central African rainforests they call home. The zebralike stripes make it easier for an okapi calf to keep an eye on its mother as they make their way through their dimly lit habitat.

SPOOKIEST SONG

This seemingly sweet songbird has a beautiful call—and an eerie way of eating. Australia's pied butcherbird sings to mark a group's territory and communicate over long distances. But the most chilling thing about this bird? The gruesome way it hacks away at its prey, including lizards and mice.

MOST COLORFUL

Somewhere over the rainbow ... you'll find a nudibranch displaying a vibrant visage of blue, orange, purple, pink, and yellow. These stunning sea slugs, which can be toxic to other sea animals, are typically found in warm coastal waters, where their unique appearance warns predators to stay away.

AMAZING ANIMALS

BEST TEAMWORK

High five! Meerkat pups often bond soon after birth and spend most of their time together exploring their environment and playing. Native to Africa's Kalahari Desert, the extremely social animals are super supportive of one another, with a community working together to share the load of raising and protecting their pups.

BEST HEADGEAR

The tropical royal flycatcher, which lives in tropical lowlands from Mexico to Brazil, breaks out its brightly colored crest as a way to attract potential mates. This distinct crownlike feature gives this species the royal part of its name, while flycatcher speaks to its habit of catching and eating flies and other insects.

BEST SPIKES

The spikes on porcupinefish say "don't mess with me" to predators. These fish can also balloon their bodies up to three times their normal size when threatened. A coat of spiky scales adds an extra layer of defense.

BEST NAPPER

Tigers love their catnaps! In fact, the animals snooze some 18 hours a day—snagging z's whenever and wherever they can. Why so sleepy? The big cats usually rest after a big meal, which helps them conserve energy for their next hunt. Once they're up, they're recharged and ready to go.

ANIMAL FUN

LONGEST EYELASHES

Given their size, it's no wonder that elephants have the longest eyelashes of any land animal—up to five inches (12.7 cm) long! Along with a third eyelid, these luxurious lashes keep dust and sand out of elephants' eyes.

LONGEST LEAPER

The athletic snow leopard can jump farther than 49 feet (15 m), more than the length of an average school bus! This big cat's short, sturdy forelimbs and long hind limbs help it make such big leaps.

HEAVIEST TOAD

Known for its extraordinary size, the warty, poisonous cane toad is native to South and Central America and is invasive to many places. One cane toad recently discovered in an Australian rainforest weighed nearly six pounds (2.7 kg), the largest on record.

FASTEST-GROWING FISH

So much for being a kid! Just about 18 days after it's hatched, a female African killifish grows to its full body size, lays eggs, and produces its own young, making it the fastest-maturing vertebrate in the animal kingdom.

AMAZING ANIMALS

BEST CAMOUFLAGE

Now you see it ... now you don't. The leaf-tailed gecko, a nocturnal reptile found on Madagascar, gets its name from its cool camo, which allows it to blend into tree trunks, leaf piles, branches, and other vegetation as it moves throughout its forested environment.

FANCIEST FEATHERS

Proud as a peacock! This male bird isn't afraid to show off its bold blue-green tail feathers as a way to attract a potential mate or to intimidate rivals. The feathers, which span to five feet (1.5 m) long—longer than the peacock's body—actually grow from the bird's back, not its tail.

WEIRDEST FEET

The platypus's funky flippers serve several important purposes. Wide, webbed, and punctuated with sharp claws, the paddlelike feet act as rudders in the water, making the platypus a quick and efficient swimmer. While the platypus is on land, its claws are key to climbing and constructing dirt burrows at the water's edge. And males can fight off rivals during mating season using pointy spurs packed with enough venom to paralyze a foe.

FARTHEST FLYING BAT

The Nathusius' pipistrelle is an itty-bitty bat that can fly super far. One of these thumb-size bats recently set a record by flying from Russia to the French Alps, a total distance of some 1,500 miles (2,200 km).

43

CLASSIFICATION

WHAT IS Taxonomy?

Because our planet has billions and billions of living things called organisms, people need a way of classifying them. Scientists created a system called taxonomy, which helps to classify all living things into ordered groups. By putting organisms into categories, we are better able to understand how they are the same and how they are different. There are eight levels of taxonomic classification, beginning with the broadest group, called a domain, followed by kingdom, down to the most specific group, called a species.

Biologists divide life based on evolutionary history, and they place organisms into three domains depending on their genetic structure: Archaea, Bacteria, and Eukarya. (See page 195 for "The Three Domains of Life.")

Where do animals come in?

Animals are a part of the Eukarya domain, which means they are organisms made of cells with nuclei. More than one million species of animals, including humans, have been named. Like all living things, animals can be divided into smaller groups, called phyla. Most scientists believe there are more than 30 phyla into which animals can be grouped based on certain scientific criteria, such as body type or whether or not the animal has a backbone. It can be pretty complicated, so another, less complicated system is used to group animals into two categories: vertebrates and invertebrates.

HEDGEHOG

SAMPLE CLASSIFICATION
FIRE SALAMANDER

Domain:	Eukarya
Kingdom:	Animalia
Phylum:	Chordata
Class:	Amphibia
Order:	Caudata
Family:	Salamandridae
Genus:	*Salamandra*
Species:	*Salamandra salamandra*

TIP: Here's a sentence to help you remember the classification order: **D**id **K**ing **P**hillip **C**ome **O**ver **F**or **G**ood **S**oup?

BY THE NUMBERS

There are 17,658 vulnerable or endangered animal species in the world. The list includes:

- **1,338 mammals,** such as the snow leopard, the polar bear, and the fishing cat
- **1,354 birds,** including the Steller's sea eagle and the black-banded plover
- **3,927 fish,** such as the Mekong giant catfish
- **1,844 reptiles,** including the Round Island day gecko
- **2,415 insects,** such as the Macedonian grayling
- **2,873 amphibians,** such as the emperor newt
- **And more,** including 272 arachnids, 747 crustaceans, 256 sea anemones and corals, 228 bivalves, and 2,216 snails and slugs

ROUND ISLAND DAY GECKO

AMAZING ANIMALS

Vertebrates Animals WITH Backbones

Fish are cold-blooded and live in water. They breathe with gills, lay eggs, and usually have scales.

Amphibians are cold-blooded. Their young live in water and breathe with gills. Adults live on land and breathe with lungs.

Reptiles are cold-blooded and breathe with lungs. They live both on land and in water.

Birds are warm-blooded and have feathers and wings. They lay eggs, breathe with lungs, and are usually able to fly. Some birds live on land, some in water, and some on both.

Mammals are warm-blooded and feed on their mothers' milk. They also have skin that is usually covered with hair. Mammals live both on land and in water.

BIRD: MANDARIN DUCK

AMPHIBIAN: POISON FROG

Invertebrates Animals WITHOUT Backbones

Sponges are a very basic form of animal life. They live in water and do not move on their own.

Echinoderms have external skeletons and live in seawater.

Mollusks have soft bodies and can live either in or out of shells, on land or in water.

Arthropods are the largest group of animals. They have external skeletons, called exoskeletons, and segmented bodies with appendages. Arthropods live in water and on land.

Worms are soft-bodied animals with no true legs. Worms live in soil.

Cnidaria live in water and have mouths surrounded by tentacles.

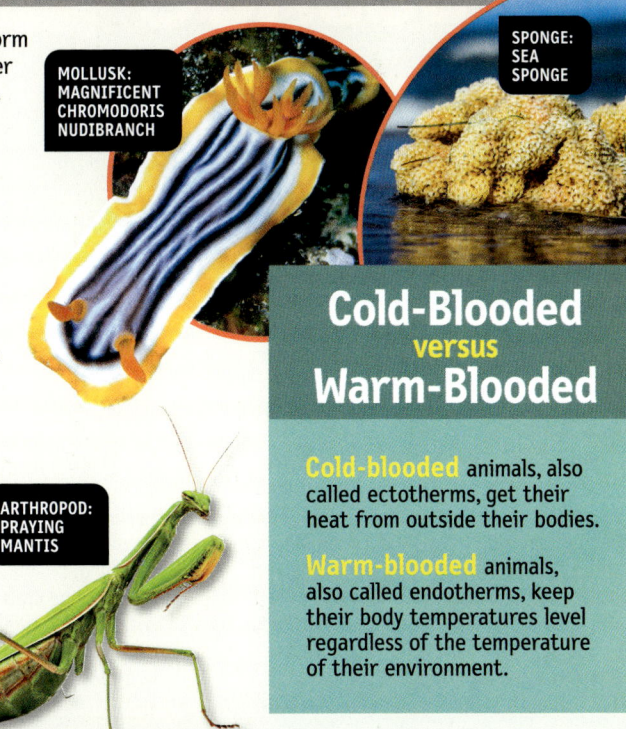

MOLLUSK: MAGNIFICENT CHROMODORIS NUDIBRANCH

SPONGE: SEA SPONGE

ARTHROPOD: PRAYING MANTIS

Cold-Blooded versus Warm-Blooded

Cold-blooded animals, also called ectotherms, get their heat from outside their bodies.

Warm-blooded animals, also called endotherms, keep their body temperatures level regardless of the temperature of their environment.

ANIMALS IN PERIL

I'M CRAB-ULOUS!

Comeback Critter: Horseshoe Crab

Pangatalan Island Marine Protected Area, the Philippines

With a spiky tail, a helmet-shaped shell, and sharp pincers at the end of eight of its 10 legs, the tri-spine horseshoe crab seems indestructible. But over the past 60 years, the number of these critters—native to the western Pacific Ocean—decreased by more than half.

Horseshoe crabs are sometimes taken for food or used as bait, and their habitats are often destroyed by human activities. Around Pangatalan Island, people burned mangrove shrubs for fuel (mangroves are important nurseries for horseshoe crabs) and fished using dynamite and poison on coral reefs.

But in 2017, conservationists created a protected area around Pangatalan. They planted mangroves and ended harmful fishing practices. Today, horseshoe crabs are thriving around the island, and other animals, like eight-foot (2.4-m)-long giant groupers, are returning.

Horseshoe crabs have been scuttling around Earth for 450 million years. Thanks to actions like these, conservationists hope they'll be here for many more.

AMAZING ANIMALS

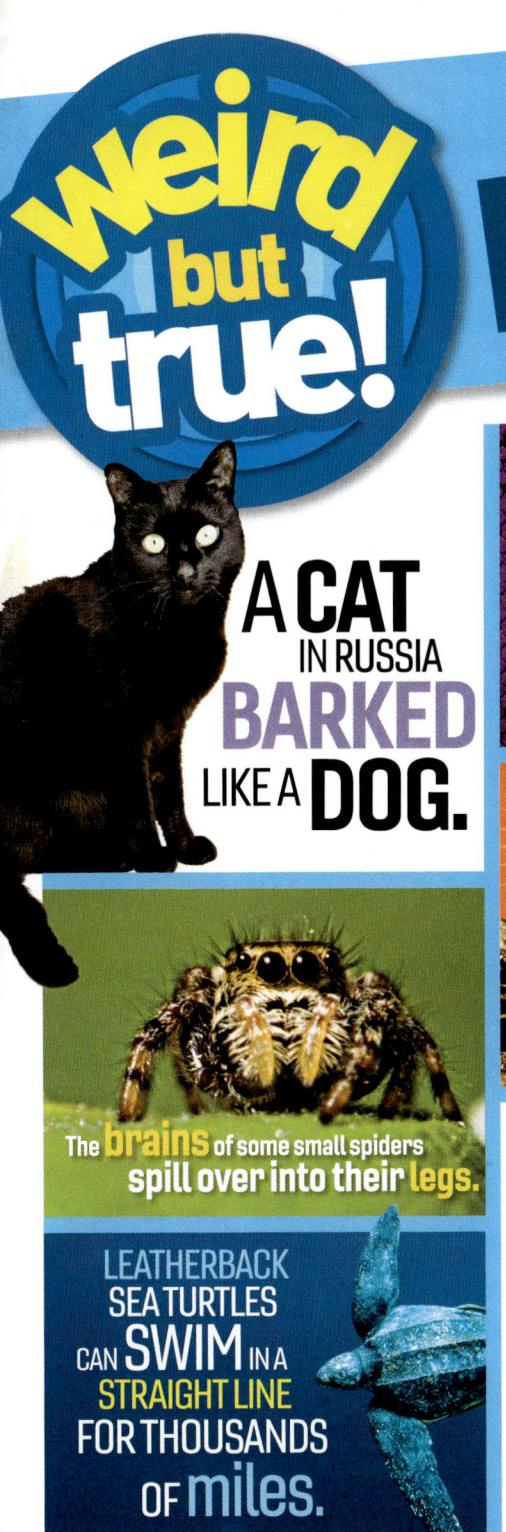

Weird but true!

Animal Oddities

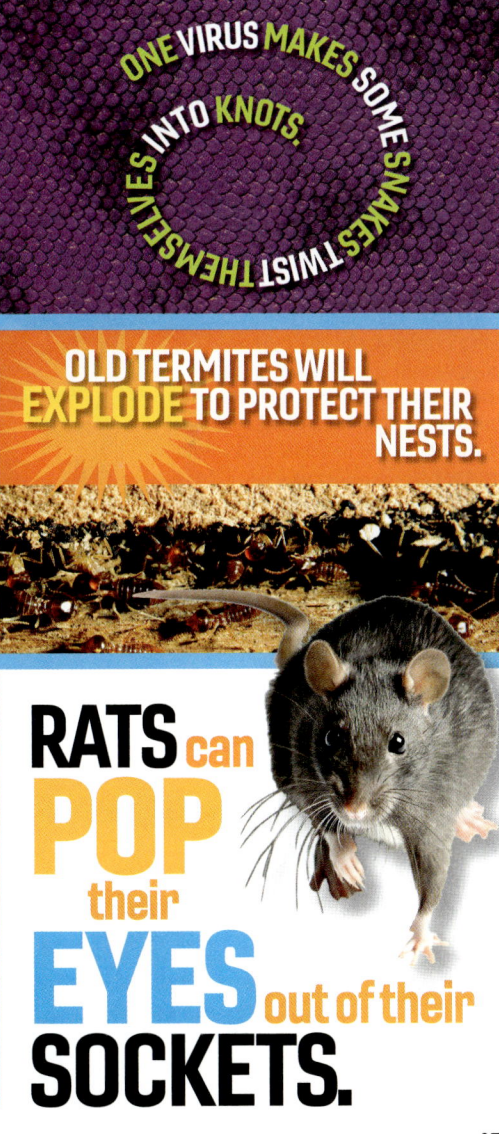

A CAT IN RUSSIA **BARKED** LIKE A **DOG**.

ONE VIRUS MAKES SOME SNAKES TWIST THEMSELVES INTO KNOTS.

OLD TERMITES WILL **EXPLODE** TO PROTECT THEIR NESTS.

The **brains** of some small spiders spill over into their **legs**.

LEATHERBACK SEA TURTLES CAN SWIM IN A STRAIGHT LINE FOR THOUSANDS OF miles.

RATS can **POP** their **EYES** out of their **SOCKETS**.

ANIMALS IN PERIL

Comeback Critter: Scarlet Macaw

POACHING PROBLEMS

With their colorful feathers, curious nature, and ability to mimic human speech, many people wanted scarlet macaws as pets throughout the 1900s, especially in the United States. So local people would climb trees in Central American forests to nab scarlet macaw chicks. One bird could be worth an entire month's wages.

When macaw numbers were crashing, the Honduran government passed a law in 1990 that made it illegal to take the birds. They also hoped that making it the country's national bird would protect it.

The U.S. Endangered Species Act listed scarlet macaws as endangered in 2019, which made it illegal to import wild-caught birds to the United States. But poachers continued to pluck and sell the birds illegally.

SPREADING THE BIRD WORD

Back in 2001, conservationist Lloyd Davidson built a park called Macaw Mountain near the Copán ruins in Honduras to care for about a hundred neglected or abused pet macaws. In 2010, James Gilardi, an ecologist from the World Parrot Trust, suggested releasing some of the captive birds back into the wild. "But I was worried at first," Davidson says. "Some people might still try to illegally harm or steal the birds."

So the conservationists set up an education program at nearby schools to teach kids why it's better to have macaws in the wild than as pets. Then they invited locals to come watch the macaws being released as they flew over

MACAW SCULPTURE

ONLOOKERS CELEBRATE AS A SCARLET MACAW IS RELEASED BACK INTO THE WILD IN HONDURAS.

AMAZING ANIMALS

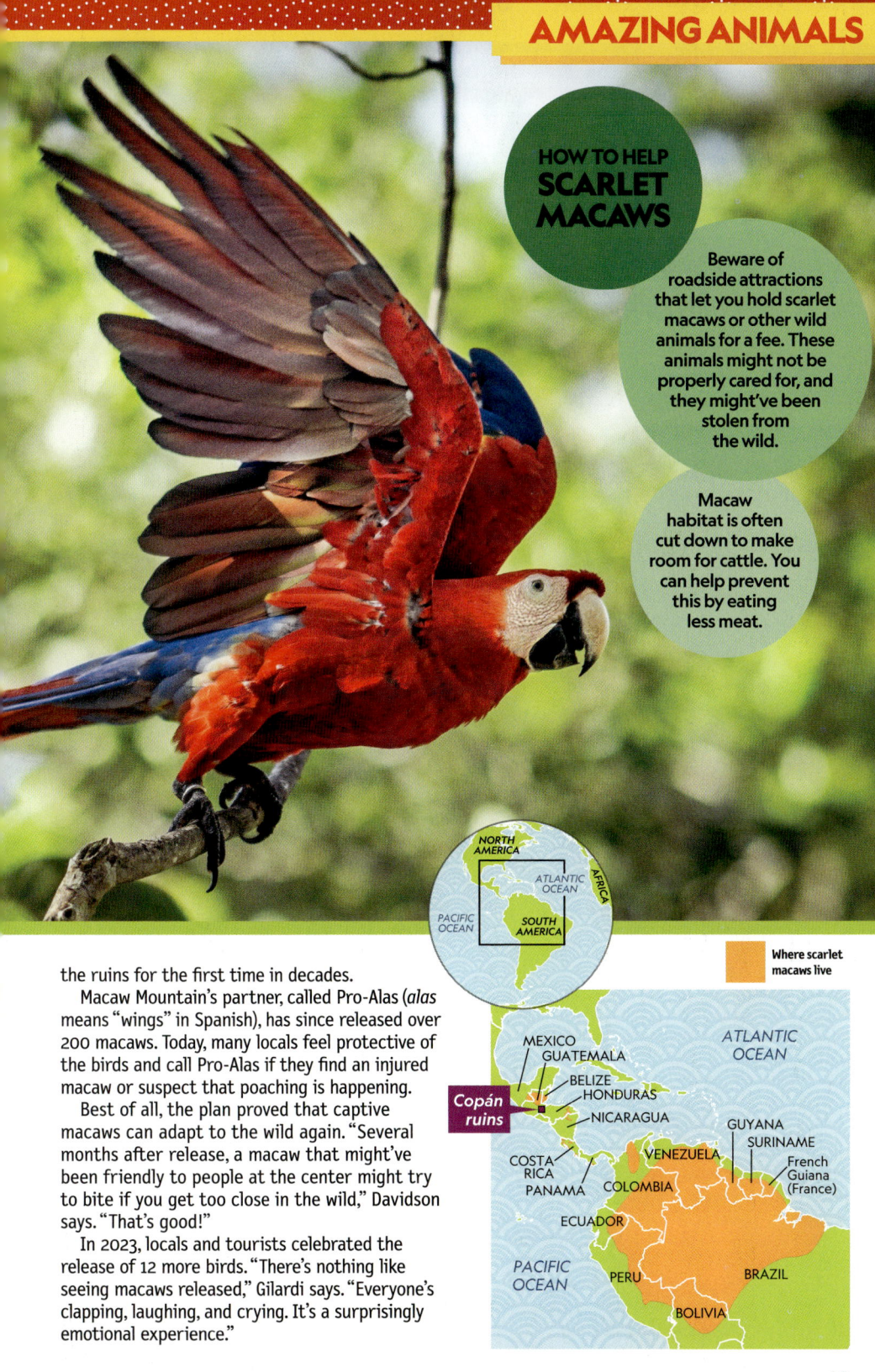

HOW TO HELP SCARLET MACAWS

Beware of roadside attractions that let you hold scarlet macaws or other wild animals for a fee. These animals might not be properly cared for, and they might've been stolen from the wild.

Macaw habitat is often cut down to make room for cattle. You can help prevent this by eating less meat.

Where scarlet macaws live

the ruins for the first time in decades.

Macaw Mountain's partner, called Pro-Alas (*alas* means "wings" in Spanish), has since released over 200 macaws. Today, many locals feel protective of the birds and call Pro-Alas if they find an injured macaw or suspect that poaching is happening.

Best of all, the plan proved that captive macaws can adapt to the wild again. "Several months after release, a macaw that might've been friendly to people at the center might try to bite if you get too close in the wild," Davidson says. "That's good!"

In 2023, locals and tourists celebrated the release of 12 more birds. "There's nothing like seeing macaws released," Gilardi says. "Everyone's clapping, laughing, and crying. It's a surprisingly emotional experience."

INTO THE WATER

So. Many. Penguins!

A recently discovered giant colony helps scientists understand why **Adélies** rule the roost.

ADÉLIE PENGUINS LIVE IN ANTARCTICA, THE DRIEST, COLDEST, AND WINDIEST CONTINENT ON EARTH.

Just two penguin species live only in Antarctica: Adélies and emperor penguins.

Squawk! Gurgle! Honk!

Along the bustling "highways" crisscrossing Antarctica's Danger Islands, more than a million Adélie penguins waddle to and from the ocean. It's a lot of traffic and noise—but until recently scientists didn't even know this metropolis existed.

That is, until penguin poo helped them find it.

Few people have ever explored the Danger Islands. Researchers could never get close enough because of heavy sea ice that could trap their boats. So no one really knew how much wildlife was there.

Then satellite imagery from space spotted guano, or poo, stains on the islands, hinting that a large number of penguins might be present.

"Penguin guano is a pinkish red color and looks like practically nothing else in the Antarctic," ecologist Heather Lynch says. "Once we viewed the images, we figured there had to be penguins on the Danger Islands."

Then Lynch's team got another surprise: The Danger Islands are home to more than 1.5 million Adélie penguins.

Before the discovery, scientists had been concerned that Adélies were disappearing, possibly because of climate change. But now that they've uncovered this super colony, they know that the Adélie population in Antarctica is not only thriving but super busy, too.

PENGUIN LIFE

Throughout the year, Adélies log more than 8,000 miles (12,875 km) on the "road," commuting back and forth from their nests to the ocean to hunt for krill, squid, lanternfish, or jellyfish for dinner. With so many residents on the move, traffic can be tricky.

AMAZING ANIMALS

"The Adélies have fairly distinct highways," seabird ecologist Barbara Wienecke says. "The paths get incredibly congested, so like humans, the birds sometimes have to take detours to avoid getting stuck in traffic."

And like a bustling city, the noise never stops. Adélie chicks and parents identify each other mostly by sound—not by sight. So they squawk on their commute to let their family know they're coming back from fishing for the day. And if they've been away on a long hunting trip, each bird sings a unique tune to make sure they've found the correct partner.

The chatter isn't all sweet, though.

"If a neighbor gets too close, an Adélie can sound a nest alarm by making loud, sharp calls, which basically mean 'This is my nest! Go away!'" Wienecke says.

And don't forget the splat sounds they make while pooing. Adélies go often, and even all over each other! They're not trying to hit each other, though—the wind tends to blow the guano toward other nests.

ADÉLIES DIVE FOR FOOD TO FEED THEMSELVES AND THEIR CHICKS.

NOSY NEIGHBORS

All that noise can be distracting, but Adélies have to stay focused to prevent a big-city theft of their valuables—that is, their pebbles.

Penguins use the small rocks to build nests for their chicks. Because pebbles can be scarce on the island, one Adélie might swipe a few stones from another. In rare cases, if the parents and chicks are away from the nest, a nonbreeding neighbor might try to steal the entire nest and connect it to their own nest to build an even bigger home. The birds fight back against these intruders by biting them or slapping them with their wings to scare them off.

Despite squabbles, neighbors can be helpful. "When the nests are all built within pecking distance of each other, it makes it harder for predatory seabirds like south polar skuas and giant petrels to target the colony," Wienecke says. "If they did, they'd have a lot of Adélies banding together against them."

Scientists have gotten involved to protect Adélies, too. The Danger Islands are now a protected area that can only be visited with a special permit. "And," Lynch says, "the area's dangerous sea ice will likely keep out most of the people curious about the Adélie penguins."

That way, penguin cities can keep hustling, bustling, and making noise for years to come.

Emperors reach nearly four feet (1.2 m) tall and can weigh up to 50 pounds (23 kg); Adélies only stand up to two feet (0.6 m) tall and weigh about 10 pounds (5 kg).

MORE THAN 1.5 MILLION ADÉLIE PENGUINS LIVE IN THIS CROWDED COLONY ON THE DANGER ISLANDS.

INTO THE WATER

10 COOL FACTS ABOUT PENGUINS

African penguins have a **PINK GLAND** above their eyes that allows **EXCESS HEAT TO ESCAPE** their bodies.

THANKS TO THE PINK KRILL THEY EAT, ADÉLIE PENGUINS' POOP IS PINK.

An emperor penguin has about **100 feathers** on every square inch (15 feathers/sq cm) of its body.

One emperor penguin dove to a depth of **1,850 FEET** (564 m)—**the deepest dive** for a bird that scientists have tracked.

AMAZING ANIMALS

Penguins can **adjust blood flow** to their feet to **keep them from freezing** on the ice.

SOME MALE PENGUINS USE SMOOTH PEBBLES TO "PROPOSE" TO FEMALES.

The fastest swimming bird, a gentoo penguin, glides through water at **22 miles** an hour (35 km/h).

EVERY PENGUIN HAS ITS **OWN UNIQUE VOICE**, WHICH HELPS IT **FIND ITS MATE** OR CHICK IN A CROWD.

An emperor **penguin dad incubates** a single egg in a **special pouch** on his feet while the **mom forages for food** at sea.

Some species of penguins spend up to **75 PERCENT** of their lives **in the water**.

53

STANDOUT SPECIES

awes8me

THESE ANIMALS ARE AT THE TOP OF THEIR CLASS IN SMARTS.

An octopus's arms can think independently from its brain.

1

SNEAKY SMARTS
Octopuses are curious creatures. They can open the lids of jars, and some have even found escape routes from their aquarium enclosures. They can also wriggle their boneless bodies through passages as small as a quarter! Octopuses learn quickly and can recognize individual human faces.

CLEVER CREATURES

NO BIRDBRAIN
African gray parrots are known for being chatterboxes. They're excellent at mimicking humans and can form simple sentences. They're also one of a few animals capable of reasoning, or coming up with an answer based on information they already have. They can figure out puzzles and work together to solve problems.

2

3

SMART LITTLE PIGGY
They might like to wallow in mud, but **domestic pigs** clean up in the intelligence department. Pigs can learn tasks, like operating levers to get food, and they are one of a few animal species that understand how mirrors work.

AMAZING ANIMALS

5. ALL FOR ONE
Talk about teamwork! These **army ants** are joining together to build a living ant tower so some individuals can climb to this plant stem and retrieve food for the community. Researchers discovered that no single ant calls the shots in the tower-building; they make decisions as a colony.

4. THIRST FOR KNOWLEDGE
Chimpanzees, one of the closest relatives to humans, use things in nature such as leaves and spongelike mosses to soak up water for drinking. They pass on this trick to other family members, which is a type of social learning only the smartest of animals achieve.

6. NUTS FOR LEARNING
When it comes to finding nuts, **gray squirrels** are the experts. In one study, researchers hid several hazelnuts to discover how squirrels solve a puzzle. The squirrels were quick learners, and they even changed tactics to get their nut reward more quickly.

7. CRAFTY CROW
If a **New Caledonian crow** can't find a tool for the job, it just makes one! The South Pacific bird can bend twigs into hooks to retrieve insects hidden in logs.

8. CATCH ME IF YOU CAN!
Being playful is considered a sign of intelligence—which puts **dolphins** near the top of the list of smartest animals. Several species of dolphins ride the waves created by boats, and some dolphins play tag by nudging each other and then swimming away for a high-speed chase!

STANDOUT SPECIES

INVISIBLE Frogs

These freaky amphibians can nearly disappear!

The best way to hide in a rainforest full of hungry animals? Disappear! Named for their nearly see-through skin, the 160 known species of glass frogs hang out in trees in the tropical forests of Central and South America. Discover the science behind their ability to appear almost invisible.

LIVER
HEART
EGGS
DIGESTIVE SYSTEM
SUN GLASS FROG

LIGHT BRIGHT

We see color because light bounces off objects and reflects those colors to our eyes. Sometimes light bounces off substances called pigments to give off a color. And if something has no pigments—like plain glass—it appears totally clear.

Glass frogs' undersides have very few pigments, allowing more than 90 percent of light to shoot straight through. "So you can actually see through their bellies and look at many of their organs—and even watch their tiny hearts beat," says Jesse Delia, a National Geographic Explorer who studies these frogs.

SAFE SLEEP

Glass frogs sleep during the day, when predators like birds and snakes are hunting. That can be dangerous for the snoozing frogs if hungry animals see them. But scientists recently discovered that while northern glass frogs sleep, they hide up to 89 percent of their bright red blood cells in their liver. Without all those cells reflecting the light, the frogs can become two to three times more translucent—meaning more light passes through them—than when they're awake. Talk about hide-and-sleep!

NORTHERN GLASS FROGS SLEEPING ON A LEAF

AMAZING ANIMALS

CLEARLY COOL CRITTERS

Take a look at—and through!—a few other translucent animals.

RETICULATED GLASS FROG

LEAFLIKE

Glass frogs have more pigments in their backs than their tummies. That means less light passes through their backs and instead reflects color. The color reflecting off their backs matches the color of the leaves these frogs sit on. This might mean the frogs have another way to hide. Experts think that the different levels of light passing through a frog's back and tummy—that is, the different levels of translucency—is what makes these frogs so tough to spot: The amount of light passing through the frogs matches how much light comes through the tops and bottoms of leaves. So to predators, the frog might look like part of the leaf. "Translucency is really weird, and a cool camouflage trick!" Delia says.

LIMON GIANT GLASS FROG

Comb jelly

Barreleye fish

Domed land snail

Glass octopus

Glass shrimp

Barton Springs salamander

57

ANIMAL FRIENDS

INCREDIBLE ANIMAL FRIENDS

MONKEY DOTES ON IGUANA

Krefeld, Germany

This white-faced saki rarely scaled back her affection for her green iguana bestie. The saki, a type of monkey, loved petting and snuggling her reptile pal as they lounged together on tree branches at the Krefeld Zoo.

The saki and iguana met after they were placed in the zoo's Rainforest House, a tree-filled enclosure that's home to 40 different types of animals from tropical areas. "Both green iguanas and white-faced sakis spend most of their time in treetops," zoo spokesperson Petra Schwinn says. "One day these two crossed paths." The curious saki examined the reptile, patting its skin with her long fingers.

The pals continued to have hangout sessions, eating together at the enclosure's feeding station. But most of their "playdates" were in the trees and involved the saki petting the iguana and tickling its chin. The reptile, meanwhile, seemed to soak up the attention.

The animals have since moved to separate zoos. But keepers and visitors haven't forgotten about their friendship. "They made a good team," Schwinn says.

WHITE-FACED SAKI

RANGE South America

WEIGHT Around 4 pounds (2 kg)

FACE-OFF Only the male white-faced saki has white fur covering its face. The fur on a female's face is mostly brown.

SWEET TREATS Sakis eat fruit, honey, leaves, and flowers.

GREEN IGUANA

RANGE Central and South America

WEIGHT Up to 17 pounds (8 kg)

TALL TAIL If it's caught by a predator, the green iguana can detach its tail and grow another.

FUNNY NAME These animals are sometimes referred to as "bamboo chickens."

HOW ABOUT A NECK RUB?

MONKEY

IGUANA

AMAZING ANIMALS

BIRD HANGS OUT WITH BUNNY

YOU'RE MY BFF: BIRD FRIEND FOREVER.

Kildare, Ireland

Bunny the European rabbit and Pidg the common pigeon didn't let anything come between their friendship—not even a wall!

After being found weak and alone, the animals were brought separately to what was then the Kildare Animal Foundation Wildlife Unit. Both needed warmth to survive, but volunteer Aideen Magee had only one incubator. So she put the rabbit and the bird inside together, setting a cardboard wall between them so that they'd each have their own space. When Magee went to check on the duo a little later, she saw that Bunny had knocked down the barrier and was cuddling with Pidg!

Magee took the cardboard wall away so that the animals could snuggle 24/7. Soon after, Bunny became sick, and Pidg refused to leave the rabbit's side.

"The bird comforted Bunny and kept him going," says animal manager Dan Donoher. Once Bunny recovered, the friends spent their time eating together, grooming each other, and curling up at nap time.

After about six months, Pidg and Bunny were released back into the wild. They're no longer side by side, but when they needed it most, these critters had each other's backs.

COMMON PIGEON
WEIGHT About 13 ounces (369 g)
DIET Seeds, grains, and fruit
EGG ALERT It takes about 17 days for their eggs to hatch.
ROCK ON They're sometimes called rock doves.

EUROPEAN RABBIT
WEIGHT Up to 5 pounds (2.2 kg)
DIET Grass, bark, buds, and roots
ALL GROWN UP Bunnies become independent after about a month.
DISTRESS SIGNAL They thump their feet when threatened.

PIDG   BUNNY

INTO THE WILD

10 TIPS
TO HELP ANIMALS

Animals need more than laws to protect them—they need you, too! See how small actions can help make big changes.

WEST INDIAN MANATEE

1 SPACED OUT
Don't give **wild animals** food or water. It might seem kind, but doing this encourages critters like **manatees** to approach people and boats, which puts them in danger. (Plus, people food can make animals sick.) And don't toss food out of the car window—it encourages animals like opossums, coyotes, and turtles to get close to the road, where they can get hurt. (Bird feeders and birdbaths are OK!)

2 DRAIN-OH-NO!
Be careful what you pour down the drain or flush down the toilet. Substances like paint, hydrogen peroxide, grease, medicine, and more can cause great harm to plants, **animals,** and water quality.

3 BIRD BUDDY
Put stickers, paint, or tape on the outside of your house's windows to keep **birds** from flying into these reflective surfaces. On spring or fall evenings, close the curtains so that artificial light won't confuse migrating birds.

DECALS CAN ALSO HELP PREVENT BIRD CRASHES.

4 PLASTIC BUSTER
Plastic that blows out of trash cans can look like food to some animals, and it can make them sick if they eat it. Get our guide for how to talk to businesses about reducing their plastic waste: natgeokids.com/kidsvsplastic.

AMAZING ANIMALS

CLOVER

5 BEST MESS
Flowering clover and dandelions provide food for **bees** and **butterflies**, and dead leaves are cozy spots for lots of insects to hibernate in during the winter. So go ahead—let your backyard be messy!

FLORIDA PANTHERS

6 PROTECT YOUR STATE
Research which **endangered animals** live in your state or territory. Start with groups like the U.S. Fish and Wildlife Service.

VERMILION SEA STAR

7 FIREFLY FRIEND
It's OK to gently catch **fireflies** in your hands, but don't put them in a glass jar or other container. Some species of these insects are in danger of going extinct, so let them fly free.

8 WILDLIFE WATCH
If you see people feeding, chasing, or touching a wild animal like a **seal, sea turtle,** or **dolphin,** ask an adult to call for help. They can call the police or a special hotline managed by the National Oceanic and Atmospheric Administration to report a problem.

9 BEACH BODYGUARD
Never take live **sea stars, sand dollars,** or **urchins** from the ocean—these living animals can't survive out of the water. And leave shells at the beach—whole ones are homes for **hermit crabs,** and broken shells are important hiding places for **fish** and **octopuses.**

HAWAIIAN MONK SEAL

10 GORILLA GUARDIAN
Phones, computers, and other electronics contain coltan, a mineral extracted from **gorilla** habitats. You can be a hero for these animals by using your old devices as long as you can, then recycling the tech at your local electronics store or electronics recycling center.

61

INTO THE WILD

Moment of Huh?

No, your eyes are not playing tricks on you!

Extra Feet? How many legs does this **piping plover** have? Just two—plus a lot of **chicks**. For the first few weeks of their lives, the baby birds hide under Mom or Dad for warmth and protection.

Snake Fake Birds and frogs are in for a big surprise. When this kind of **hawk moth caterpillar** is disturbed, it hangs off a twig to reveal a scaly, snakelike belly. Then it puffs up to create a triangle-shaped "face" and sways like a real serpent.

Clear for Landing Take a look at this—if you can. The transparent wing membranes of the **glasswing butterfly** allow the insect to almost disappear while in flight, avoiding hungry birds.

Catching Air This **Kenyan rock agama** isn't a lizard wizard that can levitate. Strong jumpers, these creatures use their tails to balance their body weight as they prep for a perfect landing. Smooth moves!

AMAZING ANIMALS

Bet You Didn't Know!

7 terrific facts about tails

1 A **spider monkey** can use its **tail** as a fifth **"arm"** to hang from branches.

2 When chasing prey, a **cheetah** swings its tail to one side to **balance** while turning quickly.

3 One type of **snake** has a tail that looks like a **spider** to **lure prey** like birds.

4 Zebras can aim the **tips** of their tails to **swat flies.**

5 To attract mates, the **superb lyrebird** fans its tail over its head like an **umbrella,** then dances and chirps.

6 Lions sometimes display **friendliness** by draping their tails over each other.

7 A **giraffe's** tail can grow up to **8 feet** (2.4 m)— as long as a **surfboard!**

63

INSECTS

GLOWWORM CAVE

How these insects create a glittery underground world

A river flows through a dimly lit cave in New Zealand. It's so dark that you can't see the water from your boat—you can only hear it. Then, as your boat turns a corner, thousands of twinkling blue-green lights appear overhead.

This is Glowworm Grotto, part of the Waitomo Caves network on the North Island of New Zealand. The spot's shimmering lights look otherworldly, but they're actually created by a species of insect found only in New Zealand. How do these bugs put on such a cool light show? Read on to find out.

LIGHTS ON

Waitomo's limestone caves have existed for about 30 million years. But humans only discovered them some 400 years ago, when the Maori (MOW-ree)—the first people to come to New Zealand—found the cave system's entrance. Still, nobody explored the underground network until Maori chief Tane Tinorau and English explorer Fred Mace built a raft in 1887 to float through part of the 180 miles (290 km) of pitch-dark caves.

Below Earth's surface, Tinorau and Mace found a surprise: Some of the walls and ceilings were sparkling like stars. The dazzling display was coming from thousands of insects called New Zealand glowworms.

GLOW ON, "WORMS"

These glowworms aren't actually worms, though. They're the larvae of fungus gnats, a type of fly about the size of a mosquito. "Similar to how caterpillars eventually become butterflies, these larvae will one day become flies," biochemist Kurt Krause says.

Adult fungus gnats lay their eggs in Waitomo Caves because they're a good spot for larvae to hunt after they hatch. "The larvae build delicate snares to catch their meals," Krause says. These snares work best in calm, wind-free habitats like caves to lure buggy prey like midges.

Here's how it works: A single glowworm—which grows to the length of two U.S. nickels placed side by side—makes dozens of long, silky-looking fishing lines in its mouth and hangs them from a cave ceiling. Then it spits droplets of mucus to make the lines sticky.

Next, the bug emits its blue-green light thanks to a chemical reaction in the creature's tail. Animals that glow like this are called bioluminescent (by-oh-loo-meh-NEH-sent). The glowing light attracts other insects, which then get trapped on the sticky threads.

That's when the glowworm zips

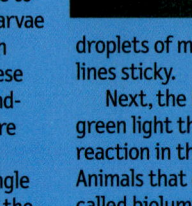

Wellington, New Zealand, is the southernmost national capital on the planet.

64

AMAZING ANIMALS

SNARES

TO CATCH PREY, GLOWWORMS HANG THESE STICKY SNARES FROM CAVE CEILINGS.

GLOWWORM

LIGHT

THE LARVAE THEN LIGHT UP TO ATTRACT PREY TO THE "FISHING LINES."

GLOWWORM

PREY

LURED BY THE LIGHT, AN INSECT GETS STUCK ON THE MUCUS-DOTTED TRAP.

New Zealand has more sheep than people.

The Maori—the first people to come to New Zealand—call the island nation "Land of the Long White Cloud."

down to snatch its snack. And when thousands of glowworms do this at once, tourists watching from below get an amazing light show.

GLOW GUARDIANS

Too many tourists, however, can be bad for the glowworms' habitat. Carbon dioxide from people's breath can damage the limestone walls that the glowworms hang their snares from.

That's why Native cave guides like Hiria Kohe-Love are working to protect the caves' most famous residents.

"We've put sensors underground so we can monitor the temperature, humidity, water levels, carbon dioxide levels, and wind speed in the caves," says Kohe-Love, a great-great-great-granddaughter of Chief Tinorau, Waitomo's first explorer. "If conditions aren't good for the glowworms, we'll delay tours."

Most of the other guides are also related to Tinorau and consider themselves *kaitiaki* (ky-tee-AH-kee), or guardians of the caves. "We look after this spot for future generations," Kohe-Love says. "To us, these caves are *taonga* (ton-GUH), or treasure—they're cherished."

65

INSECTS

Bizarre BUGS

Butterflies are beautiful, and fireflies are fantastic. But zoom in on the insect world, and you'll find zombie-makers, explosive tushies, and more.

BUTT BLASTER
Beware this bottom! **Bombardier beetles** take precise aim and blast stinky, boiling-hot acid from their butts to fend off predators. Why doesn't the liquid hurt the beetles while it's inside them? These insects have a series of chambers in their bodies that keep two chemicals separated. But when a beetle is in danger, it opens the valves and combines the chemicals. Then ... boom!

The beetles can even use the gassy defense after they've been swallowed: Scientists have watched unlucky frogs puke up bombardier beetles.

ZOMBIE-MAKER
In some scary movies, scientists accidentally create zombies. But female **jewel wasps** turn bugs into brainless beings on purpose. When she's ready to lay an egg, the wasp stings a **cockroach** to paralyze it. Then she sticks her stinger into the roach's brain, probing around for just the right spot to inject mind-altering chemicals.

After the first sting wears off and the roach can move again, the wasp leads the insect zombie by its antenna to a burrow and lays her egg on the roach's leg. A healthy cockroach would fight back or run away. But this roach sits still while the wasp seals up the burrow with small pebbles—and the roach inside. Three days later, the wasp larva hatches and eventually feasts on the cockroach.

AMAZING ANIMALS

COSTUME DESIGNER

With their long, slender bodies and soft abdomens, **caddisfly** larvae look like lunch to every fish in the stream. So after hatching, they quickly construct a dashing disguise. First the youngsters find pebbles, sticks, shells, or pieces of leaves. Then using special silk produced in glands around their mouths, they paste their collection together.

The silk acts like double-sided tape to build the one-inch (2.5-cm)-long portable shelters that the larvae will use for up to two years. As adults, caddisflies only survive a few weeks. But soon new caddisfly youngsters will get dressed up all over again.

HEAT GENERATOR

A group of **northern giant hornets**—the world's largest hornet—are unstoppable when attacking a bee or wasp hive. The nearly two-inch (5-cm)-long invaders bite off their prey's heads, chomping all the adults in the colony. Then they take over the hive, feeding the bee or wasp larvae to their own young.

But **Japanese honeybees** have outsmarted these warriors. When a hornet comes to scope out the hive, up to 500 honeybees surround the scout, wiggling and buzzing for an hour. Their body heat raises the temperature at the center of the ball to 117°F (47°C), killing the hornet. (The bees can survive up to 122°F [50°C].) The dead hornet scout can't tell its buddies about the hive, and the bees stay safe.

ROYAL FIGHTERS

A few hours after the reigning queen in a colony of **Indian jumping ants** dies, an epic battle begins. For about a month, female worker ants jab each other with their antennae and nip each other with their superlong jaws, which they normally use for hunting. Exhausted, the losers give up and get back to work hunting other insects and tending to the young.

But a few of the toughest females become sort of like princesses. Worker ants can never be true queens, but these royal ladies can help keep the colony alive for years and years. As they prepare to produce eggs, their brains shrink up to 25 percent, which might give them more energy for this regal duty. Good thing they don't have to wear crowns.

WILD CATS

BIG CATS

Not all wild cats are big cats, so what are big cats? To wildlife experts, this group includes tigers, lions, leopards, snow leopards, jaguars, cougars, and cheetahs. As carnivores, they survive solely on the flesh of other animals. Big cats are excellent hunters thanks to powerful jaws; long, sharp claws; and daggerlike teeth.

A JAGUAR AND HER CUBS

AMAZING ANIMALS

WHO'S WHO?

BIG CATS IN THE *PANTHERA* GENUS MAY HAVE a lot of features in common, but if you know what to look for, you'll be able to tell who's who in no time.

FUR

SNOW LEOPARD
A snow leopard's thick, spotted fur helps the cat hide in its mountain habitat, no matter the season. In winter its fur is off-white to blend in with the snow, and in summer it's yellowish gray to blend in with plants and the mountains.

JAGUAR 
A jaguar's coat pattern looks similar to that of a leopard, as both have dark spots called rosettes. The difference? The rosettes on a jaguar's torso have irregularly shaped borders and at least one black dot in the center.

TIGER 
Most tigers are orange-colored with vertical black stripes on their bodies. This coloring helps the cats blend in with tall grasses as they sneak up on prey. These markings are like fingerprints: No two stripe patterns are alike.

LION 
Lions have light brown, or tawny, coats and a tuft of black hair at the end of their tails. When they reach their prime, most male lions have shaggy manes that help them look larger and more intimidating.

LEOPARD
A leopard's yellowy coat has dark spots called rosettes on its back and sides. In leopards, the rosettes' edges are smooth and circular. This color combo and pattern help leopards blend into their surroundings.

LEOPARD
Up to 198 pounds (90 KG)
4.25 to 6.25 feet long (1.3 TO 1.9 M)

BENGAL TIGER
Up to 716 pounds (325 KG)
5 to 6 feet long (1.5 TO 1.8 M)

JAGUAR
Up to 348 pounds (158 KG)
5 to 6 feet long (1.5 TO 1.8 M)

SNOW LEOPARD
Up to 121 pounds (55 KG)
4 to 5 feet long (1.2 TO 1.5 M)

AFRICAN LION
Up to 575 pounds (261 KG)
4.5 to 6.5 feet long (1.4 TO 2 M)

WILD CATS

10 COOL FACTS ABOUT BIG CATS

A lion pride can be as few as **three lions** or as many as **30.**

Bobcats are named for their **short, bobbed tails.**

An adult lion's **roar** can be **heard** up to **five miles** (8 km) **away.**

A leopard can **drag prey heavier** than itself **50 feet** (15 m) **up a tree.**

AMAZING ANIMALS

A jaguar's **eyesight** is **twice** as powerful at **night** to help it **stalk prey** in the **dark.**

A leopard's **roar** sounds like a **handsaw cutting wood.**

A big cat's **sense of smell** is **20 times stronger** than **a human's.**

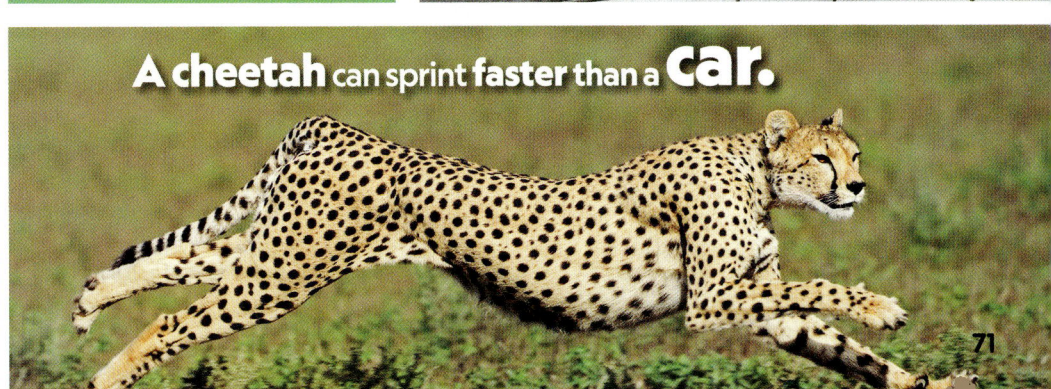

Lion cubs are born **spotted** to help them **camouflage** in the grass.

Bobcats can **pounce 10 feet** (3 m) to catch **prey.**

A **cheetah** can sprint **faster** than a **car.**

71

WILD CATS

CHEETAH RESCUE

AFTER BEING RESCUED FROM WILDLIFE TRAFFICKERS, FIVE SIX-WEEK-OLD CHEETAHS KEEP WARM IN FRONT OF A HEATER.

How conservationists are saving these cats from smugglers

In the back seat of an SUV, a cheetah cub bared his teeth and hissed. Around his neck was a rope, which not too long ago had been used to tie him to the base of a tree. His eyes darted in every direction, taking in his surroundings.

The people who peered into the vehicle meant only one thing to the alarmed cheetah: danger. Stolen from his mother to be someone's pet, the wild cat probably hadn't had many good interactions with humans.

What the cheetah, called Astur, didn't know was that the faces outside were friendly—these people came to rescue him.

ASTUR THE CHEETAH CUB PEEKS OUT OF A CRATE AT HIS RESCUERS.

Cheetah brothers often stay together for life. A female is usually solitary until she has cubs.

Tracking Astur

The people are part of a team of wildlife conservationists who work to stop smugglers from selling cheetahs in Somaliland, an independent region in the East African country of Somalia. The rescuers heard about Astur from informants who keep a lookout for animals that are being trafficked, or illegally traded, in the area. The conservationists learned that Astur had been stolen from the wild and might be sold to a wildlife trafficker. Then that trafficker would sell the cheetah as a pet.

Many people in Somaliland don't know that taking cubs from the wild is against the law. People there who attempt to sell the cats are often trying to make extra money for their families and protect their goat herds from the predators. The rescuers hoped they could convince the man trying to sell Astur to give the cat to them instead of a pet smuggler.

"Sometimes sellers do the right thing and give up the animals when asked," says National Geographic Explorer Timothy Spalla, who is working to end the cheetah trade in Africa and the Middle East.

But before the team could talk to the seller, he drove away. He *did* know that having a cub was illegal and was afraid of being arrested. But the police quickly caught up to the vehicle and handed Astur over to the rescuers.

AMAZING ANIMALS

Check-Up Time

Veterinarian Asma Bile Hersi tried to treat the cub as soon as he was picked up by the team. She checked him as best she could for obvious injuries like open wounds and broken bones. At about seven months old, Astur was older than most cheetah cubs Hersi had treated—and *much* fiercer.

"The people who were keeping him didn't feed him very well," Hersi says. "He was hungry, so that's why he was fighting everyone."

Hersi and the others wanted to get Astur to Hargeysa, Somaliland's capital, so the anxious cub could get a full medical examination. After two days of driving, the team arrived at a rescue center run by the Cheetah Conservation Fund, an organization that cares for cheetahs that were removed from the wild at a young age. There, veterinarian Anna Ciezarek took over examining a distressed Astur. Ciezarek sedated Astur before examining him carefully.

"Ultimately, Astur didn't need treatment," Ciezarek says. "Other cubs aren't so lucky—many of them arrive in very poor condition."

A New Home

To help Astur adjust to the rescue center and feel safe, caregivers put him in a comfortable enclosure. They also focused on having short, friendly interactions with the cat so he'd begin to trust his human caretakers. According to Joe Bottiglieri, the center's cheetah care manager when Astur arrived, just being near the cub without looking scary can be helpful. "Gaining their trust takes time and patience," Bottiglieri says.

Now that he's older, Astur has become more settled at the rescue center. He lives with other male cheetahs. His caregivers say Astur still doesn't like people very much, but he's learned to respond to commands like "come here" and "down." When Astur cooperates, he gets treats like antelope, a favorite cheetah snack.

Protecting Cheetahs

Because he was taken from the wild so young, Astur doesn't know how to survive on his own; he'll spend the rest of his life at the rescue center. Still, he'll hang out with fellow cheetahs, play on plenty of climbing structures, chase around lots of toys, and be cared for by experts who know how to keep him healthy.

Meanwhile, the fight against cheetah smuggling in this region continues. "These animals belong to the wild, not in a sanctuary," says Shukri Haji Ismail Mohamoud, Somaliland's environment minister. "We'll keep fighting for cheetahs like Astur to be safe."

THIS SIX-WEEK-OLD ORPHAN BOTTLE-FEEDS EVERY FEW HOURS TO GET THE NUTRIENTS IT WOULD'VE RECEIVED FROM MOM.

Cheetah cubs chirp to communicate.

Most big cats hunt at night, but cheetahs hunt during the day.

ASTUR THE CHEETAH IS EXAMINED FOR INJURIES. TISSUES IN HIS EARS AND AN EYE MASK HELP KEEP HIM CALM.

ANIMALS IN ACTION

Poo Powers Zoo

I'M POOPED.

BRICKS MADE FROM POOP

THESE AFRICAN WILD DONKEYS "WORK" BY EATING AND POOPING!

ZOOKEEPERS SCOOP THE VALUABLE DROPPINGS.

Colden Common, England
The donkeys, zebras, and giraffes at Marwell Zoo are creating renewable energy—by pooping! In the past, zookeepers sent off the animal waste to be composted. "But then we thought: We might as well use it!" says Duncan East, the zoo's head of sustainability.

Buildings are sometimes heated by burning oil. But oil is a limited resource that releases climate-warming carbon dioxide into the atmosphere. So when this zoo built a new structure to house tropical plants and animals, they decided to heat it with animal poop instead.

Keepers first mix poo from grass-eating animals with leftover bedding material like straw and wood. Then they dry and press the mixture into bricks.

They burn the bricks to heat water that warms a building where sloths, crocodiles, and lizards live. (The bricks do release carbon dioxide when burned, but growing new plants to feed the animals absorbs carbon, reducing the environmental impact.) Zookeeper Zoe Newnham says, "It's a good thing the heating doesn't smell like the poo!"

AMAZING ANIMALS

REAL ANIMAL HEROES

DOLPHINS PROTECT SWIMMER

DOLPHIN

A BOTTLENOSE DOLPHIN COASTS ALONGSIDE ADAM WALKER AS HE SWIMS TOWARD THE NEW ZEALAND SHORE.

Cook Strait, New Zealand
Long-distance swimmer Adam Walker had been swimming for three hours when he found himself surrounded by a pod of 12 bottlenose dolphins. Then he saw something swimming beneath him that was a different size and shape from the others: a great white shark.

The swimmer didn't know how long the shark had been trailing him, but he thinks the dolphins were trying to shield him from the shark. "They swam with me until the shark left," Walker says. "One dolphin rolled on its side and swam facing me, as if to say, 'We've got your back.'"

Scientist Rochelle Constantine, who studies marine mammals, can't say for sure that the animals were protecting Walker. "But dolphins are known for helping helpless things," she says. "And a pod of dolphins can do some damage to a solo shark, so the shark likely backed off because they were there."

Whatever the dolphins were up to, Walker is thankful for their presence.

TALK ABOUT POD SQUAD GOALS.

DOG RESCUES KITTY

Billings, Montana, U.S.A.
Chloe the pug rarely barks. She only acts excited when she wants a carrot snack. Then she spins like a top and points toward the refrigerator. But one freezing cold morning this normally quiet pup went berserk.

Owner Amanda Bjelland was dressing for work when Chloe asked to go out. But as soon as Bjelland closed the door, Chloe barked to come in. Yapping loudly, she followed her owner from room to room. Bjelland was frustrated. "What do you want?" she asked, and let the dog out again.

This time, Chloe ran straight to their backyard pond. She spun around and sat. "Now I know something is wrong," Bjelland said. She raced to the pond herself.

Her Siamese cat, Willow, had fallen through the ice! Bjelland rescued the half-frozen kitty and wrapped her in blankets. For two days, the pug stayed by Willow's side. "It's amazing," Bjelland says. "I never would have known if it hadn't been for Chloe."

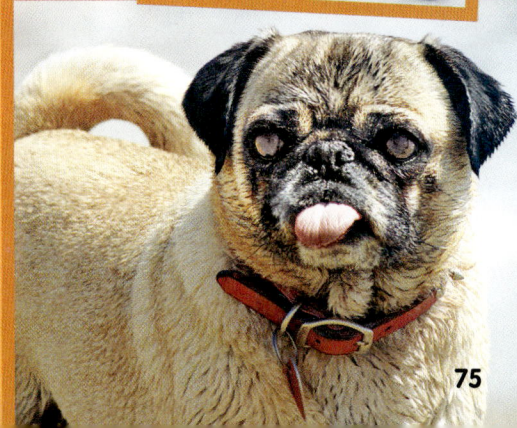

DINOSAURS

Prehistoric TIMELINE

HUMANS HAVE WALKED on Earth for some 300,000 years, a mere blip in the planet's 4.5-billion-year history. A lot has happened during that time. Earth formed, and oxygen levels rose in the millions of years of the Precambrian time. The productive Paleozoic era gave rise to hard-shell organisms, vertebrates, amphibians, and reptiles.

Dinosaurs ruled Earth in the mighty Mesozoic. And 66 million years after dinosaurs became extinct, modern humans emerged in the Cenozoic era. From the first tiny mollusks to the dinosaur giants of the Jurassic and beyond, Earth has seen a lot of transformation.

THE PRECAMBRIAN TIME
4.5 billion to 539 million years ago
- Earth (and other planets) formed from gas and dust left over from a giant cloud that collapsed to form the sun. The giant cloud's collapse was triggered when nearby stars exploded.
- Low levels of oxygen made Earth a suffocating place.
- Early life-forms appeared as oxygen levels rose.

THE PALEOZOIC ERA
539 million to 252 million years ago
- The first insects and other animals appeared on land.
- 450 million years ago (mya), the ancestors of sharks began to swim in the oceans.
- 430 mya, plants began to take root on land.
- More than 360 mya, amphibians emerged from the water.
- Slowly, the major landmasses began to come together, creating Pangaea, a single supercontinent.
- By 300 mya, reptiles had begun to dominate the land.

What Killed the Dinosaurs?

It's a mystery that boggles the minds of scientists: What happened to the dinosaurs? Although various theories have bounced around, a recent study confirms that the most likely culprit is an asteroid or comet that created a giant crater. Researchers say that the impact set off a series of natural disasters like tsunamis, earthquakes, and temperature swings that plagued the dinosaurs' ecosystems and disrupted their food chains. This, paired with intense volcanic eruptions that caused drastic climate changes, is thought to be why about three-quarters of the world's species—including the non-avian dinosaurs—died in a mass extinction.

AMAZING ANIMALS

DINO TIMES

THE MESOZOIC ERA
252 million to 66 million years ago
The Mesozoic era, or the age of the reptiles, consisted of three consecutive time periods (shown below). This is when the first dinosaurs began to appear. They would reign supreme for more than 150 million years.

TRIASSIC PERIOD
252 million to 201 million years ago
- The first mammals appeared. They were rodent-size.
- The first dinosaurs appeared.
- Ferns were the dominant plants on land.
- The giant supercontinent of Pangaea began breaking up toward the end of the Triassic.

JURASSIC PERIOD
201 million to 145 million years ago
- Giant dinosaurs dominated the land.
- Pangaea continued its breakup, and oceans formed in the spaces between the drifting landmasses, allowing sea life, including sharks and marine crocodiles, to thrive.
- Conifer trees spread across the land.

CRETACEOUS PERIOD
145 million to 66 million years ago
- The modern continents developed.
- The largest dinosaurs developed.
- Flowering plants spread across the landscape.
- Mammals flourished, and giant pterosaurs ruled the skies over small birds.
- Temperatures grew more extreme. Dinosaurs lived in deserts, swamps, and forests from the Antarctic to the Arctic.

THE CENOZOIC ERA—PALEOGENE AND NEOGENE PERIODS
66 million to 2.6 million years ago
- Following the dinosaur extinction, mammals rose as the dominant species.
- Birds continued to flourish.
- Volcanic activity was widespread.
- Temperatures began to cool, eventually ending in an ice age.
- The period ended with land bridges forming, which allowed plants and animals to spread to new areas.

DINOSAURS

FIELD NOTES FROM A PALEONTOLOGIST

Meet paleontologist Rodolfo M. Salas-Gismondi

Salas-Gismondi has made it his mission to uncover everything there is to know about prehistoric animals in Amazonia. As one of the first Peruvian vertebrate paleontologists, he's unearthed fossils for creatures like the giant penguin, ground sloths, saber-toothed cats, and crocodilian species that lived long ago. Here, Salas-Gismondi shares what it's like to study fossils for a living.

Q: How did you get into paleontology?

A: As a kid, even as young as five years old, I was fascinated with dinosaurs. I drew them and read everything I could about them. I eventually started going out on my own to look for fossils and got into studying prehistoric marine animals, specifically those that lived in South America.

Q: How do you go about finding fossils?

A: We talk to local people who know the area well and have seen fossils. They'll take us to a site, and then we start to explore the area, and then it can take several days for us to find fossils. We've found fossils in caves and in rocks near rivers. You look everywhere.

AMAZING ANIMALS

Q: What, exactly, do you look for?

A: Skulls and teeth are important for diagnostics, or to determine when these species lived. One big discovery we had lately was a complete skull of a dolphin from the early Miocene epoch in the Napo riverbank, a tributary of the Amazon River. The river was low in the dry season, exposing 20-million-year-old rock where the skull was partially embedded.

Q: What has been your biggest discovery to date?

A: Finding of the skull of *Gnatusuchus*, a 13-million-year-old species of crocodile. It's one of several different species of crocodiles that hunted clams and snails in the swampy waters of proto-Amazonia, in what is now northwestern Peru. That was part of a discovery of the largest number of crocodile species—seven different species!—coexisting in one place at any time in Earth's history.

Q: What are the tools you can't live without in the field?

A: We travel by boat to most sites, so we have to pack pretty light. I pack all of my tools: picks, chisels, brushes, and plaster to stabilize the fossils. We also have to bring a tent because we camp out most of the places we go.

DINOSAURS

DINO Classification

Classifying dinosaurs and all other living things can be a complicated matter, so scientists have devised a system to help with the process. Dinosaurs are put into groups based on a very large range of characteristics.

Scientists divided dinosaurs into two major groups: the bird-hipped ornithischians and the lizard-hipped saurischians.

Ornithischian

ILIUM
PUBIS
ISCHIUM

"Bird-hipped"
(pubis bone in hips points backward)

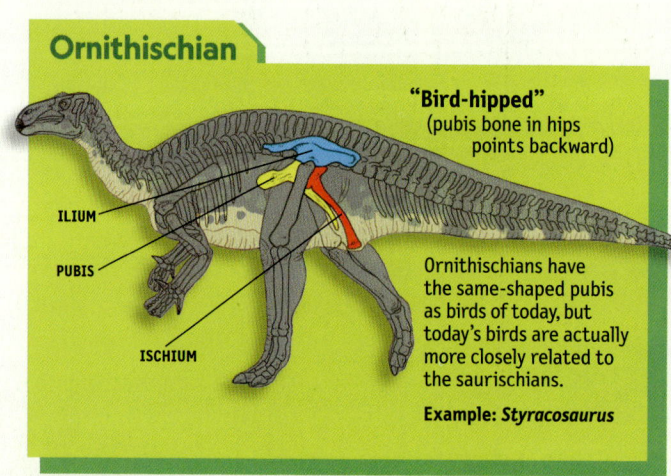

Ornithischians have the same-shaped pubis as birds of today, but today's birds are actually more closely related to the saurischians.

Example: *Styracosaurus*

Saurischian

ILIUM
PUBIS
ISCHIUM

"Lizard-hipped"
(pubis bone in hips points forward)

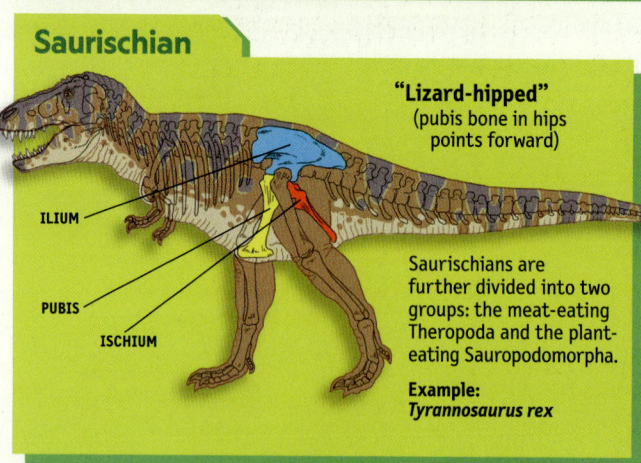

Saurischians are further divided into two groups: the meat-eating Theropoda and the plant-eating Sauropodomorpha.

Example: *Tyrannosaurus rex*

Within these two main divisions, dinosaurs are then separated into orders and then families, such as Stegosauridae. Like other members of the Stegosauria, *Stegosaurus* had spines and plates along its back, neck, and tail.

DINOSAURS SURVIVED MORE THAN **800 TIMES LONGER** THAN HUMANS HAVE LIVED ON EARTH.

T. REX COULD GULP **100 POUNDS** (45.4 KG) OF MEAT AT ONCE.

SOME DINOSAURS WERE **NO BIGGER THAN CHICKENS.**

BRACHIOSAURUS WOULD BE TALL ENOUGH TO LOOK THROUGH A **FIFTH-FLOOR WINDOW.**

AMAZING ANIMALS

4 NEWLY DISCOVERED DINOS

Humans have been searching for—and discovering—dinosaur remains for centuries. In that time, at least 1,000 different kinds of dinos have been found all over the world, and thousands more may still be out there waiting to be unearthed. Recent finds include the largest long-necked dinosaur and a giant sea-dwelling lizard with screwdriver-like teeth.

1
Iani smithi (ornithischian)
Name Meaning: Named after the two-faced Roman god of change, Janus; also honors paleontologist Joshua Aaron Smith
Length: 10 feet (3 m)
Time Range: Mid Cretaceous period
Where: Utah, U.S.A.

2
Vectipelta barretti (ornithischian)
Name Meaning: "Isle of Wight shield"; also refers to paleontologist Paul Barrett
Length: 10 feet (3 m)
Time Range: Early Cretaceous period
Where: Isle of Wight in the United Kingdom

3
Chucarosaurus diripienda (saurischian)
Name Meaning: "Indomitable reptile"
Length: 100 feet (30 m)
Time Range: Mid Cretaceous period
Where: Argentina

4
Stelladens mysteriosus (saurischian)
Name Meaning: "Star-toothed mystery"
Length: 13 feet (4 m)
Time Range: Late Cretaceous period
Where: Morocco

DINOSAURS

WOULD YOU SURVIVE IN THE AGE OF DINOSAURS?

Take this *claw*-some quiz to find out.

Look out! You've been transported back to when dinosaurs roamed planet Earth, and now a dino (*T. rex*) is coming your way.

The age of dinosaurs started some 252 million years ago and lasted until about 66 million years ago. That's when scientists think a huge asteroid wiped out all the dinosaurs on the planet.

Modern humans have only been around for about 300,000 years. If humans had lived during dinosaur times, they would've had to dodge deadly predators, ride out extreme hurricanes, and escape other prehistoric perils.

So ... would you survive in the age of dinosaurs? Answer these questions to find out.

START HERE

SOMETHING IS MOVING IN THE BUSHES NEARBY. WHAT DO YOU DO?

CHECK IT OUT, OF COURSE.

RUN. DUH.

WITHOUT ELECTRICITY, HOW DO YOU SEE AT NIGHT?

YOU DON'T. YOU PREFER THE DARK.

CHOOSE A DINOSAUR TO SPEND TIME WITH.

BRACHIOSAURUS

VELOCIRAPTOR

THINGS AREN'T GOING GREAT ON LAND. DO YOU HEAD TO THE SEA INSTEAD?

HONESTLY? EW.

IT PROBABLY WON'T TASTE *THAT* BAD.

YES—IT'S PROBABLY SAFER THERE.

HOW DOES A TERMITE-AND-CRICKET SANDWICH SOUND?

PICK AN ITEM TO TAKE WITH YOU TO THE PAST.

A MAP

CHOCOLATE!

AMAZING ANIMALS

RESULTS

If these descriptions don't match your personality, don't worry. These questions are just for fun!

WOW, YOU'VE GOT THIS.

Scary dinos ... what scary dinos? **T. rex, Spinosaurus,** and other giant predatory creatures don't spook you. You might be much (much!) smaller than many dinos, but you're also smarter. Meat-eating **Allosaurus,** for example, stretched some 28 feet (8.5 m) in length and weighed three tons (2.7 t). But these dinos were likely only as smart as dogs today. Your ability to remain calm when face-to-face with a hungry carnivore means you'd probably last in this wild world.

Allosaurus

YOU *MIGHT* MAKE IT ... BUT JUST BARELY.

Maybe you'd survive in the age of the dinosaurs. But would you *thrive*? Nah. And that's OK! You wouldn't be the only creature struggling to avoid herds of **Titanosaurus** kicking up clouds of dust with feet about as large as twin-size mattresses! Even sleeping would be stressful: Many meat-eating dinos hunted at night, aided by awesome eyesight and a keen sense of smell. Your problem-solving skills would be helpful, but your best bet would be to hide as much as possible.

Titanosaurus

UH, YOU'RE TOAST.

So you're better suited for a more modern era—so what? After all, the age of dinosaurs didn't have air-conditioning or indoor plumbing—and life is *definitely* better with those things. Your curious nature would mean you'd enjoy observing plant-eating herbivores like **Ankylosaurus.** But once you spotted the bony club on its tail that it probably used to fight predators, your common sense would kick in: "Take me back to the 21st century, please!" (And we wouldn't blame you.)

Ankylosaurus

BY BUILDING A CAMPFIRE

CLIMB A TREE.

A HUGE HURRICANE CAUSES EXTREME FLOODING AND MUDSLIDES. WHAT DO YOU DO?

TAKE SHELTER IN AN ABOVE-GROUND CAVE.

NO—I'M NOT REALLY SURE WHAT'S BELOW THE SURFACE.

BACK AWAY. IMMEDIATELY.

AW! SOMEONE SHOULD WATCH OVER THEM ...

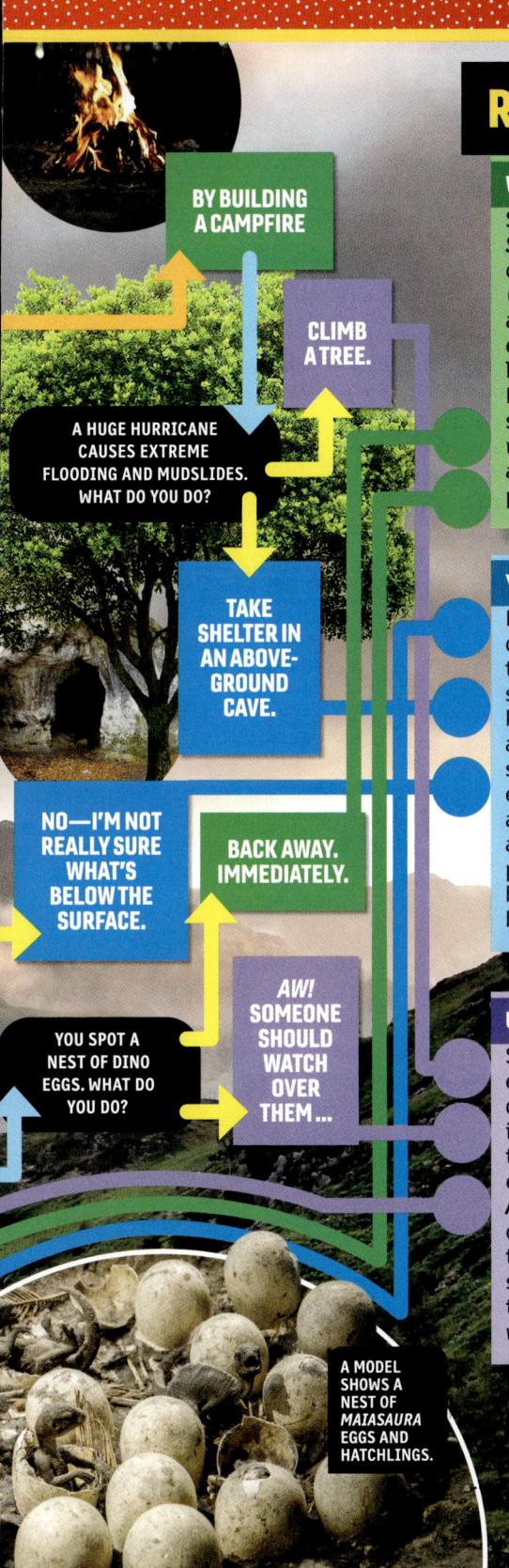

YOU SPOT A NEST OF DINO EGGS. WHAT DO YOU DO?

A MODEL SHOWS A NEST OF *MAIASAURA* EGGS AND HATCHLINGS.

83

MORE FOR YOU

QUIZ WHIZ

Explore just how much you know about animals with this quiz! Write your answers on a piece of paper. Then check them below.

1. Which animal helps prevent wildfires by eating dead brush on hillsides?
a. bears
b. vultures
c. goats
d. pigs

2. True or false? Black cats are bad luck.

3. A peacock's long, showy feathers grow from its ____.
a. back
b. tail
c. head
d. feet

4. A cave in New Zealand is lit inside by _____.
a. the sun
b. iridescent grass
c. phosphorescence in the water
d. bioluminescent worms

5. True or false? People make heating fuel out of animal poop.

Not **STUMPED** yet? Check out the *NATIONAL GEOGRAPHIC KIDS QUIZ WHIZ* collection for more fun **ANIMAL** questions!

ANSWERS: 1. c; 2. False; 3. a; 4. d; 5. True

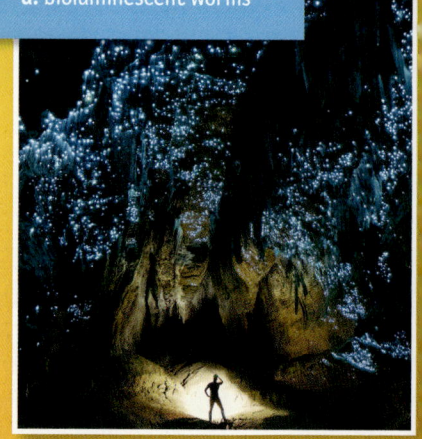

AMAZING ANIMALS

HOMEWORK HELP

Wildly Good Animal Reports

SEAHORSE

Your teacher wants a report on the seahorse. Not to worry. Use these organizational tools so you can stay afloat while writing a report or creating a digital presentation.

STEPS TO SUCCESS: Your report will follow the format of a descriptive or expository essay (see page 127 for "How to Write a Perfect Essay") and should consist of a main idea, followed by supporting details and a conclusion. Use this basic structure for each paragraph, as well as the whole report, and you'll be on the right track.

1. Introduction
State your **main idea**.
> Seahorses are fascinating fish with many unique characteristics.

2. Body
Provide **supporting points** for your main idea.
> Seahorses are very small fish.
> Seahorses are named for their head shape.
> Seahorses display behavior that is rare among almost all other animals on Earth.

Then **expand** on those points with further description, explanation, or discussion.
> Seahorses are very small fish.
> Seahorses are about the size of an M&M at birth, and most adult seahorses would fit in a teacup.
> Seahorses are named for their head shape.
> With long, tubelike snouts, seahorses are named for their resemblance to horses.
> A group of seahorses is called a herd.
> Seahorses display behavior that is rare among almost all other animals on Earth.
> Unlike most other fish, seahorses stay with one mate their entire lives. They are also among the only species in which dads, not moms, give birth to the babies.

3. Conclusion
Wrap it up with a **summary** of your whole report.
> Because of their unique shape and unusual behavior, seahorses are among the most fascinating and easily distinguishable animals in the ocean.

KEY INFORMATION

Here are some things you should consider including in your report:

What does your animal look like?
To what other species is it related?
How does it move?
Where does it live?
What does it eat?
What are its predators?
How long does it live?
Is it endangered?
Why do you find it interesting?

SEPARATE FACT FROM FICTION: Your animal may have been featured in a movie or in myths and legends. Compare and contrast how the animal has been portrayed with how it behaves in reality. For example, penguins can't dance the way they do in the movie *Happy Feet*.

PROOFREAD AND REVISE: As you would do with any essay, when you're finished, check for misspellings, grammatical mistakes, and punctuation errors. It often helps to have someone else proofread your work, too, as that person may catch things you have missed. Also, look for ways to make your sentences and paragraphs even better. Add more descriptive language, choosing just the right verbs, adverbs, and adjectives to make your writing come alive.

BE CREATIVE: Use visual aids to add interest to your report. Include animal photos you find online, or draw your own! You can also build a miniature animal habitat diorama or create a simulated virtual habitat. Use creativity to help communicate your passion for the subject.

THE FINAL RESULT: Put it all together in one final, polished draft. Make it neat and clean, and remember to cite your references.

SPACE and EARTH

Scientists work on the James Webb Space Telescope before its 2021 launch.

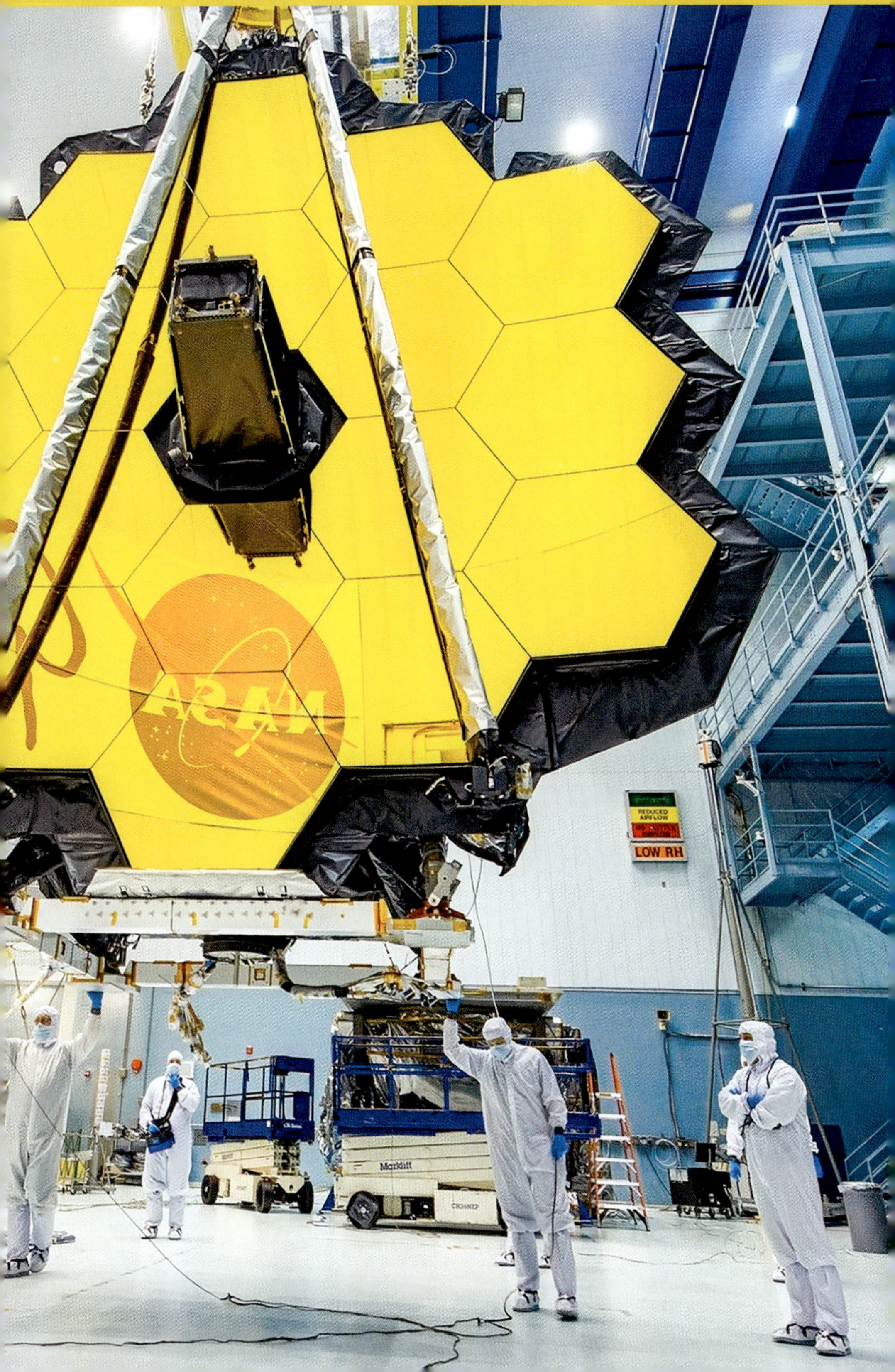
REDUCED AIRFLOW
LOW RH
Marklift

SPACE

ARTIST'S INTERPRETATION OF THE MILKY WAY

1 It could take up to **8 years** to fly from **Earth to Neptune.**

2 An asteroid called **Cucula** was named after the **cuckoo bird.**

3 From Earth you always look at the **same side** of the moon.

4 The temperature on **Uranus's surface can plunge to -357°F** (-216°C).

5 A star at **the center** of the **Crab Nebula** formation rotates **30 times a second.**

SPACE AND EARTH

Out-of-This-World
Facts About
Space

6 **Mars** has **blue** sunsets.

7 Astronauts have **grown potatoes** on the **space shuttle.**

8 The north pole of **Uranus** doesn't get sunlight for almost **42 years** at a time.

9 A recent **lightning storm** on Saturn was nearly big enough to cover the **entire United States.**

10 One year on **Neptune** lasts about **165 Earth years.**

89

SPACE

PLANETS

MERCURY

VENUS

EARTH

MARS

CERES

JUPITER

SUN

MERCURY
Average distance from the sun: 35,983,125 miles (57,909,227 km)
Position from the sun in orbit: 1st
Equatorial diameter: 3,032 miles (4,879 km)
Length of day: 59 Earth days
Length of year: 88 Earth days
Known moons: 0

VENUS
Average distance from the sun: 67,238,251 miles (108,209,475 km)
Position from the sun in orbit: 2nd
Equatorial diameter: 7,520 miles (12,103 km)
Length of day: 243 Earth days
Length of year: 225 Earth days
Known moons: 0

EARTH
Average distance from the sun: 92,956,050 miles (149,598,262 km)
Position from the sun in orbit: 3rd
Equatorial diameter: 7,900 miles (12,750 km)
Length of day: 24 hours
Length of year: 365.25 days
Known moons: 1

MARS
Average distance from the sun: 141,637,725 miles (227,943,824 km)
Position from the sun in orbit: 4th
Equatorial diameter: 4,220 miles (6,792 km)
Length of day: 24.6 Earth hours
Length of year: 1.88 Earth years
Known moons: 2

SPACE AND EARTH

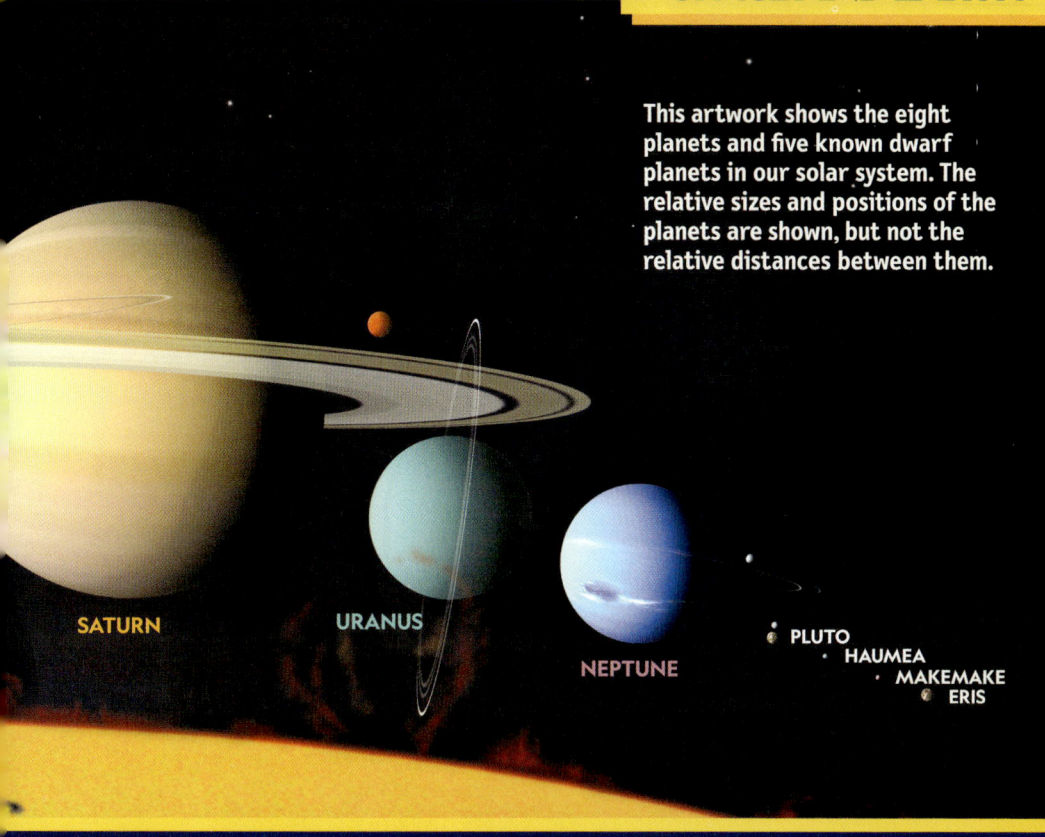

This artwork shows the eight planets and five known dwarf planets in our solar system. The relative sizes and positions of the planets are shown, but not the relative distances between them.

SATURN
URANUS
NEPTUNE
PLUTO
HAUMEA
MAKEMAKE
ERIS

JUPITER
Average distance from the sun: 483,638,564 miles (778,340,821 km)
Position from the sun in orbit: 6th
Equatorial diameter: 86,880 miles (139,820 km)
Length of day: 9.9 Earth hours
Length of year: 11.9 Earth years
Known moons: At least 95*

SATURN
Average distance from the sun: 886,489,415 miles (1,426,666,422 km)
Position from the sun in orbit: 7th
Equatorial diameter: 72,367 miles (116,464 km)
Length of day: 10.7 Earth hours
Length of year: 30 Earth years
Known moons: 146*

URANUS
Average distance from the sun: 1,783,744,300 miles (2,870,658,186 km)
Position from the sun in orbit: 8th
Equatorial diameter: 31,518 miles (50,724 km)
Length of day: 17.2 Earth hours
Length of year: 84 Earth years
Known moons: 28

NEPTUNE
Average distance from the sun: 2,795,173,960 miles (4,498,396,441 km)
Position from the sun in orbit: 9th
Equatorial diameter: 30,599 miles (49,244 km)
Length of day: 16.1 Earth hours
Length of year: 164.8 Earth years
Known moons: 16

*Includes provisional moons, which await confirmation and naming from the International Astronomical Union.

For information about dwarf planets, see page 92.

SPACE

DWARF PLANETS

Haumea

Eris

Pluto

CERES
Position from the sun in orbit: 5th
Length of day: 9 Earth hours
Length of year: 4.39 Earth years
Known moons: 0

PLUTO
Position from the sun in orbit: 10th
Length of day: 6.39 Earth days
Length of year: 248 Earth years
Known moons: 5

HAUMEA
Position from the sun in orbit: 11th
Length of day: 3.9 Earth hours
Length of year: 285 Earth years
Known moons: 2

MAKEMAKE
Position from the sun in orbit: 12th
Length of day: 22.5 Earth hours
Length of year: 305.34 Earth years
Known moons: 1*

ERIS
Position from the sun in orbit: 13th
Length of day: 1.1 Earth days
Length of year: 558 Earth years
Known moons: 1

Thanks to advanced technology, astronomers have been spotting many never-before-seen celestial bodies with their telescopes. One recent discovery? A population of icy objects orbiting the sun beyond Pluto. The largest, like Pluto itself, are classified as dwarf planets. Smaller than the moon but still massive enough to pull themselves into a ball, dwarf planets nevertheless lack the gravitational "oomph" to clear their neighborhood of other sizable objects. So, although larger, more massive planets pretty much have their orbits to themselves, dwarf planets orbit the sun in swarms that include other dwarf planets, as well as smaller chunks of rock or ice.

So far, astronomers have identified five dwarf planets in our solar system: Ceres, Pluto, Haumea, Makemake, and Eris. There are many more newly discovered dwarf planets that will need additional study before they are named. Astronomers are observing hundreds of newly found objects in the frigid outer solar system. As time and technology advance, the family of known dwarf planets will surely continue to grow.

*Includes provisional moons, which await confirmation and naming from the International Astronomical Union.

SPACE AND EARTH

BLACK HOLE TURNS STAR INTO DOUGHNUT AND EATS IT

What does a hungry black hole snack on? How about a doughnut? That's *kind of* what the Hubble Telescope captured happening in space: a black hole stretching a star into a giant "doughnut" the size of our solar system. The black hole, perched some 300 million light-years away, then used its incredibly strong gravitational pull to "swallow" the stellar doughnut.

This phenomenon is known as tidal disruption. It occurs when a star gets too close to a black hole and the tidal forces of the black hole rip the star apart. It's sort of like how the moon pulls tides in Earth's oceans, but way more dramatic!

About 100 tidal disruption events around black holes have been detected by astronomers through the years. Still, a star stretching—and shredding—at this magnitude is fairly rare. Now, the only question is: What's the black hole's favorite flavor of doughnut?

What if aliens came to Earth?

Humans haven't explored our own solar system (or the universe beyond) well enough to rule out the presence of extraterrestrials. How cool would it be if we found out aliens do exist? Aliens that could pay us a visit from outside our solar system would possess amazing technology light-years ahead of our own. After all, these travelers figured out how to cross vast distances between stars. But not everyone is ready to welcome aliens to Earth. Physicist Stephen Hawking believed in extraterrestrials and feared that any alien visitors would likely use their technology to ransack our planet for its resources. He thought Earthlings might be enslaved or wiped out. But who knows for sure? For now, those extraterrestrials are staying extra hidden.

SPACE

Weird but true!

Check out these outrageous space facts.

Astronauts' **PEE** goes into a **cleaning system** and is **turned back** into **DRINKING WATER!**

Crew members were treated to a **PIZZA NIGHT IN SPACE** when NASA sent them a special meal kit.

The **INTERNATIONAL SPACE STATION** orbits **EARTH** every **92 minutes,** which means **ASTRONAUTS** on board get to see **16 sunsets and sunrises a day!**

The **LACK OF GRAVITY** means that astronauts **GROW UP TO TWO INCHES** (5 cm) **TALLER** during a stay on the space station.

Working **SEVEN HOURS STRAIGHT** in mega-constricting suits means that astronauts must sometimes **WEAR DIAPERS.**

94

SPACE AND EARTH

Sky Calendar 2026

LOOK UP! From lunar eclipses to meteor showers—which are often named after a nearby star or constellation—here are some of the major events dazzling the night sky in 2026.

- **JANUARY 3-4**
  QUADRANTIDS METEOR SHOWER PEAK. At its peak, this shower can produce some 100 meteors an hour, making it one of the most impressive meteor events.

- **JANUARY 10**
  JUPITER AT OPPOSITION. Jupiter—and its moons—are at their closest approach to Earth, giving the planet a brighter and larger appearance in the evening sky.

- **MARCH 3**
  TOTAL LUNAR ECLIPSE. Visible throughout most of eastern Asia, Australia, the Pacific Ocean, and North America. Watch as Earth passes directly between the sun and the moon, causing Earth's shadow to completely cover the moon.

- **MARCH 20**
  MARCH EQUINOX. Earth's orbit and axis line up so the Northern and Southern Hemispheres get the same amount of sunlight.

- **APRIL 22-23**
  LYRIDS METEOR SHOWER. Best viewed after midnight, this shower sends some 20 meteors streaking through the sky each hour.

- **MAY 31**
  FULL MOON, BLUE MOON. Despite its name, the moon is not actually blue; the name just refers to the semi-rare occurrence of two full moons in one month.

- **AUGUST 12**
  TOTAL SOLAR ECLIPSE. The moon moves between Earth and the sun, almost completely obscuring the sun. Best visibility is in parts of Europe.

- **AUGUST 12-13**
  PERSEIDS METEOR SHOWER. See up to 100 meteors an hour at its peak! Best viewing is in the direction of the constellation Perseus.

- **AUGUST 28**
  PARTIAL LUNAR ECLIPSE. Grab your telescope (or even a pair of binoculars) and watch as Earth's shadow briefly covers a small portion of the moon.

- **OCTOBER 21-22**
  ORIONIDS METEOR SHOWER. View up to 20 meteors an hour. Look toward the constellation Orion for the best show.

- **NOVEMBER 20**
  MERCURY AT GREATEST WESTERN ELONGATION. Just before sunrise, Mercury will be at its highest point above the horizon. Look for the planet in the eastern sky.

- **NOVEMBER 24**
  FULL MOON, SUPERMOON. Also known as the Frosty moon, the moon will be near its closest approach to Earth and may look larger and brighter than usual.

- **DECEMBER 21**
  DECEMBER SOLSTICE. The shortest day of the year in the Northern Hemisphere, when the sun reaches its lowest point in the sky. In the Southern Hemisphere, it's the longest day of the year.

- **DECEMBER 23**
  FULL MOON, SUPERMOON. The last of three supermoons in 2026, the moon will be near its closest approach to Earth, appearing lighter and brighter.

Note: Dates may vary slightly depending on your location. Check with a local planetarium for the best viewing times in your area.

EARTH

A LOOK INSIDE

The distance from Earth's surface to its center is about 3,950 miles (6,435 km) at the Equator. There are four layers: a thin, rigid crust; the rocky mantle; the outer core, which is a layer of molten iron and nickel; and finally the inner core, which is believed to be mostly solid iron and nickel.

The **CRUST** includes tectonic plates, landmasses, and the ocean. Its average thickness varies from 5 to 25 miles (8 to 40 km).

The **MANTLE** is about 1,800 miles (2,900 km) of hot, thick, solid rock.

The **OUTER CORE** is liquid molten rock made mostly of iron and nickel.

The **INNER CORE** is a solid center made mostly of iron and nickel.

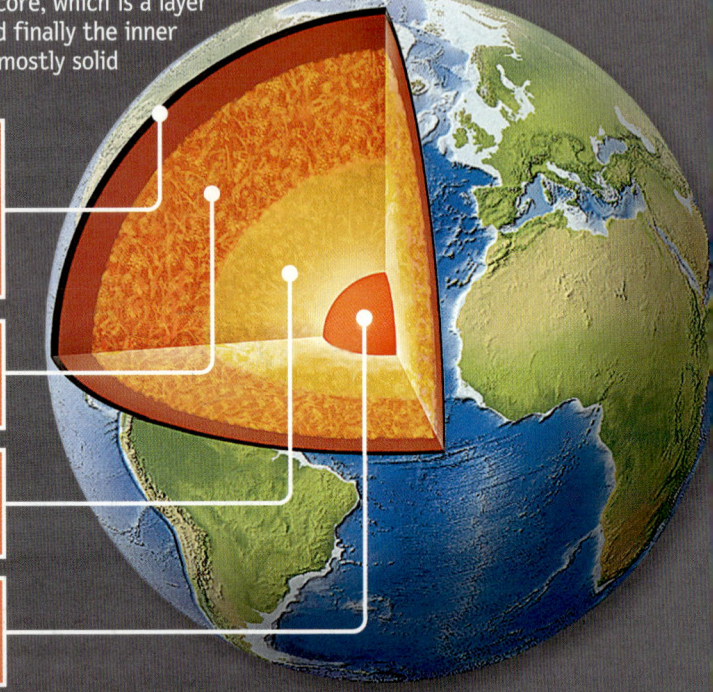

What if you could dig to the other side of Earth?

Got a magma-proof suit and a magical drill that can cut through any surface? Then you're ready to dig some 7,900 miles (12,714 km) to Earth's other side. First you'd need to drill up to 25 miles (40 km) through the planet's ultra-tough crust to its mantle. The heat and pressure at the mantle are intense enough to turn carbon into diamonds—and to, um, crush you. If you were able to survive, you'd still have to bore 1,800 more miles (2,897 km) to hit Earth's Mars-size core that can reach 11,000°F (6093°C). Now just keep drilling through the core and then the mantle and crust on the opposite side until you resurface on the planet's other side. But exit your tunnel fast. A hole dug through Earth would close quickly as surrounding rock filled in the empty space. The closing of the tunnel might cause small earthquakes, and your path home would definitely be blocked. Happy digging!

SPACE AND EARTH

ROCK STARS

Rocks and minerals are everywhere on Earth! And it can be a challenge to tell one from the other. So what's the difference between a rock and a mineral? A rock is a naturally occurring solid object made mostly from minerals. Minerals are solid, nonliving substances that occur in nature—and the basic components of most rocks. Rocks can be made of just one mineral or, like granite, of many minerals. But not all rocks are made of minerals: Coal comes from plant material, while amber is formed from ancient tree resin.

Igneous

Named for the Greek word meaning "from fire," igneous rocks form when hot, molten liquid called magma cools. Pools of magma form deep underground and slowly work their way to Earth's surface. If they make it all the way, the liquid rock erupts and is called lava. As the layers of lava build up, they form a mountain called a volcano. Typical igneous rocks include obsidian, basalt, and pumice, which is so chock-full of gas bubbles that it actually floats in water.

ANDESITE **GRANITE PORPHYRY**

Metamorphic

Metamorphic rocks are the masters of change! These rocks were once igneous or sedimentary, but thanks to intense heat and pressure deep within Earth, they have undergone a total transformation from their original form. These rocks never truly melt; instead, the heat twists and bends them until their shapes substantially change. Metamorphic rocks include slate as well as marble, which is used for buildings, monuments, and sculptures.

MICA SCHIST **BANDED GNEISS**

Sedimentary

When wind, water, and ice constantly wear away and weather rocks, smaller pieces called sediment are left behind. These are sedimentary rocks, also known as gravel, sand, silt, and clay. As water flows downhill, it carries the sedimentary grains into lakes and oceans, where they are deposited. As the loose sediment piles up, the grains eventually get compacted or cemented back together again. The result is new sedimentary rock. Sandstone, gypsum, limestone, and shale are sedimentary rocks that are formed this way.

LIMESTONE **HALITE**

EARTH

MINERALS
• THE INSIDE STORY •

Mohs definitely

BY THE NUMBERS

Geologists rate the hardness of rocks and minerals on a scale from 1 to 10. It's named for the man who created it, Friedrich Mohs.

MINERAL	HARDNESS
Talc	1
Gypsum	2
Calcite	3
Fluorite	4
Apatite	5
Orthoclase	6
Quartz	7
Topaz	8
Corundum	9
Diamond	10

When you look at a rock, you see a solid chunk of stuff. What you might not be able to see are the minerals that are inside almost all rocks. Minerals are everywhere—there are more than 5,000 different ones on Earth, and they exist on other planets, too. Not all of them are commonly found in rocks—fewer than a hundred make up most of Earth's crust. Of these, a handful of minerals, like feldspar, mica, and quartz, are extremely common "ingredients" in rocks. They're sort of like salt, sugar, and flour to a baker—you couldn't make much without them.

What makes one mineral different from another? The key lies in things you cannot even see, even with a powerful microscope. All substances are made up of tiny particles called atoms. Each mineral's atoms come together to form crystals in a particular way. This crystal structure is one way geologists tell minerals apart.

IT'S ELEMENTAL

Most minerals are made up of two or more elements—these are substances that can't be broken down into simpler substances with the same chemical properties. They're the basic building blocks of all the gas, liquids, and solids in the world, and some help keep you alive, like oxygen. It's part of the air you breathe and the water you drink. And it turns up in lots of rocks, too, because lots of minerals have oxygen in them. Oxygen is one of the 118 chemical elements known to exist.

SPACE AND EARTH

A PROPER LOOK AT MINERAL PROPERTIES

A property might be a nice piece of land, so minerals must be pretty rich since they have lots of properties! Not exactly. Properties are what geologists call the various traits or features that make one mineral different from another. Crystal form is one property. Some of the others are how hard the mineral is and its luster, which describes how light reflects off a mineral. (Some shine in the light, while others are dull.) Another mineral property is its streak—the color it leaves when it's rubbed on a white porcelain tile.

You probably share some traits with other students in your classes, like your age and where you live. Well, minerals are like that, too. Depending on the elements inside of them, minerals are grouped into different classes. The biggest mineral clan is the silicates—minerals made up primarily of oxygen and silicon, with some other elements mixed in. Here's a quick look at the other major mineral classes.

BORATE: formed when oxygen combines with a form of the element boron

CARBONATES: minerals with carbon and oxygen, along with an element, such as calcium

HALIDES: any of several elements, such as chlorine or fluorine, combined with a metal

HYDROXIDES: formed when water combines with a metallic element

OXIDES: formed when oxygen combines with a metal, such as iron

NATIVE ELEMENTS: minerals that have only one element, such as gold and silver

SULFATES: chemical compounds composed of one sulfur atom with four oxygen atoms surrounding it

SULFIDES: formed when sulphur combines with a metal, such as lead

99

EARTH

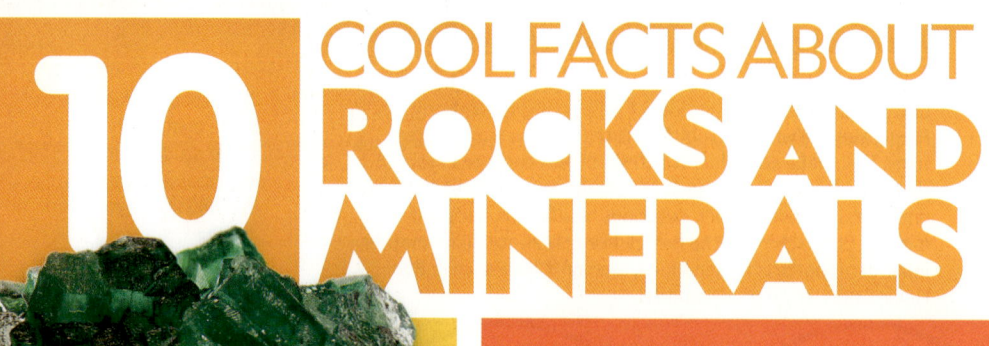

10 COOL FACTS ABOUT ROCKS AND MINERALS

Found in **South Africa**, **the oldest known emeralds,** a mineral, are almost **3 billion years old.**

Scientists study **how lava flows** by **melting** billion-year-old **basalt rock.**

A professional rock expert is called a **petrologist.**

The inside of a **geode rock** discovered in Brazil looks just like **Cookie Monster.**

Called **fool's gold,** a mineral called **pyrite** is often **mistaken for gold.**

100

SPACE AND EARTH

According to legend, the **giant rock formations** of Ha Long Bay in Vietnam were created by **dragons** to keep out invaders.

In India, thin sheets called **varak** are made from the **mineral silver** to decorate **desserts.**

If you heat a diamond to **1405°F** (763°C), the mineral will **vaporize.**

STALACTITES

Some **stalactite mineral formations** have been **growing in caves** for nearly **200,000 years!**

Different layers of **sandstone mountains** in **China's Zhangye National Geopark** show off **rainbow-like colors.**

EARTH

A HOT TOPIC

WHAT GOES ON INSIDE A STEAMING, BREWING VOLCANO?

If you could look inside a volcano, you'd see something that looks like a long pipe, called a conduit. This leads from inside the magma chamber under the crust up to a vent, or opening, at the top of the mountain. Some conduits have branches that shoot off to the side, called fissures.

When pressure builds from gases inside the volcano, the gases must find an escape, and they head up toward the surface! An eruption occurs when lava, gases, ash, and rocks explode out of the vent.

- CRATER
- VENT
- CONDUIT
- FISSURE
- MAGMA CHAMBER
- HARDENED LAVA AND ASH LAYERS

102

SPACE AND EARTH

TYPES OF VOLCANOES

CINDER CONE VOLCANO
Eve Cone, Canada

Cinder cone volcanoes look like an upside-down bowl. They spew cinder and hot ash. Some of these volcanoes smoke and erupt for years at a time.

COMPOSITE VOLCANO
Licancábur, Chile

Composite volcanoes, or stratovolcanoes, form as lava, ash, and cinder from previous eruptions harden and build up over time. These volcanoes spit out pyroclastic flows, or thick explosions of hot ash and gas that travel at hundreds of miles an hour.

SHIELD VOLCANO
Mauna Loa, Hawaii, U.S.A.

The gentle, broad slopes of a shield volcano look like an ancient warrior's shield. Its eruptions are often slower. Lava splatters and bubbles rather than shooting forcefully into the air.

LAVA DOME VOLCANO
Mount St. Helens, Washington, U.S.A.

Dome volcanoes have steep sides. Hardened lava often plugs the vent at the top of a dome volcano. Pressure builds beneath the surface until the top blows.

RING OF FIRE

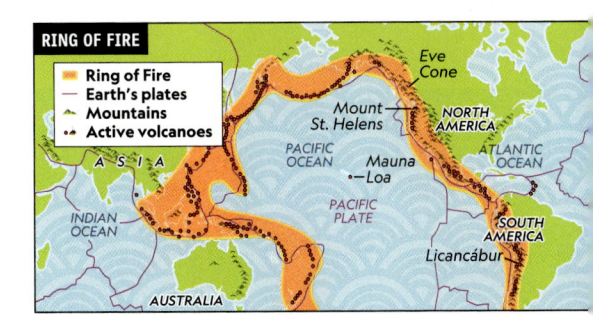

RING OF FIRE
- Ring of Fire
- Earth's plates
- Mountains
- Active volcanoes

Although volcanoes are found on every continent, most are located along an arc known as the Ring of Fire. This area, which forms a horseshoe shape in the Pacific Ocean, stretches some 24,900 miles (40,000 km). Several of the large, rigid plates that make up Earth's surface are found here, and they are prone to shifting toward each other and colliding. The result? Volcanic eruptions and earthquakes—and plenty of them. In fact, the Ring of Fire hosts 90 percent of the world's recorded earthquakes and about 75 percent of its active volcanoes.

103

EARTH

SUPER-VOLCANOES

MAUNA LOA, IN HAWAII, IS THE LARGEST ACTIVE VOLCANO ON EARTH.

THE BIGGEST

How do you determine the size of a volcano? One way is to measure its height. In this category, Mauna Kea in Hawaii, U.S.A., is the clear winner. Its summit is 13,797 feet (4,205 m) above sea level. But if you measure it from where it actually begins, under the Pacific Ocean, it's almost three times as tall: 33,500 feet (10,211 m)! It's not only the world's tallest volcano, but also the world's tallest mountain. It's taller even than Mount Everest—in Nepal's Himalaya mountains—which is 29,032 feet (8,849 m) from bottom to top. Mauna Kea is still considered active, even though its last eruption was about 4,500 years ago. That's because there's still magma beneath it, which means it likely won't stay asleep forever.

In terms of how much space it takes up on land—also known as the footprint—the world's biggest volcano is Tamu Massif, located about 1,000 miles (1,609 km) off the coast of Japan. This extinct, bowl-shaped shield volcano covers an area of more than 100,000 square miles (258,999 sq km), which is bigger than the entire state of New Mexico, U.S.A. That's roughly 50 times the size of the world's largest active volcano: Hawaii's Mauna Loa, which covers an area of just 2,000 square miles (5,180 sq km).

SPACE AND EARTH

CASTLE GEYSER AT YELLOWSTONE NATIONAL PARK

ANAK KRAKATAU, "CHILD OF KRAKATAU," VOLCANO, INDONESIA

Scientists didn't discover Tamu Massif until 1993, and, at first, they mistakenly thought it was three separate volcanoes. That's because, believe it or not, Tamu Massif is not easy to see: It sits 6,500 feet (1,981 m) under the Pacific Ocean!

THE MOST POWERFUL

Yellowstone National Park—located in Wyoming, Montana, and Idaho—is the oldest national park in the United States. But it's also home to a supervolcano, a kind of volcano that's thousands of times more powerful than a regular volcano. Supervolcanoes aren't shaped like mountains—instead, they usually look like giant depressions in the ground. These depressions, called calderas, have huge magma chambers under Earth's crust. They form after an eruption, when the ground above the now semi-empty magma chamber collapses, creating a giant depression. Yellowstone is actually made up of three calderas, which were created after massive eruptions 2.1 million years ago, 1.3 million years ago, and 640,000 years ago. Thankfully, there's no evidence that magma is building up beneath Yellowstone's calderas, and scientists don't predict any eruptions in the near future.

Unfortunately, scientists in 1600 couldn't predict that a small Peruvian volcano called Huaynaputina would be responsible for the largest volcanic eruption in South America, and one of the largest eruptions on Earth. Before it blew, Huaynaputina caused four days of serious earthquakes. Once it erupted, it sent an ash plume almost 22 miles (35.5 km) into the sky. The eruption set off deafening thunder and 40 hours of darkness. By the time it was over, it had sent hot mud pouring into the ocean 75 miles (121 km) away.

More than 200 years later, on the island of Krakatau, in Indonesia, another huge eruption took place. In 1883, the Krakatau volcano produced a fast-moving, superhot surge of gas and rock that traveled across water to an island some 24 miles (38.6 km) away. The volcano's explosion could be heard almost 3,000 miles (4,828 km) away. Ash spewed from the volcano and traveled almost 3,800 miles (6,116 km). The eruption was so powerful that, within a year of the explosion, it caused temperatures to drop, and they didn't climb back to normal for another four years. Even now, Krakatau is experiencing small eruptions, getting ready for another big bang, but no one knows when it might erupt again.

1938 POSTER FOR YELLOWSTONE NATIONAL PARK

MORE FOR YOU

QUIZ WHIZ

Are your space and Earth smarts out of this world? Take this quiz!

Write your answers on a piece of paper. Then check them below.

1 **True or false?** Sedimentary rock is formed from cooled lava.

2 In the phenomenon known as a tidal disruption, a black hole pulls a star into the shape of:
a. a doughnut
b. an ice-cream cone
c. a pizza
d. a hot dog

3 How long does it take for the International Space Station to orbit Earth?
a. 92 minutes
b. 92 days
c. 92 hours
d. 92 years

4 What color are sunsets on Mars?
a. purple
b. red
c. green
d. blue

5 **True or false?** Some mountains in China have rainbow-colored stripes.

Not **STUMPED** yet? Check out the *NATIONAL GEOGRAPHIC KIDS QUIZ WHIZ* book collection for more fun **SPACE AND EARTH** questions!

ANSWERS: 1. False; 2. a; 3. a; 4. d; 5. True

SPACE AND EARTH

HOMEWORK HELP

ACE YOUR SCIENCE FAIR

You can learn a lot about science from books, but to really experience it firsthand, you need to get into the lab and "do" some science. Whether you're entering a science fair or just want to learn more on your own, there are many scientific projects you can do. So put on your goggles and lab coat, and start experimenting.

Most likely, the topic of the project will be up to you. So remember to choose something that is interesting to you.

THE BASIS OF ALL SCIENTIFIC INVESTIGATION AND DISCOVERY IS THE SCIENTIFIC METHOD. CONDUCT YOUR EXPERIMENT USING THESE STEPS:

Observation/Research—Ask a question or identify a problem.

Hypothesis—Once you've asked a question, do some thinking and come up with some possible answers.

Experimentation—How can you determine if your hypothesis is correct? You test it. You perform an experiment. Make sure the experiment you design will produce an answer to your question.

Analysis—Gather your results, and use a consistent process to carefully measure the results.

Conclusion—Do the results support your hypothesis?

Report Your Findings—Communicate your results in the form of a paper that summarizes your entire experiment.

Bonus!
Take your project one step further. Your school may have an annual science fair, but there are also local, state, regional, and national science fair competitions. Compete with other students for awards, prizes, and scholarships!

EXPERIMENT DESIGN
There are three types of experiments you can do.

MODEL KIT—a display, such as an erupting volcano model. Simple and to the point.

DEMONSTRATION—shows the scientific principles in action, such as a tornado in a wind tunnel.

INVESTIGATION—the home run of science projects, and just the type of project for science fairs. This kind demonstrates proper scientific experimentation and uses the scientific method to reveal answers to questions.

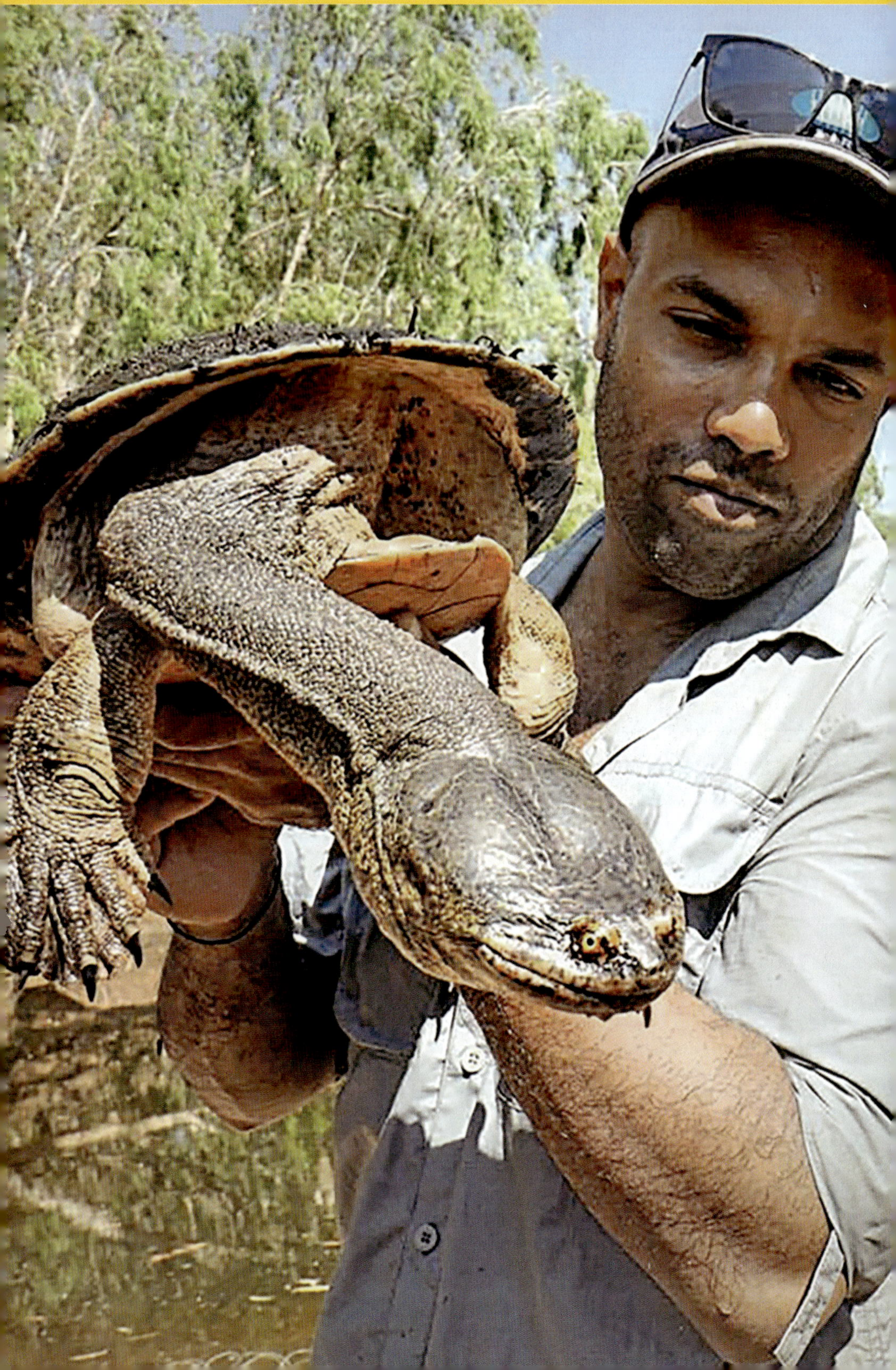

AWESOME
EXPLORATION

National Geographic Explorer Ru Somaweera holds a sandstone long-neck turtle in the Australian outback.

EXPLORERS

DARE TO EXPLORE

How three Nat Geo Explorers are traveling the world to study animals, nature, and human history

BROWN HOWLER MONKEYS MAKE CHILLING NOISES IN A BRAZILIAN RAINFOREST.

THE BIOLOGIST

Bruno Alves Buzatto studies spiders all over the globe. Below, he describes searching for Australia's Sydney funnel-web spider, one of the most venomous spiders on the planet.

TRACKING DEVICE

A SYDNEY FUNNEL-WEB SPIDER WEARS A TRACKING DEVICE ON ITS BACK.

"Sydney funnel-web spiders live mostly underground. But when my tracking device showed one high up in some rocks, I thought I had discovered a new hiding spot. But then a gecko suddenly appeared. "That's when I realized the signal I'd been tracking was emitting from the gecko—it had eaten my spider! [The gecko eventually pooped out the transmitter in a lab.] I didn't discover a new hiding spot for these spiders, but I *did* discover another animal that preys on them.

"Tracking these spiders is always dangerous, no matter how many times you've handled one. They're the size of your palm with huge fangs, and if one bites you, you need to go to the hospital—fast.

"But we need to learn more about the mysterious species. So when we spot one, we use carbon dioxide to make it sleep. Then we carefully attach transmitters to track them. That *is*, when a gecko doesn't eat our subject!"

"More people should be observers of nature and not try to conquer it. Appreciating the creatures we share the Earth with is important."

BUZATTO TRACKS A SIGNAL FROM A SYDNEY FUNNEL-WEB SPIDER.

WANT TO BE A BIOLOGIST?
STUDY Biology, entomology
READ *Braiding Sweetgrass for Young Adults* by Robin Wall Kimmerer, adapted by Monique Gray Smith
WATCH *A Bug's Life*

AWESOME EXPLORATION

THE PRIMATOLOGIST

AJ Hardie studies brown howler monkeys in southeastern Brazil. Here, Hardie talks about listening to these animals communicate in the tropical rainforests where they live.

"I've been chased by angry armadillo wasps and tracked by six-foot (2-m)-long boa constrictors. But some animals in the rainforest welcome me to their home.

"I study brown howler monkeys, which live in parts of Central and South America. I studied three groups for months, and they learned to recognize me and would make excited noises when they saw me.

"Their 'howling' is actually a roaring sound they make in their throats. They have a bone called a hyoid that's as big as a golf ball but hollow like a balloon. It allows them to create the sounds they make when they're expressing excitement or communicating their location.

"Once, I was relaxing on a hammock close to a troop I'd been observing. Several younger monkeys studied me closely, but one of the adults took a nap! Most animals won't sleep in front of you unless they *really* trust you. That made me feel special, like I was part of the forest, too."

"When you see animals like monkeys up close, you get a sense of how closely we're related to them and how much our lives are tied together."

WANT TO BE A PRIMATOLOGIST?
STUDY Anthropology, ecology
READ *Mad About Monkeys* by Owen Davey
WATCH *Jane*, a documentary about primatologist Jane Goodall

THE ARCHAEOLOGIST

Veena Mushrif-Tripathy studies human skeletal remains found at archaeological sites. Here, she recalls navigating an ancient cave in India.

"I collect bones at archaeological dig sites to piece together and study human remains. Sometimes these skeletons have been there for hundreds, even thousands, of years.

"One time, I had just discovered another room in a cave called the Old Lady Spider Cave. I needed to slide down to the new room with only my headlamp light to guide me. And I had to move very slowly—if I moved too quickly, the loose sandstone roof might fall in. Bones were scattered everywhere, so I needed to be careful not to crush them.

"Studying ancient DNA gives us a glimpse into where humans have come from. Being in caves helps me feel the cultures that came before me. There's a major sense of connection to these people and their lives."

MUSHRIF-TRIPATHY WEARS GLOVES TO PROTECT THE HUMAN BONES SHE'S MEASURING IN OLD LADY SPIDER CAVE.

"Working in science is like putting together a puzzle. The more pieces we find and place, the more we learn about our world."

WANT TO BE AN ARCHAEOLOGIST?
STUDY History, archaeology
READ *A Street Through Time* by Anne Millard and Steve Noon
WATCH The *Indiana Jones* movies

EXPLORERS

SCIENCE BLOOPERS

EVEN NAT GEO EXPLORERS MAKE MISTAKES—AND LAUGH ABOUT THEM LATER.

SPERM WHALES NEAR SRI LANKA DO THEIR BUSINESS IN THE OCEAN.

POOP

WHOSE POO?

THE SCIENTIST
Mauricio Cantor

COOL JOB
Behavioral ecologist

THE LOCATION
Galápagos Islands, Ecuador

"We were on a boat following sperm whales and scooping their poop from the ocean's surface. Back at the lab, I could study the stuff to learn more about the whales' social lives. So I placed each poo sample into a vial labeled with the animal's name and social group. Then I put the tubes into a container of liquid nitrogen—it's minus 320°F [–196°C] and instantly freezes the poop, which keeps it fresh.

"Back at the lab, I opened the container—and all the labels had fallen off the vials! I didn't know which poop sample belonged to which whale. I'd ordered the wrong stickers, which fell off in the super-cold temperature. I was not the most popular person at the lab that day—but instead the most '*poop*-ular.'

"This is how science works: You fail a lot, and you learn from it. Luckily, I could use other data I had collected on that trip for my research. And I definitely learned not to buy the wrong labels!"

AWESOME EXPLORATION

CAVE CONFUSION

THE SCIENTIST
Violeta Zhelyazkova

COOL JOB
Biologist and mycologist (a fungi scientist)

THE LOCATION
Raychova Dupka cave, Bulgaria

ZHELYAZKOVA COLLECTS FUNGUS SAMPLES IN BULGARIA'S IVANOVA VODA CAVE.

HORSESHOE BAT

"My research partner and I entered one of the deepest caves in Bulgaria to study the horseshoe bats that live inside. Many people had explored this cave before, so I thought that we'd see a sign telling visitors when to turn back before the cave became too small for a person to pass through.

"We traveled over a thousand feet [300 m] beneath the Earth's surface, swabbing the bats' noses and cave walls with cotton to gather samples along the way. (We were studying if a fungus might be growing on these animals.) As we went on, the cave got smaller and smaller until ... I got stuck! I was so confused: Hadn't lots of other people been down here? I had no choice but to turn back.

"I wiggled backward while my teammate behind me laughed at my strange moves. Defeated, we headed toward the entrance. And then we spotted the sign!

"Although we'd gathered what we needed from the bats that day, we learned an important lesson about paying closer attention while doing science!"

FISHY FAIL

THE EXPLORER
Hannah Nordhaus

COOL JOB
Science journalist

THE LOCATION
Syr Darya River, Kazakhstan

NORDHAUS'S TEAM FOUND FISH LIKE THIS ASP—BUT NO SYR DARYA STURGEON.

"We were searching for a fish that hadn't been seen in 50 years, a sturgeon called the Syr Darya shovelnose. Around midnight after the first day, I woke up to a strange feeling—hundreds of tiny ants were crawling on my neck and biting me!

"I brushed them off, but their bites left big, red welts. Then I saw where the ants were walking: straight from the front door to my bag, climbing over me and my teammates to get there.

"Turns out, a container of sugary powder that I mix with water to keep me hydrated broke in my bag on my flight to the site. I didn't know it—but the ants did!

"Even after I cleaned up the mess, the ants returned each night. I learned to pack more carefully and always check my bag upon arrival.

"My teammates spent two weeks dredging sections of the river with nets, finding 10 different species of fish. But they didn't find any Syr Darya sturgeon and are planning a return trip to search again for this ghost fish. So I also learned from them to never give up."

113

EXPLORERS

awes8me
AGE WAS ONLY A NUMBER FOR THESE YOUNG EXPLORERS.

1 ROCK ON

As a teenager, **Ashima Shiraishi** set rock-climbing records that adults only dream about. Shiraishi, seen here in 2008 climbing in Central Park in her hometown of New York City, excels at bouldering, or scaling 20-foot (6-m)-tall rocks without ropes or harnesses.

Kids on a Mission

2 RECORD BREAKER

In 2014, 16-year-old **Lewis Clarke** became the youngest person to ski to the South Pole from the Antarctic coast, a journey of 702 miles (1,130 km). With below-freezing temperatures and winds gusting at 120 miles an hour (193 km/h), his Antarctic adventure lasted for almost 50 days.

AWESOME EXPLORATION

3 WAGON TRAIL

Let's go West! A family crosses the Great Plains in a covered wagon on the **Oregon Trail**. Some kids in the mid-19th century journeyed nearly 2,000 miles (3,200 km) over four tiring months to reach Oregon or California—and a whole new life.

4 POLAR PUSH

In April 2016, at age 14, Australian adventurer **Jade Hameister** became the youngest person to ski to the North Pole—all without the help of any reindeer! Hameister dragged a heavy sled for 93 miles (150 km) on this epic trek.

5 DYNAMIC DUO

Like father, like daughter. In late 2011, the British team of **Amelia Hempleman-Adams** and her explorer father, David Hempleman-Adams, braved Antarctica's deep freeze for 17 nights to ski 97 miles (156 km) to the South Pole. At 16, Amelia became the youngest person at the time to achieve this feat.

6 DRUM BEAT

Children as young as 14 served in the American Civil War (1861–1865). This **drummer boy** would have played different drumrolls to convey the orders from the officers, such as "retreat" and "attack," to the soldiers in battle.

7 SURF'S UP

Kyllian Guerin started shredding the waves when he was four years old. As a teenager, he was a pro-surfer and divided his time between France and Costa Rica when he wasn't traveling the world and seeking out the best barrels the oceans had to offer.

8 MAIDEN VOYAGE

Sixteen-year-old Australian **Jessica Watson** arrived in Sydney Harbor, Australia, in May 2010, after finishing her record-setting, 210-day journey to sail around the world by herself unassisted. She navigated more than 23,000 nautical miles (42,600 km) in a 34-foot (10-m) yacht.

PLANET PROTECTION

10 WAYS TO PROTECT THE PLANET

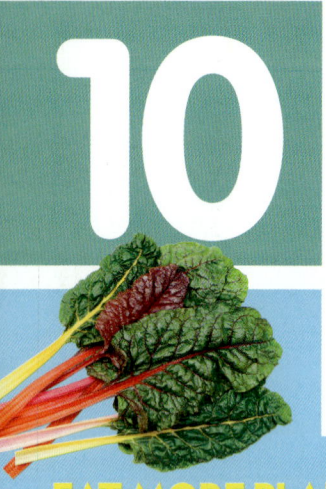

Our Earth needs extra love, and here's how you can help! *National Geographic Kids* editor Allyson Shaw shares 10 tips for making an impact.

EAT MORE PLANTS.
"Cattle ranching is the top reason people cut down trees in the Amazon rainforest. By reducing the amount of meat we eat and swapping in other protein sources, we can potentially limit the demand and avoid losing so many trees."

SWITCH YOUR TP!
"Ask your parents to buy toilet paper made of sustainable bamboo, recycled content, or wheat straw. Why? Twenty-eight pounds (12.7 kg) per person gets flushed each year, and much of that comes from old-growth forests. You'll save trees by going sustainable."

WATCH WHAT YOU FLUSH.
"On the topic of flushing, make sure you're only putting human waste and toilet paper in the toilet. Things like medicine and pet waste don't get processed by wastewater treatments and go right back into our oceans. This can make sea animals sick."

ORGANIZE A FUND RAISER.
"Find an eco-friendly cause close to your heart. Then, with your parents' permission, whip up something sweet to sell to your neighbors, with all proceeds going to a related organization."

VISIT YOUR LOCAL RECYCLING CENTER.
"By getting to see how it all works, you'll understand how to become a better recycler. You'll learn things that you'll remember forever about carefully recycling."

AWESOME EXPLORATION

PLAN A NEIGHBORHOOD CLEANUP.

"Grab some gloves and a trash bag and pick up trash in your neighborhood. Not only does it make your surroundings cleaner, but you can prevent trash from winding up in the ocean—or worse, in a marine animal's mouth—if it lands in a sewer or a nearby waterway."

BUY LESS STUFF.

"Overconsumption is a huge global problem. It takes natural resources like oil to make new things, not to mention that people's junk winds up clogging landfills. Heading to a birthday party? Gift your friend with a membership to an accredited zoo or aquarium instead of buying a toy."

SAY NO TO EXPLOITING WILD ANIMALS.

"Wild animals living in roadside attractions or in people's homes are in distress. So discourage your parents and relatives from supporting people who keep these animals as pets, whether it's on social media or in a facility. These animals deserve to be in the wild or appropriate animal shelter."

LEAVE SHELLS ON THE BEACH.

"Scientists are discovering that shells are disappearing from shores around the world. They're important for beach ecosystems, as they become houses for hermit crabs, places for fish and octopuses to hide in the water, and attachment systems for seagrass and algae. Fragments of shells on the shoreline can also prevent erosion. If you find a pretty shell, take a picture and leave it."

VISIT LOCAL ZOOS AND AQUARIUMS.

"Just be sure they are accredited by the Association of Zoos and Aquariums, which gives money back to important causes that support animals. The Smithsonian's National Zoo in Washington, D.C., for example, was able to save golden lion tamarins from extinction through this type of funding." The Association of Zoos and Aquariums provides a list of accredited zoos online.

PHOTOGRAPHY

PHOTO SECRETS REVEALED

HOW FOUR SNEAKY PHOTOGRAPHERS GOT THE SHOT

Wildlife photographers often use some tricky tactics to get amazing shots. Check out four incredible pictures—and hear straight from the photographers about how they used their own sneaky methods to get the pics.

SPOTTING JAGUARS

PHOTOGRAPHER: Steve Winter
ANIMAL: Jaguar
LOCATION: Brazil's Pantanal region

"Jaguars are big cats. But they're extremely good at hiding. I needed to set a trap—a camera trap—to get a photo of this juvenile.

"Camera traps take pictures when an animal steps into an invisible beam of light. The tricky part is figuring out where to put one. For help, I got advice from scientists who monitored jaguar movements with GPS collars.

"I set my camera trap on a large tree limb. Just three weeks later, this 10-month-old jaguar tripped the beam ... and even looked into the camera!"

BIRD HERD

PHOTOGRAPHER: Jay Fleming
ANIMAL: Great egret chicks
LOCATION: Chesapeake Bay, Maryland, U.S.A.

"Wading birds like egrets raise their chicks on small islands. I had to paddle about five miles (8 km) in a kayak and search very carefully for these birds' nest because the chicks' green skin helps them blend in with the grasses.

"These two-week-old chicks were only about a foot (30 cm) tall, so to photograph them at their level, I was lying all the way back in my kayak. I had to plant my foot in the mud to keep the kayak steady and set up my camera to take multiple shots with just one click."

AWESOME EXPLORATION

SPLASHDOWN

PHOTOGRAPHER: Paul Nicklen
ANIMAL: Emperor penguins
LOCATION: Ross Sea, Antarctica

"Emperor penguins are not known for their climbing ability. They basically have to rocket out of the ocean to get back onto the sea ice. To do this, they dive deep and then swim upward at a sharp angle to accelerate. I really wanted to get a shot of a penguin launching out of the water.

"I spent six weeks with some penguins to figure out their favorite landing spots. Knowing that penguins can zoom up to six feet (1.8 m) in the air and land beyond the edge of the ice, I spread myself out on the ice where I had seen these birds appear and waited for an explosion of penguins, making sure not to block their path from the water. But I didn't get the picture I wanted. Finally, I figured out that I was too close to the water. I moved back and waited behind a block of ice. My new placement allowed me to capture this one as it landed, while another penguin catapulted into the air behind him."

FISH FACE

PHOTOGRAPHER: Birgitte Wilms
ANIMAL: Clownfish
LOCATION: Off the coast of Papua New Guinea

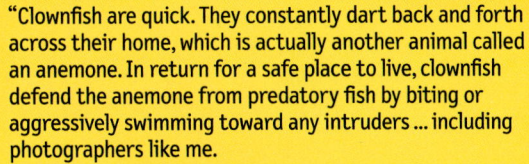

"Clownfish are quick. They constantly dart back and forth across their home, which is actually another animal called an anemone. In return for a safe place to live, clownfish defend the anemone from predatory fish by biting or aggressively swimming toward any intruders ... including photographers like me.

"All the clownfish I tried to photograph before this one were too fast. My pictures were a split second too late, catching only a tail or no fish at all. So I had to use some tricks. I quietly steadied myself on the bottom so the ocean current wouldn't push me away, and patiently waited—clownfish get defensive if you approach their home. Then I focused my camera on where I thought the fish would appear and waited for it to come out in search of food. Getting a shot with eye contact was a moment of joy!"

PHOTOGRAPHY

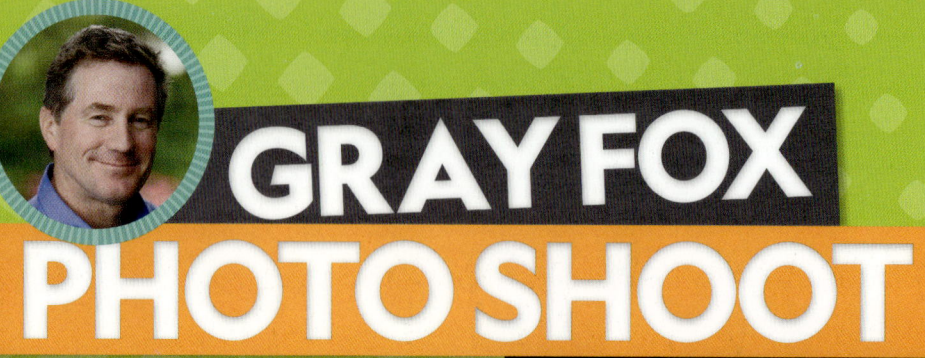

GRAY FOX PHOTO SHOOT

When National Geographic Explorer **Joel Sartore** gets the chance to photograph a species for the first time, he's there in a snap!

NATIONAL GEOGRAPHIC PHOTO ARK
JOEL SARTORE

This gray fox was rescued after falling into a window well at a St. Paul, Minnesota, U.S.A., church. After the fox had recovered, the staff at the Wildlife Rehabilitation Center called National Geographic Explorer Joel Sartore. This photographer is on a mission to take close-up photos of every species living in zoos, aquariums, and rescue centers. Hoping to inspire people to protect animals, Sartore has photographed nearly 16,000 species so far for his project, called the National Geographic Photo Ark.

Sartore lives a few hours away in Nebraska, and he hadn't yet shot this subspecies—a prairie gray fox. So rescuers asked if he would come take photos of the youngster. Sartore always photographs his subjects on white or black backgrounds to remove distractions in the photo to show that each animal he photographs is just as important as any other. He chose to capture pictures of this fox in a small, white photo tent.

"The fox sniffed around, then stood in the back of the tent like he was waiting to see what was going to happen," Sartore says.

AWESOME EXPLORATION

Ru Somaweera:
THE REPTILE MAN

Snakes and crocodiles may strike fear in the hearts of many people, but for National Geographic Explorer Ru Somaweera, interacting with these reptiles is all part of the job. Born in Sri Lanka, Somaweera has studied slithery and scaly creatures all over the world. Here's more about this awesome explorer!

LEAF-NOSED LIZARD

NGK: Have you always loved reptiles?

Ru: Growing up in Sri Lanka, which is a biodiversity hot spot, there was a lot to play with. When I was eight years old, I caught a water snake in a net while playing in a paddy field and it fascinated me, and ignited a passion for reptiles.

NGK: Why did you decide to focus your career on snakes and crocodiles?

Ru: They are the underdogs in the animal world. They're not cute and cuddly, but they're mysterious—and misunderstood. The more I studied them, the more interested I got.

NGK: What's the scariest thing that's happened to you in the field?

Ru: I got bit by an Indian cobra, a highly venomous snake, and I've had two crocodile bites. That was dramatic! Fortunately, I am certified in remote-area first aid, so I was able to initially treat myself before I got to an emergency room.

NGK: What's the coolest discovery you've made to date?

Ru: We recently found a species of sea snakes in the Indian Ocean off the coast of Indonesia that hunt in packs! Imagine a pack of like 20 snakes going after fish together—it's incredible. Someone who was deep-sea diving in the area actually posted a photo of these snakes together on social media, because he didn't know what was going on. So we went to that area to explore and observe their coordinated hunting methods.

NGK: What's next for you?

Ru: I'm studying the evolution of the Komodo dragon, the world's largest lizard, which has been around for millions of years. I'm looking into how they've been able to exist for so long when other species have gone extinct. Hint: They likely have survived because they benefit from human interaction and eating our food! It's an example of animals benefiting from humans.

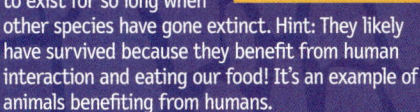

NGK: What's one myth you'd like to bust about reptiles?

Ru: The most common misconception is that reptiles are dangerous. That's simply not true. Take snakes, for example. No snake is dangerous if you don't bother it. Making venom costs a lot of energy for the snakes, so they don't want to actually use it unless they have to, like if it is scared for its life or if it's surprised. Besides, most snakes aren't venomous. So leave snakes alone and they'll leave you alone!

121

NO LIMITS

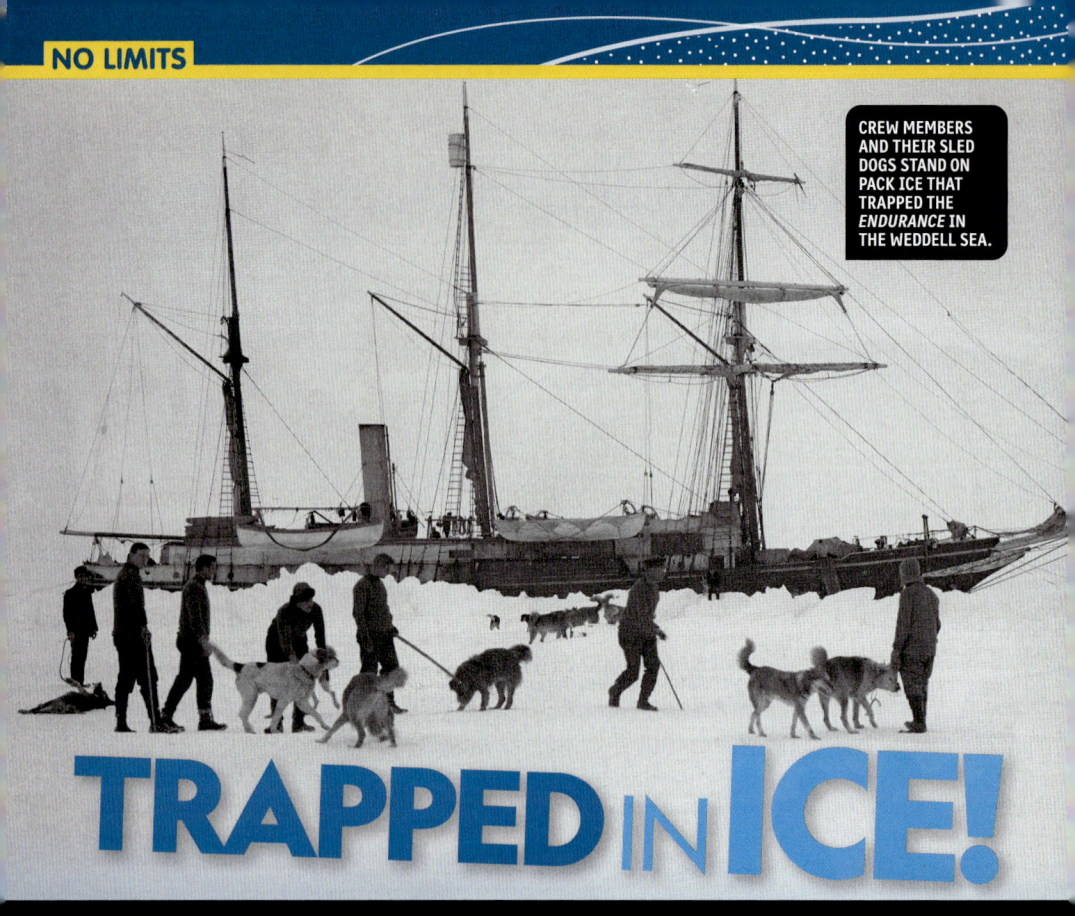

CREW MEMBERS AND THEIR SLED DOGS STAND ON PACK ICE THAT TRAPPED THE *ENDURANCE* IN THE WEDDELL SEA.

TRAPPED IN ICE!

HOW EXPLORERS FOUND THIS MISSING SHIP 100 YEARS AFTER IT SANK

The sailors couldn't stop shivering. It was November 21, 1915, and they were stranded on sea ice off the coast of Antarctica. In the distance, they could see their abandoned ship, named *Endurance*, stuck in the ice and flooding with seawater.

Suddenly, the crew heard the ship's wood groan and crack. The ice forced itself against the vessel, then quickly retreated. The ship "then gave one quick dive and the ice closed over her forever," wrote the expedition leader, Ernest Shackleton. For the next 106 years, *Endurance* would remain lost 10,000 feet (3,048 m) beneath the sea.

ADVENTURE GONE WRONG

Shackleton and 27 crew members set out in 1914 to try to cross Antarctica by land—but they had to sail there first. The 144-foot (44-m)-long ship was specially built for the chilly polar waters, with extra-thick wood planks to keep the dangerous pack ice floating in the ocean from damaging the ship.

But just three months after setting sail from Buenos Aires, Argentina, the boat became stuck in pack ice too thick to sail through. The worthy vessel held up for nine months as the ice pushed it north. But in October, the pressure from the ice buckled the planks, and water slowly

ERNEST SHACKLETON

ICE FORCED *ENDURANCE* ONTO ITS SIDE.

122

AWESOME EXPLORATION

UNDERWATER CAMERAS TOOK THESE IMAGES OF THE SUNKEN SHIP.

THE SHIP'S NAME

poured in. On October 27, Shackleton ordered his crew to gather their equipment and supplies and abandon the ship, pitching tents on the ice about a mile and a half (2.4 km) away. A few weeks later, they watched *Endurance* sink beneath the Weddell Sea.

LONG JOURNEY HOME
At first, the crew tried to drag their lifeboats over the ice, but the snowy and icy terrain was too difficult to cross on foot. So the group camped out on the pack ice as it drifted north. The crew survived the next five months by living off penguins, seals, and seaweed.

Finally, the ice broke up enough to allow the crew to sail in the lifeboats. For seven days, they sailed more than a hundred miles (161 km) till they arrived at the uninhabited Elephant Island. But the crew couldn't survive there for long. So with five crew members, Shackleton made a dangerous attempt to get help: They sailed 800 miles (1,287 km) over 16 days across freezing, stormy seas to South Georgia Island. Once they arrived, the six men hiked for 36 hours across the island to reach a whaling station. They were dirty, cold, and exhausted—but alive.

With a new ship, Shackleton returned to the uninhabited island to rescue the rest of his crew. All 28 people survived the ordeal. But the *Endurance* remained lost under the sea.

LOST SHIP FOUND
Ocean archaeologist Mensun Bound grew up on the Falkland Islands, not far from the Weddell Sea. Inspired by the adventurers, he was determined to find the lost ship.

In 2019, Bound and his team tried unsuccessfully to find the ship. They set out again in February 2022 and—just like the *Endurance*—got stuck in pack ice. Luckily, the tide rose a few hours later, and the explorers could sail on.

Bound carefully reviewed the original sailors' records to choose the search area. The team scanned 107 square miles (277 sq km) of the seafloor with remote-controlled underwater cameras for more than three weeks. With only three days before the ship had to be back in port, drifting sea ice forced Bound to search elsewhere.

On March 5, 2022, the cameras revealed exciting images: broken masts, ropes, a crewman's boot, and the ship's bell. The next day, nearly two miles (3.2 km) below the surface, the explorers saw the ship's name in brass letters on the stern, or back. They had found the lost *Endurance*. "You see that, and your eyes pop out," Bound says. "It felt like I was tumbling back in time. I could feel the breath of Shackleton on my neck."

The *Endurance* is now a protected historic site, which means that people need a permit to study or film it; even then, explorers can't touch it. A team of experts is working on a conservation plan to protect the ship from looters as well as the effects of a warming ocean due to climate change. For now, the *Endurance* remains safe beneath the sea.

IN THE KNOW

WHAT'S THE BUZZ ON BUGS?

As an entomologist, Samuel Ramsey (also known as "Dr. Sammy") gets to play with insects all day. A National Geographic Explorer, he also uses his research to educate others on topics like the importance of protecting insects, like honeybees. Here, Dr. Sammy shares the buzz on studying bugs for a living.

Is there a difference between a bug and an insect?
The scientific difference is that a bug is a very specific group of insects. Not all insects are bugs, but every bug is an insect. True bugs have a straw for a mouth, called a stylet, and they eat only fluids. Bedbugs and cicadas are examples of true bugs. A praying mantis is not a true bug, because it can chew.

Did you always like to play with insects?
When I was a little kid, it was really all that I did. And when I found out there was a job where people would pay you money to pick up bugs and learn about them, I could not have been more excited. I was seven years old when I told my parents I wanted to be an entomologist.

What do you find most fascinating about insects?
They're really cool—they have emotions, they have motivation, and they're intelligent. And there's no more diverse group of organisms.

What do you hope you'll accomplish through your work as an entomologist?
I would absolutely love to solve real-world problems through my scientific research.

I want people to know how important insects are in our lives. Like bees, which are integral to the food we eat on a regular basis because our crops rely on pollinators. My lab is doing everything we can to fix our current pollinator pandemic and protect the bee population.

Are you afraid of getting stung?
We wear protective gear, but sometimes accidents do happen. It's usually no big deal, but when you're working with hornets at the top of a mountain in Japan where it's hard to get medical attention, you have to be careful.

What's your wildest story from the field?
Once, in Thailand, I was working with a bunch of bees inside an old burrow in the ground. I was digging when I noticed one that looked like it was crawling around inside my suit. It's a sealed suit, but I forgot to zip it up, so bees got in and were flying around my face. Fortunately, they got stuck in my hair, so I did not get stung. But I still had to run down the mountain to a clearing, take off the suit, and shake the bees out. The guys I was working with thought it was hilarious.

What are the items you never leave home without?
Protective gear, mosquito nets, and bug spray. We have collection tubes and a jug of nitrogen to preserve samples. And I use my trusty net to catch bugs right out of the air.

What's your advice for kids who are interested in entomology?
Read a lot! Keep asking questions, and find good books that can answer them. Consider studying Latin or Greek to help you learn the insects' scientific names.

Finally, tell us: What's your favorite insect?
The praying mantis! Some hang upside down from branches, grab snakes off the ground, and eat them alive. That's so cool.

AWESOME EXPLORATION

AMAZING INSECTS!

HOW OFTEN DO YOU THINK ABOUT INSECTS? You probably think about them when you get bitten by a mosquito. Or when fireflies come out at night. Or, when something really big happens—like, say, millions of cicadas emerge from beneath the ground in the United States. (2024 was a big year for bugs!) Well, guess what? Even when you don't see them, insects are behind-the-scenes superstars. When you spot a field of beautiful flowers, listen to the birds sing, eat yummy honey on toast, or harvest some veggies from your garden—you have insects to thank! Not only are they incredibly diverse and cool, but they play a vital role in the environment and our lives.

Insects pollinate most of the world's plants, including the crops we use for food. They eat other bugs that damage crops or bite humans, and they help prevent overpopulation of some species. Insects clean up animal waste on land and break down debris in aquatic ecosystems, contributing to a healthier environment. They are a source of food for many species, including birds, fish, reptiles, amphibians, bats, and humans in several parts of the world. They create many products we enjoy, such as honey, beeswax, silk, and dyes. And that's just part of what they do.

So instead of ignoring or, even worse, fearing them, let's take some time to get to know and appreciate our insect neighbors!

MORE FOR YOU

QUIZ WHIZ

Discover just how much you know about exploration with this quiz!

Write your answers on a piece of paper. Then check them below.

1. **True or false?** One way to help protect the planet is to buy less stuff.

2. How many animal species has Nat Geo Explorer Joel Sartore photographed?
a. 16,000
b. 1,600
c. 160
d. 160,000

3. Sydney funnel-web spiders live mostly _____.
a. in trees
b. under leaves
c. underground
d. between rocks

4. Nat Geo Explorer Ru Somaweera discovered a species of _____ that hunt in packs.
a. giraffes
b. sea snakes
c. turtles
d. mice

5. **True or false?** Scientists never make mistakes.

Not **STUMPED** yet? Check out the *NATIONAL GEOGRAPHIC KIDS QUIZ WHIZ* collection for more fun **EXPLORATION** questions!

ANSWERS: 1. True; 2. a; 3. c; 4. b; 5. False

AWESOME EXPLORATION

HOMEWORK HELP

How to Write a Perfect Essay

Need to write an essay? Does the assignment feel as big as climbing Mount Everest? Fear not. You're up to the challenge! The following step-by-step tips will help you with this monumental task.

1. BRAINSTORM. Sometimes the subject matter of your essay is assigned to you; sometimes it's not. Either way, you have to decide what you want to say. Start by brainstorming some ideas, writing down any thoughts you have about the subject. Then read over everything you've come up with and consider which idea you think is the strongest. Ask yourself what you want to write about the most. Keep in mind the goal of your essay. Can you achieve the goal of the assignment with this topic? If so, you're good to go.

2. WRITE A TOPIC SENTENCE. This is the main idea of your essay, a statement of your thoughts on the subject. Again, consider the goal of your essay. Think of the topic sentence as an introduction that tells your readers what the rest of your essay will be about.

3. OUTLINE YOUR IDEAS. Once you have a good topic sentence, you then need to support that main idea with more detailed information, facts, thoughts, and examples. These supporting points answer one question about your topic sentence—"Why?" This is where research and perhaps more brainstorming come in. Then organize these points in the way you think makes the most sense, probably in order of importance. Now you have an outline for your essay.

4. ON YOUR MARK, GET SET, WRITE! Follow your outline, using each of your supporting points as the topic sentence of its own paragraph. Use descriptive words to get your ideas across to readers. Go into detail, using specific information to tell your story or make your point. Stay on track, making sure that everything you include is somehow related to the main idea of your essay. Use transitions to make your writing flow.

5. WRAP IT UP. Finish your essay with a conclusion that summarizes your entire essay and restates your main idea.

6. PROOFREAD AND REVISE. Check for errors in spelling, capitalization, punctuation, and grammar. Look for ways to make your writing clear, understandable, and interesting. Use descriptive verbs, adjectives, and adverbs when possible. It also helps to have someone else read your work to point out things you might have missed. Then make the necessary corrections and changes in a second draft. Repeat this revision process once more to make your final draft as good as you can.

127

A lion cub in Kenya clings playfully to its mother's head.

FUN and GAMES

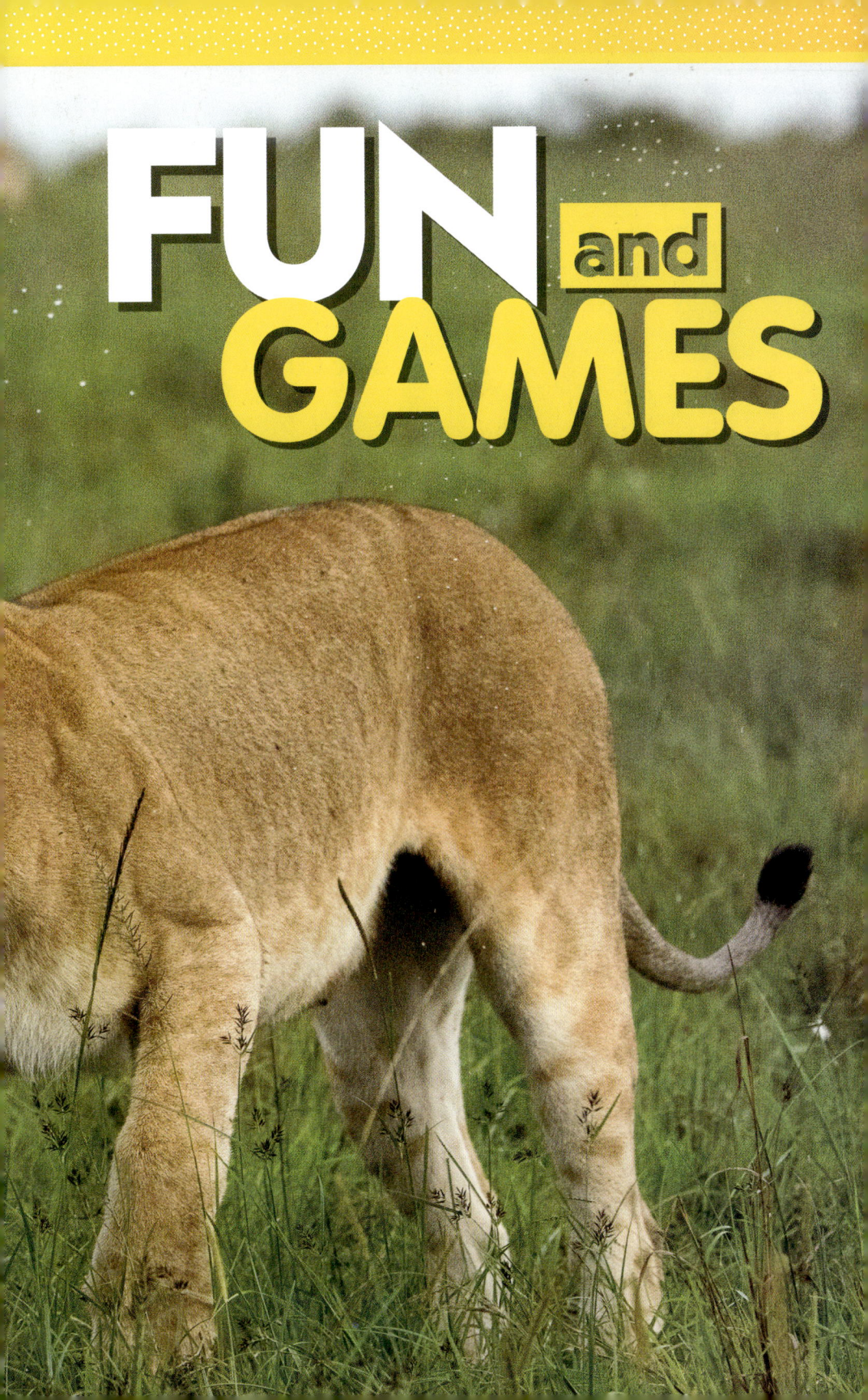

SHIVERING SHAPES

A winter wind has given these photos of cold-weather animals a frosty twist. Look at each photo and the clues. On a separate sheet of paper, unscramble the letters to identify what's in each picture.

ANSWERS ON PAGE 354

1
NAGTI
_____

ADPNA
_____

CLUE: These animals living in China's mountainous forests answer the question, "What's black and white and loved all over?"

2
ESNAPJAE
_____

QECAUAM
_____

CLUE: For this Asian primate, snowy weather is a great excuse to take a dip in a hot spring with friends.

3
RMAU
____

DPORALE
_____

CLUE: Thick fur keeps this spotted feline warm in chilly forests in eastern Russia and northern China. Its first name happens to rhyme with fur.

4
RHONNERT
_____

ALRCNDIA
_____

CLUE: This North American singer adds a warm pop of color to trees during dark and cold winter days.

130

FUN AND GAMES

CRITTER CHAT

WELCOME TO MY WORLD!

If animals used social media, what would they say? Follow this *T. rex*'s day as it updates its feed.

TYRANNOSAURUS REX

SCREEN NAME: DinoQueen
LIVES IN: Western North America, about 68 million years ago
FRIENDS

TRICERATOPS	ANKYLOSAURUS	EDMONTOSAURUS
TripleThreat	TailTrouble	ShovelMuzzle

---

9 a.m.

DinoQueen: Teeth? Sharp. Feet? Stompy. Nose? Sniff-tastic. Stomach? Hungry. You better hide—I'm on the prowl.

TailTrouble: Don't smell me! I'll smack you with my heavy tail! KA-POW!

ShovelMuzzle: Sending out the honk alert to my herd: **DinoQueen** is hunting. Run! #SheIsScaryButSlow #TRexRace

TripleThreat: Don't even think about tangling with my three horns, **DinoQueen**. I'm no pushover. #16,000Pounds

10 a.m.

DinoQueen: I sniffed out some leftovers, aka dead meat. Now I get to play with my food. #TossAndCatch

TailTrouble: Glad you found something, er ... tasty? #Plant-Eater

TripleThreat: Whew! Now I can use my horns to impress my mate—not to fight **DinoQueen**. #PeaceAndLove ♥

ShovelMuzzle: And my herd and I can go back to relaxing in the swamp. #ChillingOut

3 p.m.

DinoQueen: I think my hatchling should win #CutestBabyDino. 🏆

ShovelMuzzle: Whoa, **DinoQueen** has a soft side! My tiny tots are pretty cute, too. They're just 1/20 of my length—and supersweet.

TripleThreat: *T. rex* chicks might be cute, but the teenagers are terrors! I had to battle a few last year.

TailTrouble: And one day they'll be 40 feet long with a bite that can crush bones. #NotThatCute

DinoQueen: Hey, I'm one of the fiercest predators of all time—maybe you should just agree with me.

131

WHAT IN THE WORLD?

AWESOME OVALS
These photographs show close-up views of oval shapes you might recognize. On a separate sheet of paper, unscramble the letters to identify what's in each picture.
ANSWERS ON PAGE 354

YLELJ NEBA	DWNWOI	IHFS
PMLBI	ASC'T YEE	UMITSDA
ETEBLE	ALOP	WIIK IRTFU

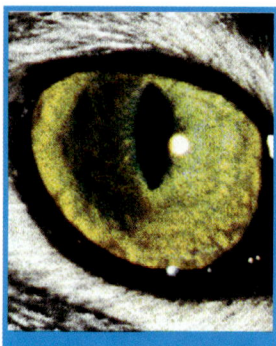

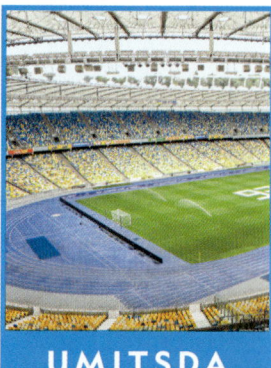

FUN AND GAMES

FUNNY FILL-IN

FARM FRENZY

Ask a friend to give you words to fill in the blanks in this story without showing it to them. Then read it out loud for a laugh.

At _____ a.m., my family and I piled into the car for our annual camping trip. We were
    small number

singing along to _____ when we heard a(n) _____. Our car had a flat _____!
                     pop star   *loud noise*   *noun*

Soon a pickup truck pulled over. "I'm Farmer _____. Can I offer y'all a ride?" the
                                                                  friend's name

driver asked. That's how we spent the day on a(n) _____ farm. I sat on a(n) _____
                                                                           noun   *piece of furniture*

next to the farmer to learn to milk a cow. But the cow started _____ my hair. So instead,
                                                                                                 verb ending in -ing

I tried to run the _____ milk machine. As I pulled a lever, my _____ disconnected
                    adjective   *body part*

a tube, and _____ started _____ everywhere. I _____ from
              type of liquid   *verb ending in -ing*   *past-tense verb*

the machine, right into a(n) _____ pile of _____. A bunch of _____
                                      adjective   *something gross*   *animal, plural*

ran to lap up the spill, so I _____ toward the door. On the way I slipped and fell into the
                             past-tense verb

_____ pen. I hope our next vacation is a little less exciting.
 animal

FIND THE HIDDEN ANIMALS

Animals often blend in with their environment to hide. Find each animal listed below in one of the pictures. On a separate sheet of paper, write the letter of the correct picture and the animal's name.

ANSWERS ON PAGE 354

1. orchid mantis
2. harlequin ghost pipefish
3. pallid scops owl
4. eyelash viper
5. Texas horned lizard
6. giant Pacific octopus
7. red-shouldered macaws

FUN AND GAMES

135

CRITTER CHAT

If wild animals used social media, what would they say? Follow this orca's day as it updates its feed.

ORCA
SCREEN NAME: SeaPanda
LIVES IN: Antarctic Ocean **Likes:** High fins and fast swims
FRIENDS

ANTARCTIC KRILL	WEDDELL SEAL	EMPEROR PENGUIN
ChillKrill	VerySealious	KingBird

10 a.m.

SeaPanda: Can I get a few likes for my new profile pic? #SpyHopSelfie

ChillKrill: What are you doing?

VerySealious: That's **SeaPanda**'s way of getting to the surface to look for prey like me. So I'll steer clear of a photo bomb and dive deep.

KingBird: Yeah, thanks for the selfie, **SeaPanda**. It gives me a chance to catch up with **VerySealious**.

ChillKrill: Plus all the action's underwater anyway. No offense, but on land **VerySealious** just thumps around, and **KingBird** shuffles on the ice.

KingBird: Yeah, but you can't touch me when I'm swimming—I can move 11 feet (3 m) a second in the water!

SeaPanda: Wanna race?

2:30 p.m.

SeaPanda: Anybody seen my pod? About 40 orcas? I used our special call but ... no answer.

ChillKrill: Only 40? My swarm has BILLIONS of krill—people can see us from space!

VerySealious: **SeaPanda**, I think I saw your pod, um, north! Yeah, that's it! Like *way* north.

KingBird: Here, I'll GPS it for you. I think you'll love the change in latitude.

VerySealious: Say hi to the Brazilian surfers for us! #I'mSoSeally

4:30 p.m.

SeaPanda: Found my pod! Whew. My mom would have been stressed if I'd gotten lost. BIG trouble.

VerySealious: Trouble like when you're trapped on an ice floe surrounded by orcas? Seriously, you don't know the MEANING of trouble.

ChillKrill: Chill, bros. Just go with the flow and float with the current like me and my swarm. It's all good.

KingBird: **SeaPanda**'s just worried his mom will be mad. I don't get it! My three-month-old chick will be on his own in just a few months.

SeaPanda: I admit it ... I'm a momma's whale. #CanIGetAHighFin

136

FUN AND GAMES

STUMP
YOUR PARENTS

DENALI NATIONAL PARK AND PRESERVE, ALASKA, U.S.A.

If your parents can't answer these questions, maybe *they* should go to school instead of you!

ANSWERS ON PAGE 354

1 The _____ protects millions of acres (ha) of land.
A. Louisiana Purchase
B. Department of Parks and Recreation
C. U.S. National Park Service
D. National Basketball Association

2 Besides laundry detergent, what liquid, when mixed with water, can be used to remove stains?
A. mouthwash   C. buttermilk
B. ginger ale   D. vinegar

IF YOU TRY THIS, GET A PARENT'S PERMISSION.

3 The energy used to fill up a bathtub could power a _____ for eight minutes. 
A. television
B. microwave
C. lightbulb
D. Taylor Swift concert

4 Every day, about _____ species become extinct.
A. 1 to 20
B. 30 to 70
C. 80 to 120
D. 150 to 200

5 Which alternative form of transportation burns the most calories during 30 minutes of use?
A. skateboard
B. tricycle
C. inline skates
D. scooter

6 The _____ is one of the world's critically endangered animals.
A. mountain gorilla   C. red panda
B. humpback whale   D. jaguar

7 Which of these products can be made from corn? 
A. straws
B. tape
C. balloons
D. toilet paper

8 By 2050, scientists estimate that people will be unable to live on which group of islands because of rising sea levels?
A. the Bahamas   C. the Philippines
B. the Cayman Islands   D. the Maldives

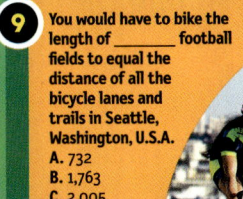

9 You would have to bike the length of _____ football fields to equal the distance of all the bicycle lanes and trails in Seattle, Washington, U.S.A.
A. 732
B. 1,763
C. 2,005
D. 3,104

137

SIGNS OF THE TIMES

Seeing isn't always believing. Two of these funny signs aren't real. Can you figure out which two are fake?
ANSWERS ON PAGE 354

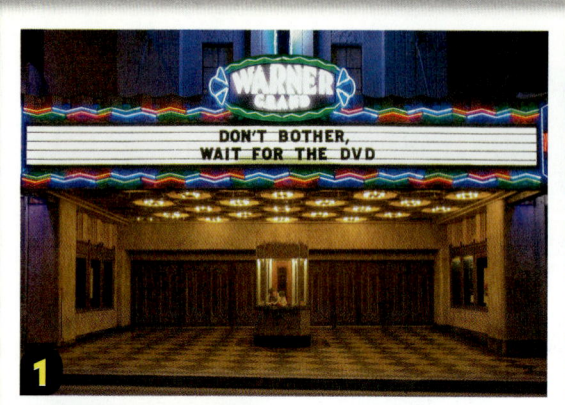

1. WARNER — DON'T BOTHER, WAIT FOR THE DVD

2. THIS SIGN WILL ACCOMPLISH NOTHING

3. EARTH 3

4. DON'T THINK — $350 PENALTY — DEPARTMENT OF MENTAL PROTECTION

5. PLEASE DO NOT FEED ANIMALS (BE COUGAR & BEAR AWARE)

6. DON'T EVEN THINK OF PARKING HERE / NO PARKING HERE TO THERE

7. WHY

138

FUN AND GAMES

FUNNY FILL-IN

PARTY ANIMALS

Ask a friend to give you words to fill in the blanks in this story without showing it to them. Then read it out loud for a laugh.

My two friends and I were hosting a(n) _____ Fan Club meeting at my house to
                                              celebrity
start a letter-writing campaign. _____ showed up first with a pet _____!
                                  friend's name   *animal*
Then _____ more friends _____ with animals.
      large number   *past-tense verb*
So I reread my invitation. Instead of "Bring your own *pen*," I had written "Bring your own *pet!*"

Now a(n) _____ was _____ over our heads while a(n)
          type of bird   *verb ending in -ing*
_____ slid up my _____. Soon a dog was _____
   reptile   *body part*   *verb ending in -ing*
from the _____, and somehow _____ were swimming
          noun   *sea creature, plural*
in the punch bowl. A(n) _____ _____ was even chasing a cat around
                         adjective   *rodent*
the _____, knocking over the _____. It's going to take a lot of
     noun   *type of liquid*
_____ to clean up this mess!
   something gross

139

WHAT IN THE WORLD?

GET IN LINE
These photographs show close-up and faraway views of objects in rows. Unscramble the letters to identify what's in each picture.
ANSWERS ON PAGE 354

LFUOESWSNR	ESPA	ACSR
SLYBCCIE	GARCHINM NABD	IATNP TSE
ESUHOS	MDOSNEOI	AUSMTDI ATSES

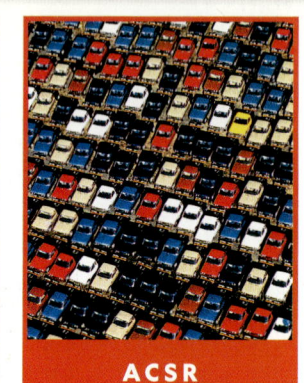

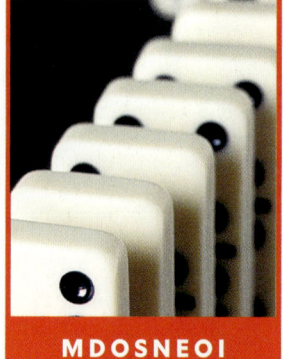

140

FUN AND GAMES

STUMP YOUR PARENTS

If your parents can't answer these questions, maybe *they* should go to school instead of you!
ANSWERS ON PAGE 354

1 The idea that sparked the Hula-Hoop craze of the late 1950s came from _____.
A. circular branches used by monkeys
B. tire rims used by Swedish kids
C. metal hoops used by factory workers
D. bamboo hoops used by Australian kids

2 Most people lose _____ strands of hair every day.
A. 75   C. 95
B. 85   D. 105

3 In the Netherlands, it is most polite to eat your bread with _____.
A. your hands
B. a knife and fork
C. your feet
D. chopsticks

4 The pirate Blackbeard put _____ under his hat to scare captured sailors.
A. black dye   C. daggers
B. burning ropes   D. rats

5 What is Iron Man's true identity?
A. Peter Parker
B. Scott Lang
C. Tony Stark
D. Bruce Banner

6 Why do cats get stuck in trees?
A. They like the view.
B. They're afraid of heights.
C. Their claws are curved so that they can climb *up* easily, but not down.
D. They're secret BFFs with birds.

7 A group of adult alligators is called a _____. 
A. herd   C. crash
B. congregation D. hive

8 In which country do about half the highways have no speed limit?
A. Switzerland   C. Japan
B. Germany   D. Botswana

9 In *The Incredibles*, which accessory does Edna Mode refuse to incorporate into the superhero family's costumes?
A. capes   C. belts
B. masks   D. gloves

10 In 1922, which cookie recipe were U.S. Girl Scouts encouraged to bake and sell?
A. chocolate chip
B. Thin Mints
C. oatmeal
D. sugar

CRITTER CHAT

If animals were online, what would they say? Read these just-for-fun posts to find out.

YiPadvisor

Too risky!

Ocean cruise on a lemon shark
Slender sharksucker

Like all sharksuckers, I travel in style. I've got a natural suction cup on my head that helps me stick to whales, sharks, rays, and more. So I get to relax while my host carries me to new and exciting places.

Recently, I decided to take an ocean cruise on a lemon shark. At first, I was having tons of fun. My shark ate a lot of prey, so I got to feed on plenty of leftovers. Usually sharks leave me alone to do my thing, but this time another lemon shark tried to eat *me*! I think I'll stick with laid-back sea turtles on future vacations.

yowl

Read my review!

ANT "ROOM"

Whistling thorn tree
Giraffe
★☆☆☆☆

When I first saw this tree, I thought its leaves looked tasty. I stretched my neck, opened my mouth, stuck out my long tongue, and ... *ow!* An ant bit me! This tree grows hollow bulbs that ants use as rooms to live in. The ants get a home, and they protect the tree from harm. But I don't like it when my meal bites back!

Never again!

FUN AND GAMES

Dolphinstagram
clouded_leopard
📍 Southeast Asia

♥ 127 likes

clouded_leopard Welcome to my catwalk: the forest! I bet you've never seen style like mine. I'm a tree climber, and my cloudy spots help me hide among branches and leaves. You could say I'm sitting pretty. #WildStyleInspo

bharmony
matches | profile | my photos

SparkleButt
ANIMAL Peacock spider
LIKES Crickets, hanging out on the forest floor
DISLIKES Dance clubs that won't let spiders in

ABOUT ME If you're looking for a dance partner, search no further. You'll be wowed by my rainbow-colored backside and the steps I use to show it off. I'll flail my legs, tap on a twig, and sway back and forth. Just one request: Don't be a hater. Some females will eat a male for lunch if they don't like his groove. I'd rather live to dance another day.

Connect with me!

I wanna dance with some spider!

llamazon
the **BEAST** place to shop

gifts for marsupial ...

🔍 flavorful flowers

Bouquet of flowers

CUSTOMER REVIEWS
★☆☆☆☆
Decidedly not yummy
Koala Verified Customer

My pal sent me this pretty bouquet of flowers for my birthday. It was a nice gesture, but I only eat eucalyptus, so I couldn't chow down on most of these plants. What am I supposed to do—just *look* at them?

Better shop elsewhere.

143

FUN STUFF
GAMES, LAUGHS, AND LOTS TO DO!

SURF'S UP!
Something totally gnarly is happening at the Supreme Surfing Tournament in South Africa, where ocean animals show off their natural bodysurfing talents. Find 20 things wrong at this kooky competition.

ANSWERS ON PAGE 354

144

FUN AND GAMES

STRIKA ENTERTAINMENT
UnLeaShed
1
NOT THERE ...
MUST BE HERE SOMEWHERE!
WHERE IS IT?
ATLAS, WHAT ARE YOU LOOKING FOR?
2
MAJOR'S NEW RUBBER BONE! HE LET ME BORROW IT, AND I FORGOT WHERE I BURIED IT!
HAVE YOU TRIED SNIFFING IT OUT?
OR RETRACING YOUR STEPS?
3
I'VE LOOKED EVERYWHERE!
PLEASE HELP ME FIND IT BEFORE MAJOR WAKES UP FROM HIS NAP!
4
HMM ... LOOKS LIKE THIS SITUATION CALLS FOR SOME PALEONTOLOGISTS!
SOME WHAT?
5
PROFESSIONAL FOSSIL FINDERS!
6
SOON ...
PALEONTOLOGISTS ARE PROFESSIONAL FOSSIL FINDERS. THEY LOOK FOR FOSSILIZED BONES, PLANTS, PAW PRINTS ...
WHATEVER WE ARE, WE'VE GOT COOL OUTFITS! I REALLY LIKE YOURS, PRINCESS TALULLAH!
IT'S JUST LULU!
BUT YOU CAN CALL ME INDIANA BONES!

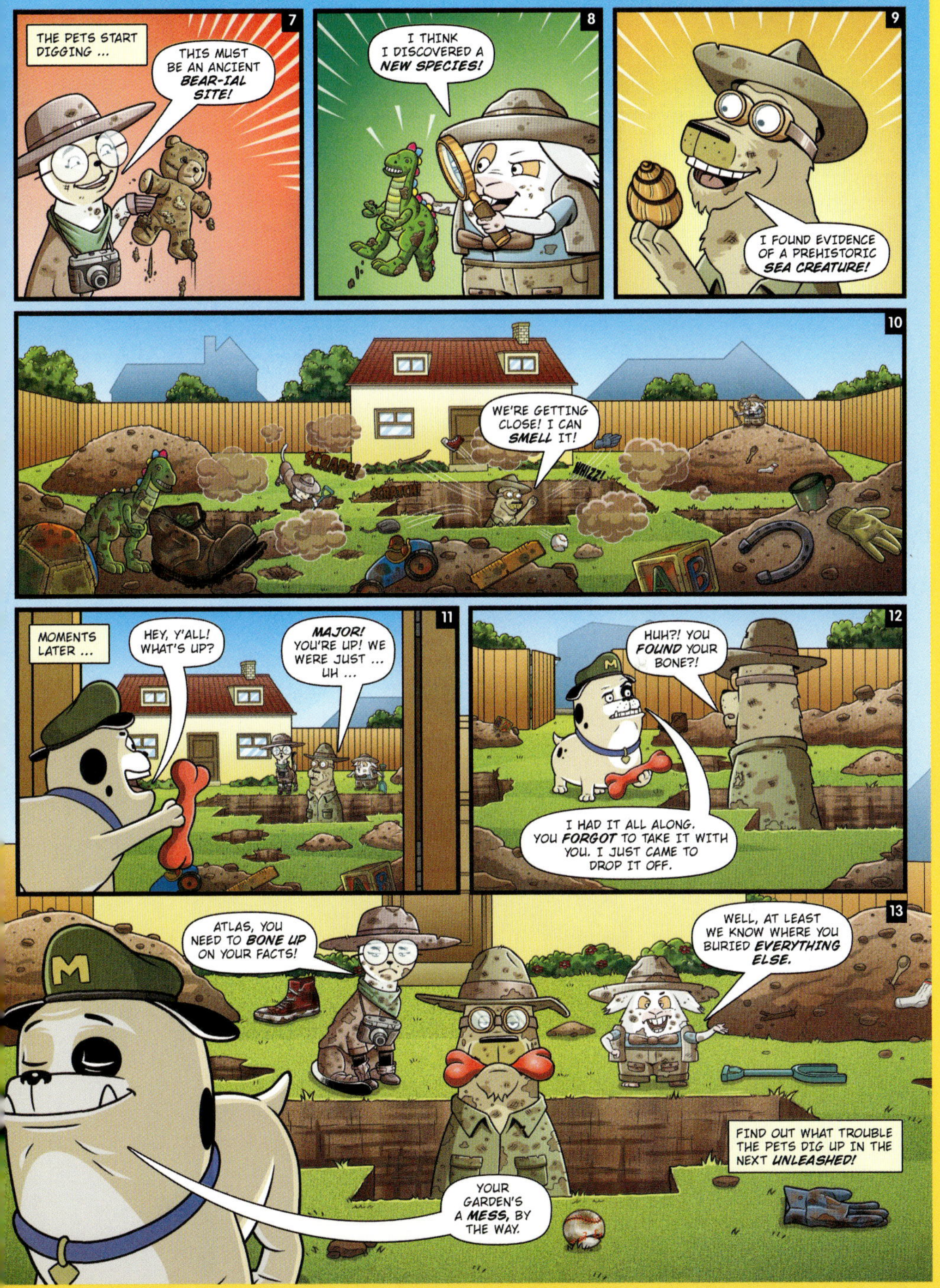
7
THE PETS START DIGGING ...
THIS MUST BE AN ANCIENT BEAR-IAL SITE!
8
I THINK I DISCOVERED A NEW SPECIES!
9
I FOUND EVIDENCE OF A PREHISTORIC SEA CREATURE!
10
SCRAPE!
SCRATCH!
WHIZZ!
WE'RE GETTING CLOSE! I CAN SMELL IT!
11
MOMENTS LATER ...
HEY, Y'ALL! WHAT'S UP?
MAJOR! YOU'RE UP! WE WERE JUST ... UH ...
12
HUH?! YOU FOUND YOUR BONE?!
I HAD IT ALL ALONG. YOU FORGOT TO TAKE IT WITH YOU. I JUST CAME TO DROP IT OFF.
13
ATLAS, YOU NEED TO BONE UP ON YOUR FACTS!
WELL, AT LEAST WE KNOW WHERE YOU BURIED EVERYTHING ELSE.
FIND OUT WHAT TROUBLE THE PETS DIG UP IN THE NEXT UNLEASHED!
YOUR GARDEN'S A MESS, BY THE WAY.

LAUGH OUT LOUD

What's so funny? These raccoons are in on the joke.

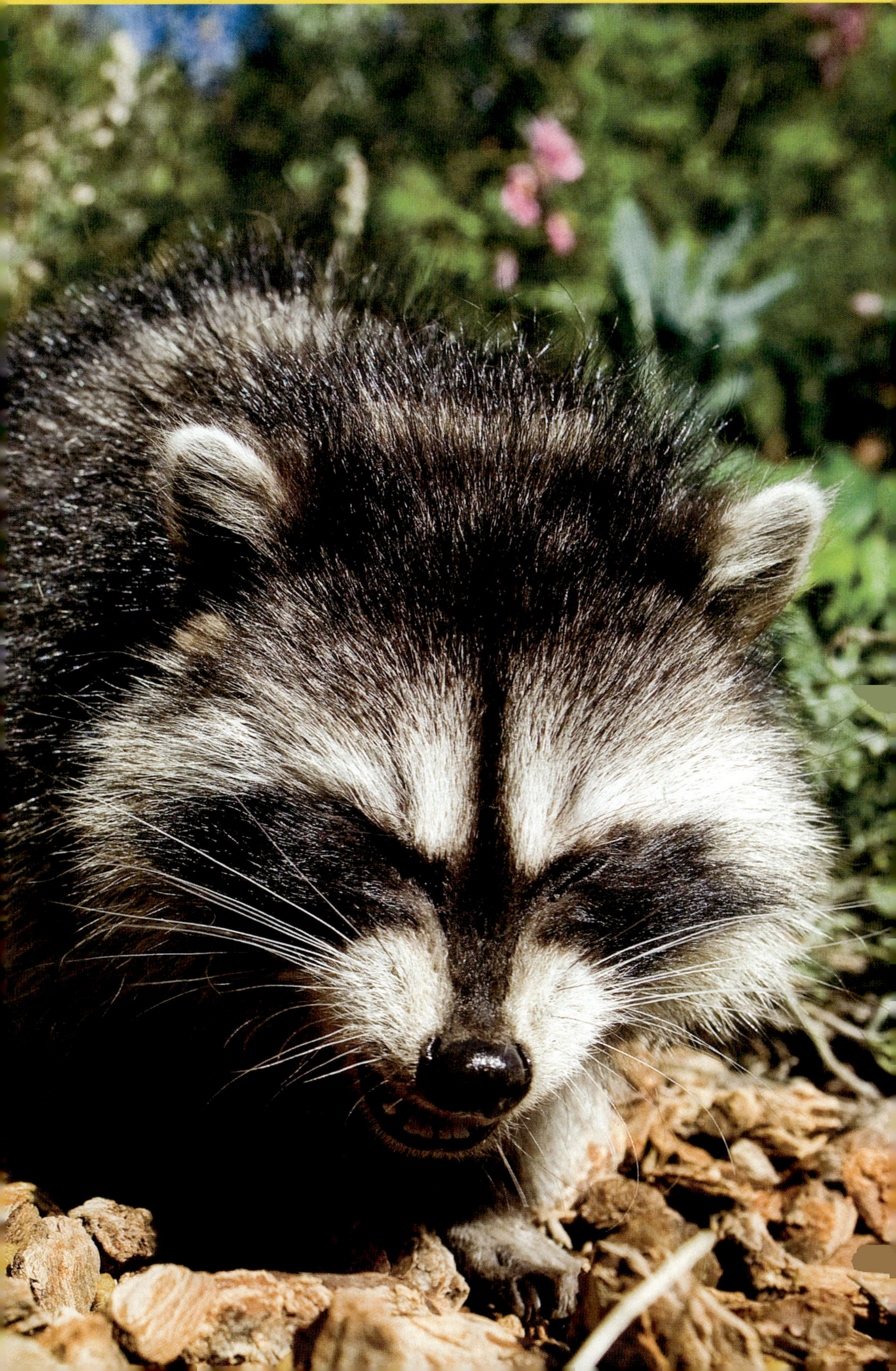

JUST JOKING

Say this fast three times:
Three free-thinking frogs think friendly thoughts.

WAITER: Why do you laugh while cooking breakfast?
CHEF: Because the egg always cracks a yolk.

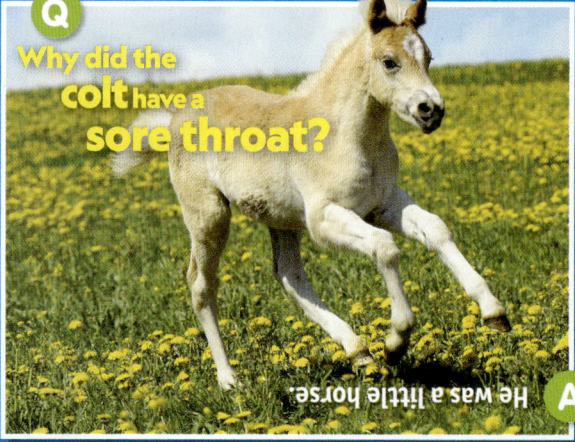

KNOCK, KNOCK.
Who's there?
Amos.
Amos who?
Amos-quito bit me!

Q Why did the **colt** have a **sore throat?**
A He was a little horse.

Q What part of the fish weighs the most?
A The scales.

150

LAUGH OUT LOUD

Animal BLOOPERS
Animals make mistakes, too!

I DIDN'T SAY I WANTED A WATERBED!

ANIMAL
Bearded seal

RANGE
Arctic Ocean

SLIPUP SPOT
Near Spitsbergen, Norway

PHOTO FAIL
Bearded seals often rest on stable ice floes before they feed, but it looks like this frozen raft is getting a little off-balance.

HEY, WHO'S STEPPING ON MY NECK?

ANIMAL
Galápagos tortoise

RANGE
Galápagos Islands, Ecuador

SLIPUP SPOT
Isabela Island

PHOTO FAIL
This tortoise's long neck can stretch upward to grab tasty leaves ... as long as it doesn't get all twisted up!

ANIMAL
European rabbits

RANGE
Native to Europe and northwest Africa; today found on every continent except Antarctica

SLIPUP SPOT
Okunoshima, Japan

PHOTO FAIL
Young rabbits play together by nipping at each other and then hopping backward. These two jumped *way* back.

YOU ARE ONE FUNNY BUNNY!

Say What?

NAMES Galileo, Hubble, and Halley

FAVORITE ACTIVITY Staring up at the night sky from our treetops

FAVORITE TOY A telescope

PET PEEVE Cloudy nights

If space is a vacuum, who changes the bags?

The moon looks broke. It must be down to its last quarter.

Adult male orangutans grow flappy cheek pads called flanges. Their faces have been likened to the man in the moon.

An astronaut took a book to read on his mission, but he couldn't put it down!

LAUGH OUT LOUD

Was that the phone ringing? Who-rang-u-tan?

KNOCK, KNOCK.
Who's there?
Police.
Police who?
Police hurry up! We're about to blast off!

RIDDLE ME THIS

What is easy for a baby *Brachiosaurus* to get into, but difficult to get out of?

Trouble.

Princess Mary's father has four daughters named A, E, I, and O. What is his fifth daughter's name?

Mary.

What's harder to catch the more that you run?

Your breath.

A container without hinges, lock, or key; a golden treasure lies inside me. What am I?

An egg.

What has six legs, four ears, and a suit of armor?

A prince on horseback.

A fairy lives in a one-story house with a blue couch, blue walls, and blue carpets. What color are her stairs?

There are no stairs in a one-story house.

What is full of keys but can't open any doors?

A piano.

What is light as a feather, but Hercules can't hold it for five minutes?

His breath.

154

LAUGH OUT LOUD

FUNNY BITES

"I'M TAKING MY FROG FOR A WALK!"

"DIDN'T I TELL YOU TO CLEAN OFF YOUR BELLY BEFORE SNACK TIME?"

"IT'S JUST UNTIL THE BRACES COME OFF."

"THE BABY'S BOTTLE IS ALMOST READY!"

JUST JOKING

Q What do you call lunch that takes you places in London?

A A double-decker.

Q What kind of **public transportation** do **goblins** use?

A A troll-ey.

Q What underwater train systems do humpbacks take?

A Whale ways.

BRAD: A mother called the traffic police to report her seven-year-old son.
STACY: Report him for what?
BRAD: Driving her up a wall.

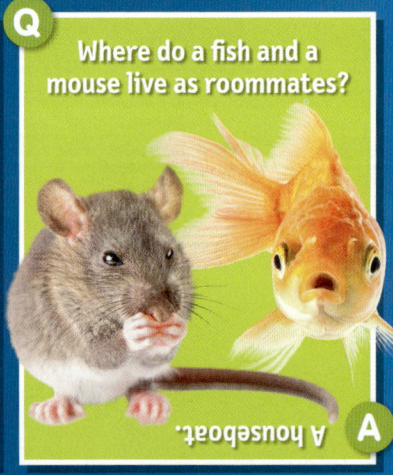

Q Where do a fish and a mouse live as roommates?

A A houseboat.

Q What did **one oar say** to the other?

A "Canoe help me row to shore?"

Q Why did the man throw his guitar overboard?

A His friends told him not to rock the boat.

LAUGH OUT LOUD

PUN FUN

Biologists have good cell service.

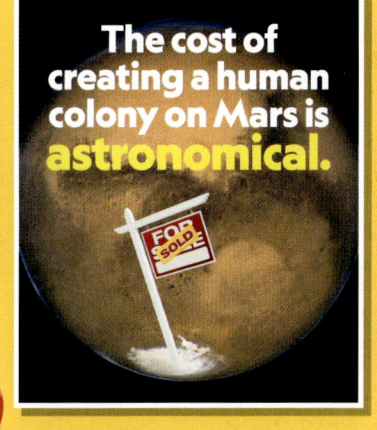

The cost of creating a human colony on Mars is **astronomical.**

A baker's job is a piece of cake.

Most people look up to basketball players.

Popcorn jokes are **corny.**

The rabbit gave his love a 24-carrot ring. It was delicious.

The ocean is so friendly. It always waves.

Never tell your secret to a pig. They're bound to squeal.

157

Say What?

NAME Sir Screech-a-lot

FAVORITE ACTIVITY Hanging out with other knight owls

FAVORITE OUTFIT A medieval hoot of armor

PET PEEVE When the visor on my helmet slips and I'm left totally in the dark

The best magician in history was Hoo-dini.

History was owl-ways my favorite subject!

Call me owl-fashioned, but I like a good yarn.

KNOCK, KNOCK.
Who's there?
Manny.
Manny who?
Manny years ago they didn't have so much history to learn!

In ancient Greece, owls were symbols of wisdom. In medieval Europe, however, they were associated with witches.

LAUGH OUT LOUD

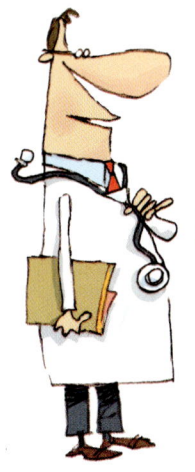

FUNNY BITES

"WHAT KIND OF MILEAGE DOES THAT THING GET?"

"YOU SAY YOU'VE BEEN FEELING RATHER JUMPY LATELY?"

"I HATE GETTING STUCK BEHIND A SCHOOL BUS."

159

JUST JOKING

KNOCK, KNOCK.
Who's there?
Nobel.
Nobel who?
No bell. That's why I'm knocking.

Q What do chefs in Alaska call the dessert known as baked Alaska?

A Baked here.

Say this fast three times:
Eleven benevolent elephants took the elevator.

Q What do you get when you put a Tasmanian devil in a chicken coop?

A Deviled eggs.

PRESIDENT: If George Washington and Abe Lincoln were alive today, what would be the most amazing thing about them?
VICE PRESIDENT: Their hairstyles?
PRESIDENT: No, their ages!

LAUGH OUT LOUD

It's a LONG story...

IT WAS THE LAST MINUTE OF SCIENCE CLASS and Mrs. Baines, the teacher, stood up and addressed the students.

"Now, class," Mrs. Baines said. "It's time to turn in your homework on your favorite element."

"Mine's right here!" replied John. "I chose helium, because I like balloons."

"Nice work, John," said Mrs. Baines.

"I've got mine, too!" Kate exclaimed. "I chose copper, because that's the name of my dog."

"Always a good one," Mrs. Baines replied. "Freddie, can I have yours, please?"

"Sure, Mrs. Baines," Freddie said. "I think you'll like it."

"Why, Freddie, this is just a blank piece of paper. Where's your assignment on your favorite element?" Mrs. Baines asked.

"It's right there," Freddie explained. "I WAS GOING FOR THE ELEMENT OF SURPRISE!"

JUST JOKING

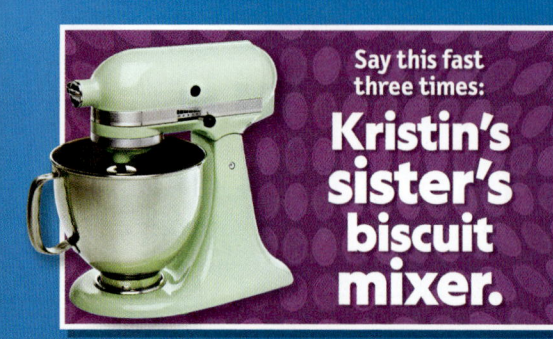

Say this fast three times:
Kristin's sister's biscuit mixer.

A **sloth** was climbing a **tree** when **three snails** attacked him. After **recovering**, he went to the police. **An officer** asked, "Can you describe **the snails?**" The sloth replied, "Not well. It all happened **too fast.**"

Q
Why do giraffes have long necks?

A Because they have smelly feet.

Q
What's the difference between Superman and an ordinary man?

A Superman wears his underwear over his pants.

KNOCK, KNOCK.
Who's there?
Avenue.
Avenue who?
Avenue heard enough of these jokes?

162

LAUGH OUT LOUD

TONGUE TWISTERS
SAY THESE FAST THREE TIMES

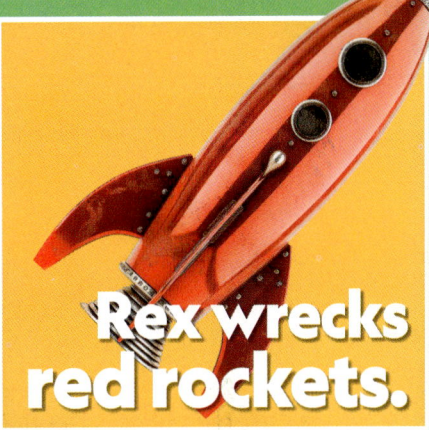

Patsy's perfect puff pastries.

Rex wrecks red rockets.

Theo throws three free throws.

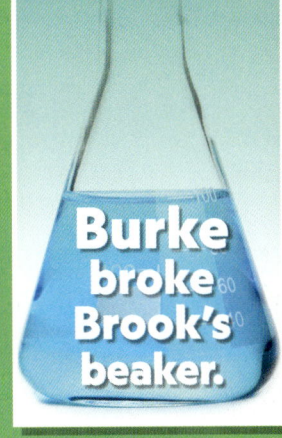

Burke broke Brook's beaker.

Which fish wished a fish's wish?

Becky gave Brett the black bat back.

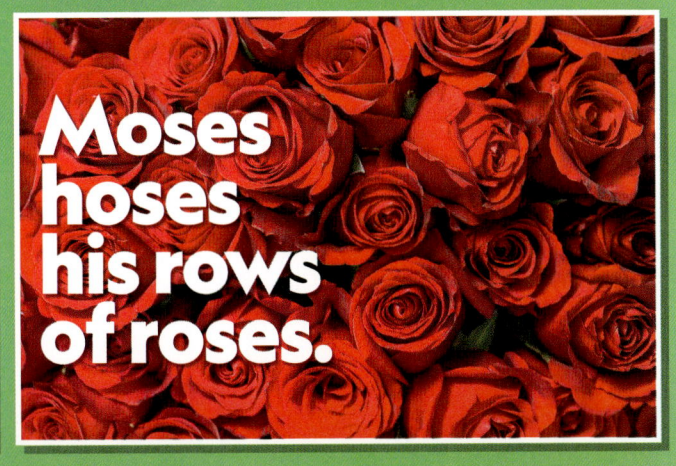

Moses hoses his rows of roses.

163

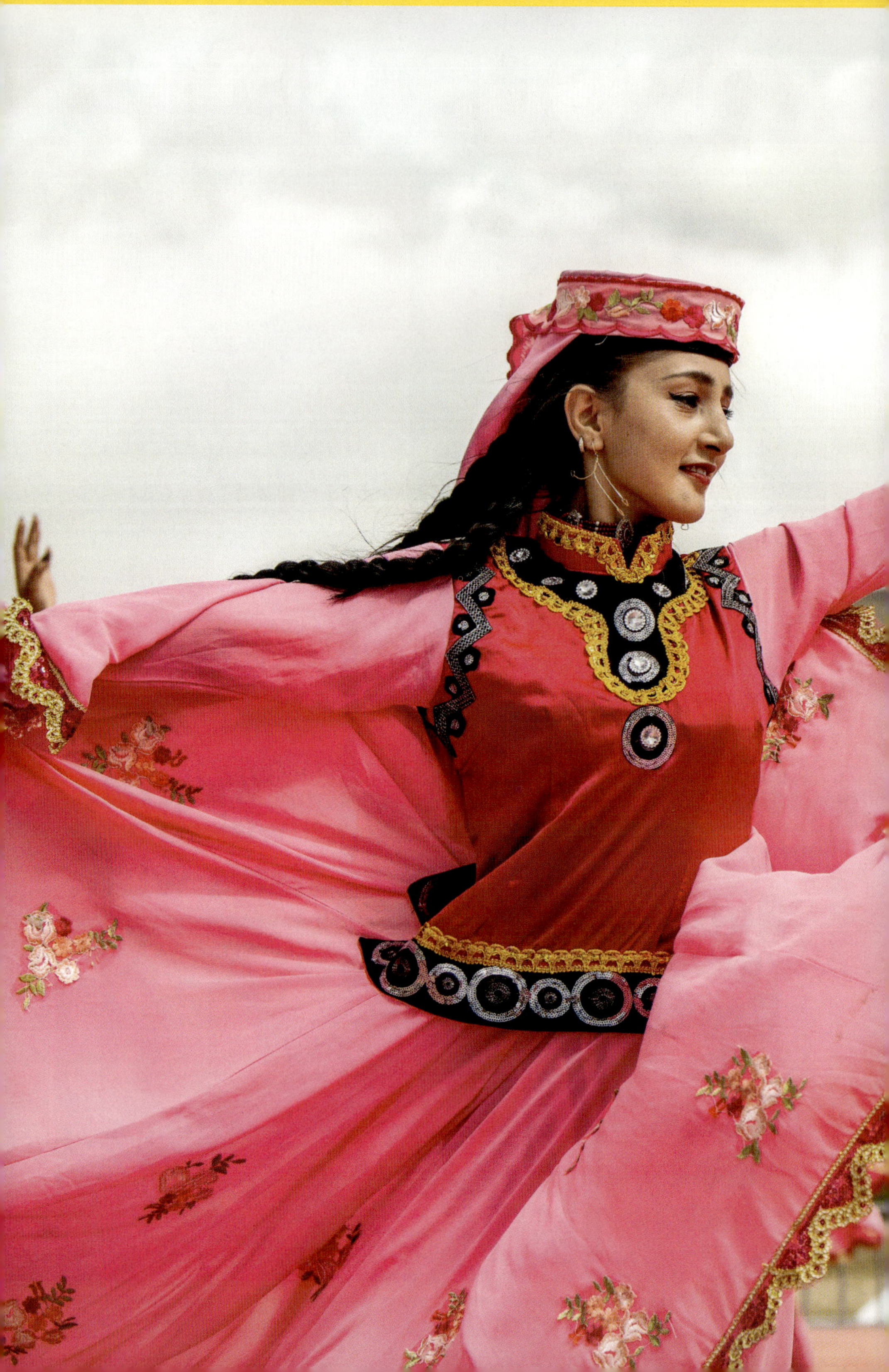

CULTURE CONNECTION

Dancers at the Dragon Boat Festival in northwest China

HOLIDAYS

CELEBRATIONS

LOSAR (TIBETAN NEW YEAR)

Begins February 18

A multiday celebration of the Tibetan New Year, Losar is a time for families to gather together for cultural events, traditional food, dancing, and singing. Tibetans also perform religious rituals to mark the start of the new year.

RAMADAN AND EID AL-FITR

February 18**– March 20

Muslims worldwide spend the ninth month of the Islamic lunar calendar in prayer and reflection and fasting from dawn until sunset to focus on worship and good deeds. The end of Ramadan is marked by the holiday of Eid al-Fitr, a breaking-the-fast holiday celebrated with prayer, feasts, and time spent together.

SONGKRAN

April 13–15

Thailand's New Year's festival, Songkran, is celebrated with street parties, giant friendly water fights, and other types of splashy fun as a symbolic way to "wash away" the previous year.

MARCH EQUINOX

March 20

The start of spring in the Northern Hemisphere—and autumn in the Southern Hemisphere—the March equinox features nearly equal hours of day and night. In certain parts of the world, cultures celebrate the arrival of spring with festivals and rituals.

MIDSUMMER

June 21

Also known as the June solstice, the longest day of the year in the Northern Hemisphere is honored with events often associated with summery celebrations, like bonfires and outdoor gatherings.

YOM KIPPUR

September 20*

Yom Kippur, a day of atonement for Jewish people, includes fasting and prayer, during which Jewish people ask for forgiveness of their sins. At the end of services, the fast is broken with a traditional meal.

MAKE A DIFFERENCE DAY

October 24

Volunteering is encouraged on this day of service, where communities come together to give back and make contributions big and small in an effort to make an impact and create positive change.

CULTURE CONNECTION

Around the World

HANUKKAH
December 4*–12

This eight-day Jewish holiday, also known as the Festival of Lights, pays homage to religious freedom and triumph over adversity. Each of the eight nights is marked by lighting the menorah, eating foods cooked in oil, exchanging gifts, singing songs, and playing games.

DAY OF RECONCILIATION
December 16

This annual event honors the end of apartheid, or segregation based on race, and the start of democracy in South Africa. Around the country, programs and events center around diversity, culture, and forgiveness.

CHRISTMAS DAY
December 25

A Christian holiday marking the birth of Jesus Christ, Christmas is usually celebrated by decorating trees, exchanging presents, and having festive gatherings.

*Begins at sundown.
**Dates may vary slightly by location.

2026 CALENDAR

JANUARY						
S	M	T	W	T	F	S
				1	2	3
4	5	6	7	8	9	10
11	12	13	14	15	16	17
18	19	20	21	22	23	24
25	26	27	28	29	30	31

FEBRUARY						
S	M	T	W	T	F	S
1	2	3	4	5	6	7
8	9	10	11	12	13	14
15	16	17	18	19	20	21
22	23	24	25	26	27	28

MARCH						
S	M	T	W	T	F	S
1	2	3	4	5	6	7
8	9	10	11	12	13	14
15	16	17	18	19	20	21
22	23	24	25	26	27	28
29	30	31				

APRIL						
S	M	T	W	T	F	S
			1	2	3	4
5	6	7	8	9	10	11
12	13	14	15	16	17	18
19	20	21	22	23	24	25
26	27	28	29	30		

MAY						
S	M	T	W	T	F	S
					1	2
3	4	5	6	7	8	9
10	11	12	13	14	15	16
17	18	19	20	21	22	23
24	25	26	27	28	29	30
31						

JUNE						
S	M	T	W	T	F	S
	1	2	3	4	5	6
7	8	9	10	11	12	13
14	15	16	17	18	19	20
21	22	23	24	25	26	27
28	29	30				

JULY						
S	M	T	W	T	F	S
			1	2	3	4
5	6	7	8	9	10	11
12	13	14	15	16	17	18
19	20	21	22	23	24	25
26	27	28	29	30	31	

AUGUST						
S	M	T	W	T	F	S
						1
2	3	4	5	6	7	8
9	10	11	12	13	14	15
16	17	18	19	20	21	22
23	24	25	26	27	28	29
30	31					

SEPTEMBER						
S	M	T	W	T	F	S
		1	2	3	4	5
6	7	8	9	10	11	12
13	14	15	16	17	18	19
20	21	22	23	24	25	26
27	28	29	30			

OCTOBER						
S	M	T	W	T	F	S
				1	2	3
4	5	6	7	8	9	10
11	12	13	14	15	16	17
18	19	20	21	22	23	24
25	26	27	28	29	30	31

NOVEMBER						
S	M	T	W	T	F	S
1	2	3	4	5	6	7
8	9	10	11	12	13	14
15	16	17	18	19	20	21
22	23	24	25	26	27	28
29	30					

DECEMBER						
S	M	T	W	T	F	S
		1	2	3	4	5
6	7	8	9	10	11	12
13	14	15	16	17	18	19
20	21	22	23	24	25	26
27	28	29	30	31		

HOLIDAYS

DIWALI
The Hindu Festival of Lights

Diwali is India's biggest holiday. In October or November each year, millions of Hindus, Sikhs, and Buddhists around the world celebrate for five days.

DIWALI, sometimes called Deepavali or Dipawali, means "rows of lights." People use lamps and lanterns to decorate their homes and public spaces. Fireworks fill the skies. The light symbolizes the victory of good over evil. People in different parts of India have different beliefs about the origins of the holiday. In southern India, people celebrate it as the day the Hindu god Krishna defeated a demon. In western India, it marks the day another god, Vishnu, sent the demon king Bali to rule the underworld.

Each of Diwali's five days has its own set of traditions. The first day is considered a lucky day for shopping and cleaning the house. On the second day, people decorate their homes. On the third day, families come together to feast and celebrate. The fourth day is for exchanging gifts. On the last day of Diwali, brothers visit their married sisters, who welcome them with a meal.

Today, setting off fireworks with a hiss and pop is Diwali's biggest tradition. But it's a new addition to this otherwise ancient holiday. Until the 1900s, pyrotechnics were so expensive they were for royals only.

> Some people believe that the sound of Diwali fireworks sends a message to the gods about the joy of people on Earth.

168

CULTURE CONNECTION

During Diwali, Hindus light rows of small clay lamps called *diyas*, which are filled with oil.

HOLIDAYS

Bet You Didn't Know!

6 winter feast facts to fill up on

1 Deep-fried jelly doughnuts called *sufganiyot* are eaten during Hanukkah to represent an **ancient miracle** involving long-lasting **lamp oil.**

2 A harvest festival called **Basega** honors ancestors of the **Mossi people** in the African country of Burkina Faso.

3 During **Dongzhi,** a festival celebrated in parts of Asia, families eat sweet dumplings called *tangyuan* to symbolize togetherness.

4 During a Japanese celebration called **Toji,** people take **baths filled with citrus fruits** and eat pumpkin for good luck.

5 *Hallacas,* a type of **tamale** eaten in Venezuela on **Christmas Eve,** can be stuffed with as many as 20 different ingredients.

6 Celebrated by many Black Americans, **Kwanzaa** gets its name from the phrase "first fruits of the harvest" in Swahili, an African language.

CULTURE CONNECTION

What's Your Chinese Horoscope?
Locate your birth year to find out.

In Chinese astrology, the zodiac runs on a 12-year cycle, based on the lunar calendar. Each year corresponds to one of 12 animals, each representing one of 12 personality types. Read on to find out which animal year you were born in and what that might say about you.

RAT
1972, '84, '96, 2008, '20
Say cheese! You're attractive, charming, and creative. When you get mad, you can have really sharp teeth!

HORSE
1966, '78, '90, 2002, '14
Being happy is your *mane* goal. And though you're smart and hardworking, your teacher may get upset if you talk too much.

OX
1973, '85, '97, 2009, '21
You're smart, patient, and as strong as an ... well, you know. Though you're a leader, you never brag.

SHEEP
1967, '79, '91, 2003, '15
Gentle as a lamb, you're also artistic, compassionate, and wise. You're often shy.

TIGER
1974, '86, '98, 2010, '22
You may be a nice person, but no one should ever enter your room without asking—you might attack!

MONKEY
1968, '80, '92, 2004, '16
No "monkey see, monkey do" for you. You're a clever problem-solver with an excellent memory.

RABBIT
1975, '87, '99, 2011, '23
Your ambition and talent make you jump at opportunity. You also keep your ears open for gossip.

ROOSTER
1969, '81, '93, 2005, '17
You crow about your adventures, but inside you're really shy. You're thoughtful, capable, brave, and talented.

DRAGON
1976, '88, 2000, '12, '24
You're on fire! Health, energy, honesty, and bravery make you a living legend.

DOG
1970, '82, '94, 2006, '18
Often the leader of the pack, you're loyal and honest. You can also keep a secret.

SNAKE
1977, '89, 2001, '13, '25
You may not speak often, but you're very smart. You always seem to have a stash of cash.

PIG
1971, '83, '95, 2007, '19
Even though you're courageous, honest, and kind, you never hog all the attention.

HOLIDAYS

The Secret History of
HALLOWEEN

No tricks, just treats in this bone-chilling timeline

GHOST-FOOLING CLOTH SOLD HERE

You probably love putting on a Halloween costume and getting candy, but that's totally different from how the event used to be celebrated. In fact, the holiday has gone through many changes in the 2,000 years it's been around. Check out this timeline to get the spooky scoop on Halloween through the centuries.

Sometimes historians don't know the exact date of long-ago events. That's why you might see "ca" next to a year. It stands for "circa," meaning "around."

1 ca 50 B.C. You might celebrate the new year on January 1, but ancient Celtic people in Ireland (Celts once lived throughout central and western Europe) had their parties on November 1. And they believed that spirits of the dead might rise the night before and ruin all the fun. So on October 31, these Irish Celts built bonfires to scare away ghosts and wore disguises so spirits wouldn't recognize them. The next day, people marked the new year with a festival called Samhain (pronounced SAH-win).

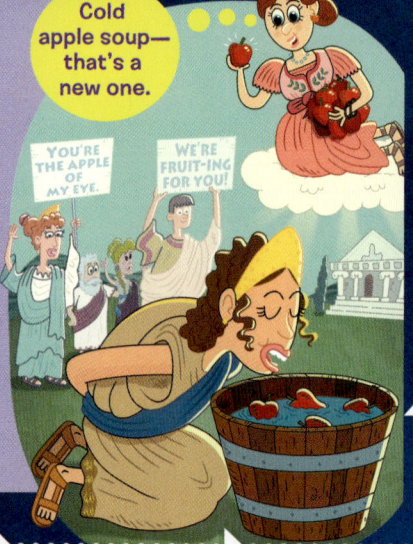

3 SEVENTH CENTURY A.D. By now, the Romans had been replaced by Christian conquerors—and they were *not* big fans of Samhain fun. Leaders swapped it with a religious holiday called All Saints' Day, or All Hallows' Day, on November 1. But people still lit bonfires and wore costumes the night before. They called it All Hallows' Eve—and later, Halloween.

2 A.D. 43 About a hundred years later, the Romans had conquered most Celtic territories. But that didn't mean they squashed the parties. They blended some of their fall festivities with Samhain and celebrated from sunset on October 31 to sunset on November 1. One of those Roman events honored Pomona, the goddess of fruit and trees. Pomona's symbol was the apple. *Hmm* … what do we bob for on Halloween again?

Cold apple soup—that's a new one.

YOU'RE THE APPLE OF MY EYE.

WE'RE FRUIT-ING FOR YOU!

4 1400s Samhain was now a big no-no. But the tradition of scaring away ghouls the night before didn't totally disappear. People in Ireland—and parts of England and Scotland now, too—kept celebrating the holiday. Folks still wore masks and costumes on All Hallows' Eve, but they also started going door-to-door to sing a song or do a trick. Performers were rewarded with food or small gifts. Sound like trick-or-treating? In those days, it was called mumming.

172

CULTURE CONNECTION

5 EARLY 1600s When the British established colonies in what would later become the United States, they brought All Hallows' Eve traditions with them. Although the Puritans who settled in New England didn't approve of the holiday, people in southern colonies like Maryland and Virginia celebrated with ghost stories, fortune telling, and dancing.

6 MID-1800s After 1845, millions of immigrants from Ireland began arriving in the United States. These newcomers helped spread Halloween celebrations throughout the country. One Irish tradition involved hollowing out turnips, carving faces into them, and placing a candle inside. The turnips were meant to protect them from an evil spirit called Stingy Jack—and were called jack-o'-lanterns! Later, people also carved potatoes, beets, and pumpkins to protect themselves from harm.

7 EARLY 1900s By the 20th century, Halloween had become a pranking holiday. Adults rattled windows and tied doors shut to make people think supernatural forces were around. Some began offering sweets to convince jokesters to leave their homes alone. (This is probably why we now say "trick or treat.") Hoping to change the way the holiday was celebrated, local leaders encouraged parents to take their costumed children door-to-door to politely ask for goodies.

8 1960s Trick-or-treating really took off during the mid-20th century. Before then, kids usually scored toys, money, and fruit—not necessarily candy. It wasn't until companies began selling miniature candy bars around the 1960s that Halloween became the "sugar fest" it is today.

For two loaves, I'll juggle *six* balls.

9 NOW Halloween is back as a holiday for kids *and* adults. Entire families—including pets!—celebrate by dressing in costume and trick-or-treating. In 2023, people in the United States spent about $12 billion on costumes, candy, and decorations for the holiday.

AROUND THE WORLD

awes8me
HOT-AIR BALLOONS FLOAT TO ALL NEW LEVELS OF EXTREME.

1 UP WE GO!

Adventure is out there! Straight from the movie, this hot-air balloon re-creates the scene in **Pixar's** *Up* where a house goes airborne with the help of balloons. This one was made by sewing 600 small balloons onto the outer skin of a regular hot-air balloon.

Uplifting Balloons

2 THE DARK SIDE RISES

Help us, Obi-Wan! This **Darth Vader** balloon (86 feet [26 m] tall) took to the skies in Taiwan. Kept top secret, manufacturing took eight weeks. To balance out the Force, the makers have also created a Yoda, which is smaller, but, of course, just as mighty.

CULTURE CONNECTION

3 WHERE ARE THE PIGS?

No slingshot needed: This **Angry Bird** floated through the Albuquerque International Balloon Fiesta without any green pigs in its way. At 80 feet (24 m), it was one of hundreds of balloons that took to the skies in 2014 at the annual event in New Mexico, U.S.A.

4 FISH OUT OF WATER

This **fish** appears to be swimming through the blue—but that isn't water! It's blue skies. You might be surprised to learn the first passengers to go up in a hot-air balloon were animals. In 1783, a sheep, duck, and rooster were the passengers aboard the first flight.

5 MAKE A WISH!

Good luck blowing out these candles! This three-tiered **birthday cake** flew over León, Mexico, in 2011 at the International Balloon Festival. Some 200 balloons fly here annually, making it the biggest hot-air balloon event in Latin America. Light shows, music, and other festivities accompany the event.

6 RISE AND SHINE

This fresh-squeezed balloon floated over the Malaysian city of Putrajaya for an international hot-air festival. The balloon is flat on one side, mimicking an **orange** with the end sliced off.

7 TWEET, TWEET!

I thought I saw a **Tweety** balloon! The famous yellow canary made an appearance at the Adirondack Balloon Festival in Glens Falls, New York, U.S.A., in 2016—and a balloon depicting his nemesis Sylvester was hovering nearby. Some 100 balloons launched while spectators watched from below.

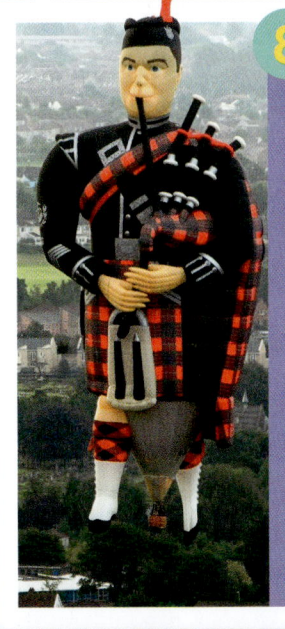

8 A LOT OF HOT AIR

The **Flying Scotsman** is just that—a 156-foot (47.5-m)-tall bagpiper that flies through the skies. It's dressed in traditional Scottish clothes—the tartan design was created using ink-jet technology. And the balloon is captained by a real Scotsman. Though eye-catching, the balloon is not aerodynamic or designed for long distances.

FOOD

10 COOL THINGS ABOUT FOOD

Vanilla is used to **make chocolate.**

THE **1904 WORLD'S FAIR** FEATURED A LIFE-SIZE ELEPHANT MADE OF **ALMONDS.**

Asparagus stalks can grow **10 inches** (25 cm) in **one day.**

You can visit a **gelato museum** in Italy.

The stringy parts of a **banana** are called **phloem** (FLO-em).

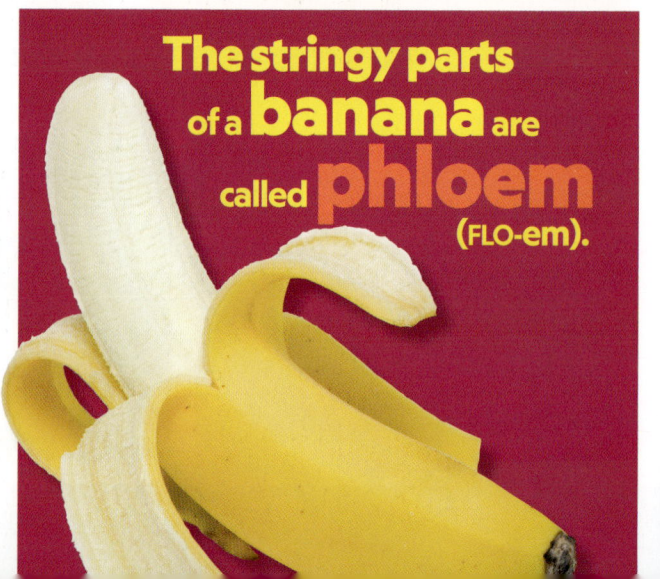

CULTURE CONNECTION

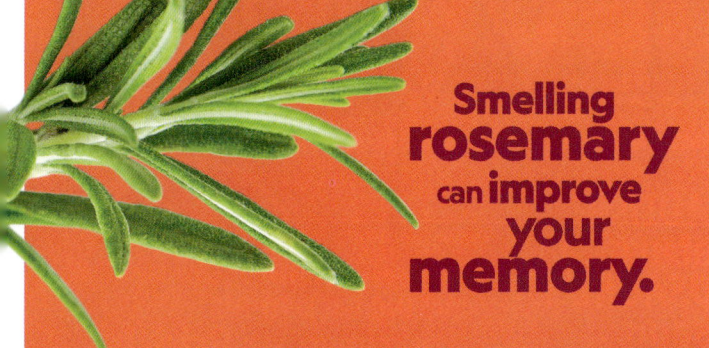

Smelling **rosemary** can **improve your memory.**

Red food coloring is often made from **crushed bugs.**

IT CAN TAKE UP TO **21 DAYS TO MAKE** A SINGLE **JELLY BEAN.**

Some **dogs' paws** smell like **corn chips.**

If you **ate one variety** of **apple** a day, you'd need **20 years** to try them all.

177

MONEY

MONEY AROUND THE WORLD!

A **RARE CANADIAN QUARTER** features a *PACHYRHINOSAURUS*, a dinosaur that was discovered in Canada.

DATING BACK TO THE 8TH CENTURY, THE **British pound** is the world's **oldest currency** STILL IN USE.

In the United States, more **$100 bills** are in circulation than **$1 bills**.

The **colón banknotes** of **Costa Rica** show native animals like the **brown-throated sloth**.

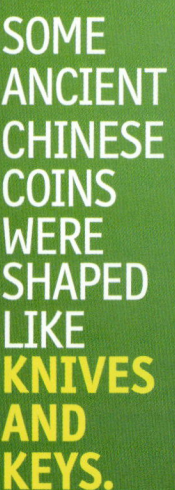

SOME ANCIENT CHINESE COINS WERE SHAPED LIKE KNIVES AND KEYS.

CULTURE CONNECTION

In Norway, **butter** was once accepted as **currency**.

The **Australian dollar** is also called a **BUCK** or the **AUSSIE**.

During the Middle Ages, people in Italy paid each other with wheels of **PARMESAN CHEESE**.

The newest design on British banknotes features **King Charles III** instead of his mother, **Queen Elizabeth II**, who died in 2022.

COINS IN THE BAHAMAS HAVE **SEA STARS AND PINEAPPLES** ON THEM.

The Aztec of ancient Mexico used **CACAO BEANS** as money.

SHIMMERING **BUTTERFLY WINGS** INSPIRED THE **ANTI-COUNTERFEIT** WINDOW ON MANY BANKNOTES.

MONEY TIP!
CLIP COUPONS FOR YOUR PARENTS. Ask if they'll put the money they save into your piggy bank.

179

LANGUAGE

Weird but true! Word Power

THE WORLD'S SHORTEST **ALPHABET** HAS **12 LETTERS;** THE WORLD'S LONGEST HAS **74 LETTERS.**

AROUND **7,100** LANGUAGES ARE SPOKEN WORLDWIDE.

N|uu, A LANGUAGE OF SOUTHERN AFRICA, USES **CLICKING SOUNDS** FOR ITS **52 CONSONANTS.**

SINCE THE 1500s, **115** LANGUAGES HAVE BECOME **EXTINCT** IN THE **UNITED STATES.**

CULTURE CONNECTION

ABOUT 15 PERCENT OF THE **WORLD'S POPULATION SPEAKS MANDARIN,** A CHINESE LANGUAGE.

AT LEAST 12 LANGUAGES USE THE WORD **"huh"** TO EXPRESS CONFUSION.

2,300 OF THE **WORLD'S LANGUAGES** ARE SPOKEN IN **ASIA.**

THE WORD **"SET"** HAS **464 DEFINITIONS** IN THE **OXFORD ENGLISH DICTIONARY.**

ENGLISH IS AN OFFICIAL **LANGUAGE** OF MORE THAN **50 COUNTRIES.**

ANCIENT BELIEFS

Monster MASH

Before Frankenstein's monster or King Kong, there were the magnificent creatures of Greek mythology. Some had sharp teeth and claws and breathed fire, and others made you solve riddles and brainteasers. These Greek beasties could be pretty scary—especially if you had to fight them—but they're kind of cool, too!

FROM THE HIT PODCAST AND BOOK *GREEKING OUT!*

THE SPHINX

This giant monster had the body of a lion, the head of a woman, wings of an eagle, and, depending upon who you ask, a snake's tail. She would pounce upon her unsuspecting victims and force them to solve a riddle: Which creature has only one voice, but has four legs in the morning, two legs in the afternoon, and three legs at night? Anyone who didn't answer the riddle correctly was devoured. P.S. Should you ever encounter the Sphinx, the answer is: a human. (The times of day represent important stages of human life!)

CULTURE CONNECTION

TYPHON

Often described as the "father of all monsters," Typhon was one of Gaea's children. He was an incredibly tall giant with multiple dragon heads, snakes for legs, and hundreds of wings. Oh, and he could breathe fire. He once tried to destroy the gods, but Zeus was able to defeat Typhon and imprison him deep inside the Underworld. Then Zeus plopped a mountain on top of the prison for good measure.

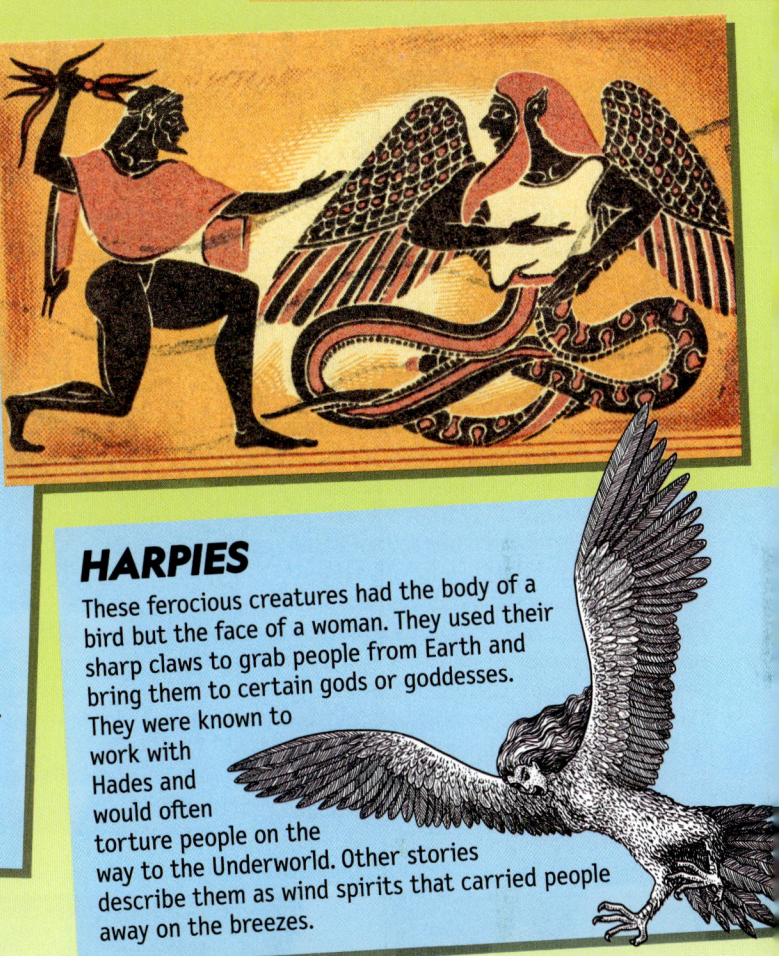

HARPIES

These ferocious creatures had the body of a bird but the face of a woman. They used their sharp claws to grab people from Earth and bring them to certain gods or goddesses. They were known to work with Hades and would often torture people on the way to the Underworld. Other stories describe them as wind spirits that carried people away on the breezes.

SIRENS

Sirens were beautiful, alluring creatures that were half bird, half human. They would sit on top of rocks near the ocean and sing for any passing ships. Sounds kinda nice, right? Well, the songs were actually enchanted. Anyone who heard them would jump off the ship and swim through the water to the sirens, providing them with a nice meal for lunch. And if sirens sound familiar, it's because they served as inspiration for what we now call mermaids.

RELIGION

World Religions

Around the world, religion takes many forms. Some belief systems, such as Christianity, Islam, and Judaism, are monotheistic, meaning that followers believe in just one supreme being. Others, like Hinduism, Shintoism, and most Native belief systems, are polytheistic, meaning that their followers believe in multiple gods.

All of the major religions have their origins in Asia, but they have spread around the world. Christianity, with the largest number of followers, has three divisions—Roman Catholic, Eastern Orthodox, and Protestant. Islam, with about one-quarter of all believers, has two main divisions—Sunni and Shiite. Hinduism and Buddhism account for about another one-fifth of believers. Judaism, dating back some 4,000 years, has some 15 million followers, about 2 percent of all believers.

CHRISTIANITY

Based on the teachings of Jesus Christ, who was born some 2,000 years ago in the area of modern-day Israel, Christianity has spread worldwide and actively seeks converts. Followers in Switzerland (above) participate in an Easter season procession with lanterns and crosses.

BUDDHISM

Founded about 2,400 years ago in northern India by the Hindu prince Gautama Buddha, Buddhism spread throughout East and Southeast Asia. Buddhist temples have statues, such as the Mihintale Buddha (above) in Sri Lanka.

HINDUISM

Dating back more than 4,000 years, Hinduism is practiced mainly in India. Hindus follow sacred texts known as the Vedas and believe in reincarnation. During the festival of Navratri, which honors the goddess Durga, the Garba dance is performed (above).

CULTURE CONNECTION

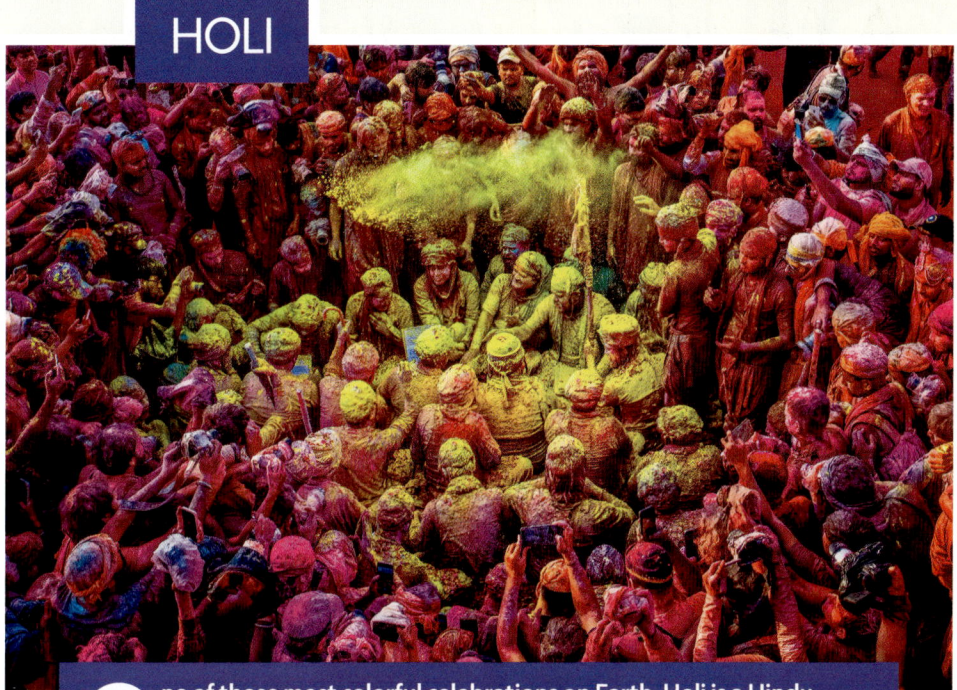

HOLI

One of those most colorful celebrations on Earth, Holi is a Hindu festival popular in India and Nepal. Also known as the Festival of Colors, Holi is marked by street parties where people throw brightly hued powders and water on friends and family to usher in the new season.

ISLAM

Muslims believe that the Quran, Islam's sacred book, records the words of Allah (God) as revealed to the Prophet Muhammad beginning around A.D. 610. Believers circle the Kaaba (above) in the Grand Mosque in Mecca, Saudi Arabia, the spiritual center of the faith.

JUDAISM

The traditions, laws, and beliefs of Judaism date back to Abraham (the patriarch) and the Torah (the first five books of the Old Testament). Followers pray before the Western Wall (above), which stands below Islam's Dome of the Rock in Jerusalem.

185

MORE FOR YOU

QUIZ WHIZ

How vast is your knowledge about the world around you? Quiz yourself!

Write your answers on a piece of paper. Then check them below.

1 Diwali is the Hindu festival of _____.
a. friendship   c. summer
b. lights   d. community

2 Much of red food coloring is made from _____.
a. fish scales   c. crushed bugs
b. beets   d. flowers

3 True or false? Trick-or-treating became popular in the 1700s.

4 What percentage of the world speaks Mandarin Chinese?
a. 15 percent   c. 25 percent
b. 5 percent   d. 40 percent

5 True or false? Harpies have the body of a bird and the face of a woman.

Not **STUMPED** yet? Check out the *NATIONAL GEOGRAPHIC KIDS QUIZ WHIZ* collection for more fun **CULTURE** questions!

ANSWERS: 1. b; 2. c; 3. False; 4. a; 5. True

CULTURE CONNECTION

HOMEWORK HELP

Explore a New Culture

YOU'RE A STUDENT, but you're also a citizen of the world. Writing a report on another country or your own country is a great way to better understand and appreciate how different people live. Pick the country of your ancestors, one that's been in the news, or one that you'd like to visit someday.

STAMPS OF BRAZIL

CURRENCY AND COINS OF BRAZIL

FLAG OF BRAZIL

Passport to Success
A country report follows the format of an expository essay because you're "exposing" information about the country you choose.

The following step-by-step tips will help you with this international task.

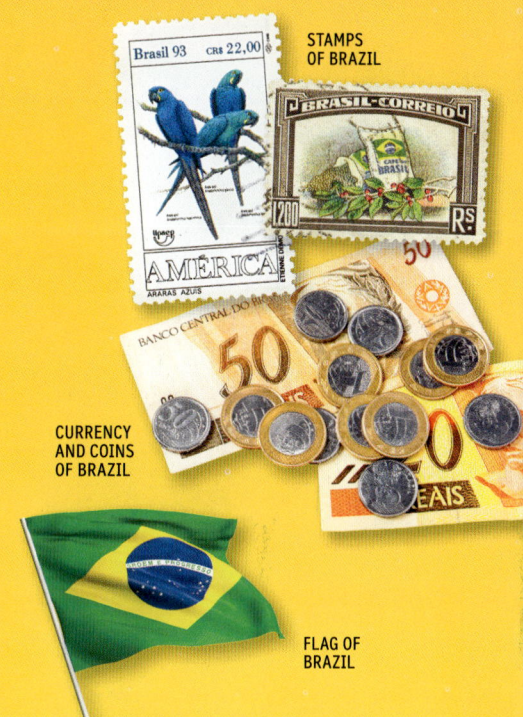

1 RESEARCH. Gathering information is the most important step in writing a good country report. Look to internet sources, encyclopedias, books, magazine and newspaper articles, and other sources to find important and interesting details about your subject.

2 ORGANIZE YOUR NOTES. Put the information you gather into a rough outline. For example, sort everything you found about the country's system of government, climate, etc.

3 WRITE IT UP. Follow the basic structure of good writing: introduction, body, and conclusion. Remember that each paragraph should have a topic sentence that is then supported by facts and details. Incorporate the information from your notes, but make sure it's in your own words. And make your writing flow with good transitions and descriptive language.

4 ADD VISUALS. Include maps, diagrams, photos, and other visual aids.

5 PROOFREAD AND REVISE. Correct any mistakes, and polish your language. Do your best!

6 CITE YOUR SOURCES. Be sure to keep a record of your sources.

Two thousand drones create a dragon pattern over Nanning, Guangxi Province, China.

SCIENCE and TECHNOLOGY

INVENTIONS AND TECHNOLOGY

10 FANTASTIC FUTURE TECHNOLOGIES

Ever wonder what the future will look like? Here are 10 types of technology scientists are working on right now!

Oceangoing pioneers plan to **build a floating city,** complete with **swimming pools** and **tree-filled parks.**

REMOTE-CONTROLLED **COCKROACHES** WILL BE ABLE TO CRAWL INSIDE RUBBLE TO **SEARCH FOR EARTHQUAKE VICTIMS.**

Imagine a house like a tree, with a roof that **captures sunlight for energy** and **walls that heal like bark** when scratched.

SCIENCE AND TECHNOLOGY

Wireless electricity will be beamed **through the air** to power homes, cars, and airplanes.

SENSORS SEWN INTO YOUR JACKET **WILL WARN OF ONCOMING TRAFFIC** IF YOU FORGET TO LOOK BOTH WAYS.

Flying cars might sound too out there. But **electric vertical take-off and landing vehicles,** or eVTOLs, are actually being developed by companies around the world right now!

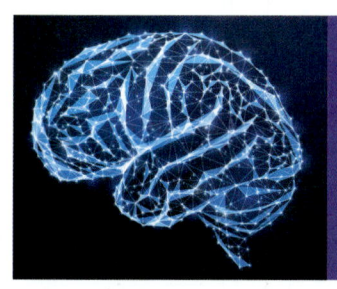

IN 30 YEARS **SOME ROBOTS** MAY HAVE **REAL BRAINS** GROWN FROM HUMAN BRAIN CELLS.

Soldiers of the future will **feel like superheroes** when they strap on **strength-boosting robotic outfits** called exosuits.

SPECIAL DESKTOP OBJECT PRINTERS will print complete products—from a **COMB TO A CELL PHONE TO ANOTHER PRINTER.**

Multimedia wallpaper will turn walls and ceilings into **larger-than-life video displays.**

191

INVENTIONS AND TECHNOLOGY

awes8me

3D PRINTING GIVES DESIGNERS THE FREEDOM TO PRINT EVERYTHING FROM TINY TOYS TO HUMONGOUS HOUSES.

1 ROYAL RESIDENCE

This 3D-printed creation is fit for a prince—or a princess. Andrey Rudenko built this **cement castle** in his own Minnesota, U.S.A., backyard, but first he had to tailor the nozzle on a 3D printer that usually worked with plastic to use cement instead.

Eye-Popping Creations

2 ECO-CHIC CAR

The two-seater **Strati**, the world's first 3D-printed car, is not only for the space age, it's also eco-friendly. Printed in Detroit, Michigan, U.S.A., with the help of the Oak Ridge National Laboratory, the electric car was made from carbon-fiber-reinforced plastic and is 100 percent recyclable.

SCIENCE AND TECHNOLOGY

5 NANO NANO

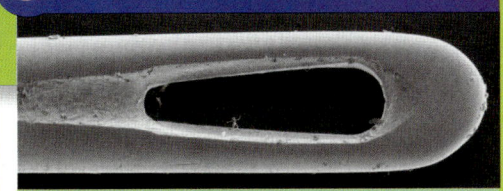

Artist Jonty Hurwitz likes things small ... very small. He printed a human form so small she is dwarfed by the eye of a needle and impossible to see without a powerful microscope. At 80 x 100 x 20 microns, she fits on a strand of human hair.

4 PENNY PINCHER

This cute **piggy bank** was made at the offices of MakerBot in New York City. The company supports classrooms with 3D printing resources, tools, and education.

3 SWEET HOME

This two-story **concrete house** was printed in one piece in a neighborhood in Beijing, China. At 4,305 square feet (400 sq m), the home is about the size of a U.S. high school basketball court.

6 ROCK ON

The Secret Jazz Band from Los Angeles entertained the crowd at an awards ceremony by playing on a 3D-printed **guitar and drums.** Rocking out on this innovative, red instrument shows off how this new technology can carry its own tune.

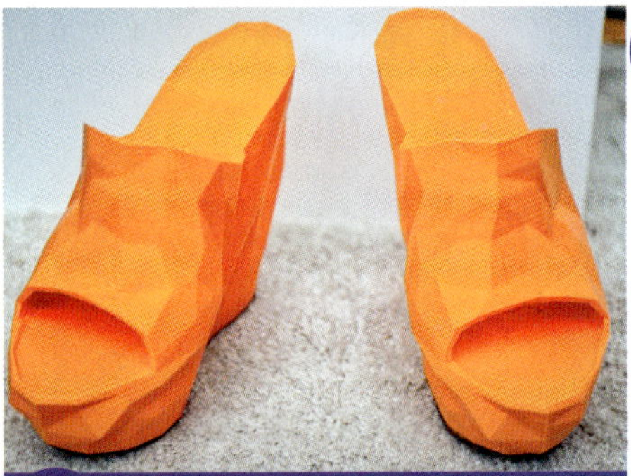

8 FANTASTIC FLIER

It's a bird, it's a plane, it's a 3D-printed drone called **Thor!** Created by the large airplane manufacturer Airbus, Thor is 13 feet (4 m) long and weighs 46 pounds (21 kg). The only part that's not printed? Its electrical system.

7 UNIQUE SHOES

The geometric folds in these orange, 3D-printed **shoes** are crystal sharp. Style and function join forces with this new technology as artists and designers can realize unique designs and create custom shoes designed for the perfect fit.

BIOLOGY

WHAT IS LIFE?

This seems like such an easy question to answer. Everybody knows that singing birds are alive and rocks are not. But when we start studying bacteria and other microscopic creatures, things get more complicated.

SO WHAT EXACTLY IS LIFE?
Most scientists agree that something is alive if it can reproduce, grow in size to become more complex in structure, take in nutrients to survive, give off waste products, and respond to external stimuli, such as increased sunlight or changes in temperature.

KINDS OF LIFE
Biologists classify living organisms by how they get their energy. Organisms such as algae, green plants, and some bacteria use sunlight as an energy source. Animals (like humans), fungi, and some single-celled microscopic organisms called Archaea use chemicals to provide energy. When we eat food, chemical reactions within our digestive system turn our food into fuel.

Living things inhabit land, sea, and air. In fact, life thrives deep beneath the oceans, embedded in rocks miles below Earth's crust, in ice, and in other extreme environments. The life-forms that thrive in these challenging environments are called extremophiles. Some of these draw directly upon the chemicals surrounding them for energy. Because these are very different forms of life from what we're used to, we may not think of them as alive, but they are.

HOW IT ALL WORKS
To understand how a living organism works, it helps to look at one example of its simplest form: the single-celled bacterium called *Streptococcus*. There are many kinds of these tiny organisms, and some are responsible for human illnesses. What makes us sick or uncomfortable are the toxins the bacteria give off in our bodies.

A single *Streptococcus* bacterium is so small that at least 500 of them could fit on the dot above this letter *i*. These bacteria are some of the simplest forms of life we know. They have no moving parts, no lungs, no brain, no heart, no liver, and no leaves or fruit. Yet this life-form reproduces. It grows in size by producing long-chain structures, takes in nutrients, and gives off waste products. This tiny life-form is alive, just as you are alive.

What makes something alive is a question scientists grapple with when they study viruses, such as the ones that cause the common cold and COVID-19. They can grow and reproduce within host cells, such as those that make up your body. Because viruses lack cells and cannot metabolize nutrients for energy or reproduce without a host, scientists ask if they are indeed alive. And don't go looking for them without a strong microscope—viruses are a hundred times smaller than bacteria.

Scientists think life began on Earth more than four billion years ago, but no fossils exist from that time. The earliest fossils ever found are from the primitive life that existed 3.5 billion years ago. Other life-forms, some of which are shown below, soon followed. Scientists continue to study how life evolved on Earth and whether it is possible that life exists on other planets.

MICROSCOPIC ORGANISMS

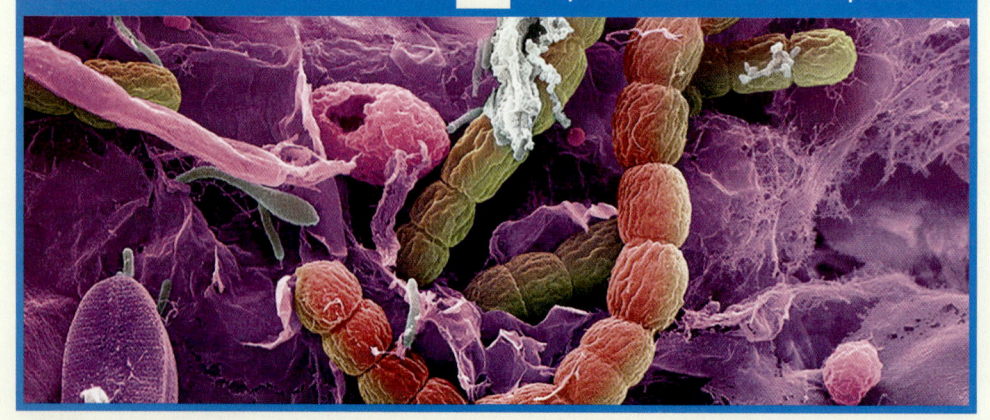

SCIENCE AND TECHNOLOGY

The Three Domains of Life

Biologists divide all living organisms into three domains, or groups: Bacteria, Archaea, and Eukarya. Archaea and Bacteria cells do not have nuclei—cellular parts that are essential to reproduction and other cell functions—but they are different from each other in many ways. Because human cells have a nucleus, we belong to the Eukarya domain.

1 BACTERIA

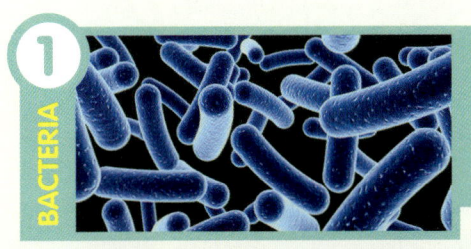

DOMAIN BACTERIA: These single-celled microorganisms are found almost everywhere in the world. Bacteria are small and do not have nuclei. They can be shaped like rods, spirals, or spheres. Some of them are helpful to humans, and some are harmful.

2 ARCHAEA

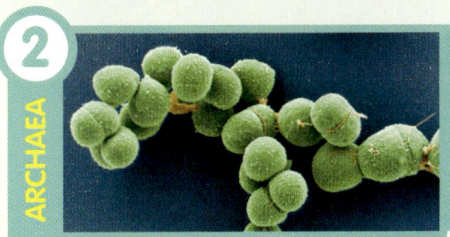

DOMAIN ARCHAEA: These single-celled microorganisms are often found in extremely hostile environments. Like Bacteria, Archaea do not have nuclei, but they have some genes in common with Eukarya. For this reason, scientists think the Archaea living today most closely resemble the earliest forms of life on Earth.

3 EUKARYA

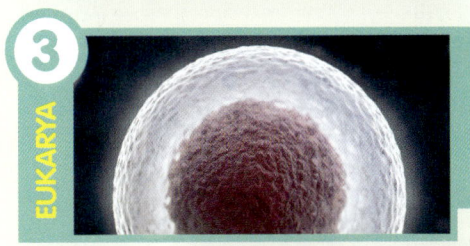

DOMAIN EUKARYA: This diverse group of life-forms is more complicated than Bacteria and Archaea, as Eukarya have one or more cells with nuclei. These are the tiny cells that make up your whole body. Eukarya are divided into four groups: fungi, protists, plants, and animals.

FUNGI
KINGDOM FUNGI: Mainly multicellular organisms, fungi cannot make their own food. Mushrooms and yeast are fungi.

PROTISTS
PROTISTS: Once considered a kingdom, this group is a "grab bag" that includes unicellular and multicellular organisms of great variety.

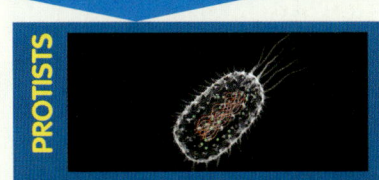

PLANTS
KINGDOM PLANTAE: Plants are multicellular, and many can make their own food using photosynthesis.

ANIMALS
KINGDOM ANIMALIA: Most animals, which are multicellular, have their own organ systems. Animals do not make their own food.

FYI — **WHAT IS A DOMAIN?** Scientifically speaking, a domain is a major taxonomic division into which natural objects are classified (see page 44 for "What Is Taxonomy?").

PLANTS

Freaky Plants

Wondering what could be so peculiar about a plant? Then you'll be amazed by these strange sprouts with odd smells, funny "faces," and more.

The fruit on the doll's eye plant looks like human eyeballs.

THE POISON GARDEN in northern England is a public garden filled with **DEADLY PLANTS**.

ANTS THAT LIVE ON BULLHORN ACACIAS SWARM ANY INTRUDING BUGS AND THROW THEM OFF THE TREE.

Petals of the skeleton flower become see-through when wet, then turn back to white as they dry.

The trunk of the **baobab tree** swells into the **shape of a bottle** as it collects **rainwater**.

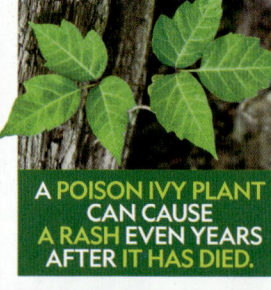

A **POISON IVY PLANT** CAN CAUSE A **RASH** EVEN YEARS AFTER **IT HAS DIED**.

AFTER CLOSING ITS "MOUTH" AROUND AN INSECT, A CARNIVOROUS VENUS FLYTRAP CAN TAKE UP TO 12 DAYS TO REOPEN.

The **Darth Vader flower** from Central America **resembles** the *Star Wars* villain.

196

SCIENCE AND TECHNOLOGY

WEIRD AND WONDERFUL TREES

WORLD'S TALLEST TREE
You'd think you could find the world's tallest tree, named **Hyperion**, pretty easily. But its location—somewhere in Redwood National Park in California, U.S.A.—is kept quiet to make sure it isn't damaged. (Scientists have climbed it and measured it.) The coast redwood stands at an incredible 381 feet (116 m)—taller than the Statue of Liberty.

ROBIN HOOD'S HANGOUT
According to folklore, this 1,000-year-old oak tree in England's Sherwood Forest is the legendary hideaway for Robin Hood and his Merry Men. Known as **Major Oak**, it is the biggest oak tree in Britain. In a good year, the tree produces around 150,000 acorns.

SUPER SOLAR
These "trees" are the ultimate multi-taskers. Standing up to 164 feet (50 m) tall, the trees in Singapore's **Supertree Grove** are sculptures covered in living plants, making them look like real trees. Their massive canopies provide shade for pedestrians during the day, and in the evening they glow with a solar-powered light display.

OPEN-AIR MUSEUM
Art meets nature in the **Oma Forest,** located in Spain's Basque Country. Painter and sculptor Agustín Ibarrola painted colorful patterns, shapes, and figures on pine trees, combining techniques from the Paleolithic period as well as from the modern era.

HUMAN BODY

Your Amazing Body!

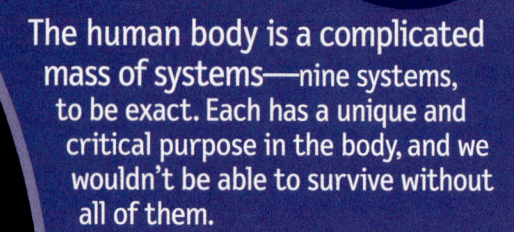

HUMANS ARE THE ONLY SPECIES KNOWN TO BLUSH.

The human body is a complicated mass of systems—nine systems, to be exact. Each has a unique and critical purpose in the body, and we wouldn't be able to survive without all of them.

The **NERVOUS** system controls the body.

The **MUSCULAR** system makes movement possible.

The **SKELETAL** system supports the body.

The **CIRCULATORY** system moves blood throughout the body.

The **RESPIRATORY** system provides the body with oxygen.

The **DIGESTIVE** system breaks down food into nutrients and gets rid of waste.

The **IMMUNE** system protects the body against disease and infection.

The **ENDOCRINE** system regulates the body's functions.

The **REPRODUCTIVE** system enables people to produce offspring.

Weird but true!

BRAIN CELLS LIVE LONGER THAN ALL THE OTHER CELLS IN YOUR BODY.

PEOPLE'S TONGUE PRINTS ARE AS UNIQUE AS THEIR FINGERPRINTS.

YOUR HAIR GROWS FASTER IN WARMER WEATHER.

SCIENCE AND TECHNOLOGY

WHAT Are GENES?

HUMANS and CHIMPANZEES SHARE about 99 PERCENT of their DNA.

In each of your cells, you have microscopic threadlike structures called chromosomes. These chromosomes are made up of something called DNA, or deoxyribonucleic acid. DNA is found in every single living thing, from a tiny fruit fly to an enormous elephant. In your chromosomes, DNA is grouped into units. Each unit acts as the instructions for making a protein. Larger sections of these units are called genes.

Proteins are your body's building blocks, and your genes tell the proteins what to build and how. Genes determine how your body functions and how it grows. They also influence some of the things that make you YOU. This includes how you look—from your hair color to your eye color to your height—how you act, some of the things you like ... and so much more! Many of the things that genes influence are known as traits.

DNA double helix

HUMAN BODY

Why do our teeth fall out?

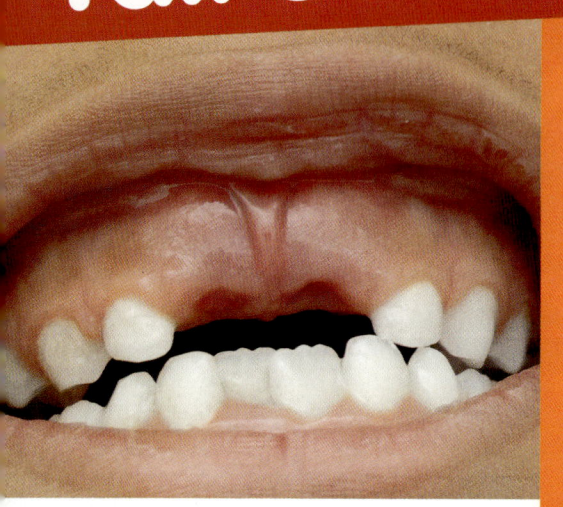

Do animals lose baby teeth, too?

Animals, they're just like us! Well, some of them. Most mammals are born with two sets of teeth, like humans. Puppies, kittens, and even lion cubs have tiny baby teeth that will fall out and be replaced with stronger ones. But there are some exceptions. Manatees, elephants, and kangaroos all have multiple sets of teeth that they go through in a lifetime. Other animals lose and grow new teeth almost constantly. Take the shark, for example, which can go through thousands of teeth in its lifetime!

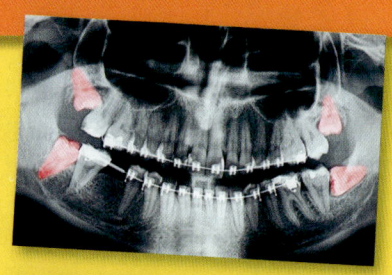

Wiggly baby teeth are commonplace among kids, but did you ever wonder why you lose those tiny chompers? Most of us are born with a full set of 20 baby teeth, which are embedded in the jaw and eventually grow in when we're between five months and two years old. These teeth help you chew and formulate speech patterns as you learn to talk, but they're not meant to stick around forever. Instead, they're placeholders until our adult teeth, which become permanent, are ready to come in. Adult teeth are stronger and more durable than baby teeth. (After all, they're meant to last for a very, very long time!) As you grow, so does your jaw, creating more space in your mouth for your permanent teeth. When adult teeth push on your baby teeth, the baby teeth get loose. Soon enough, they'll fall out one by one—and maybe with a little help from you, if you can't resist wiggling them back and forth!

Will wisdom teeth make me smarter?

Despite their name, wisdom teeth have nothing to do with your smarts! These teeth are your third and final set of molars—the flat teeth at the back of your mouth that help you crush and grind food. And they're named for the time they usually appear in your life. This set of four teeth tends to crop up in your late teens or early twenties—when you're thought to have more, well, wisdom! And it's a good thing they don't provide any intellectual value: Dentists often remove wisdom teeth if they're crowding your other teeth or causing other issues in your mouth.

SCIENCE AND TECHNOLOGY

WHY do I have 10 FINGERS?

Scientists have several ideas about why humans can high-five each other instead of, say, high-four or high-six. One theory suggests four fingers and a thumb on each hand are the perfect number and length to grip objects firmly. (Another study suggests we can grasp most things with just our thumb and index finger if necessary; the other three fingers are spares.)

The process of evolution determined the most beneficial number of fingers and toes for our survival. Pandas, after all, have thumblike digits to help them grasp bamboo shoots, while some birds have quadruple digits for perching and tucking away during flight. Occasionally, babies are born with extra fingers and toes (a condition known as polydactyly), but those additional digits have never offered enough of an edge to survive to later generations. In other words, evolution determined that five fingers on each hand are just right for humans.

HUMAN BODY

How Viruses Spread

IMAGINE YOU'RE AT BASKETBALL PRACTICE when your teammate coughs. He covers his mouth, but tiny droplets—hardly visible to the naked eye—escape. You don't notice, and you keep playing. The next day, your teammate stays home from school. A few days later, you have a fever and a sore throat. Did you get sick from your teammate?

It's hard to pinpoint the source of a virus. Some germs spread through the air, while others can be picked up from surfaces, such as doorknobs, light switches, and desks. If you're around someone who's carrying a virus and that person coughs, sneezes, or even talks near you, you could be in the virus's direct line of fire. Once you're exposed to infectious particles, your immune system will do its best to protect you from getting sick.

But if the virus muscles its way past your body's line of defense, it then has to find a host to stay alive. If it does, the virus invades the host cells in your body and begins to replicate, or make copies of itself. This causes a disease (such as the flu or COVID-19) that usually makes you feel sick. Meanwhile, your immune system continues to work hard against the virus. For example, you might get a fever, which is a sign that your body's fighting off those germs.

What can you do? It's best to rest, hydrate, and lie low while your body rids itself of the virus. Then hopefully within a few days, both you and your teammate will be back on the basketball court!

Germy Terms!

BACTERIA: Microorganisms that can cause sicknesses like ear infections or strep throat. But some are good for your health, like the kind that break down food in your gut.

EPIDEMIC: A sudden increase in the number of people in a certain area—like a town, city, or state—with the same disease.

PANDEMIC: A worldwide outbreak of a disease. This happens when a virus spreads easily and infects a lot of people.

VIRUSES: Tiny organisms found all around—in dirt, water, and the air—that need a host's energy to grow and survive. Once inside a host, a virus can multiply and attack cells.

SCIENCE AND TECHNOLOGY

HOW VACCINES WORK

PICTURE THIS: You are heading to the doctor for your annual checkup when your parent casually mentions that you're due for your shots. Your heart races at just the thought of the needle piercing your skin (ouch!), but at the same time, you know the quick blip of pain is worth it to help protect your health in the long run.

THAT NEEDLE (OR SOMETIMES A NASAL SPRAY) is the vehicle through which vaccines are delivered to your body. Throughout your life, you may receive at least 25 vaccines in order to prevent serious diseases and help keep you healthy. In the past, illnesses like measles, influenza, polio, and COVID-19 posed a very serious threat to all humans, and some of them were especially dangerous for children. But because scientists developed vaccines to fight off those diseases, childhood vaccination prevents some four million deaths worldwide every year.

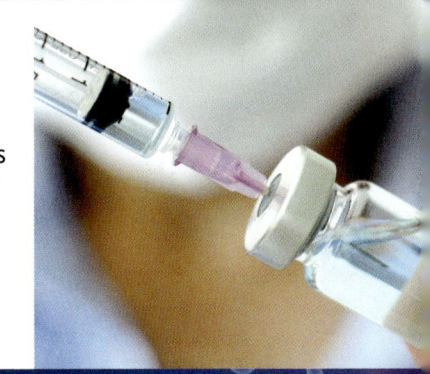

HOW DO VACCINES WORK? Simply put, a vaccine gives you a tiny piece of a disease-causing germ or a version of the germ that is dead or very weak, also known as an antigen. It's not enough to make you really sick; instead, the antigen teaches your immune system to recognize the germ and fight it off by activating antibodies that get rid of the virus or bacteria. These antibodies live in your immune system, and they have great memories. So they know exactly what to do if you're exposed to those germs in the future.

We are all exposed to germs every day. Even if you're vaccinated, you may still pick up a virus, like flu or COVID-19. But thanks to vaccinations, your body is armed with the ability to fight off those germs, so instead of getting really sick, you'll likely get only a mild case of the illness.

HUMAN BODY

The Science of Cute

How these adorable animals affect your brain

Waking from a nap, a fluffy kitten blinks its big blue eyes and yawns to reveal a tiny pink tongue. Then it stretches its body, exposing a furry little tummy. Curling back into a ball, the kitten lets out a soft meow and goes back into snooze mode. *So adorable!*

Whether it's a sleepy kitty or a bumbling baby elephant, certain traits drive our cute-o-meters wild. And it turns out that science can explain our need to squee over critters.

Scientists think our tendency to value cuteness has to do with species survival. Human babies are born helpless—they need adults to look after them. Having features that grown-ups find irresistible helps make sure that a baby is cared for and played with so that it's healthy and learns social skills. So over hundreds of thousands of years, humans developed a fondness for certain traits in babies. And when we see similar characteristics in animals, we find them *aw*-worthy as well.

What is it about human babies and animals that we find so adorable? In 1943, Austrian zoologist Konrad Lorenz came up with a list of cuteness traits—from big eyes to clumsiness—that make us feel affection. "People have an automatic response to these features," says scientist Sookyung Cho. Discover which traits give us warm fuzzies, and why.

head-to-head

Adorable Animal: An arctic fox pokes its fluffy head out from behind a snowbank. Living in its rugged habitat on the Arctic tundra, the animal sports a thick layer of fur in winter that makes its head look big.

Cuteness Factor: A large head is one of the traits that humans find adorable. Some scientists believe that we're drawn to animals with big heads because they remind us of a human baby's noggin. When humans are born, our brains are more developed than other parts of our bodies. Our skulls must then be big enough to hold those brains. So when humans see other animals with similarly large heads, we feel the need to protect them.

SCIENCE AND TECHNOLOGY

round it out

Adorable Animal: A koala rests its rump on a tree branch in an Australian forest as it munches eucalyptus leaves. Its body looks like a furry ball clinging to a branch. The koala swallows the last of its leafy snack.

Cuteness Factor: One quality that people tend to find irresistible in koalas is **a rounded body,** rather than a sharp one like a sea urchin has. In general, humans prefer curving geometric shapes. "We're more drawn to roundness than sharp lines," says researcher Hiroshi Nittono of Japan's Osaka University.

eye got it

Adorable Animal: A baby giraffe on the African savanna blinks, showing off its huge peepers. Lots of young animals have large eyes, from giraffes to puppies to gorillas. Baby humans do, too—a human's eyes grow fastest during the first few years of life, then slow down while the body catches up.

Cuteness Factor: Large eyes are often associated with sweetness and innocence, creating a major adorable alert in your brain. Looking at the big peepers of certain animals and human babies can even prompt some people to produce natural chemicals called dopamine and oxytocin, which boost feelings of happiness.

sweet sounds

Adorable Animal: An emperor penguin chick nestles underneath its father for warmth. The chick opens its beak and squeaks—it's now toasty beneath the dad's belly.

Cuteness Factor: Squeals and trills from animals can make a human want to coo. "Unlike a loud roar or sharp squawk, the sounds made by baby animals aren't threatening," says Joshua Paul Dale, a professor at Japan's Chuo University who studies the concept of cuteness. So humans are able to see the critters as lovable.

205

FUTURE TECHNOLOGY

FUTURE WORLD:

Future fashion won't be just for wearing—clothes will monitor the weather, give directions, and even wash themselves.

WEATHER REPORT
Through a connection with your smartphone, this umbrella can alert you when it's about to rain and even let you know if you've accidentally left it behind.

NICE AND TOASTY
The temperatures were below freezing when U.S. athletes put on their team uniforms for the 2022 Winter Games in Beijing, China. But the competitors were warm. The fabric on their parkas contained materials that adapt to changes in temperature. As temperatures drop, the materials contract at different rates. This forms air pockets, which create insulation. So the jacket becomes a puffer when it's cold and a regular parka when it warms up. And this technology could be part of your wardrobe soon.

SMART CLOTHES
What do you do if you need directions while you're on your bike? This looks like a normal denim jacket. But sensors built into the sleeve will allow cyclists to simply touch a cuff to safely pause their music, answer a call, or check that next turn.

206

SCIENCE AND TECHNOLOGY

Clothing

LATER, LAUNDRY
Say goodbye to sweaty sports uniforms. Researchers are developing clothes covered with special microscopic structures to keep them clean. When exposed to light, the structures release a burst of energy that breaks down everything from soil to paint to tomato sauce.

A CONTACT LENS TOOK THIS PHOTO!

POWER UP
Device about to die? No problem: Simply plug it into your outfit. A Dutch designer has already sent a line of sunlight-capturing clothes down the runway. Small, flexible solar panels collect energy when worn in direct sunlight, storing power for charging smartphones and more.

IT'S A SNAP
These contact lenses help the wearer take a picture in the blink of an eye—literally. They come with a built-in, microscopic camera that can be controlled by eye movements and blinking.

No one really knows what the future holds. These predictions are just for fun!

207

FUTURE TECHNOLOGY

FUTURE WORLD:

Scientists are dreaming up ways to cool down Earth. Check out a few of their brainiest—and zaniest!—ideas to slow climate change.

SPACE UMBRELLA

When you get too hot at the beach, you sit under an umbrella, so why not do the same for the planet? Scientists estimate we would need to decrease the sun's glare by only 2 to 4 percent to make the planet's temperature healthy again. One idea is to deploy trillions of butterfly-size robots that would form a sunshade 60,000 miles (96,560 km) wide. But how to launch them is a puzzle—this technology doesn't exist yet.

PAINTING MOUNTAINS

Glaciers help keep the planet cool because their icy white color reflects light and heat from the sun. But as Earth warms, glacier ice melts, which then heats the planet even more. One Peruvian inventor came up with a possible solution: painting a former glacier—now a dark mountain—bright white. Like snow and ice, the white paint would reflect light and heat to help keep the planet cool.

CARBON EATERS

Carbon dioxide—a heat-trapping gas released by burning coal, oil, and natural gas—is dangerously warming the planet. Luckily, phytoplankton (microscopic plantlike creatures that live on the surface of the ocean) suck small amounts of this gas out of the air for food. So scientists dumped iron, which phytoplankton need to grow, into an area of the ocean. The result? A huge growth of hungry phytoplankton that gobbled up the CO_2, causing levels in the area to drop.

SCIENCE AND TECHNOLOGY

Climate Tech

CREATING CLOUDS

When volcanoes erupt, the ash can form a shield that reflects the sun's heat into space and lowers Earth's temperature by one degree Fahrenheit (.55°C) for a short time. This inspired scientists to look into spraying sea salt into the sky from airplanes. There, water vapor would collect on the salt particles and form clouds that would help reflect the sun's heat. But once started, the process would have to go on forever, or the planet would quickly rewarm.

MORE FOR YOU

QUIZ WHIZ

Test your science and technology smarts by taking this quiz!

Write your answers on a piece of paper. Then check them below.

1. The world's tallest tree is in _____.
a. Mongolia
b. Thailand
c. Peru
d. the United States

2. **True or false?** Humans find animals with rounded bodies unappealing.

3. Humans belong to which domain?
a. Bacteria
b. Archaea
c. Eukarya
d. Internet

4. How many systems are in the human body?
a. three
b. seven
c. nine
d. twenty

5. **True or false?** Some vaccines can be given by a spray in your nose.

Not **STUMPED** yet? Check out the *NATIONAL GEOGRAPHIC KIDS QUIZ WHIZ* collection for more fun **SCIENCE AND TECHNOLOGY** questions!

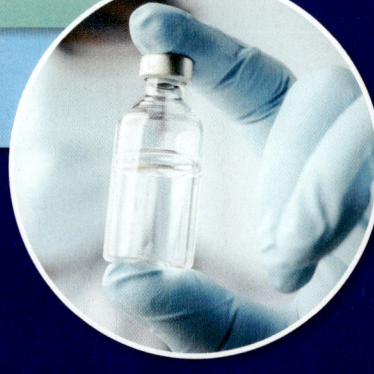

ANSWERS: 1. d; 2. False; 3. c; 4. c; 5. True

SCIENCE AND TECHNOLOGY

HOMEWORK HELP

This Is How It's Done!

Sometimes, the most complicated problems are solved with step-by-step directions. These "how-to" instructions are also known as a process analysis essay. Although scientists and engineers use this tool to program robots and write computer code, you also use process analysis every day, from following a recipe to putting together a new toy or gadget. Here's how to write a basic process analysis essay.

Step 1: Choose Your Topic Sentence
Start with a clear and concise topic sentence that describes what you're writing about. Be sure to explain to the readers why the task is important—and how many steps there are to complete it.

Step 2: List Materials
Do you need specific ingredients or equipment to complete your process? Mention these right away so the readers will have all they need to do the activity.

Step 3: Write Your Directions
Your directions should be clear and easy to follow. Assume that you are explaining the process for the first time, and define any unfamiliar terms. List your steps in the exact order the readers will need to follow to complete the activity. Try to keep your essay limited to no more than six steps.

Step 4: Restate Your Main Idea
Your closing should revisit your topic sentence, drawing a conclusion relating to the importance of the subject.

EXAMPLE OF A PROCESS ANALYSIS ESSAY

Downloading an app is a simple way to enhance your tablet. Today, I'd like to show you how to search for and add an app to your tablet. First, you will need a tablet with the ability to access the internet. You'll also want to ask a parent for permission before you download anything onto your tablet. Next, select the specific app you want by going to the app store on your tablet and entering the app's name into the search bar. Once you find the app you're seeking, select "download" and wait for the app to load. When you see that the app has fully loaded, tap on the icon and you will be able to access it. Now you can enjoy your app and have more fun with your tablet.

WONDERS of NATURE

When conditions are just right, sunlight on Yosemite National Park's Horsetail Falls in California, U.S.A., makes the water look like molten lava.

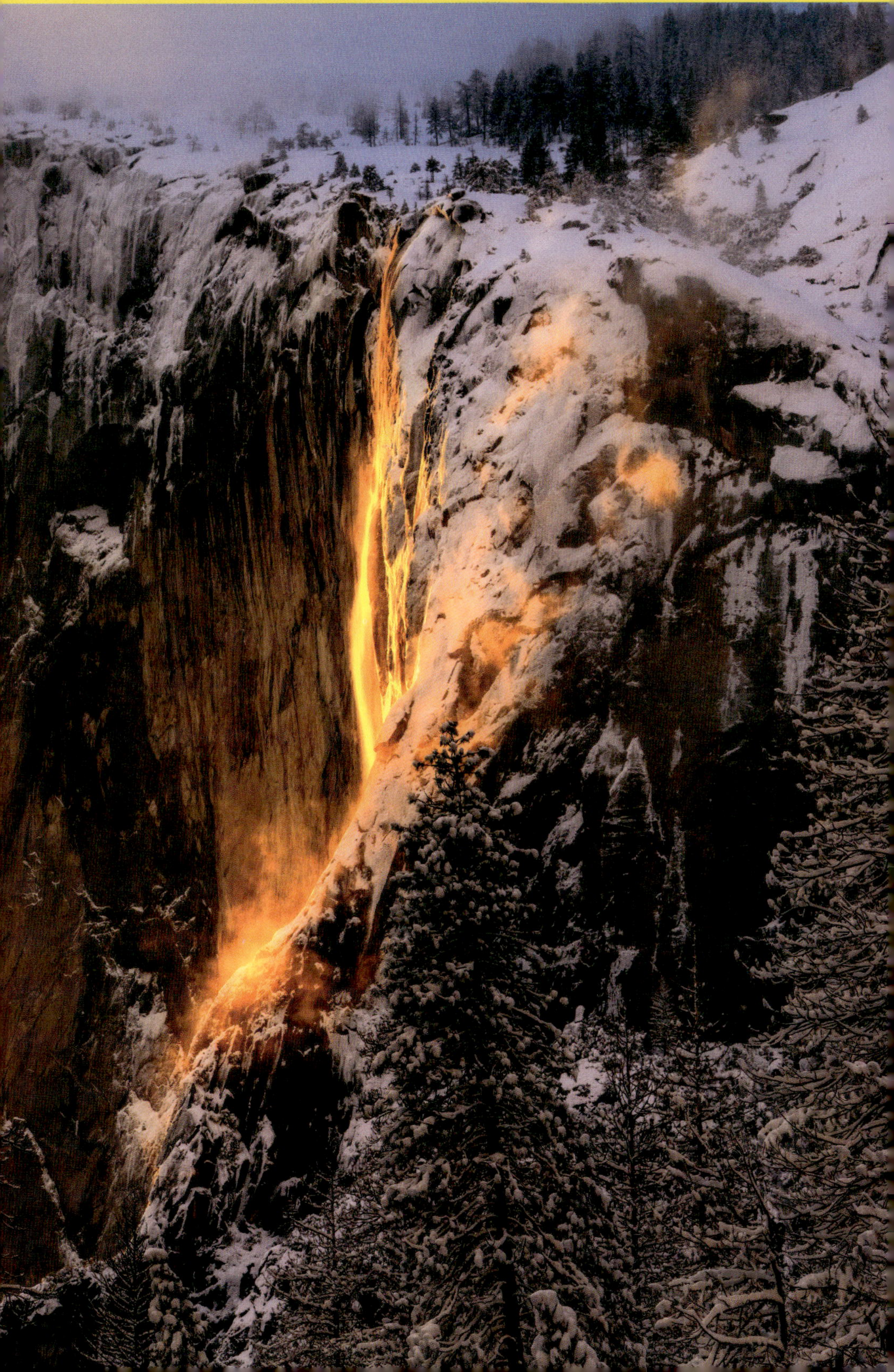

BIOMES

Biomes

A BIOME, OFTEN CALLED A MAJOR LIFE ZONE, is one of the natural world's major communities where plants and animals adapt to their specific surroundings. Biomes are classified depending on the predominant vegetation, climate, and geography of a region. They can be divided into six major types: forest, freshwater, marine, desert, grassland, and tundra. Each biome consists of many ecosystems.

Biomes are extremely important. Balanced ecological relationships among biomes help maintain the environment and life on Earth as we know it. For example, an increase in one species of plant, such as an invasive one, can cause a ripple effect throughout a whole biome.

FOREST

Forests occupy about one-third of Earth's land area. There are three major types of forests: tropical, temperate, and boreal (taiga). Forests are home to a diversity of plants, some of which may hold medicinal qualities for humans, as well as thousands of animal species, some still undiscovered. Forests can also absorb carbon dioxide, a greenhouse gas, and give off oxygen.

Trees in the top layer of a rainforest, the canopy, can be as tall as a 20-story building.

FRESHWATER

Most water on Earth is salty, but freshwater ecosystems—including lakes, ponds, wetlands, rivers, and streams—usually contain water with less than one percent salt concentration. The countless animal and plant species that live in freshwater biomes vary from continent to continent, but they include algae, frogs, turtles, fish, and the larvae of many insects.

Even though the world is covered with rivers, lakes, ponds, and streams, fresh water makes up less than 3 percent of Earth's water.

WONDERS OF NATURE

MARINE

The marine biome covers almost three-fourths of Earth's surface, making it the largest habitat on our planet. Oceans make up the majority of the saltwater marine biome. Coral reefs are considered to be the most biodiverse of any of the biome habitats. The marine biome is home to more than one million plant and animal species.

If all the oceans' salt content could be collected and dried out, it would cover all of Earth's continents in five feet (1.5 m) of sodium.

DESERT

Covering about one-fifth of Earth's surface, deserts are places where precipitation is less than 10 inches (25 cm) a year. Although most deserts are hot, there are other kinds as well. The four major kinds of deserts are hot, semiarid, coastal, and cold. Far from being barren wastelands, deserts are biologically rich habitats.

The Sahara in North Africa is the largest hot desert on Earth, with temperatures that can reach 136°F (58°C).

GRASSLAND

Biomes called grasslands are characterized by having grasses instead of large shrubs or trees. Some of the world's largest land animals, such as elephants, live there. Grasslands generally have precipitation for only about half to three-fourths of the year. If it were more, they would become forests. Grasslands can be divided into two types: tropical (savannas) and temperate.

Grasslands cover more than 40 percent of Africa: more than five million square miles (13 million sq km).

TUNDRA

The coldest of all biomes, a tundra is characterized by an extremely cold climate, simple vegetation, little precipitation, poor nutrients, and a short growing season. There are two types of tundra: Arctic and alpine. A tundra is home to few kinds of vegetation. Surprisingly, though, quite a few animal species can survive the tundra's extremes, such as wolves and caribou, and even mosquitoes.

Though the treeless Arctic tundra is barren for much of the year, grasses and lichens can completely cover it during its short, three-month-long growing period.

BIOMES

ANTARCTICA

NATIONAL GEOGRAPHIC EXPLORER CARSTEN PETER'S EXTREME ADVENTURE TO THE WORLD'S SOUTHERNMOST CONTINENT

HERE'S THE THING ABOUT ANTARCTICA—
IT'S BIG.

No, not just big—vast!
Dictionaries define "vast" as immense, empty, and boundless. All of these words describe Antarctica. But so do these words—fantastic, awesome, otherworldly, and beautiful.

When I first stepped from the plane onto the Antarctic ice, I knew I was in a place like no other. I was struck by the sameness of my surroundings. A nearly flat plain of ice stretched to the horizon in most directions. We were on an island, but you'd never know it. Thick sea ice connected the island to the mainland about 45 miles (72 km) away.

The dry air was crystal clear, making the sky overhead a deep blue. Brilliant sunshine reflected off the landscape. Sunglasses were a must—both day and night. It was summer, and the sun would not be setting the entire three weeks of the expedition.

The constant sunshine did little to warm the air. Temperatures mostly stayed in the negative numbers. Lows were down to minus 30°F (-34°C). Strange things happen when it gets that cold.

The slightest amount of moisture glazes ropes with ice. That makes them tricky to hold. Eating is a challenge, too. My parents used to say, "Eat your food before it gets cold." Here we say, "Eat your food before it freezes." You might end up chiseling frozen soup from a bowl that was hot from the stove a few minutes earlier.

The vastness of Antarctica really makes you feel exposed to the weather, especially when the wind blows. I often had to turn away from the stinging ice crystals that the wind whipped at us. During some days (or were they nights?), the tents rattled and flapped so much I thought for sure they were going to fly away.

Everything about Antarctica was extreme and beautiful. But the sight I'll remember most occurred several days into the expedition. We took a short helicopter ride from our base camp. We landed about halfway up a mountain. I stepped off. I looked up. I don't know how long I gawked at the steaming volcano, Mount Erebus, that loomed before me.

WONDERS OF NATURE

Expert Tips

STAY HYDRATED! That's the advice of polar explorers such as Will Steger. He should know. His team was the first to cross Antarctica by dogsled:

Despite the cold, Antarctica is a desert. The air is dry, and very little precipitation falls. The body loses moisture easily to the dry air. Walking and working on ice can be exhausting. You sweat, breathe heavily, and lose more moisture. As explorers, we make sure we keep our water bottles full. How? By melting ice and snow and then, while the water is hot, pouring it into thermoses!

Gear & Gadgets

WHEN IT COMES TO STAYING WARM, the point isn't to keep cold air out. It's to keep your body heat in. Sometimes when sleeping on the tent floor, the heat from my body melted the ice beneath my sleeping bag. To keep my body heat from escaping, I dress in layers. I sleep in layers, too. In Antarctica, my "bed" consisted of a fleece liner inside a sleeping bag stuffed inside another sleeping bag. I laid the double bags on top of a sheepskin rug on top of an air mattress on top of a foam mat. It took six layers of bedding and as many layers of clothing to keep me warm.

In Antarctica, there's a 30-30-30 rule: When the temperature is minus 30°F (-34°C) and the wind is 30 miles an hour (48 km/h), human skin freezes in 30 seconds.

In some parts of Antarctica, the ice is three miles (4.8 km) thick.

A LAVA LAKE STEAMS INSIDE MOUNT EREBUS.

A SEAL PUP ON ANTARCTICA'S ROSS ISLAND

USING A GIANT DRILL, SCIENTISTS ON ROSS ISLAND GATHER A CORE SAMPLE OF ICE.

SCIENTISTS EXPLORE THE CRATER OF MOUNT EREBUS.

OCEANS

THE OCEANS

PACIFIC OCEAN

STATS

Surface area
65,100,000 sq mi (168,600,000 sq km)

Percentage of all oceans
46 percent

Surface temperatures
Summer high: 90°F (32°C)
Winter low: 28°F (-2°C)

Tides
Highest: 30 ft (9 m) near Korean Peninsula
Lowest: 1 ft (0.3 m) near Midway Islands

Cool creatures: giant Pacific octopus, bottlenose whale, clownfish, great white shark

CLOWNFISH

ATLANTIC OCEAN

STATS

Surface area
33,100,000 sq mi (85,600,000 sq km)

Percentage of all oceans
24 percent

Surface temperatures
Summer high: 90°F (32°C)
Winter low: 28°F (-2°C)

Tides
Highest: 52 ft (16 m) Bay of Fundy, Canada
Lowest: 1.5 ft (0.5 m) Gulf of Mexico and Mediterranean Sea

Cool creatures: blue whale, Atlantic spotted dolphin, sea turtle, bottlenose dolphin

BOTTLENOSE DOLPHIN

WONDERS OF NATURE

INDIAN OCEAN

STATS

Surface area
27,500,000 sq mi (71,200,000 sq km)

Percentage of all oceans
20 percent

Surface temperatures
Summer high: 93°F (34°C)
Winter low: 28°F (-2°C)

Tides
Highest: 36 ft (11 m)
Lowest: 2 ft (0.6 m)
Both along Australia's west coast

Cool creatures: humpback whale, Portuguese man-of-war, dugong (sea cow), leatherback turtle

LEATHERBACK TURTLE

ARCTIC OCEAN

STATS

Surface area
6,100,000 sq mi (15,700,000 sq km)

Percentage of all oceans
4 percent

Surface temperatures
Summer high: 41°F (5°C)
Winter low: 28°F (-2°C)

Tides
Less than 1 ft (0.3 m) variation throughout the ocean

Cool creatures: beluga whale, orca, harp seal, narwhal

NARWHAL

SOUTHERN OCEAN

STATS

Surface area
8,500,000 sq mi (21,900,000 sq km)

Percentage of all oceans
6 percent

Surface temperatures
Summer high: 50°F (10°C)
Winter low: 28°F (-2°C)

Tides
Less than 2 ft (0.6 m) variation throughout the ocean

Cool creatures: emperor penguin, colossal squid, mackerel icefish, Antarctic toothfish

EMPEROR PENGUIN

To see the major oceans and bays in relation to landmasses, look at the map on pages 272 and 273.

AWESOME NATURE

awes8me

FEAST YOUR EYES ON SOME OF NATURE'S WILDEST ATTRACTIONS.

1 AMAZING CRATER

Algae, sulfur, salt, and other minerals help create this brightly colored crater of the **Dallol volcano**. It's Earth's lowest land volcano, located in the Danakil Depression on the border of Ethiopia and Eritrea.

WEIRD WONDERS

COOL CAVES 2

Deep underground in Virginia's Shenandoah Valley, **Luray Caverns** is filled with rock formations called stalactites (hanging from the ceiling) and stalagmites (rising from the floor). All of these towering formations—some up to five stories long—are calcite, a form of limestone.

The formations in Luray Caverns, Virginia, U.S.A., grow one cubic inch (16.4 cu cm) every 120 years.

220

WONDERS OF NATURE

3
ALL CRACKED UP

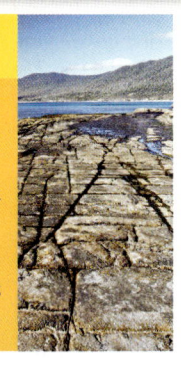

These brown rectangular shapes at **Eaglehawk Neck** in Tasmania, an island state in Australia, look like they were carved in mud. But this geological formation, called a tessellated pavement, was caused when pressure at Earth's crust created these linear cracks millions of years ago.

4
HUMONGOUS HOLE

The massive 570-foot (174-m)-deep **Barringer Crater** in the Arizona desert was caused by a meteorite slamming into Earth some 50,000 years ago. The 150,000-ton (134,000-t) space rock hit the ground at a speed of 7.4 miles a second (12 km/s)—more than 100 times faster than a race car at top speed!

5
MIGHTY WATERFALL

On the border of Zambia and Zimbabwe, Africa's **Victoria Falls** is the largest waterfall in the world. Spanning a width of 5,600 feet (1,700 m), it's more than 15 times wider than the length of a football field.

6
THINK PINK!

No one knows exactly why this 1,970-foot (600-m)-long lake in western Australia is the color of bubblegum. Scientists think that **Lake Hillier's** color might come from algae, bacteria, or salt in the water.

7
SALTY SITE

Spreading for thousands of square miles in southwestern Bolivia is **Salar de Uyuni**, the world's largest salt flat. Formed when a lake dried up, the remote site is also home to the Luna Salada hotel, where almost everything—including floors, walls, tables, and chairs—is made of salt.

8
RAINBOW RIVER

A plant called *Macarenia clavigera* needs just the right water level and sunlight to make this river dazzle. For a few months a year, Colombia's **Caño Cristales** (commonly called the River of Five Colors) turns bright red—and, in some places, hot pink, bright green, blue, yellow, and orange. It's like a liquid rainbow.

WEATHER

Weather and Climate

Weather is the condition of the atmosphere—temperature, wind, humidity, and precipitation—at a given place at a given time. Climate, however, is the average weather for a particular place over a long period of time. Different places on Earth have different climates, but climate is not a random occurrence. It is a pattern that is controlled by factors such as latitude, elevation, prevailing winds, the temperature of ocean currents, and location on land relative to water. Climate is generally constant, but evidence indicates that human activity is causing a change in its patterns—a long-term shift called climate change.

WEATHER EXTREMES

HURRICANE FORCE: With maximum sustained winds of 213 mph (343 km/h), Hurricane Patricia, which struck Mexico's Pacific Coast in 2015, is one of the most intense hurricanes on record.

HOTTEST MONTH: July 2024, when average temperatures were .05 degrees Fahrenheit (.03°C) higher than July 2023, which was previously the hottest on record since 1850.

RAINIEST YEAR: Over 12 months in 1860–1861, it rained 1,042 inches (26.47 m) in Cherrapunji, India.

GLOBAL CLIMATE ZONES

Climatologists, people who study climate, have created different systems for classifying climates. One that is often used is called the Köppen system, which classifies climate zones according to precipitation, temperature, and vegetation. It has five major categories—tropical, dry, temperate, cold, and polar—with a sixth category for locations where high elevations override other factors.

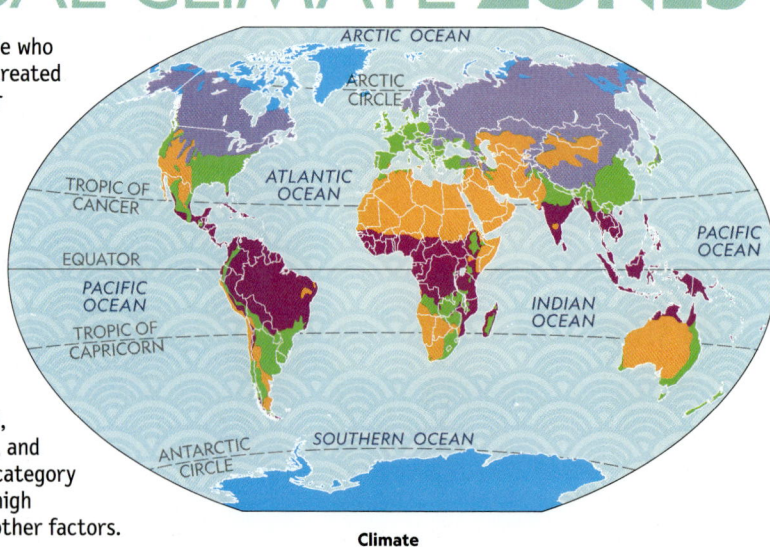

Climate: Tropical | Dry | Temperate | Cold | Polar

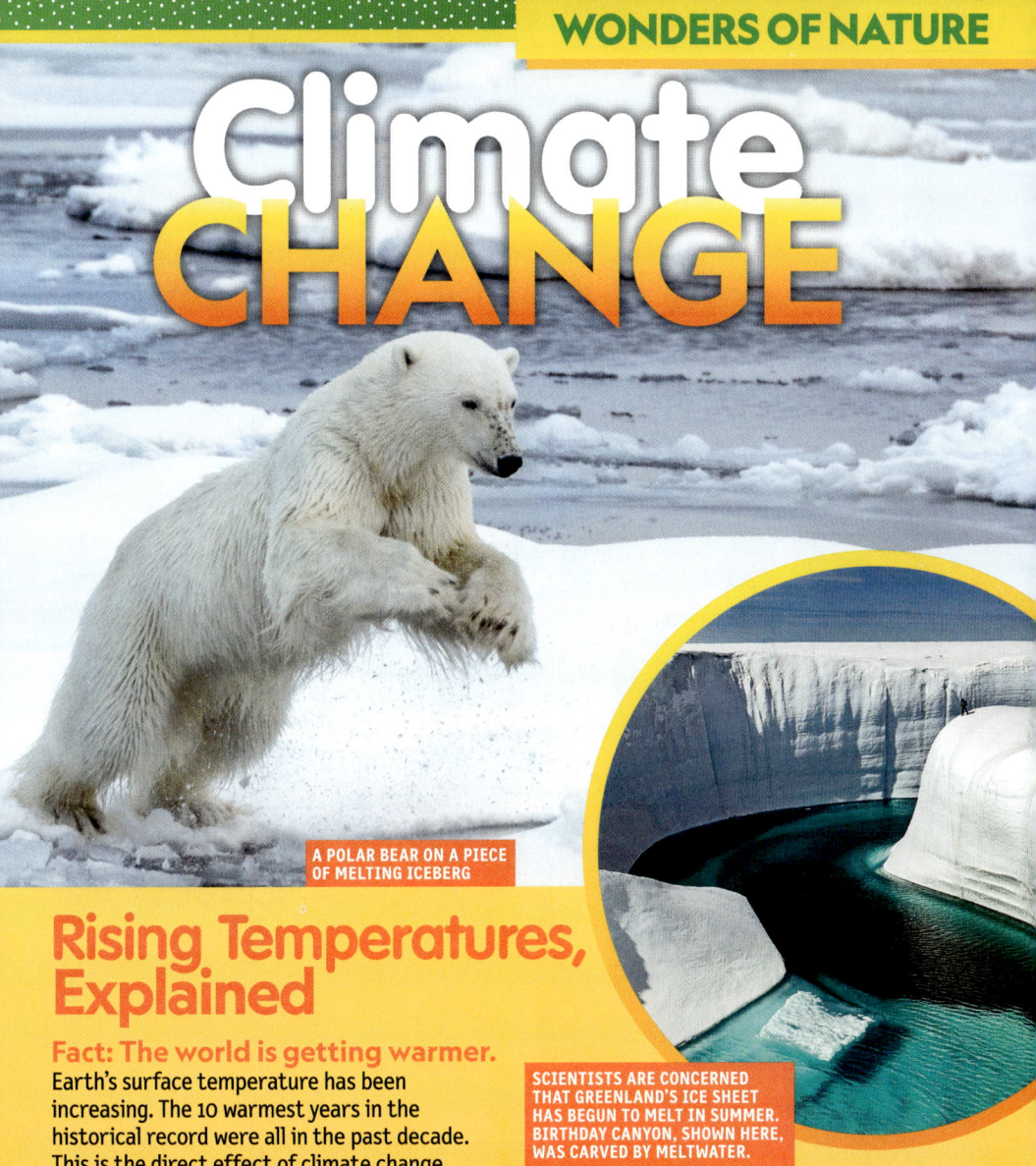

WONDERS OF NATURE

Climate CHANGE

A POLAR BEAR ON A PIECE OF MELTING ICEBERG

Rising Temperatures, Explained

Fact: The world is getting warmer.
Earth's surface temperature has been increasing. The 10 warmest years in the historical record were all in the past decade. This is the direct effect of climate change, which refers not only to the increase in Earth's average temperature (known as global warming), but also to its long-term effects on winds, rain, and ocean currents. Global warming is the reason glaciers and polar ice sheets are melting—resulting in rising sea levels and shrinking habitats. This makes survival for some animals a big challenge. Warming also means more flooding along coasts and drought for inland areas.

Why are temperatures climbing?
While some of the recent climate changes can be tied to natural causes—such as changes in the sun's intensity, the unusually warm ocean currents of El Niño, and volcanic activity—human activities are the greatest contributor.

Activities that require burning fossil fuels, such as driving gasoline-powered cars, contribute to global warming. These activities produce greenhouse gases, which enter the atmosphere and trap heat. At the current rate, by the end of this century, Earth's global average temperature is projected to rise at least 5 degrees Fahrenheit (3°C) higher than the average temperature from 1900 to 1960—and it will likely get even warmer after that. This warming will unfortunately continue to affect the environment and our society in many ways.

SCIENTISTS ARE CONCERNED THAT GREENLAND'S ICE SHEET HAS BEGUN TO MELT IN SUMMER. BIRTHDAY CANYON, SHOWN HERE, WAS CARVED BY MELTWATER.

WEATHER

10 FACTS ABOUT FREAKY FORCES OF NATURE

A **pyroclastic flow**, which is created by a volcano, is a cloud of gas and rock that **can reach temperatures above 1000°F (538°C).**

Thousands of small frogs once rained down on a town in **Serbia,** a country in Europe, sending people scurrying for cover.

Flame-throwing tornadoes, called fire whirls, can be **50 feet** (15 m) **wide** and grow as tall as a **40-story** building.

A **hailstorm** in the Himalayan mountain range in Asia **dropped chunks of ice** the size of baseballs **at more than 100 miles an hour** (161 km/h).

Mysterious rogue waves, which can appear without any warning in the open sea, can be **10 STORIES TALL.**

WONDERS OF NATURE

SNOW ROLLERS form when wet snow falls on icy ground that snow can't stick to. Pushed by strong winds, the snow rolls into logs.

Usually seen once a **thunderstorm has passed,** mammatus clouds form from pouches of sinking air.

Underwater hot springs, called hydrothermal vents, occur when water seeps through cracks in the ocean floor after being heated by magma inside Earth.

The fastest wind speed ever recorded— **some 300 miles an hour** (480 km/h)— occurred during a tornado near Oklahoma City, Oklahoma, U.S.A., in 1999.

Vast glowing rings called **AURORAS** often appear far above the North and South Poles. These rings can be more than **12,000 miles** (19,300 km) around.

WEATHER

Water on the Move: THE WATER CYCLE EXPLAINED

CONDENSATION In the atmosphere, the water vapor cools and condenses into clouds. For a water molecule to condense, it needs to find a particle that has a radius of at least 1/250,000 of an inch (one millionth of a meter) to bond to. These teeny-tiny particles, called condensation nuclei, might be specks of dirt, dust, or salt (from the ocean, for example). So every cloud droplet has a little something extra at its core—like smoke particles from a volcano or fire, wind-blown dirt, or salt from sea spray.

» Earth contains a finite amount of water, and it is constantly moving in, on, and above the planet in a natural water cycle. This rotation of water is necessary for the survival of all the living things on Earth, and it connects us to one another. The water we drink today could be the same water that cycled through a dinosaur, erupted as steam from a volcano, was used to make George Washington's coffee, or was bathed in by an ancient Neanderthal!

PRECIPITATION Carried on air currents, clouds move all around the world. They grow and sometimes combine with other clouds. When they become too full, the water falls as rain, hail, sleet, or snow, aka precipitation.

SUN HEATS WATER The sun heats the water on Earth's surface, causing it to evaporate from places like oceans, rivers, and lakes. Water molecules then rise as vapor into the atmosphere.

GROUNDWATER If water falls to cold parts of Earth's surface, it may freeze and accumulate as ice caps and glaciers. If it falls on warm areas of Earth, gravity pulls it back into bodies of water, or into the groundwater.

TRANSPIRATION Water also rises into the atmosphere through transpiration. Water from the soil is absorbed by plants and trees through their roots, then travels up to the leaves and evaporates, returning to the atmosphere.

The amount of water on Earth is more or less constant— only the form changes. As the sun warms Earth's surface, liquid water is changed into water vapor in a process called **evaporation**. Water on the surface of plants' leaves turns into water vapor in a process called **transpiration**. As water vapor rises into the air, it cools and changes form again. This time, it becomes clouds in a process called **condensation**. Water droplets fall from the clouds as **precipitation**, which then travels as groundwater or runoff back to the lakes, rivers, and oceans, where the cycle (shown above) starts all over again.

To a meteorologist—a person who studies the weather—a "light rain" is less than 1/48 inch (0.5 mm) an hour. A "heavy rain" is more than 1/6 inch (4 mm) an hour.

You drink the same water as the dinosaurs! Earth has been recycling water for more than four billion years.

226

WONDERS OF NATURE

Types of Clouds

If you want a clue about the weather, look up at the clouds. They'll tell a lot about the condition of the air and what weather might be on the way. Clouds are made of both air and water. On fair days, warm air currents rise and push against the water in clouds, keeping it from falling. But as the raindrops in a cloud get bigger, it's time to set them free. The bigger raindrops become too heavy for the air currents to hold up, and they fall to the ground.

How Much Does a Cloud Weigh?
A light, fluffy cumulus cloud typically weighs about 216,000 pounds (98,000 kg). That's about the weight of 18 elephants. A rain-soaked cumulonimbus cloud typically weighs 105.8 million pounds (48 million kg), or about the same as 9,000 elephants.

1 STRATUS These clouds make the sky look like a bowl of thick gray porridge. They hang low in the sky, blanketing the day in dreary darkness. Stratus clouds form when cold, moist air close to the ground moves over a region.

2 CIRRUS These wispy tufts of clouds are thin and hang high up in the atmosphere where the air is extremely cold. Cirrus clouds are made of tiny ice crystals.

3 CUMULUS These white, fluffy clouds make people sing, "Oh, what a beautiful morning!" They form low in the atmosphere and look like marshmallows. They often mix with large patches of blue sky. Formed when hot air rises, cumulus clouds usually disappear when the air cools at night.

4 CUMULONIMBUS These are the monster clouds. Rising air currents force fluffy cumulus clouds to swell and shoot upward, as much as 70,000 feet (21,000 m). When these clouds bump against the top of the troposphere, known as the tropopause, they flatten out on top like tabletops.

227

WEATHER

weird but true!

WEIRD
WEATHER

Red Sprite

Red sprites are still a bit mysterious to scientists. They happen in the upper atmosphere, miles above thunderstorms that are ending. After much of the electric charge is removed from a storm through lightning strikes, these glowing streamers may appear. Red sprites are rarely seen from Earth.

Haboob

A haboob is a giant desert dust storm. The thick blanket of dust can swallow up a city, knock over power lines, and cause traffic accidents because of reduced visibility. Cover your mouth and nose and run for cover if a haboob comes your way.

Double Rainbow

Light reflecting inside water droplets causes one rainbow, but it's actually possible for light to be reflected more than once inside a raindrop. The rare secondary rainbow is formed above the first and is usually fainter—and the colors are seen in the reverse order. Intense!

WONDERS OF NATURE

TIRED OF SUN, CLOUDS, AND ALL THE USUAL STUFF WHEN YOU PEEK OUT YOUR WINDOW? CHECK OUT THESE EXCITING WEATHER CONDITIONS THAT WILL **BLOW YOU AWAY!**

St. Elmo's Fire

It's not actually fire at all—it's a gas called plasma. Metallic or pointy objects often become supercharged during thunderstorms. When the charges are high enough, the air around the object also becomes charged, or ionized. The nitrogen and oxygen in the air cause the glow to be blue or violet, and the St. Elmo's light can continue for several minutes.

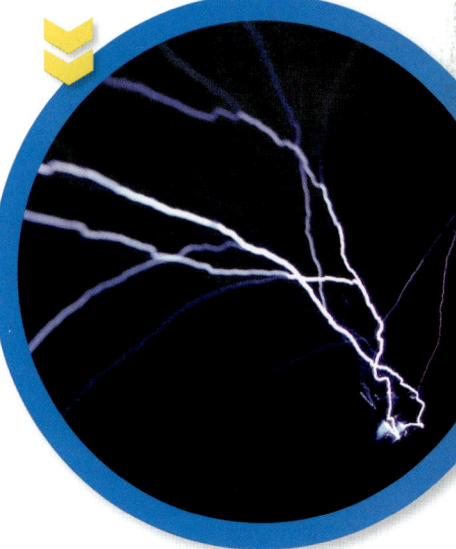

Sky Punch

Sometimes you'll see a stretch of clouds across the sky, and then a few minutes later there's a hole punched right through them! This phenomenon is caused when an airplane flies through supercooled clouds floating in a blanket-like layer in the sky. The broken cloud section then falls as snow.

Waterspout

These water funnels form in two ways: when a tornado moves over water, or when wind is light but cumulus clouds have begun to develop. (Cumulus clouds are the white, fluffy-looking clouds.) The second kind starts swirling at the surface of the water and moves upward. They'll fall apart quickly if they reach land.

TURBULENT EARTH

HURRICANE HAPPENINGS

A storm is brewing—but is this a tropical cyclone, a hurricane, or a typhoon? These weather events go by different names depending on where they form, how fast their winds get, or both. Strong tropical cyclones are called hurricanes in the Atlantic and parts of the Pacific Ocean; in the western Pacific, they are called typhoons. But any way you look at it, these storms pack a punch. And they all form when warm moist air rises from the ocean, causing air from surrounding areas to be "sucked" in. That air then becomes warm and moist and rises, too, beginning a cycle that forms clouds, which rotate with the spin of Earth. If there is enough warm water to feed the storm, it will result in a hurricane. And the warmer the water and the more moisture in the air, the more powerful the hurricane.

HURRICANE NAMES FOR 2026

Atlantic hurricane names come from six official international lists. The names alternate between male and female. When a storm becomes a hurricane, a name from the list is used, in alphabetical order. (If the hurricane season is especially active and the list runs out, the World Meteorological Organization will provide extra names to draw from.) Each list is reused every six years. A name is "retired" if that hurricane caused a lot of damage or many deaths.

Arthur	Gonzalo	Marco	Sally
Bertha	Hanna	Nana	Teddy
Cristobal	Isaias	Omar	Vicky
Dolly	Josephine	Paulette	Wilfred
Edouard	Kyle	Rene	
Fay	Leah		

SCALE OF HURRICANE INTENSITY

CATEGORY	ONE	TWO	THREE	FOUR	FIVE
DAMAGE	Minimal	Moderate	Extensive	Extreme	Catastrophic
WINDS	74–95 mph (119–153 km/h)	96–110 mph (154–177 km/h)	111–129 mph (178–208 km/h)	130–156 mph (209–251 km/h)	157 mph or higher (252+ km/h)

(DAMAGE refers to wind and water damage combined.)

WONDERS OF NATURE

What Is a Tornado?

THE ENHANCED FUJITA SCALE
The Enhanced Fujita (EF) Scale, named after tornado expert T. Theodore Fujita, classifies tornadoes based on wind speed and the intensity of damage that they cause.

EF0
65–85 mph winds
(105–137 km/h)
Slight damage

EF1
86–110 mph winds
(138–177 km/h)
Moderate damage

EF2
111–135 mph winds
(178–217 km/h)
Substantial damage

EF3
136–165 mph winds
(218–266 km/h)
Severe damage

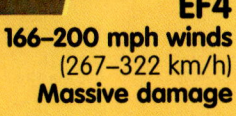

EF4
166–200 mph winds
(267–322 km/h)
Massive damage

EF5
More than 200 mph winds
(322+ km/h)
Catastrophic damage

TORNADOES, ALSO KNOWN AS TWISTERS, are funnels of rapidly rotating air that are created during thunderstorms. With wind speeds that can exceed 300 miles an hour (483 km/h), tornadoes have the power to pick up and destroy everything in their path.

THIS ROTATING FUNNEL OF AIR, formed in a cumulus or cumulonimbus cloud, became a tornado when it touched the ground.

TORNADOES HAVE OCCURRED IN ALL 50 U.S. STATES AND ON EVERY CONTINENT EXCEPT ANTARCTICA.

TURBULENT EARTH

What Is a Bomb Cyclone?

In 2024, parts of California were walloped with whipping winds, record rainfall, and widespread flooding. This wasn't your typical storm. Rather, it was part of a powerful weather phenomenon known as a bomb cyclone.

Bomb cyclones form when systems of cold air slam into warm air, creating a spinning mass of air called a cyclone. A cyclone can become stronger and faster if the air pressure at its center suddenly drops, or "bombogenesis" occurs. These storms develop rapidly and hit with excessive force, earning their explosive name.

Bomb cyclones don't just bring rain and wind. They can drop blizzards, as one did in 2018 in the northeastern United States. That massive storm saw 17 inches (43 cm) of snowfall in Boston, Massachusetts, plus whipping winds and a 15-foot (4.6-m) tidal surge that flooded a subway station.

Although not as destructive as other major weather events like hurricanes, bomb cyclones still pack a dangerous punch and can cause downed trees and electrical poles, icy temperatures, and flooding. Your best bet when a bomb cyclone's heading your way? Stay safely inside.

A SATELLITE IMAGE OF A 2023 BOMB CYCLONE

FLOODING IN THE AFTERMATH OF A 2023 BOMB CYCLONE IN CALIFORNIA

WONDERS OF NATURE

KOALA RESCUE

A young koala scrambled up a eucalyptus tree. It was not trying to grab one of the tasty leaves it loved snacking on—it was trying to get away from the flames and smoke swirling in the forest beneath it.

In 2019 and 2020, a record number of wildfires raged through woodland habitats in Australia, destroying many of the trees koalas live in and rely on for food. The fires burned across some 65,000 square miles (168,350 sq km), an area the size of Florida, U.S.A. Experts say that some 30,000 koalas might have been killed in these fires, alongside hundreds of millions of other animals.

Koalas aren't endangered, but they face many other threats in addition to wildfires. Starvation, dog attacks, car accidents, and disease have also put the fuzzy mammals in danger. Luckily, brave people step up every day to help these marsupials, like the one described below.

Instead of outrunning fires, koalas usually climb trees to escape.

The raging fire had passed, so the koala cautiously scooted down her eucalyptus tree toward the ground. But before she made it, her paws grasped part of the blackened tree trunk that was still smoldering from the fire. The koala had badly burned her paws and other parts of her body.

Hours later, wildlife rescue organization Wildcare Australia sent a team to find animals injured in the bushfire. They spotted and captured the koala—now named Maddie—and rushed her to Currumbin Wildlife Hospital.

Maddie also had burns on her nose and ears, so her caregivers applied a cooling ointment to her injuries. She was also starving. "When a koala's in pain, it won't eat," says Michael Pyne, the senior veterinarian at the hospital. "So we need her burns to heal quickly."

Less than a week later, Maddie was ready for a meal. But not just any eucalyptus leaf would do. "Koalas all have their favorite," Pyne says. Leaves that they're not used to eating are harder for them to digest, or just taste yucky. But Maddie finished off the batch of leaves she was given.

A month after the fire, she was still recovering at the hospital, but Pyne was hopeful. "It won't be long before she's taking naps in a forest instead of a hospital," he says.

MADDIE

MORE FOR YOU

QUIZ WHIZ

Quiz yourself to find out if you're a natural when it comes to nature knowledge!

Write your answers on a piece of paper. Then check them below.

1 True or false? Antarctica is a desert.

2 Bubblegum pink Lake Hillier is in _____.
a. Australia
b. Colorado
c. Scotland
d. South Africa

3 St. Elmo's Fire is _____.
a. a volcano
b. plasma
c. a campfire that never goes out
d. a tropical flower

4 What is the highest rating for a tornado?
a. EF1
b. EF5
c. EF10
d. EF100

5 True or false? The world is getting cooler.

Not **STUMPED** yet? Check out the *NATIONAL GEOGRAPHIC KIDS QUIZ WHIZ* collection for more fun **NATURE** questions!

ANSWERS: 1. True; 2. a; 3. b; 4. b; 5. False

234

WONDERS OF NATURE

HOMEWORK HELP

Oral Reports Made Easy

TIP: Make sure you practice your presentation a few times. Stand in front of a mirror or have a friend or family member record you so you can see if you need to work on anything, such as eye contact.

Does the thought of public speaking start your stomach churning like a tornado? Would you rather get caught in an avalanche than give a speech?

Giving an oral report does not have to be a natural disaster. The basic format is very similar to that of a written essay. There are two main elements that make up a good oral report—the writing and the presentation. As you write your oral report, remember that your audience will be hearing the information as opposed to reading it. Follow the guidelines below, and there will be clear skies ahead.

Writing Your Material

Follow the steps in the "How to Write a Perfect Essay" section on page 127, but prepare your report to be spoken rather than written.

Try to keep your sentences short and simple. Long, complex sentences are harder to follow. Limit yourself to just a few key points. You don't want to overwhelm your audience with too much information. To be most effective, hit your key points in the introduction, elaborate on them in the body, and then repeat them once again in your conclusion.

AN ORAL REPORT HAS THREE BASIC PARTS:

- **Introduction**—This is your chance to engage your audience and really capture their interest in the subject you are presenting. Use a funny personal experience or a dramatic story, or start with an intriguing question.

- **Body**—This is the longest part of your report. Here you elaborate on the facts and ideas you want to convey. Give information that supports your main idea, and expand on it with specific examples or details. In other words, structure your oral report in the same way you would a written essay, so that your thoughts are presented in a clear and organized manner.

- **Conclusion**—This is the time to summarize the information and emphasize your most important points to the audience one last time.

Preparing Your Delivery

1 Practice makes perfect. Practice! Practice! Practice! Confidence, enthusiasm, and energy are key to delivering an effective oral report, and they can best be achieved through rehearsal. Ask family and friends to be your practice audience and give you feedback when you're done. Were they able to follow your ideas? Did you seem knowledgeable and confident? Did you speak too slowly or too fast, too softly or too loudly? The more times you practice giving your report, the more you'll master the material. Then you won't have to rely so heavily on your notes or papers, and you will be able to give your report in a relaxed and confident manner.

2 Present with everything you've got. Be as creative as you can. Incorporate videos, sound clips, slide presentations, charts, diagrams, and photos. Visual aids help stimulate your audience's senses and keep them intrigued and engaged; they can also help to reinforce your key points. And remember that when you're giving an oral report, you're a performer. Take charge of the spotlight and be as animated and entertaining as you can. Have fun with it.

3 Keep your nerves under control. Everyone gets a little nervous when speaking in front of a group. That's normal. But the more preparation you've done— meaning plenty of researching, organizing, and rehearsing—the more confident you'll be. Preparation is the key. And if you make a mistake or stumble over your words, just regroup and keep going. Nobody's perfect, and nobody expects you to be.

Schwerin Castle, which sits on an island in Lake Schwerin, Germany, has 953 rooms.

HISTORY HAPPENS

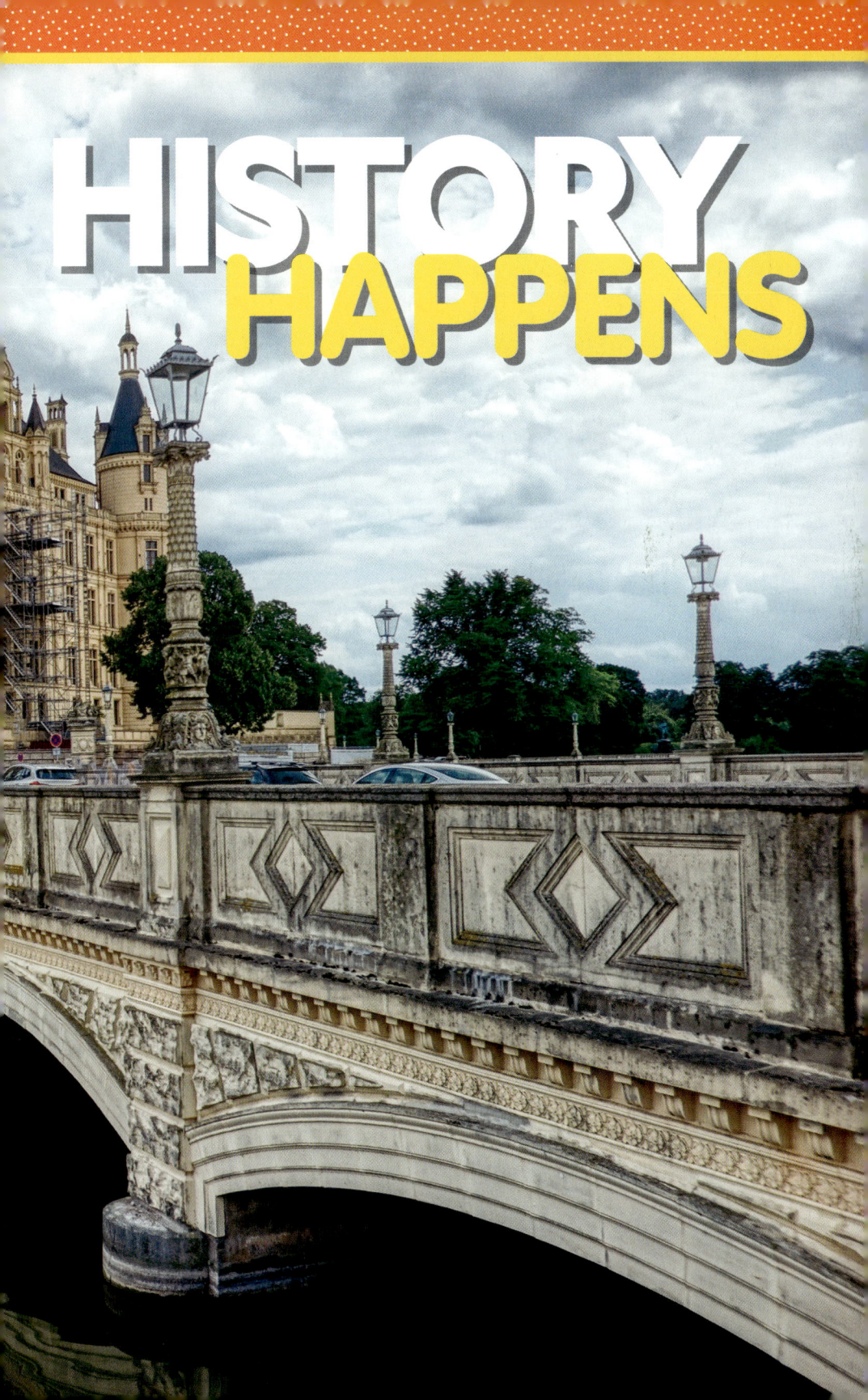

LIFE IN THE PAST

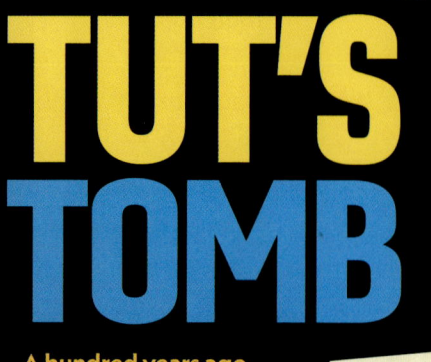

TUT'S TOMB

A hundred years ago, explorers uncovered this pharaoh's ancient resting place in Egypt's Valley of the Kings. Here's what they found inside.

❶ TOMB FOUND!
It was a mystery: British archaeologist Howard Carter had found artifacts stamped with the name of a pharaoh who didn't seem to have a tomb. One day, an Egyptian on his team uncovered stairs in the sand that led to a sealed doorway. The name on the entrance? Tutankhamun. On November 26, 1922, Carter chiseled a hole into the door to peek inside King Tut's tomb. He'd spend the next 10 years exploring its chambers and cataloging the items inside.

❷ GOLDEN GOODS
Most pharaohs had many rooms inside their tombs to hold all their treasures from when they were alive, as well as things they'd need in the afterlife. The four rooms of Tut's tomb were packed with more than 5,000 objects, including fancy chariots, a gem-encrusted throne, and even golden sandals. The tomb also contained three golden beds in the shape of a lioness, a cow, and a hippo-lion-crocodile combination. These beds were probably used during the ruler's mummification process.

❸ SNACK PACKS
Ancient Egyptians believed that the afterlife would be a lot like regular life. So workers filled Tut's tomb with items like underwear, board games, and plenty of snacks. Wooden containers full of poultry and beef were like ancient lunch boxes. Baskets of bread, grapes, garlic, spices, and a jar of honey—now totally dried out—would keep Tut from getting hungry.

❹ TUT TRUTH
King Tut took the throne when he was just nine years old and died about 10 years later, around 1323 B.C. Experts still aren't sure if his death was caused by a chariot crash, a bone disease, or a mosquito-borne illness. Although the tomb's contents have been moved to a museum, Tut himself still rests inside a glass case near his original stone sarcophagus.

❺ GOT GUTS?
To mummify the teenage pharaoh, priests removed Tut's liver, lungs, stomach, and intestines, then placed each organ in its own compartment inside a gilded shrine. A statue of Anubis, the god of mummification and the dead, seems to guard it nearby. Next, the priests wrapped the body in linens and adorned him with jewels and a gold burial mask.

238

HISTORY HAPPENS

No one is sure what King Tut's tomb looked like right after it was sealed, or where workers placed many of the items. Ancient looters made the tomb a jumbled mess!

6 SO MANY COFFINS
Tut's mummified body was placed in a solid-gold coffin. That coffin was placed inside two other coffins, each one slightly bigger than the other. Those two coffins were put into a stone sarcophagus. Next, the whole unit was placed inside four shrines, which also rested inside one another. The container was so large it filled almost the entire room.

7 QUICK JOB
Because Tut died unexpectedly at 19, workers likely had to rush to complete his tomb. That's probably why only one room is painted—and why those walls are covered in mold. The mold formed because the paint was still wet when the tomb was sealed.

8 HIDDEN TREASURES
Archaeologists have never found a more intact pharaoh's tomb than Tut's, probably because for thousands of years no one knew it existed. Why? Another tomb was carved directly on top of Tut's, hiding it from explorers.

9 PHARAOH'S CURSE?
Soon after opening the tomb, Carter's boss, Lord Carnarvon, suddenly died. Another friend who received gifts from the tomb lost his house. But Carter lived another 17 years. Did opening the tomb unleash a mummy's curse? You decide.

239

LIFE IN THE PAST

Brainy Questions

HEY, SMARTY-PANTS!

GOT BIG, WEIRD QUESTIONS?

WE'VE GOT ANSWERS!

Who is the wealthiest person of all time?

Mansa Musa. But he didn't create a social media platform or run a giant company—this person took the top spot around 700 years ago. Mansa Musa ruled the Empire of Mali in western Africa between 1312 and 1337, and he's estimated to have been worth around $400 billion in today's dollars. (By comparison, Jeff Bezos, who founded the online store Amazon, was worth "only" about $194 billion at the end of 2024.) His land was rich in gold and salt—which was extremely valuable then because it preserved food. The empire traded these items far and wide. When he traveled to what's now Saudi Arabia, Mansa Musa's caravan included 80 camels, each carrying 300 pounds (136 kg) of gold. Back home, Mansa Musa used his wealth to improve cities, adding more schools and libraries. That's a good way to spend money.

Why do beaches have sand?

Sand is mostly mountains plus time. Over millions of years, wind and rain break off little pieces of Earth's crust. These bits travel through rivers and streams, getting smaller and smaller as they flow through water and bump against other obstacles. Eventually the bits reach the ocean, where waves smash them into even smaller pieces and push them onto the shore. But some sand, like on the beaches of Hawaii, is mostly made from parrotfish poop! Parrotfish nibble on algae growing on dead coral, and sometimes they accidentally digest the coral. Then they poop it out as sand. One parrotfish's tummy can grind up enough coral to create up to 800 pounds (363 kg) of soft, white sand every year.

HISTORY HAPPENS

awes8me
BURIED TREASURE

1 BYGONE BLING
These remains from a shipwreck dating to about 60 B.C. were discovered more than a century ago by divers near the Greek island of Antikythera. Pictured here are a bronze spear from a statue and a marble bust of the Greek god Hermes (inset).

SPEAR

2 WATERY RICHES
This jewel-encrusted gold belt was recovered from the wreck of a Spanish ship called the *Nuestra Señora de Atocha* that sank in 1622 off the coast of what is now Florida, U.S.A.

4 METAL MIRACLE
More than a hundred Viking treasures, including the thousand-year-old gold pin seen here, were discovered by a retired businessman using a metal detector in a field in southwest Scotland!

3 TOMB OF TREASURES
A tomb dating back to the Zhou dynasty (1046–256 B.C.) was discovered under a hospital in China's Henan Province. This bronze drinking vessel was among the incredible finds.

5 SPECTACULAR STASH
Pieces of jewelry dating back 2,000 years were uncovered during a department store renovation near London. Archaeologists believe a Roman woman stashed her treasure here for safekeeping during a British tribe's revolt against Roman rule in A.D. 61.

THIS GOLD ARMLET WAS AMONG THE DISCOVERIES.

6 DIVING FOR GOLD
Nearly 2,000 gold coins were discovered by amateur scuba divers off the coast of the ancient city of Caesarea, in modern-day Israel. Members of the diving club first thought the thousand-year-old coins were toys!

8 SHOCKING STOCKPILE
A collection of 108 gold coins was found under a floor tile in these ancient ruins north of Tel Aviv, Israel. Researchers believe that the treasure was hidden to keep it safe from invaders in the mid-13th century.

7 UNDERSEA SWAG
This black granite sphinx—believed to have represented Ptolemy XII, the father of Cleopatra—was one of many treasures uncovered during excavations in the harbor of Alexandria, Egypt.

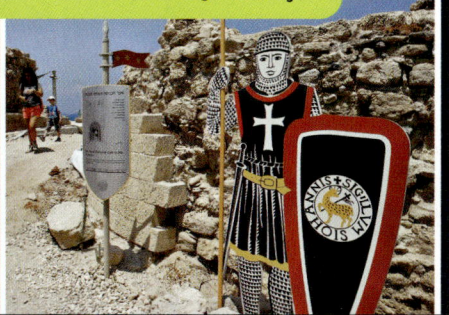

241

LIFE IN THE PAST

HISTORY'S MYSTERIES: THE ANCIENT MAYA
THE CIVILIZATION THAT WENT THE WAY OF THE DINOSAURS

THE BACKGROUND
The ancient Maya flourished in the Central American rainforest about 3,500 years ago. Their civilization was centuries before its time. They had vast cities, grand stone temples, and advances in writing, astronomy, and mathematics. Dozens of elaborate cities stretched across the areas of modern-day Guatemala, Belize, El Salvador, Honduras, and Mexico.

Then about 2,400 years ago, the Maya people all but vanished, leaving their giant stone pyramids eerily abandoned in the jungle. How could such a sophisticated society fade away? And what happened to them? To this day, nobody knows for sure.

THE DETAILS
Archaeologists dig, chisel, sweep, and ponder artifacts left behind—from piles of stone to ruins of entire cities and palaces. The Maya were known for having a sophisticated written language, spectacular art, amazing architecture, and complex mathematical and astronomical systems, which is evident from treasures unearthed from the time when they thrived. Their civilization also developed advanced agricultural techniques such as irrigation, composting, and terracing. Historians have pieced together a history of people rich in knowledge and resources. So, if their cities and temples stood the test of time, why didn't they?

THE CLUES
Over the past few decades, archaeologists have discovered hidden ruins that shed light on the destruction of individual Maya villages. And even more recently, they've used advanced technology to study the world at the time when the Maya lived—and perhaps uncover what happened to them. These three clues stand out as possible indicators of what went wrong.

JAGUAR PAW TEMPLE IN GUATEMALA

DEFORESTATION MIGHT HAVE CONTRIBUTED TO THE DOWNFALL OF THE MAYA.

242

HISTORY HAPPENS

MAYA STONE CARVING

MAYA WRITING

MAYA ARCHAEOLOGICAL SITE IN YUCATÁN STATE, MEXICO

BURIED IN ASH In 1978, archaeologists first set eyes on Joya de Cerén, a lost village in El Salvador that was accidentally discovered by construction workers. They dug through 16 feet (5 m) of volcanic ash before hitting the roof of a preserved thatched Maya house.

ALL-DRIED UP In 2009, scientists studying environmental conditions in Mexico's Yucatán Peninsula discovered there had been a sharp reduction in rainfall in the areas where the Maya lived at about the same time their numbers started to dwindle.

CROP COLLAPSE NASA conducted computer simulations and collected data that indicate there was serious deforestation during the time of the Maya—meaning the Maya people cut down a huge amount of trees. This could have affected local climate, caused erosion, and depleted the soil of its nutrients.

THE THEORIES

The question of what happened to the Maya has fascinated researchers and the public since 19th-century explorers began discovering these imposing lost cities in the jungles of Central America.

Some evidence, like the volcanic ash discovered at Joya de Cerén, suggests a sudden catastrophe, like a mega earthquake, hurricane, or volcanic eruption, led to the end of the Maya.

Some researchers believe that the collapse of the Maya civilization could have been due to a mysterious disease that wiped out the population over a period of about 200 years. Without modern medicine, disease could have spread easily from person to person in a dense city environment. However, many experts now believe the answer isn't so simple. They think it was a combination of factors, such as overpopulation, environmental damage, famine, and drought, that may have caused people to abandon their cities slowly over time. Scarce resources, like water and food, could have caused the system to crumble and led to catastrophic violence and wars with nearby civilizations.

Millions of people in Mexico and Central America today are direct descendants of the ancient Maya. Many of them still use an ancient Maya dialect as their first language. If only they also knew the secrets of what happened to this fascinating civilization.

LIFE IN THE PAST

awes8me

THESE MYSTERIES FROM HISTORY ARE COLD CASES WAITING TO BE SOLVED.

1 COLOSSAL HEADS

The Olmec people of Mesoamerica vanished around 300 B.C., and no one knows why. They left something huge behind, though: more than a dozen of these **carved stone heads**, which are as tall as 11 feet (3.4 m) and weigh 20 tons (18 t) each. Experts believe the heads are portraits of Olmec rulers.

ANCIENT MYSTERIES

2 CIRCLE OF STONES

Scientists have been examining **Stonehenge**, a 5,000-year-old monument in southern England, for centuries. Folklore says Merlin the wizard created it by moving the giant stones from Ireland. Theories today say it might have been a holy site or celestial observatory.

HISTORY HAPPENS

3 A COLONY VANISHED

More than 100 colonists who settled on **Roanoke Island**, North Carolina, U.S.A., in 1587 disappeared without a trace three years later. The only clues left behind were the words "Croatoan" carved into a gatepost of their fort and "Cro" scratched into a tree. No one knows for sure where they vanished to.

4 LOST CITY

Excavations in Türkiye (Turkey) in the late 19th century revealed that the **city of Troy**, once thought to be an imaginary city from Homer's ancient poem *The Iliad*, actually existed. Archaeologists are searching for clues about the kingdom and whether it was conquered during the Trojan War, as the 3,000-year-old legend says.

THE GREAT SPHINX MAY HAVE ONCE BEEN COVERED IN COLORFUL PAINT.

6 UNCREDITED MONUMENT

Although it's a massive monument, no one knows for sure who made the **Great Sphinx of Giza**. Some believe it was Khafre, who ruled ancient Egypt 4,600 years ago; others believe it was Khafre's father, who oversaw the building of the Great Pyramid of Giza.

5 MYSTERIOUS MANUSCRIPT

The **Voynich Manuscript** has puzzled researchers ever since it came to the public's attention in 1912, when book dealer Wilfrid M. Voynich bought it in Italy. The handwritten pages, which date back to the 1400s, contain botanical drawings, although no one has been able to identify what the plants are. And no one has been able to decode the language the book is written in.

7 MYSTERY LANGUAGE

The ancient people of Easter Island once possessed written language in the form of hieroglyphic scripts called **Rongorongo**. The script hasn't been deciphered, in part because when Europeans colonized the island, they destroyed most examples of it.

8 MYTHICAL LAND

More than 2,000 years ago, the Greek philosopher Plato wrote about **Atlantis**, a legendary island in the Atlantic Ocean filled with gold, silver, and exotic animals. The story says that Atlantis eventually sank into the sea after being destroyed by fires and earthquakes—the gods punishing its inhabitants.

LIFE IN THE PAST

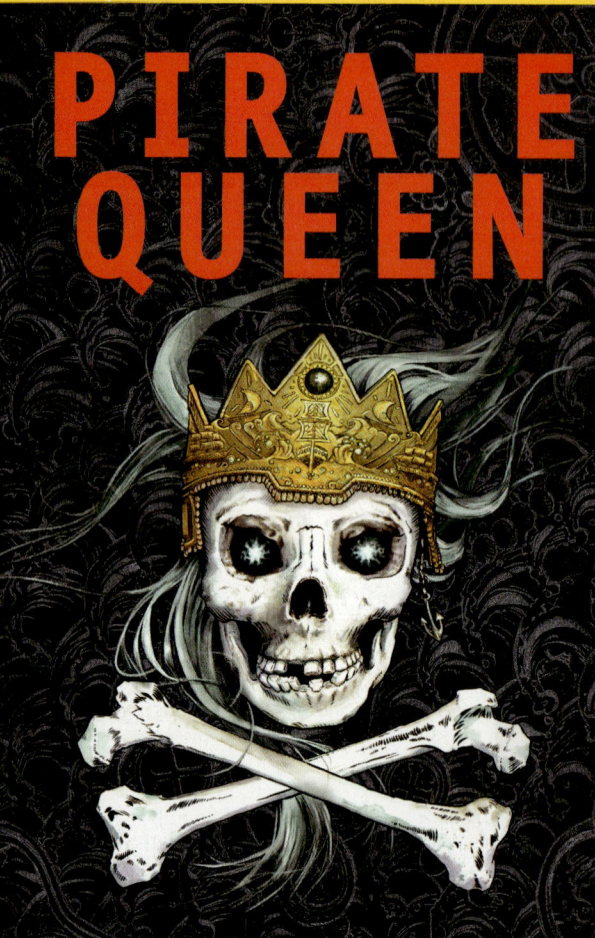

PIRATE QUEEN

CHING SHIH
FIERCE LEADER AND SAVVY NEGOTIATOR

WHEN: circa A.D. 1775 to 1844

WHERE: South China Sea

WHO: Ching Shih, whose masterful leadership made the massive Red Flag Fleet indomitable, commanded more ships and more pirates than any other pirate in history.

ALIASES: Ching Shih aka Cheng I Sao aka Zheng Yi Sao aka Madame Ching

TAKING OVER
Sailing the South China Sea, Ching Shih and her husband shared command of the powerful Red Flag Fleet. They had been married for six years when he died suddenly. Ching Shih—or Cheng I Sao, as she was sometimes called, which means "wife of Cheng I"—commandeered their pirate business, supposedly telling her fleet, "We shall see how you prove yourselves under the hand of a woman."

DREAM TEAM
The convincing new commander persuaded rival pirates to work together under her leadership. As a result, she united an enormous squadron of an estimated 1,800 ships with more than 80,000 pirates. She appointed her adopted son, Cheung Po Tsai, as captain of the fleet, which freed her to focus on business and military strategy. Before long, her pirates were not only pillaging and plundering at sea, but also expanding to schemes on land, such as extortion and blackmail. They also took over several coastal villages.

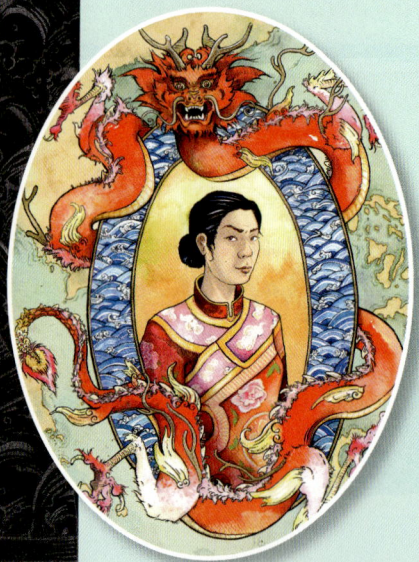

HISTORY HAPPENS

As more money flowed in, Ching Shih set up a pirates' bank to ensure her crew had savings to support their families.

LAW AND ORDER

Ching Shih wrote a set of laws for her crew to follow, and those who broke them were severely punished. Anyone caught disobeying a superior's orders, for example, faced the threat of having their ears cut off—or worse, they'd be beheaded. Often, at sea, pirates would bring women aboard their ships as enslaved people. Ching Shih refused to allow this mistreatment. She mandated that male pirates could only bring their wives on board and punished anyone who dared mistreat them.

SOVEREIGN OF THE SEAS

By 1807, the Red Flag Fleet was more organized than the Chinese navy. Chinese officials tried to stop the fleet with the help of British and Portuguese warships, but the Red Flag Fleet defeated that armada. Outmaneuvered and outnumbered at every turn, the Chinese government had no choice but to forgive Ching Shih's crimes. In exchange, they asked Ching Shih to stop pirating. She agreed, but on the condition that her entire crew be pardoned, too.

She got what she wanted—along with a small fleet of ships for her new husband to command, offers of military employment for her crew members, and money for their new life onshore. They also got to keep their loot.

SHREWD MOVES

She's often called history's most successful pirate. So just how prosperous was Ching Shih? To put it in perspective, her fleet of 1,800 ships and 80,000 men was hundreds of times larger than those of other well-known raiders of the time, like Captain Blackbeard. Managing such a colossal fleet couldn't have been easy, and it's said that Ching Shih's business savvy helped her be a better boss. Aside from overseeing the day-to-day schedules of her own army of ruffians, she was able to devise military strategy, manage the finances of her fleet, and broker business deals. One of Ching Shih's most impressive alliances? Developing a partnership with local farmers, who agreed to supply her men with food. And with 80,000 mouths to feed, that deal was certainly no small potatoes.

A LEADER'S LEGACY

A life on land didn't mean lying low for Ching Shih. Instead, she used her fortune to start new business enterprises, which by all accounts were pretty successful. She died peacefully at the age of about 69. This shrewd commander defied stereotypes and used her smarts and resourcefulness to create one of the most formidable pirate fleets the world has ever known.

LIFE IN THE PAST

HISTORY'S MYSTERIES: EASTER ISLAND (RAPA NUI) WHO CARVED THESE HEADS AND WHY?

THE BACKGROUND
On a remote island off the coast of Chile called Easter Island (Earth's most isolated spot inhabited by humans), an army of ancient monoliths has been guarding the island for centuries. The word "monolith" refers to a massive single stone, often standing upright as a monument. Ancient islanders—likely people who had come from Polynesia between A.D. 300 and 400—carved more than 1,000 of the massive figures, which were then situated to ring the island, facing inland. Called moai (MOE-eye), each one stands on a sacred platform called an ahu (AH-hoo).

THE DETAILS
The statues were discovered about 300 years ago by European explorers. Island lore says the statues are infused with the spirits of the inhabitants' ancestors. While the buildup of sediment over time has buried some of the moai, today there are still some 900 of these giant statues watching and protecting the island (others have been destroyed by erosion and weather). One thing they're not doing—speaking up about how they were built, their symbolic meaning, or how anybody moved these monstrous monoliths into place without modern machinery and equipment.

HISTORY HAPPENS

THE CLUES
The mega moai weigh about 26,000 pounds (11,800 kg) each. How ancient people made them and moved them into place with no access to metal tools or even wheels (which hadn't been invented yet) is a mystery. These clues only seem to create more questions than answers:

MEGA-MEN The many moai men were carved (using only hand tools) from porous, lightweight volcanic rock. But at an average of 13 feet (4 m) high, they are certainly not lightweight!

ON YOUR OWN TWO FEET Oral tradition says the statues walked themselves into place.

TEXT MESSAGE Along with the many moai, researchers found wooden and stone tablets filled with mysterious script, called Rongorongo.

THE THEORIES
As for where the moai came from, most archaeologists studying the island believe the big statues were carved first and then dragged into place with help from huge frames atop rolling logs. Some archaeologists have another theory. They think humans could have "walked" the statues into place. They've re-created this method of statues "walking" by being pulled with ropes and rocked from side to side. It would have been difficult and slow work but could have been possible. And that might help explain the local legend about the statues walking themselves into place. But that still doesn't answer the questions of why people would take the time to carve and haul these giant heads and what they were for.

249

INTERNATIONAL CONFLICTS

GOING TO WAR

Since the beginning of time, different countries, territories, and cultures have feuded with each other over land, power, and politics. Major military conflicts include the following wars:

1095-1291 THE CRUSADES
Starting late in the 11th century, these wars over religion were fought in the Middle East for nearly 200 years.

1337-1453 HUNDRED YEARS' WAR
France and England battled over rights to land for more than a century before the French eventually drove the English out in 1453.

1754-1763 FRENCH AND INDIAN WAR (part of Europe's Seven Years' War)
A nine-year war between the British and French for control of North America.

1775-1783 AMERICAN REVOLUTION
Thirteen British colonies in America united to reject the rule of the British government and to form the United States of America.

1861-1865 AMERICAN CIVIL WAR
This war occurred when the northern states (the Union) went to war with the southern states, which had seceded, or withdrawn, to form the Confederate States of America. Slavery was one of the key issues in the war.

1910-1920 MEXICAN REVOLUTION
The people of Mexico revolted against the rule of dictator President Porfirio Díaz, leading to his eventual defeat and to a democratic government.

1914-1918 WORLD WAR I
The assassination of Austria's Archduke Ferdinand by a Serbian nationalist sparked this wide-spreading war. The U.S. entered after Germany sank the British ship *Lusitania*, killing more than 120 Americans.

1918-1920 RUSSIAN CIVIL WAR
Following the 1917 Russian Revolution, this conflict pitted the Communist Red Army against the foreign-backed White Army. The Red Army won, leading to the establishment of the Union of Soviet Socialist Republics (U.S.S.R.) in 1922.

1936-1939 SPANISH CIVIL WAR
Aid from Italy and Germany helped Spain's Nationalists gain victory over the Communist-supported Republicans. The war resulted in the loss of more than 300,000 lives and increased tension in Europe leading up to World War II.

1939-1945 WORLD WAR II
This massive conflict in Europe, Asia, and North Africa involved many countries that aligned with the two sides: the Allies and the Axis. After the bombing of Pearl Harbor in Hawaii in 1941, the U.S. entered the war on the side of the Allies. More than 50 million people died during the war.

HISTORY HAPPENS

1946–1949 CHINESE CIVIL WAR
Also known as the "War of Liberation," this war pitted the Communist and Nationalist Parties in China against each other. The Communists won.

1950–1953 KOREAN WAR
Kicked off when the Communist forces of North Korea, with backing from the Soviet Union, invaded their democratic neighbor to the south. A coalition of 16 countries from the United Nations stepped in to support South Korea. An armistice, or temporary truce, ended active fighting in 1953.

1950s–1975 VIETNAM WAR
This war was fought between the Communist North, supported by allies including China, and the government of South Vietnam, supported by the United States and other anticommunist nations.

1967 SIX-DAY WAR
This was a battle for land between Israel and the states of Egypt, Jordan, and Syria. The outcome resulted in Israel's gaining control of coveted territory, including the Gaza Strip and the West Bank.

1991–PRESENT SOMALI CIVIL WAR
The war began when Somalia's last president, a dictator named Mohamed Siad Barre, was overthrown. This has led to years of fighting and anarchy.

2001–2014 WAR IN AFGHANISTAN
After attacks in the U.S. by the terrorist group al Qaeda, a coalition that eventually included more than 40 countries invaded Afghanistan to find Osama bin Laden and other al Qaeda members and to dismantle the Taliban. Bin Laden was killed in a U.S. covert operation in 2011. The North Atlantic Treaty Organization (NATO) took control of the coalition's combat mission in 2003. That combat mission officially ended in 2014. The United States completed its withdrawal of troops in 2021.

2003–2011 WAR IN IRAQ
A coalition led by the U.S., and including Britain, Australia, and Spain, invaded Iraq over suspicions that Iraq had weapons of mass destruction.

2022—PRESENT RUSSIA-UKRAINE WAR
Military forces led by Russian president Vladimir Putin crossed the border into Ukraine, seeking to take control of the country. Russia launched attacks on major cities across the country, including the capital city of Kyiv.

WARTIME INVENTIONS

During war, life is hard, and people need ways to make life easier. So it's no surprise that some ingenious inventions have their origins in wartime. These innovations have their origins in World War II.

MICROWAVE OVENS: Next time you pop your popcorn on movie night, thank Percy Spencer. He's the engineer who accidentally discovered that electromagnetic waves could have cooking properties while working on radar equipment during and after World War II. During an experiment, Spencer noticed that the chocolate bar in his pocket melted when he came close to equipment generating electromagnetic radiation—including waves known as microwaves. Spencer and other engineers used these waves to create the very first microwave oven, now a fixture in millions of homes around the world.

DUCT TAPE: Vesta Stoudt was working at a munitions factory during World War II when she came up with a tape to seal boxes of bullets, keeping them dry and making them safer to take into battle. The waterproof, cloth-backed tape quickly became a military fix-all for everything from leaky boots to cracked jeep fenders. When people began using it to wrap air ducts, it got the name that persists today.

SUPER GLUE: In 1942, Dr. Harry Coover unintentionally created an extra-sticky substance while manufacturing a clear plastic to make sights for guns. The super-durable compound eventually became Super Glue. During the Vietnam War, the glue was used to close wounds soldiers received on the battlefield.

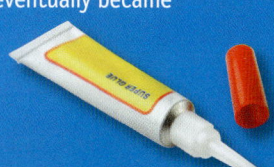

WORLD LEADERS

LEADERS OF THE WORLD

Each of the 195 independent countries in the world has its own leader or leaders. Whatever the leader is called, they take charge of the direction of the country's growth—politically, economically, and socially.

Some countries have more than one person who has an executive role in the government. That second person is often a prime minister or a chancellor. This varies depending on the type of government in the country.

Over the next several pages, the countries and their leaders are listed in alphabetical order according to the most commonly used version of each country's name. Disputed areas such as Northern Cyprus and Taiwan, and dependencies such as Bermuda, Greenland, and Puerto Rico, which belong to independent nations, are not included in this listing. The date given for leaders taking office is the date of their first term.

Note the color key at the bottom of the pages, which assigns a color to each country based on the continent on which it is located.

NOTE: These facts are current as of press time.

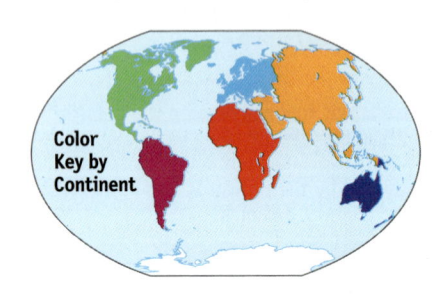

Color Key by Continent

Afghanistan
**Taliban Leader
Haybatullah Akhundzada**
Took office: August 15, 2021

Albania
President Bajram Begaj
Took office: July 24, 2022

Prime Minister Edi Rama
Took office: September 10, 2013

Algeria
**President
Abdelmadjid Tebboune**
Took office: December 12, 2019

**Prime Minister
Nadir Larbaoui**
Took office: November 11, 2023

More information on world leaders can be found on the CIA's World Factbook online.

Andorra
**Co-Prince
Emmanuel Macron**
Took office: May 14, 2017

**Co-Prince
Archbishop Joan-Enric
Vives i Sicília**
Took office: May 12, 2003

**Prime Minister
Xavier Espot Zamora**
Took office: May 16, 2019

Angola
**President João Manuel
Goncalves Lourenço**
Took office: September 26, 2017

Antigua and Barbuda
**Governor General
Rodney Williams**
Took office: August 14, 2014

**Prime Minister
Gaston Browne**
Took office: June 13, 2014

Argentina
**President
Javier Milei**
Took office: December 10, 2023

Armenia
**President
Vahagn Khachaturyan**
Took office: March 13, 2022

**Prime Minister
Nikol Pashinyan**
Took office: September 10, 2021

Australia
**Governor General
Samantha Mostyn**
Took office: July 1, 2024

**Prime Minister
Anthony Albanese**
Took office: May 23, 2022

Austria
**President
Alexander Van Der Bellen**
Took office: January 26, 2017

Chancellor Karl Nehammer
Took office: December 6, 2021

252 COLOR KEY ● Africa ● Australia, New Zealand, and Oceania

HISTORY HAPPENS

Azerbaijan
President Ilham Aliyev
Took office: October 31, 2003

**Prime Minister
Ali Asadov**
Took office: October 8, 2019

Bahamas, The
**Governor General
Cynthia A. Pratt**
Took office: September 1, 2023

**Prime Minister
Philip Edward Davis**
Took office: September 17, 2021

> **CYNTHIA A. PRATT PLAYED ON A NATIONAL SOFTBALL TEAM FOR THE BAHAMAS.**

Bahrain
King Hamad bin Isa Al-Khalifa
Began reign: March 6, 1999

**Prime Minister
Salman bin Hamad Al-Khalifa**
Took office: November 11, 2020

Bangladesh
President Mohammad Shahabuddin Chuppi
Took office: April 24, 2023

**Interim Prime Minister
Muhammad Yunus**
Took office: August 8, 2024

Barbados
**President
Sandra Mason**
Took office: November 30, 2021

**Prime Minister
Mia Mottley**
Took office: May 25, 2018

Belarus
**President
Alyaksandr Lukashenka**
Took office: July 20, 1994

**Prime Minister
Roman Golovchenko**
Took office: June 4, 2020

Belgium
King Philippe
Began reign: July 21, 2013

**Prime Minister
Alexander De Croo**
Took office: October 1, 2020

Belize
**Governor General
Froyla Tzalam**
Took office: May 27, 2021

**Prime Minister
John Briceño**
Took office: November 12, 2020

Benin
**President
Patrice Talon**
Took office: April 6, 2016

Bhutan
King Jigme Khesar Namgyel Wangchuck
Began reign: December 14, 2006

**Prime Minister
Tshering Tobgay**
Took office: January 28, 2024

Bolivia
**President
Luis Alberto Arce Catacora**
Took office: November 8, 2020

> **LUIS ALBERTO ARCE CATACORA IS OFTEN CALLED LUCHO.**

Bosnia and Herzegovina
**Presidency members:
Denis Bećirović
Željko Komšić
Željka Cvijanović**
Took office: November 16, 2022

Chairperson of the Council of Ministers Borjana Krišto
Took office: January 25, 2023

Botswana
President Duma Boko
Took office: November 1, 2024

> **DUMA BOKO ATTENDED HARVARD LAW SCHOOL IN THE UNITED STATES.**

Brazil
**President
Luiz Inácio Lula da Silva**
Took office: January 1, 2023

Brunei
Sultan Hassanal Bolkiah
Began reign: October 5, 1967

Bulgaria
President Rumen Radev
Took office: January 22, 2017

**Caretaker Prime Minister
Dimitar Glavchev**
Took office: April 9, 2024

Burkina Faso
**Transitional President
Captain Ibrahim Traore**
Took office: September 30, 2022

**Prime Minister
Rimtalba Jean Emmanuel Ouedraogo**
Took office: December 9, 2024

● Asia ● Europe ● North America ● South America

WORLD LEADERS

Burundi
President Evariste Ndayishimiye
Took office: June 18, 2020

Cabo Verde
President José Maria Neves
Took office: November 9, 2021

Prime Minister Ulisses Correia e Silva
Took office: April 22, 2016

Cambodia
King Norodom Sihamoni
Began reign: October 29, 2004

Prime Minister Hun Manet
Took office: August 22, 2023

Cameroon
President Paul Biya
Took office: November 6, 1982

Prime Minister Joseph Ngute
Took office: January 4, 2019

Canada
Governor General Mary Simon
Took office: July 6, 2021

Prime Minister Justin Trudeau
Took office: November 4, 2015

Trudeau announced his resignation in January 2025. At the time of this book's printing, his replacement had not been selected.

> JUSTIN TRUDEAU IS THE FIRST CHILD OF A CANADIAN PRIME MINISTER TO BECOME ONE HIMSELF.

Central African Republic
President Faustin-Archange Touadéra
Took office: March 30, 2016

Prime Minister Félix Moloua
Took office: February 7, 2022

Chad
President Mahamat Idriss Déby
Took office: May 23, 2024

Prime Minister Allamaye Halina
Took office: May 23, 2024

Chile
President Gabriel Boric
Took office: March 11, 2022

Hello From Cambodia

With a tongue that can stretch up to 10 inches (25 cm) long, this sun bear is ready to slurp up some tasty insects from its tropical forest home.

254 COLOR KEY ● Africa ● Australia, New Zealand, and Oceania

HISTORY HAPPENS

China
President Xi Jinping
Took office: March 14, 2013

Premier Li Qiang
Took office: March 11, 2023

Colombia
President Gustavo Francisco Petro Urrego
Took office: August 7, 2022

Comoros
President Azali Assoumani
Took office: May 26, 2016

Congo
President Denis Sassou-Nguesso
Took office: October 25, 1997

Prime Minister Anatole Collinet Makosso
Took office: May 12, 2021

Costa Rica
President Rodrigo Chaves Robles
Took office: May 8, 2022

Côte d'Ivoire (Ivory Coast)
President Alassane Dramane Ouattara
Took office: December 4, 2010

Prime Minister Robert Beugre Mambe
Took office: October 17, 2023

Croatia
President Zoran Milanovic
Took office: February 18, 2020

Prime Minister Andrej Plenkovic
Took office: October 19, 2016

Cuba
President Miguel Díaz-Canel Bermúdez
Took office: April 19, 2018

Prime Minister Manuel Marrero Cruz
Took office: December 21, 2019

Cyprus
President Nikos Christodoulidis
Took office: February 28, 2023

Czechia (Czech Republic)
President Petr Pavel
Took office: March 9, 2023

Prime Minister Petr Fiala
Took office: December 17, 2021

Democratic Republic of the Congo
President Felix Tshisekedi
Took office: January 24, 2019

Prime Minister Judith Suminwa Tuluka
Took office: May 29, 2024

Denmark
King Frederik X
Began reign: January 14, 2024

Prime Minister Mette Frederiksen
Took office: June 27, 2019

Djibouti
President Ismail Omar Guelleh
Took office: May 8, 1999

Prime Minister Abdoulkader Kamil Mohamed
Took office: April 1, 2013

Dominica
President Sylvanie Burton
Took office: October 2, 2023

Prime Minister Roosevelt Skerrit
Took office: January 8, 2004

Dominican Republic
President Luis Rodolfo Abinader Corona
Took office: August 16, 2020

Ecuador
President Daniel Noboa Azín
Took office: November 23, 2023

DANIEL NOBOA AZÍN HAS DEGREES FROM HARVARD, NORTHWESTERN, NYU, AND GEORGE WASHINGTON UNIVERSITIES IN THE U.S.

Egypt
President Abdel Fattah El-Sisi
Took office: June 8, 2014

Prime Minister Mostafa Madbouly
Took office: June 7, 2018

El Salvador
President Nayib Armando Bukele Ortez
Took office: June 1, 2019

Equatorial Guinea
President Teodoro Obiang Nguema Mbasogo
Took office: August 3, 1979

Prime Minister Manuela Roka Botey
Took office: February 1, 2023

● Asia ● Europe ● North America ● South America

WORLD LEADERS

Eritrea
President
Isaias Afwerki
Took office: May 24, 1993

Estonia
President
Alar Karis
Took office: October 11, 2021

Prime Minister
Kristen Michal
Took office: July 23, 2024

KRISTEN MICHAL WAS FORMERLY ESTONIA'S MINISTER OF CLIMATE.

Eswatini (Swaziland)
King Mswati III
Began reign: April 25, 1986

Prime Minister
Russell Dlamini
Took office: November 6, 2023

Ethiopia
President
Taye Atske Selassie
Took office: October 7, 2024

Prime Minister
Abiy Ahmed Ali
Took office: April 2018

Fiji
President
Ratu Wiliame Katonivere
Took office: November 12, 2021

Prime Minister
Sitiveni Ligamamada Rabuka
Took office: December 24, 2022

Finland
President Alexander Stubb
Took office: March 1, 2024

Prime Minister
Petteri Orpo
Took office: June 20, 2023

France
President
Emmanuel Macron
Took office: May 14, 2017

Prime Minister
François Bayrou
Took office: December 13, 2024

Gabon
Transitional President Gen. Brice Oligui Nguema
Took office: September 4, 2023

Prime Minister
Raymond Ndong Sima
Took office: September 7, 2023

Gambia, The
President Adama Barrow
Took office: January 19, 2017

Georgia
President
Salome Zourabichvili
Took office: December 16, 2018

Prime Minister
Irakli Kobakhidze
Took office: February 8, 2024

Germany
President
Frank-Walter Steinmeier
Took office: March 19, 2017

Chancellor Olaf Scholz
Took office: December 8, 2021

Ghana
President
John Dramani Mahama
Took office: January 7, 2025

Greece
President
Katerina N. Sakellaropoulou
Took office: March 13, 2020

Prime Minister
Kyriakos Mitsotakis
Took office: June 26, 2023

KATERINA SAKELLAROPOULOU IS THE FIRST FEMALE PRESIDENT OF GREECE.

Grenada
Governor General
Cécile La Grenade
Took office: May 7, 2013

Prime Minister
Dickon Mitchell
Took office: June 24, 2022

Guatemala
President
Bernardo Arévalo de León
Took office: January 15, 2024

Guinea
President
Mamady Doumbouya
Took office: October 1, 2021

Prime Minister
Mamadou Oury Bah
Took office: February 27, 2024

Guinea-Bissau
President
Umaro Sissoco Embalo
Took office: February 27, 2020

Prime Minister
Rui Duarte de Barros
Took office: December 20, 2023

COLOR KEY ● Africa ● Australia, New Zealand, and Oceania

HISTORY HAPPENS

VIKTOR ORBÁN IS A FATHER OF FIVE, AND A GRANDFATHER OF AT LEAST SIX.

Hungary
President
Tamas Sulyok
Took office: March 5, 2024

Prime Minister
Viktor Orbán
Took office: May 29, 2010

Iceland
President Halla Tómasdóttir
Took office: August 1, 2024

Prime Minister
Bjarni Benediktsson
Took office: April 9, 2024

India
President
Droupadi Murmu
Took office: July 25, 2022

Prime Minister
Narendra Modi
Took office: May 26, 2014

Indonesia
President Prabowo Subianto Djojohadikusumo
Took office: October 20, 2024

PRABOWO SUBIANTO IS THE FIRST PRESIDENT IN THE COUNTRY'S HISTORY WITHOUT A SPOUSE.

Iran
Supreme Leader
Ali Hoseini-Khamenei
Took office: June 4, 1989

President
Masoud Pezeshkian
Took office: July 30, 2024

Iraq
President Latif Rashid
Took office: October 13, 2022

Prime Minister
Mohammed Shia al-Sudani
Took office: October 27, 2022

Guyana
President
Mohammed Irfaan Ali
Took office: August 2, 2020

Haiti
President
Vacant

Prime Minister Garry Conille
Took office: June 3, 2024

Honduras
President Iris Xiomara Castro de Zelaya
Took office: January 27, 2022

Greetings From India

City Palace is perched on the edge of Pichola Lake in Udaipur, India.

● Asia ● Europe ● North America ● South America

WORLD LEADERS

Ireland (Éire)
President Michael D. Higgins
Took office: November 11, 2011

**Prime Minister
Simon Harris**
Took office: April 9, 2024

Israel
President Isaac Herzog
Took office: July 7, 2021

**Prime Minister
Benjamin Netanyahu**
Took office: December 29, 2022

Italy
President Sergio Mattarella
Took office: February 3, 2015

**Prime Minister
Giorgia Meloni**
Took office: October 22, 2022

Jamaica
**Governor General
Sir Patrick L. Allen**
Took office: February 26, 2009

**Prime Minister
Andrew Holness**
Took office: March 3, 2016

Japan
Emperor Naruhito
Began reign: May 1, 2019

Prime Minister Shigeru Ishiba
Took office: October 1, 2024

SERGIO MATTARELLA IS MODERN ITALY'S LONGEST-SERVING HEAD OF STATE.

Jordan
King Abdallah II
Began reign: February 7, 1999

**Prime Minister
Jafar Hassan**
Took office: September 15, 2024

Kazakhstan
**President
Kasym-Zhomart Tokayev**
Took office: March 20, 2019

**Prime Minister
Olzhas Bektenov**
Took office: February 6, 2024

KASYM-ZHOMART TOKAYEV IS ONLY THE SECOND PRESIDENT OF KAZAKHSTAN.

Welcome to Jamaica

A waterfall flows into the natural limestone pool at Jamaica's Blue Hole.

COLOR KEY ● Africa ● Australia, New Zealand, and Oceania

HISTORY HAPPENS

Kenya
President William Ruto
Took office: September 13, 2022

Kiribati
President Taneti Maamau
Took office: March 11, 2016

Kosovo
President Vjosa Osmani-Sadriu
Took office: April 4, 2021

Prime Minister Albin Kurti
Took office: March 22, 2021

Kuwait
Amir Mishal al-Ahmad al-Jabir al-Sabah
Began reign: December 16, 2023

Prime Minister Ahmad Abdullah Al-Ahmad al Sabah
Took office: May 15, 2024

Kyrgyzstan
President Sadyr Japarov
Took office: January 28, 2021

Laos
President Thongloun Sisoulith
Took office: March 22, 2021

Prime Minister Sonxai Siphandon
Took office: December 30, 2022

> THONGLOUN SISOULITH SPEAKS LAO, VIETNAMESE, RUSSIAN, AND ENGLISH.

Latvia
President Edgars Rinkēvičs
Took office: July 8, 2023

Prime Minister Evika Siliņa
Took office: September 15, 2023

> EVIKA SILIŅA IS THE SECOND FEMALE HEAD OF GOVERNMENT IN LATVIA.

Lebanon
President
Vacant

Caretaker Prime Minister Najib Miqati
Took office: September 20, 2021

Lesotho
King Letsie III
Began reign: February 7, 1996

Prime Minister Ntsokoane Samuel Matekane
Took office: October 28, 2022

Liberia
President Joseph Boakai
Took office: January 22, 2024

Libya
President, Presidential Council, Mohammed Al Menfi
Took office: February 5, 2021

GNU Interim Prime Minister Abdul Hamid Dubaybah
Took office: February 5, 2021

Liechtenstein
Prince Hans-Adam II
Began reign: November 13, 1989

Prime Minister Daniel Risch
Took office: March 25, 2021

Lithuania
President Gitanas Nausėda
Took office: July 12, 2019

Prime Minister Ingrida Šimonytė
Took office: November 24, 2020

Luxembourg
Grand Duke Henri
Began reign: October 7, 2000

Prime Minister Luc Frieden
Took office: November 17, 2023

> GRAND DUKE HENRI IS A MEMBER OF THE INTERNATIONAL OLYMPIC COMMITTEE.

Madagascar
President Andry Rajoelina
Took office: December 16, 2023

Prime Minister Christian Ntsay
Took office: June 6, 2018

Malawi
President Lazarus Chakwera
Took office: June 28, 2020

Malaysia
King Sultan Ibrahim ibni al-Marhum Sultan Iskandar
Began reign: January 31, 2024

Prime Minister Anwar Ibrahim
Took office: November 25, 2022

Maldives
President Mohamed Muizzu
Took office: November 17, 2023

● Asia ● Europe ● North America ● South America

WORLD LEADERS

Mali
President of transitional government: Assimi Goita
Took office: June 7, 2021

Transitional Prime Minister Abdoulaye Maïga
Took office: November 22, 2024

Malta
President Myriam Spiteri Debono
Took office: April 4, 2024

Prime Minister Robert Abela
Took office: January 13, 2020

Marshall Islands
President Hilda C. Heine
Took office: January 3, 2023

Mauritania
President Mohamed Ould Cheikh el Ghazouani
Took office: August 1, 2019

Prime Minister Moctar Ould Diay
Took office: August 2, 2024

Mauritius
President Dharam Gokhool
Took office: December 7, 2024

Prime Minister Pravind Jugnauth
Took office: January 23, 2017

Mexico
President Claudia Sheinbaum
Took office: October 1, 2024

Micronesia
President Wesley Simina
Took office: May 12, 2023

MOHAMMED VI RANKS AMONG THE RICHEST KINGS IN THE WORLD.

Moldova
President Maia Sandu
Took office: December 24, 2020

Prime Minister Dorin Recean
Took office: February 16, 2023

Monaco
Prince Albert II
Began reign: April 6, 2005

Minister of State Didier Guillaume
Took office: September 2, 2024

Mongolia
President Ukhnaagiin Khurelsukh
Took office: June 25, 2021

Prime Minister Luvsannamsrai Oyun-Erdene
Took office: January 27, 2021

Montenegro
President Jakov Milatović
Took office: May 20, 2023

Prime Minister Milojko Spajic
Took office: October 31, 2023

WESLEY SIMINA IS THE 10TH PRESIDENT OF THE FEDERATED STATES OF MICRONESIA.

Morocco
King Mohammed VI
Began reign: July 30, 1999

Prime Minister Aziz Akhannouch
Took office: October 7, 2021

Mozambique
President Filipe Jacinto Nyusi
Took office: January 15, 2015

Prime Minister Adriano Maleiane
Took office: March 3, 2022

Myanmar (Burma)
Prime Minister Min Aung Hlaing
Took office: August 1, 2021

Namibia
President Netumbo Nandi-Ndaitwah
Took office: March 2025

NETUMBO NANDI-NDAITWAH, NICKNAMED "NNN," IS THE FIRST FEMALE PRESIDENT OF NAMIBIA.

Nauru
President David Adeang
Took office: October 30, 2023

Nepal
President Ram Chandra Poudel
Took office: March 13, 2023

Prime Minister Khadga Prasad Sharma Oli
Took office: July 15, 2024

COLOR KEY ● Africa ● Australia, New Zealand, and Oceania

HISTORY HAPPENS

Netherlands
King Willem-Alexander
Began reign: April 30, 2013

Prime Minister Dick Schoof
Took office: July 2, 2024

> KING WILLEM-ALEXANDER ENTERED AN ICE-SKATING COMPETITION UNDER A PSEUDONYM WHEN HE WAS 18.

New Zealand
Governor General Dame Cindy Kiro
Took office: October 21, 2021

Prime Minister Christopher Luxon
Took office: November 27, 2023

Nicaragua
President José Daniel Ortega Saavedra
Took office: January 10, 2007

Niger
President Abdourahame Tiani
Took office: July 28, 2023

Prime Minister Ali Mahaman Lamine Zeine
Took office: August 9, 2023

Nigeria
President Bola Ahmed Adekunle Tinubu
Took office: May 29, 2023

North Korea
Supreme Leader Kim Jong-un
Took office: December 17, 2011

Assembly President Choe Ryong Hae
Took office: April 11, 2019

North Macedonia
President Gordana Siljanovska-Davkova
Took office: May 12, 2024

Norway
King Harald V
Began reign: January 17, 1991

Prime Minister Jonas Gahr Støre
Took office: October 14, 2021

Oman
Sultan Haitham bin Tarik Al Said
Began reign: January 11, 2020

Pakistan
President Asif Ali Zardari
Took office: March 10, 2024

Prime Minister Shahbaz Sharif
Took office: March 3, 2024

Palau
President Surangel Whipps, Jr.
Took office: January 21, 2021

> SURANGEL WHIPPS, JR., ENJOYS FISHING IN HIS SPARE TIME.

Panama
President José Raúl Mulino Quintero
Took office: July 1, 2024

Papua New Guinea
Governor General Bob Dadae
Took office: February 28, 2017

Prime Minister James Marape
Took office: May 30, 2019

Paraguay
President Santiago Peña Palacios
Took office: August 15, 2023

> SANTIAGO PEÑA PALACIOS IS PARAGUAY'S YOUNGEST PRESIDENT.

Peru
President Dina Ercilia Boluarte Zegarra
Took office: December 7, 2022

Philippines
President Ferdinand "Bongbong" Marcos, Jr.
Took office: June 30, 2022

> FERDINAND MARCOS, JR., PLAYS THE SAXOPHONE.

Poland
President Andrzej Duda
Took office: August 6, 2015

Prime Minister Donald Tusk
Took office: December 11, 2023

● Asia ● Europe ● North America ● South America

WORLD LEADERS

Portugal
President
Marcelo Rebelo de Sousa
Took office: March 9, 2016

Prime Minister
António Luís Montenegro
Took office: April 2, 2024

Qatar
Amir
Tamim bin Hamad Al Thani
Began reign: June 25, 2013

Prime Minister
Muhammad bin Abd al-Rahman Al Thani
Took office: March 7, 2023

Romania
President
Klaus Werner Iohannis
Took office: December 21, 2014

Prime Minister
Marcel Ciolacu
Took office: June 15, 2023

Russia
President Vladimir Vladimirovich Putin
Took office: May 7, 2012

Premier
Mikhail Vladimirovich Mishustin
Took office: January 16, 2020
Note: Russia is in both Europe and Asia, but its capital is in Europe, so it is classified here as a European country.

Rwanda
President
Paul Kagame
Took office: April 22, 2000

Prime Minister
Edouard Ngirente
Took office: August 30, 2017

Samoa
Head of State
Tuimaleali'ifano Va'aletoa Sualauvi II
Took office: July 21, 2017

Prime Minister
Fiamē Naomi Mata'afa
Took office: May 24, 2021

San Marino
Co-Chiefs of State: Captain Regents –
Francesca Civerchia
Dalibor Riccardi
Took office: October 1, 2024

Secretary of State for Foreign and Political Affairs Luca Beccari
Took office: January 8, 2020

Sao Tome and Principe
President
Carlos Manuel Vila Nova
Took office: October 2, 2021

Prime Minister
Patrice Trovoada
Took office: November 11, 2022

Saudi Arabia
King Salman bin Abd al-Aziz Al Saud
Began reign: January 23, 2015

Prime Minister Crown Prince Muhammad bin Salman bin Abd al-Aziz Al Saud
Took office: September 27, 2022

Senegal
President
Bassirou Diomaye Faye
Took office: April 2, 2024

Prime Minister
Ousmane Sonko
Took office: April 2, 2024

Serbia
President
Aleksandar Vučić
Took office: May 31, 2017

Prime Minister
Miloš Vučević
Took office: May 2, 2024

Seychelles
President
Wavel Ramkalawan
Took office: October 26, 2020

Sierra Leone
President
Julius Maada Bio
Took office: April 4, 2018

Singapore
President
Tharman Shanmugaratnam
Took office: September 14, 2023

Prime Minister
Lawrence Wong
Took office: May 15, 2024

> THARMAN SHANMUGARATNAM USED TO WRITE POETRY, SOME OF WHICH WAS PUBLISHED.

Slovakia
President Peter Pellegrini
Took office: June 15, 2024

Prime Minister
Robert Fico
Took office: October 25, 2023

Slovenia
President Nataša Pirc Musar
Took office: December 23, 2022

Prime Minister Robert Golob
Took office: June 1, 2022

COLOR KEY ● Africa ● Australia, New Zealand, and Oceania

HISTORY HAPPENS

Solomon Islands
**Governor General
David Tiva Kapu**
Took office: July 7, 2024

**Prime Minister
Jeremiah Manele**
Took office: May 2, 2024

Somalia
**President
Hassan Sheikh Mohamud**
Took office: May 23, 2022

**Prime Minister
Hamza Abdi Barre**
Took office: June 25, 2022

South Africa
**President
Matamela Cyril Ramaphosa**
Took office: February 15, 2018

South Korea
**Acting President
Choi Sang-mok**
Took office: December 2024

South Sudan
President Salva Kiir Mayardit
Took office: July 9, 2011

Spain
King Felipe VI
Began reign: June 19, 2014

President of the Government Pedro Sánchez Pérez-Castejón
Took office: June 2, 2018

Sri Lanka
**President
Anura Kumara Dissanayake**
Took office: September 23, 2024

St. Kitts and Nevis
**Governor General
Marcella Liburd**
Took office: February 1, 2023

**Prime Minister
Terrance Drew**
Took office: August 6, 2022

> MARCELLA LIBURD IS THE FIRST FEMALE GOVERNOR GENERAL OF ST. KITTS AND NEVIS.

St. Lucia
**Acting Governor General
Errol Charles**
Took office: November 11, 2021

**Prime Minister
Philip J. Pierre**
Took office: July 28, 2021

Postcard From South Africa

A common warthog pauses for a drink at a watering hole in South Africa's Kruger National Park.

● Asia ● Europe ● North America ● South America

263

WORLD LEADERS

St. Vincent and the Grenadines
Governor General Susan Dougan
Took office: August 1, 2019

Prime Minister Ralph E. Gonsalves
Took office: March 29, 2001

Sudan
Sovereign Council Chair General Abd-al-Fatah al-Burhan Abd-al-Rahman
Took office: October 2021

Suriname
President Chandrikapersad Santokhi
Took office: July 16, 2020

Sweden
King Carl XVI Gustaf
Began reign: September 15, 1973

Prime Minister Ulf Kristersson
Took office: October 18, 2022

> **ULF KRISTERSSON WAS AN ELITE GYMNAST AS A KID.**

Switzerland
President of the Swiss Confederation Karin Keller-Sutter
Took office: January 1, 2025

Federal Council members: Viola Amherd, Guy Parmelin, Ignazio Cassis, Albert Rösti, Elisabeth Baume-Schneider, Beat Jans
Took office: Dates vary

Syria
President
Vacant

Transitional Prime Minister Mohammed al-Bashir
Took office: December 10, 2024

Tajikistan
President Emomali Rahmon
Took office: November 6, 1994

Prime Minister Qohir Rasulzoda
Took office: November 23, 2013

> **EMOMALI RAHMON HAS NINE CHILDREN.**

Tanzania
President Samia Suluhu Hassan
Took office: March 19, 2021

Thailand
King Wachiralongkon
Began reign: December 1, 2016

Prime Minister Phaethongthan Chinnawat
Took office: August 18, 2024

> **PHAETHONGTHAN CHINNAWAT IS THAILAND'S YOUNGEST PRIME MINISTER.**

Timor-Leste (East Timor)
President José Ramos-Horta
Took office: May 20, 2022

Prime Minister Kay Rala Xanana Gusmao
Took office: July 1, 2023

Togo
President Faure Gnassingbé
Took office: May 4, 2005

Prime Minister Victoire Tomegah Dogbé
Took office: September 25, 2020

Tonga
King Tupou VI
Began reign: March 18, 2012

Prime Minister Aisake Valu Eke
Took office: December 2024

Trinidad and Tobago
President Christine Kangaloo
Took office: March 20, 2023

Prime Minister Keith Rowley
Took office: September 9, 2015

> **CHRISTINE KANGALOO IS A CANCER SURVIVOR.**

Tunisia
President Kais Saied
Took office: October 23, 2019

Prime Minister Kamel Maddouri
Took office: August 7, 2024

Türkiye (Turkey)
President Recep Tayyip Erdogan
Took office: August 28, 2014

COLOR KEY ● Africa ● Australia, New Zealand, and Oceania

HISTORY HAPPENS

Turkmenistan
President
Serdar Berdimuhamedov
Took office: March 19, 2022

Tuvalu
Governor General
Tofiga Vaevalu Falani
Took office: August 29, 2021

Prime Minister
Feleti Penitala Teo
Took office: February 27, 2024

Uganda
President
Yoweri Kaguta Museveni
Took office: January 26, 1986

Prime Minister
Robinah Nabbanja
Took office: June 14, 2021

Ukraine
President
Volodymyr Zelenskyy
Took office: May 20, 2019

Prime Minister
Denys Shmyhal
Took office: March 4, 2020

United Arab Emirates
President Muhammad bin Zayid Al Nuhayyan
Took office: May 14, 2022

Prime Minister Muhammad bin Rashid Al Maktum
Took office: January 5, 2006

United Kingdom
King Charles III
Began reign: September 8, 2022

Prime Minister
Keir Starmer
Took office: July 5, 2024

United States
President
Donald Trump
Took office: January 20, 2025

DONALD TRUMP IS THE SECOND U.S. PRESIDENT TO SERVE TWO NON-CONSECUTIVE TERMS.

Uruguay
President
Yamandú Orsi Martínez
Took office: March 1, 2025

Uzbekistan
President
Shavkat Mirziyoyev
Took office: December 14, 2016

Prime Minister
Abdulla Aripov
Took office: December 14, 2016

Vanuatu
President
Nikenike Vurobaravu
Took office: July 23, 2022

Prime Minister
Charlot Salwai
Took office: October 6, 2023

KING CHARLES III WROTE A CHILDREN'S BOOK ABOUT AN OLD MAN WHO LIVES IN A CAVE.

Vatican City
Supreme Pontiff
Pope Francis
Took office: March 13, 2013

President
Fernando Vergez Alzaga
Took office: October 1, 2021

Venezuela
President
Nicolas Maduro Moros
Took office: April 19, 2013

Vietnam
President
Luong Cuong
Took office: October 21, 2024

Prime Minister
Pham Minh Chinh
Took office: July 26, 2021

Yemen
Chairperson of Presidential Council
Rashad Muhammad al-Alimi
Took office: April 19, 2022

Zambia
President
Hakainde Hichilema
Took office: August 24, 2021

AS A KID, HAKAINDE HICHILEMA HELPED HIS FAMILY HERD CATTLE ON THEIR FARM.

Zimbabwe
President
Emmerson Dambudzo Mnangagwa
Took office: November 24, 2017

● Asia ● Europe ● North America ● South America

MORE FOR YOU

QUIZ WHIZ

Go back in time to seek the answers to this history quiz!

Write your answers on a piece of paper. Then check them below.

1. **True or false?** King Tut's organs were inside his body when he was mummified.

2. The stone temples of the ancient Maya are found in _____.
   a. Central America
   b. Africa
   c. Russia
   d. Canada

3. **True or false?** No one knows for sure who made the Great Sphinx of Giza.

4. About how much does each of the moai of Easter Island weigh?
   a. 100 tons (90 t)
   b. 26,000 pounds (11,800 kg)
   c. 1 ton (0.9 t)
   d. 5,000 pounds (2,300 kg)

5. Ching Shih was in charge of more _____ than anyone else in history.
   a. armies
   b. middle schools
   c. pirate ships
   d. construction sites

Not **STUMPED** yet? Check out the *NATIONAL GEOGRAPHIC KIDS QUIZ WHIZ* collection for more fun **HISTORY** questions!

ANSWERS: 1. False; 2. a; 3. True; 4. b; 5. c

HISTORY HAPPENS

HOMEWORK HELP

Brilliant Biographies

A biography is the story of a person's life. It can be a brief summary or a long book. Biographers—those who write biographies—use many different sources to learn about their subjects. You can write your own biography of a famous person you find inspiring.

How to Get Started

Choose a subject you find interesting. If you think Cleopatra is cool, you have a good chance of getting your readers interested, too. If you're bored by ancient Egypt, your readers will be snoring after your first paragraph.

Your subject can be almost anyone: an author, an inventor, a celebrity, a politician, or a member of your family. To find someone to write about, ask yourself these simple questions:
1. Who do I want to know more about?
2. What did this person do that was special?
3. How did this person change the world?

Do Your Research

- Find out as much about your subject as possible. Read books, news articles, and encyclopedia entries. Watch video clips and movies. Conduct interviews, if possible.
- Take notes, writing down important facts and interesting stories about your subject.

Write the Biography

- Come up with a title. Include the person's name.
- Write an introduction. Consider asking a probing question about your subject.
- Include information about the person's childhood. When was this person born? Where did they grow up? Whom did they admire?
- Highlight the person's talents, accomplishments, and personal attributes.
- Describe the specific events that helped to shape this person's life. Did this person ever have a problem and overcome it?
- Write a conclusion. Include your thoughts about why it is important to learn about this person.
- Once you have finished your first draft, revise and then proofread your work.

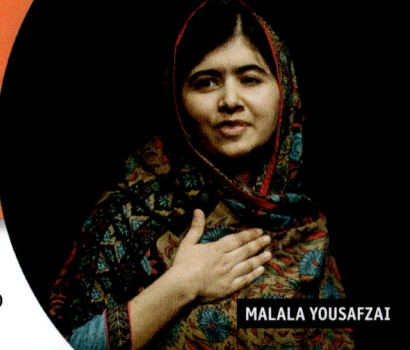

MALALA YOUSAFZAI

Here's a **SAMPLE BIOGRAPHY** of Malala Yousafzai, a human rights advocate and the youngest ever recipient of the Nobel Peace Prize. Of course, there is so much more for you to discover and write about on your own!

Malala Yousafzai

Malala Yousafzai was born in Pakistan on July 12, 1997. Malala's father, Ziauddin, a teacher, made it a priority for his daughter to receive a proper education. Malala loved school. She learned to speak three languages and even wrote a blog about her experiences as a student.

Around the time Malala turned 10, the Taliban—a group of strict Muslims who support terrorism and believe women should stay at home—took over the region where she lived. The Taliban did not approve of Malala's outspoken love of learning. One day, on her way home from school, Malala was shot in the head by a Taliban gunman. Very badly injured, she was sent to a hospital in England.

Not only did Malala survive the shooting—she thrived. She used her experience as a platform to fight for girls' education worldwide. She began speaking out about educational opportunities for all. Her efforts gained worldwide attention, and she was eventually awarded the Nobel Peace Prize in 2014 at the age of 17. She is the youngest person to earn the prestigious prize.

Each year on July 12, World Malala Day honors her heroic efforts to bring attention to human rights issues.

Bird's-eye view of the Amazon rainforest in Brazil

GEOGRAPHY ROCKS

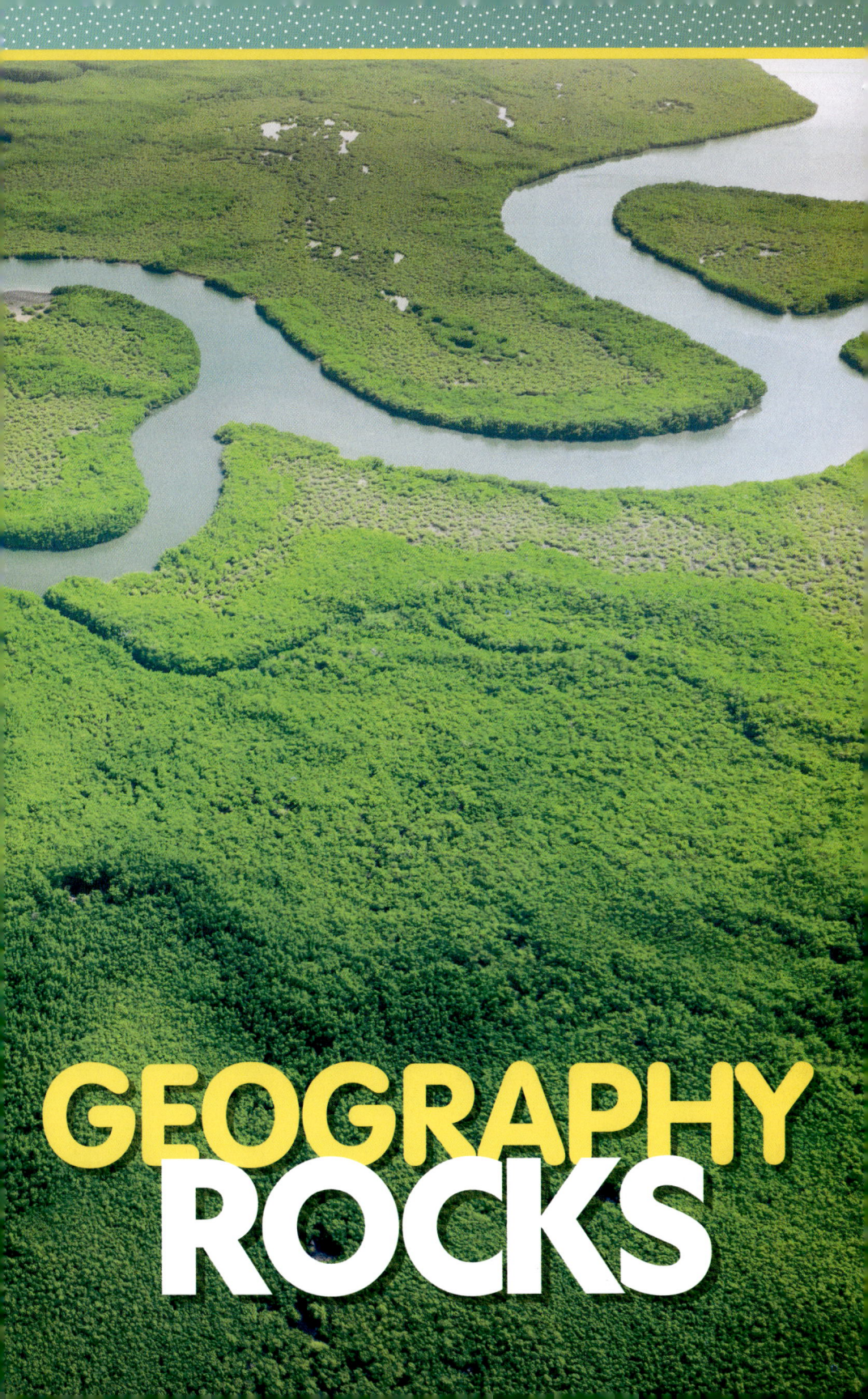

THE POLITICAL WORLD

Earth's land area is made up of seven continents, but people have divided much of the land into smaller political units called countries. Antarctica is used for scientific research. Australia is a continent made up of a single country, but the other five continents include almost 200 independent countries. The political map shown here depicts boundaries—imaginary lines created by treaties—that separate countries. Some boundaries, such as the one between the United States and Canada, are very stable and have been recognized for many years.

GEOGRAPHY ROCKS

Other boundaries, such as the one between Sudan and South Sudan in northeast Africa, are relatively new and still disputed. Countries come in all shapes and sizes. Russia and Canada are giants; others, such as El Salvador and Qatar, are small. Some countries are long and skinny—look at Chile in South America! Still other countries—such as Indonesia and Japan in Asia—are made up of groups of islands. The political map is a clue to the diversity that makes Earth so fascinating.

MAPS

THE PHYSICAL WORLD

Earth is dominated by large landmasses called continents—seven in all—and by an interconnected global ocean that is divided into five parts by the continents. More than 70 percent of Earth's surface is covered by oceans, and the rest is made up of land areas.

Different landforms give variety to the surface of the continents. The Rocky Mountains divide North America, the Andes mark the western edge of South America, and the Himalaya tower above South Asia. The Plateau of Tibet forms the rugged core of Asia,

272

GEOGRAPHY ROCKS

while the Northern European Plain extends from the North Sea to the Ural Mountains. Much of Africa is a plateau, and dry plains cover large areas of Australia. Mountains rise more than 16,000 feet (4,877 m) above Antarctica's massive ice sheets. Mountains and trenches make the ocean floors as varied as any continent. A mountain chain called the Mid-Atlantic Ridge runs the length of the Atlantic Ocean. In the western Pacific, trenches drop deep into the ocean floor.

MAPS

KINDS OF MAPS

Maps are special tools that geographers use to tell a story about Earth. Maps can be used to show just about anything related to places. Some maps show physical features, such as mountains or vegetation. Maps can also show climates or natural hazards and other things we cannot easily see. Other maps illustrate different features on Earth—political boundaries, urban centers, and economic systems.

AN IMPERFECT TOOL

Maps are not perfect. A globe is a scale model of Earth with accurate relative sizes and locations. Because maps are flat, they involve distortions of size, shape, and direction. Also, cartographers—people who create maps—make choices about what information to include. Because of this, it is important to study many different types of maps to learn the complete story of Earth. Three commonly found kinds of maps are shown on this page.

PHYSICAL MAPS Earth's natural features—landforms, water bodies, and vegetation—are shown on physical maps. The map above uses color and shading to illustrate mountains, lakes, rivers, and deserts of central South America. Country names and borders are added for reference, but they are not natural features.

POLITICAL MAPS These maps represent characteristics of the landscape created by humans, such as boundaries, cities, and place-names. Natural features are added only for reference. On the map above, capital cities are represented with a star inside a circle, while other cities are shown with black dots.

THEMATIC MAPS Patterns related to a particular topic or theme, such as population distribution, appear on these maps. The map above displays the region's climate zones, which range from tropical wet (bright green) to tropical wet and dry (light green) to semiarid (dark yellow) to arid or desert (light yellow).

GEOGRAPHY ROCKS

MAKING MAPS

Meet a Cartographer!

As a National Geographic cartographer, **Mike McNey** works with maps every day. Here, he shares more about his cool career.

National Geographic staff cartographers Mike McNey (left) and Michael Horner review a map of Africa for the *National Geographic Kids World Atlas*.

What exactly does a cartographer do?
I create maps specifically for books and atlases to help the text tell the story on the page. The maps need to fit into the size and the style of the book, with the final goal being that it's all accurate and appealing for the reader.

What kinds of stories have you told with your maps?
Once, I created a map that showed the spread of the Burmese python population in Florida, U.S.A., around the Everglades National Park. I've also made maps that show data like farmland, food production, cattle density, and fish catch in a particular location, like the United States.

How do you rely on technology in your job?
All aspects of mapmaking are on the computer. This makes it much quicker to make a map. It also makes it easier to change anything on a map. If you want to change the color of the rivers on a map, you just click the mouse.

How do you create your maps?
I work with geographic information systems (GIS), a computer software that allows us to represent any data on a specific location of the world, or even the entire world. Data can be anything, including endangered species, animal ranges, or population of a particular place. We also use remote systems, like satellites and aerial imagery, to analyze Earth's surface.

Satellites in orbit around Earth act as eyes in the sky, recording data about the planet's land and ocean areas. The data are converted to numbers transmitted back to computers specially programmed to interpret the data. They record the information in a form that cartographers can use to create maps.

What will maps of the future look like?
In the future, you'll see more and more data on maps. I also think more online maps are going to be made in a way that you can switch from a world view to a local view to see data at any scale.

What's the best part of your job?
I love the combination of science and design involved in it. It's also fun to make maps interesting for kids.

275

GEOGRAPHIC FEATURES

UNDERSTANDING MAPS

MAKING A PROJECTION
Globes present a model of Earth as it is—a sphere—but they are bulky and can be difficult to use and store. Flat maps are much more convenient, but certain problems can result from transferring Earth's curved surface to a flat piece of paper, a process called projection. Imagine a globe that has been cut in half, like the one to the right. If a light is shined into it, the lines of latitude and longitude and the shapes of the continent will cast shadows that can be "projected" onto a piece of paper, as shown here. Depending on how the paper is positioned, the shadows will be distorted in different ways.

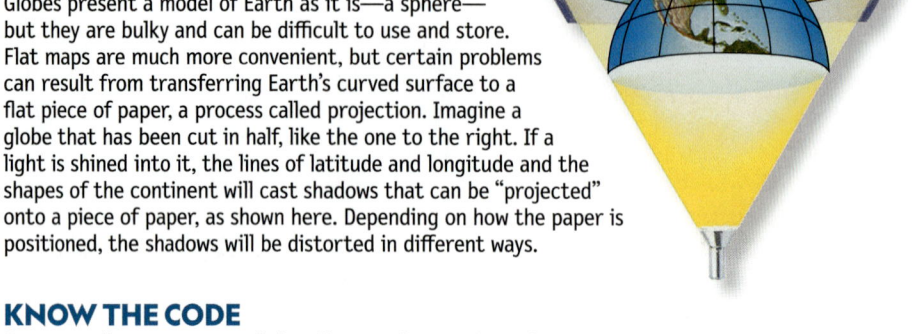

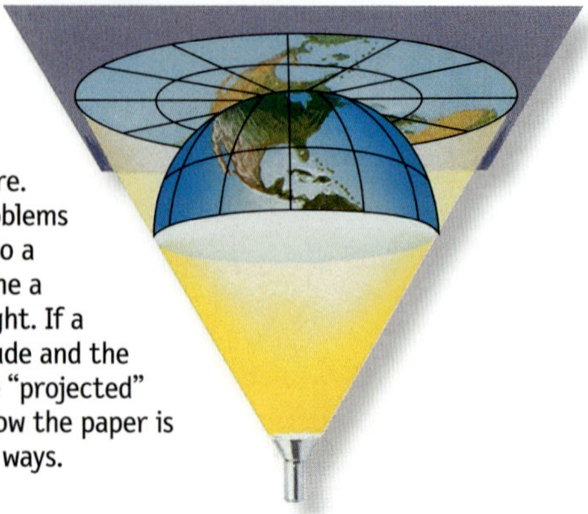

KNOW THE CODE
Every map has a story to tell, but first you have to know how to read one. Maps represent information by using a language of symbols. When you know how to read these symbols, you can access a wide range of information. For example, look at the scale and compass rose or arrow to understand distance and direction (see box below).

To find out what each symbol on a map means, you must use the key. It's your secret decoder—identifying information by each symbol on the map.

There are three main types of map symbols: points, lines, and areas. Points, which can be either dots or small icons, represent the location or the number of things, such as schools, cities, or landmarks. Lines are used to show boundaries, roads, or rivers and can vary in color or thickness. Area symbols use pattern or color to show regions, such as a sandy area or a neighborhood.

SCALE AND DIRECTION

The scale on a map can be shown as a fraction, as words, or as a line or bar. It relates distance on the map to distance in the real world. Sometimes the scale identifies the type of map projection. Maps may include an arrow to indicate north on the map or a compass rose to show all principal directions.

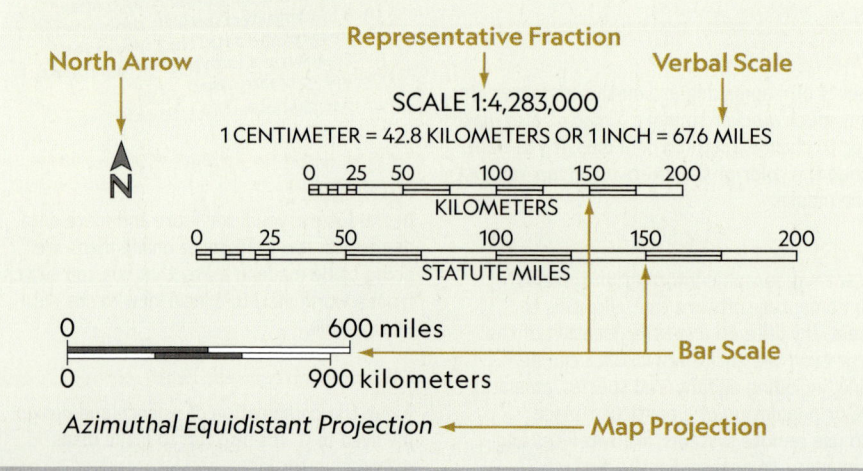

North Arrow — Representative Fraction — Verbal Scale

SCALE 1:4,283,000
1 CENTIMETER = 42.8 KILOMETERS OR 1 INCH = 67.6 MILES

0 25 50   100   150   200
KILOMETERS

0   25   50   100   150   200
STATUTE MILES

0   600 miles
0   900 kilometers

Bar Scale

Azimuthal Equidistant Projection ← Map Projection

GEOGRAPHY ROCKS

GEOGRAPHIC FEATURES

From roaring rivers to parched deserts, from underwater canyons to jagged mountains, Earth is covered with beautiful and diverse environments. Here are examples of the most common types of geographic features found around the world.

WATERFALL
Waterfalls form when rivers reach an abrupt change in elevation. At left, the Iguazú waterfall system—on the border of Brazil and Argentina—is made up of 275 falls.

VALLEY
Valleys, cut by running water or moving ice, may be broad and flat or narrow and steep, such as the Indus River Valley (above) in Ladakh, India.

RIVER
As a river moves through flatlands, it twists and turns. Above, the Rio Los Amigos winds through a rainforest in Peru.

MOUNTAIN
Mountains are Earth's tallest landforms, and Mount Everest (above) rises highest of all, at 29,031.69 feet (8,848.86 m) above sea level.

GLACIER
Glaciers—"rivers" of ice—such as Hubbard Glacier (above) in Alaska, U.S.A., move slowly from mountains to the sea. Global warming is shrinking them.

CANYON
Steep-sided valleys called canyons are created mainly by running water. Buckskin Gulch (above) in Utah, U.S.A., is the deepest "slot" canyon in the American Southwest.

DESERT
Deserts are land features created by climate, specifically by a lack of water. Here, a camel caravan crosses the Sahara in North Africa.

CONTINENTS

AFRICA

Snow sometimes falls on parts of the Sahara.

Part of the canine family, black-backed jackal pups are usually born from August to October.

Black-backed jackal pups

GEOGRAPHY ROCKS

The massive continent of Africa, where humankind began millions of years ago, is second only to Asia in size. Stretching nearly as far from west to east as it does from north to south, Africa is home to both one of the longest rivers in the world (the Nile) and the largest hot desert on Earth (the Sahara).

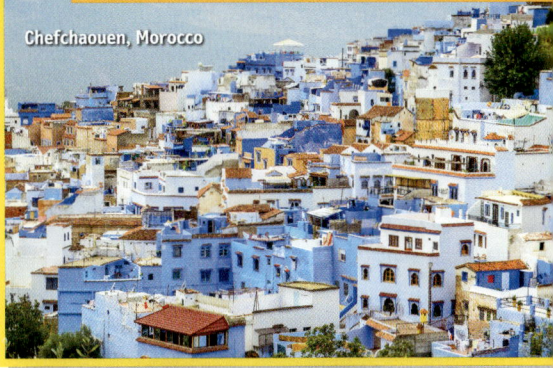

Chefchaouen, Morocco

SATANIC LEAF-TAILED GECKO

This small tree lizard from Madagascar is a master of camouflage. It's not just its tail that looks like an old, dead leaf—so does every other part of its body! Its disguise helps it to hide from predators and creep up on prey without being seen. Why is it called "satanic"? Its bright red eyes and two little horns give it a devilish look.

TWIN TOWN

In most places, twins are unusual, but in Igbo-Ora, Nigeria, they're everywhere! This small town has the highest rate of twin births in the world: At least one person in 10 is a twin. Plus, it's traditional to name twins Taiwo and Kehinde, meaning "first-born" and "second-born"—so a lot of Igbo-Ora's twins have the same names!

Great Pyramid, Great Numbers
How do the numbers for Earth's biggest pyramid stack up?

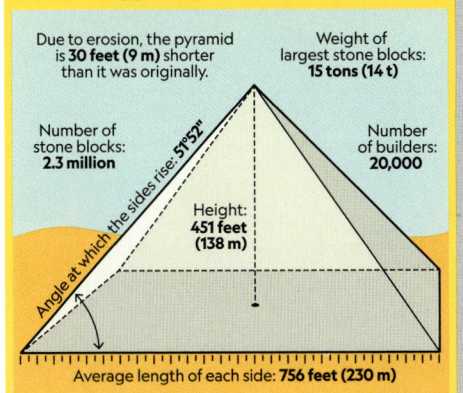

Due to erosion, the pyramid is **30 feet (9 m)** shorter than it was originally.

Weight of largest stone blocks: **15 tons (14 t)**

Number of stone blocks: **2.3 million**

Number of builders: **20,000**

Angle at which the sides rise: **51°52'**

Height: **451 feet (138 m)**

Average length of each side: **756 feet (230 m)**

REMARKABLE RIVER

Africa is home to one of the longest rivers in the world: the Nile. Flowing south to north along some 4,100 miles (6,600 km), the Nile runs through or along the border of 11 African countries. Throughout history, the Nile has been a key source of fresh water and food for both people and the animals that live nearby, including hippos, turtles, and crocodiles.

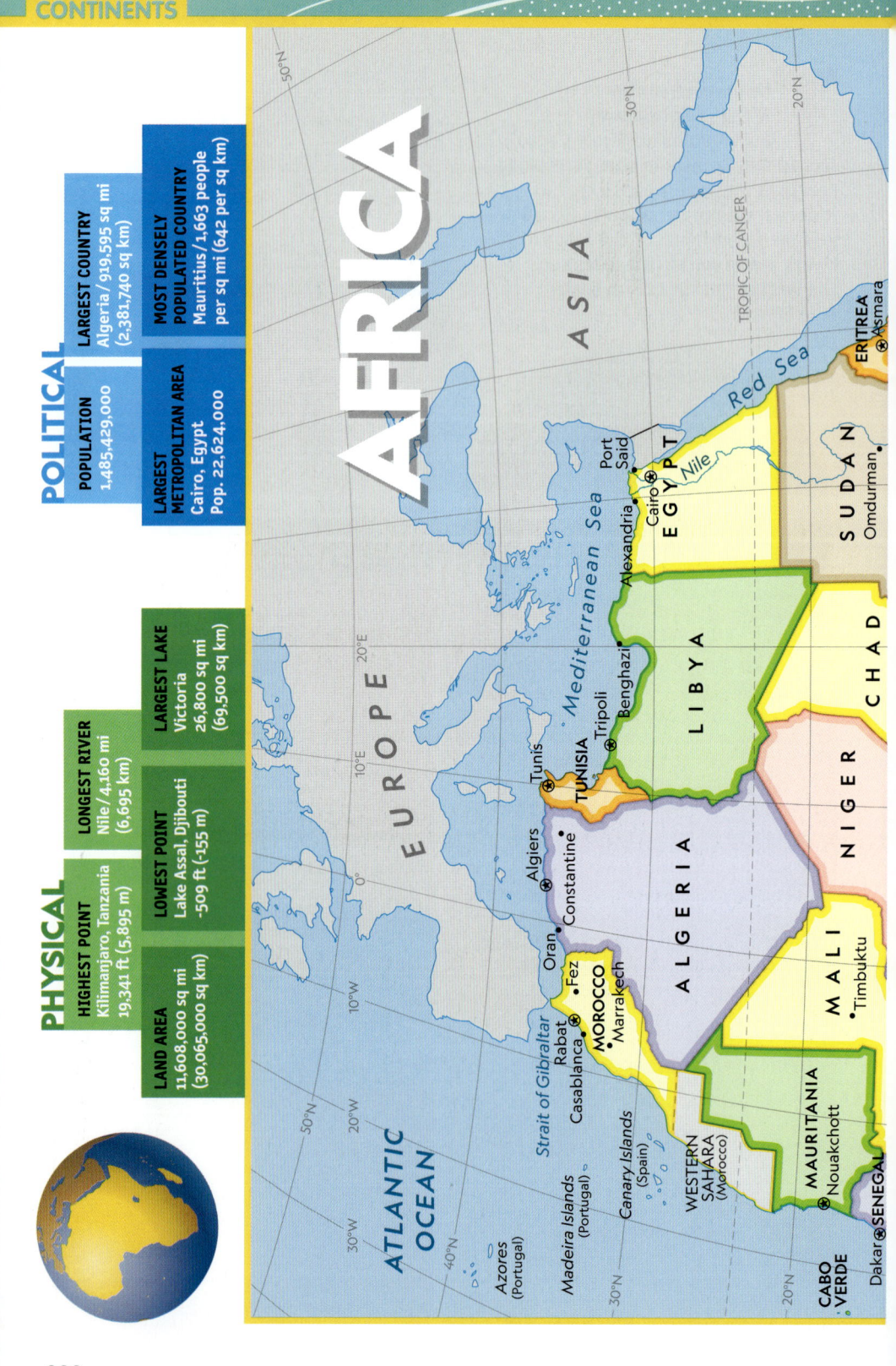

CONTINENTS

PHYSICAL

LAND AREA
11,608,000 sq mi
(30,065,000 sq km)

HIGHEST POINT
Kilimanjaro, Tanzania
19,341 ft (5,895 m)

LOWEST POINT
Lake Assal, Djibouti
-509 ft (-155 m)

LONGEST RIVER
Nile / 4,160 mi
(6,695 km)

LARGEST LAKE
Victoria
26,800 sq mi
(69,500 sq km)

POLITICAL

POPULATION
1,485,429,000

LARGEST METROPOLITAN AREA
Cairo, Egypt
Pop. 22,624,000

LARGEST COUNTRY
Algeria / 919,595 sq mi
(2,381,740 sq km)

MOST DENSELY POPULATED COUNTRY
Mauritius / 1,663 people per sq mi (642 per sq km)

AFRICA

280

GEOGRAPHY ROCKS

281

CONTINENTS

ANTARCTICA

Most of the meteorites found on Earth are in Antarctica.

Penguins can adjust blood flow to their feet to keep them from freezing on the ice.

Gentoo penguin

282

GEOGRAPHY ROCKS

This frozen continent may be a cool place to visit, but unless you're a penguin, you probably wouldn't want to hang out in Antarctica for long. The fact that it's the coldest, windiest, and driest continent helps explain why humans never colonized this ice-covered land surrounding the South Pole.

Leopard seal

SINGING ICE SHELF

Humans can't hear the eerie, low humming sound the ice shelf makes, but seismometers can. The hum is caused by wind blowing over the surface of the ice. The sound changes slightly depending on the weather conditions. Scientists can track the ice's singing to monitor whether it's in danger of cracking or collapsing.

PENGUIN PATROL

Call it a not-so-stealthy spy mission: In an effort to learn how climate change is impacting animals that live in the Antarctic region, scientists sent a battery-powered rover to follow penguins. The slow-moving robot records photos, video, and other types of data to get an up-close-and-personal look into penguin colonies.

Annual Average Snowfall

- 17 feet (5 m) — Sapporo, Japan
- 8 feet (2 m) — Buffalo, New York, U.S.A.
- 0.7 foot (0.2 m) — South Pole, Antarctica

GIANT JELLYFISH

Giant phantom jellyfish were recently spotted by cruise-goers off the coast of Antarctica. With ribbonlike bodies stretching 30 feet (9 m) and umbrellalike heads, the super-rare swimmers are now considered some of the largest invertebrate predators in the sea.

283

CONTINENTS

PHYSICAL

LAND AREA
5,100,000 sq mi
(13,209,000 sq km)

HIGHEST POINT
Vinson Massif
16,067 ft (4,897 m)

LOWEST POINT
Byrd Glacier
-9,416 ft (-2,870 m)

COLDEST PLACE
Ridge A, annual average temperature
-94°F (-70°C)

AVERAGE PRECIPITATION ON THE POLAR PLATEAU
Less than 2 in (5 cm)

POLITICAL

POPULATION
There are no Indigenous inhabitants, but there are both permanent and summer-only staffed research stations.

NUMBER OF INDEPENDENT COUNTRIES 0

NUMBER OF COUNTRIES CLAIMING LAND 7

NUMBER OF COUNTRIES OPERATING YEAR-ROUND RESEARCH STATIONS 20

NUMBER OF YEAR-ROUND RESEARCH STATIONS 40

Map Key
- ▲ Highest point (above sea level)
- ▼ Lowest point (below sea level)
- + Other mountain peak

ATLANTIC OCEAN · South Orkney Islands · **SOUTHERN OCEAN** · South Shetland Islands · Antarctic Peninsula · Graham Land · LARSEN ICE SHELF · Weddell Sea · Mount Jackson 10,446 ft (3,184 m) · Palmer Land · Coats · FILCHNER ICE SHELF · Alexander Island · RONNE ICE SHELF · Berkner Island · Bellingshausen Sea · ELLSWORTH LAND · Vinson Massif ▲ 16,067 ft (4,897 m) · ELLSWORTH MTS. · West Antarctica · SOUTHERN OCEAN · Amundsen Sea · MARIE BYRD LAND

Who owns Antarctica?
No one. Seven countries each claim a piece of this frozen continent.

ATLANTIC OCEAN · SOUTH AMERICA · ARGENTINE CLAIM · BRITISH CLAIM · CHILEAN CLAIM · NORWEGIAN CLAIM · AUSTRALIAN CLAIM · INDIAN OCEAN · SOUTHERN OCEAN · PACIFIC OCEAN · NEW ZEALAND CLAIM · FRENCH CLAIM · AUSTRALIAN CLAIM

0 600 Miles
0 600 Kilometers

GEOGRAPHY ROCKS

ANTARCTICA

FIMBUL ICE SHELF

RIISER-LARSEN ICE SHELF

Land

QUEEN MAUD LAND

ENDERBY LAND

SOUTHERN OCEAN

Valkyrie Dome

Lambert Glacier

MacKenzie Bay

AMERY ICE SHELF

AMERICAN HIGHLAND

WEST ICE SHELF

Ridge A

POLAR PLATEAU

East Antarctica

★ South Pole

TRANSANTARCTIC MOUNTAINS

SHACKLETON ICE SHELF

ROSS ICE SHELF

Roosevelt Island

Taylor Glacier

Byrd Glacier -9,416 ft (-2,870 m)

Ross Island

Mount Erebus 12,448 ft (3,794 m)

Ross Sea

VICTORIA LAND

Talos Dome

WILKES LAND

SOUTHERN OCEAN

INDIAN OCEAN

0   600 Miles
0   600 Kilometers
Azimuthal Equidistant Projection

285

CONTINENTS
ASIA

The colors on Tibetan prayer flags (like the ones top right) represent different elements, such as air, fire, earth, and water.

An annual marathon is run along part of the Great Wall of China.

Runners scale the heights in the Great Wall of China Marathon.

286

GEOGRAPHY ROCKS

Made up of 46 countries, Asia is the world's largest continent. Just how big is it? From western Türkiye (Turkey) to the eastern tip of Russia, Asia spans nearly half the globe! Home to more than four billion citizens—that's three out of five people on the planet—Asia's population is bigger than that of all the other continents combined.

The Boudhanath Temple in Kathmandu, Nepal

DANXIA LANDFORMS

Multicolored mountains? In China's Zhangye National Geopark, you can wander the boardwalks and viewing platforms to take in the awesome Rainbow Mountains, boasting all shades of red, blue, yellow, and orange. How did these mountains get their stripes? The shape and vivid colors of these landforms are a result of weathering, as well as tectonic plates shifting over millions of years. Over millennia, the sandstone and minerals have eroded to create a landscape that's out of this world.

SAVING THE GIBBONS

Javan gibbons, only found in Java, Indonesia, are extremely endangered due to threats like habitat loss and hunting. But conservation groups are working hard to change that fact. Efforts like rehabilitating captive-born gibbons and releasing them into protected areas are aimed at repopulating the primates.

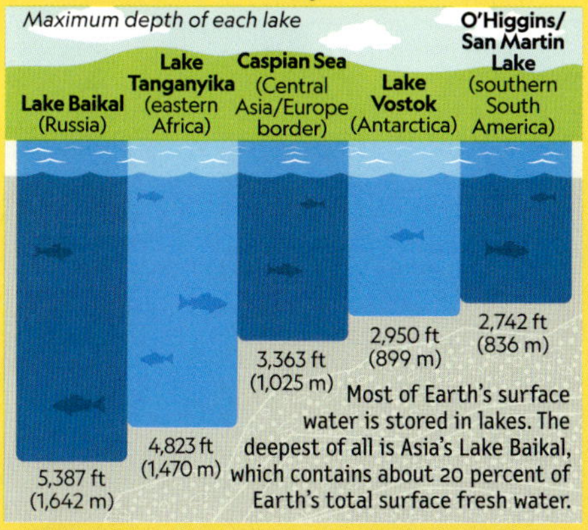

JUNGLE TEMPLE

The 900-year-old temple known as Angkor Wat sits in the jungle of northern Cambodia. Covering more than 400 acres (162 ha), the massive religious structure was built inside the capital of the Khmer Empire, a once powerful civilization in Southeast Asia. Today, the site receives millions of visitors a year.

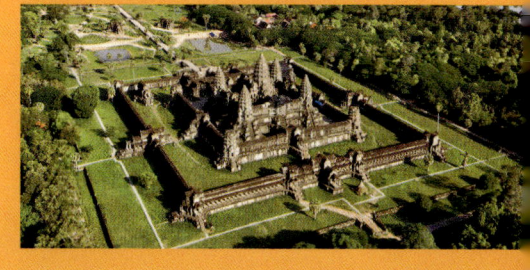

World's Deepest Lakes

Maximum depth of each lake

- **Lake Baikal** (Russia): 5,387 ft (1,642 m)
- **Lake Tanganyika** (eastern Africa): 4,823 ft (1,470 m)
- **Caspian Sea** (Central Asia/Europe border): 3,363 ft (1,025 m)
- **Lake Vostok** (Antarctica): 2,950 ft (899 m)
- **O'Higgins/San Martin Lake** (southern South America): 2,742 ft (836 m)

Most of Earth's surface water is stored in lakes. The deepest of all is Asia's Lake Baikal, which contains about 20 percent of Earth's total surface fresh water.

287

CONTINENTS

PHYSICAL

LAND AREA
17,208,000 sq mi
(44,570,000 sq km)

HIGHEST POINT
Mount Everest,
China–Nepal
29,032 ft (8,849 m)

LOWEST POINT
Dead Sea,
Israel–Jordan
-1,424 ft (-434 m)

LONGEST RIVER
Yangtze, China
3,880 mi (6,244 km)

LARGEST LAKE ENTIRELY IN ASIA
Lake Baikal, Russia
12,200 sq mi
(31,500 sq km)

POLITICAL

POPULATION
4,735,070,000

LARGEST METROPOLITAN AREA
Tokyo, Japan
Pop. 37,115,000

LARGEST COUNTRY ENTIRELY IN ASIA
China
3,705,405 sq mi
(9,596,960 sq km)

MOST DENSELY POPULATED COUNTRY
Singapore
21,685 people per sq mi
(8,385 per sq km)

Europe-Asia Boundary
A commonly accepted division between Asia and Europe — marked here by a maroon dashed line — is formed by the Ural Mountains, Ural River, Caspian Sea, Caucasus Mountains and the Black Sea with its outlets to the Bosporus and Dardanelles.

288

GEOGRAPHY ROCKS

ASIA

Map Key
- ⊛ National capital
- ○ Other capital
- • Other city
- ▲ Highest point (above sea level)
- ▼ Lowest point (below sea level)

CONTINENTS

AUSTRALIA,
NEW ZEALAND, AND OCEANIA

A baby koala catches a ride on its mom's back.

A baby koala, called a joey, stays in Mom's pouch for its first six months of life.

Papua New Guinea is home to the world's third largest tropical rainforest, behind the Amazon and the Congo Basin.

GEOGRAPHY ROCKS

G'day, mate! This vast region, about 3.3 million square miles (8.5 million sq km) in area, includes Australia—the world's smallest and flattest continent—and New Zealand, as well as a fleet of mostly tiny islands scattered across the Pacific Ocean. Also known as "down under," most of the countries in this region are in the Southern Hemisphere, below the Equator.

Indigenous dancers in Queensland, Australia

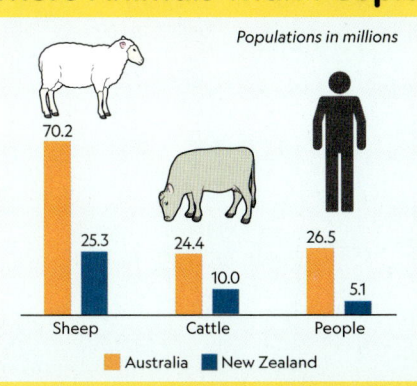

RAINBOW EUCALYPTUS

It might look like someone has been busy with a paintbrush, but these multicolored trees are absolutely natural! This species of eucalyptus thrives in wet, tropical environments in Papua New Guinea as well as Indonesia and the Philippines. The orange-tinted bark sheds in strips, revealing a bright green layer. Over time, the bark matures and the green changes to red, then orange, purple, and finally brown. And because the bark is shed at different times, one tree can display all these colors at once.

SHIPWRECK CENTRAL

Some 1,600 shipwrecks litter the coastline of Western Australia, and the area is nicknamed "Treasure Coast" for the gold, diamonds, and other booty left behind. Massive tides, extreme winds, and hidden coral reefs make these waters some of the most treacherous for boats to cross.

CHRISTMAS ISLAND CRAB

These bright red land crabs are found only in this small Australian territory. Once a year, they leave their cooler homes in the forest and begin a mammoth trek to the coast. Because their larvae can survive only in water during their first weeks of life, these crimson crawlers must travel to the ocean to breed. For up to 18 days, they swarm the island. The human residents do their best to assist—building tunnels and crab crossings to help them navigate dangerous roads.

More Animals Than People

Populations in millions

	Australia	New Zealand
Sheep	70.2	25.3
Cattle	24.4	10.0
People	26.5	5.1

291

CONTINENTS

PHYSICAL

LAND AREA
3,306,000 sq mi
(8,563,000 sq km)

HIGHEST POINT*
Mount Wilhelm,
Papua New Guinea
14,793 ft (4,509 m)
*Includes Oceania

LOWEST POINT
Lake Eyre, Australia
-49 ft (-15 m)

LONGEST RIVER
Murray, Australia
1,558 mi (2,508 km)

LARGEST LAKE
Lake Eyre, Australia
3,741 sq mi
(9,690 sq km)

POLITICAL

POPULATION
45,530,000

LARGEST METROPOLITAN AREA
Melbourne, Australia
Pop. 5,316,000

LARGEST COUNTRY
Australia
2,988,901 sq mi
(7,741,220 sq km)

MOST DENSELY POPULATED COUNTRY
Nauru
1,237 people per sq mi
(471 per sq km)

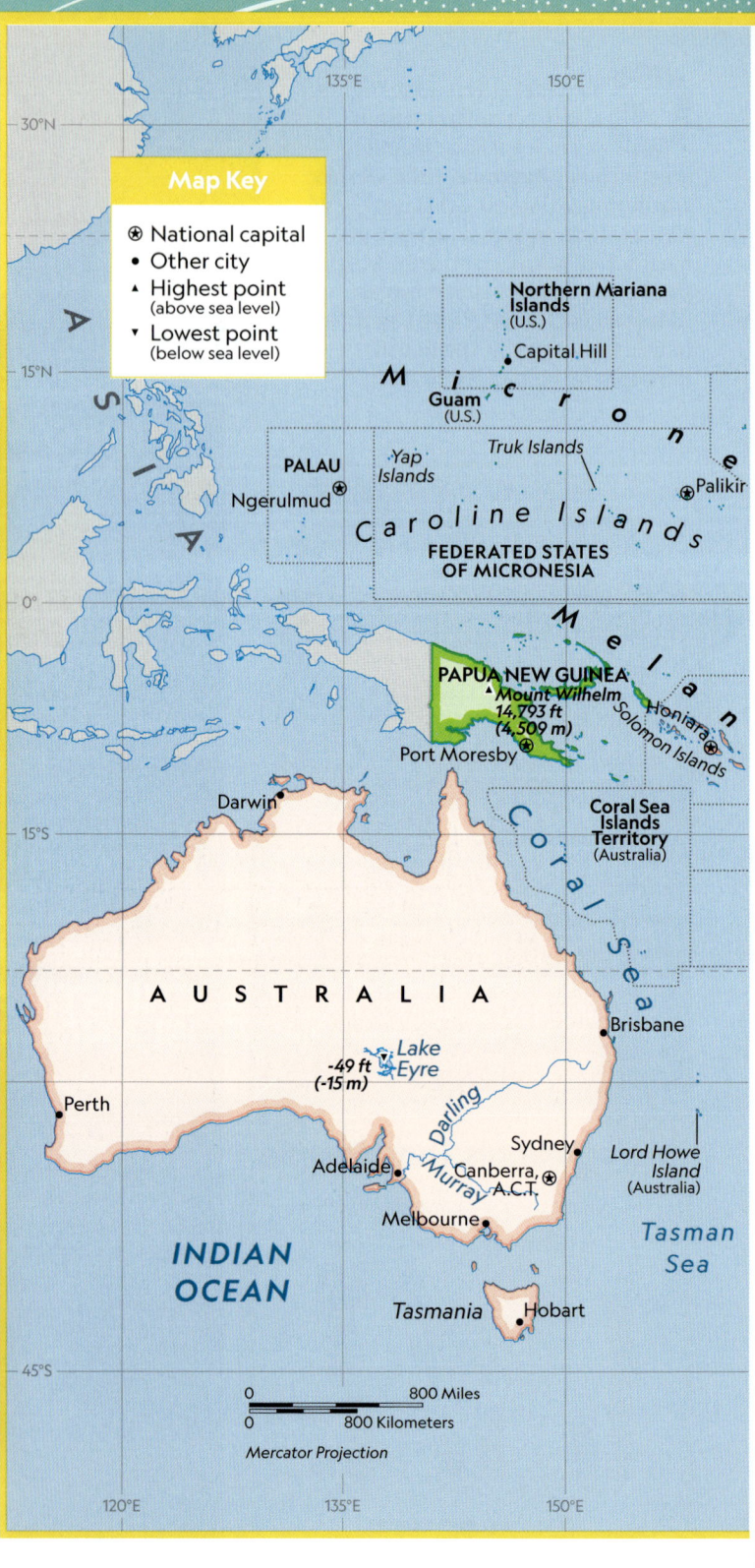

Map Key
- ⊛ National capital
- • Other city
- ▲ Highest point (above sea level)
- ▼ Lowest point (below sea level)

292

GEOGRAPHY ROCKS

AUSTRALIA, NEW ZEALAND, AND OCEANIA

NORTH PACIFIC OCEAN

- Midway Is. (U.S.)
- TROPIC OF CANCER
- Honolulu
- Hawai'i • Hilo
- Wake Island (U.S.)
- Johnston Atoll (U.S.)
- Monday / Sunday — Date Line
- Bikini Atoll
- **MARSHALL ISLANDS**
- Ratak Chain
- Ralik Chain
- Majuro
- Kingman Reef (U.S.)
- Palmyra Atoll (U.S.)
- Howland Island (U.S.)
- Baker Island (U.S.)
- Kiritimati
- Tarawa
- Gilbert Islands
- Yaren
- **NAURU**
- Jarvis I. (U.S.)
- EQUATOR
- Phoenix Is.
- **KIRIBATI**
- Line Islands
- **SOLOMON ISLANDS**
- Santa Cruz Islands
- **TUVALU** Funafuti
- Tokelau (N.Z.)
- Marquesas Islands
- Wallis and Futuna (France)
- **SAMOA** Apia
- American Samoa (U.S.)
- Pago Pago
- Cook Islands (N.Z.)
- Society Is.
- Papeete
- Tuamotu Archipelago
- Port-Vila **VANUATU**
- Suva **FIJI**
- **TONGA**
- Niue (N.Z.)
- Avarua
- **French Polynesia** (France)
- Nuku'alofa
- Austral Is.
- TROPIC OF CAPRICORN
- **New Caledonia** (France)
- Nouméa
- Norfolk Island (Australia)
- to Easter Island (Chile) →
- Kermadec Islands (N.Z.)
- Pitcairn Island (U.K.)

SOUTH PACIFIC OCEAN

- Auckland
- **NEW ZEALAND**
- Wellington
- Christchurch
- Chatham Island (N.Z.)
- Date Line

293

CONTINENTS

EUROPE

European pine marten

Europe is home to the world's smallest country, Vatican City, inside Rome, Italy.

Pine martens, a type of weasel, make nests in hollow trees.

294

GEOGRAPHY ROCKS

A cluster of peninsulas and islands jutting west from Asia, Europe is bordered by the Atlantic and Arctic Oceans and more than a dozen seas. Here you'll find a variety of scenery, from mountains to countryside to coastlines. Europe is also known for its rich cultures and fascinating history, which make it one of the most visited continents on Earth.

A traditional dance performed in Greece

FINGAL'S CAVE

The translation of this cave's original Gaelic name is the "Cave of Melody." The echoes of waves inside the huge, arched hollow inspired 19th-century composer Felix Mendelssohn to write "Fingal's Cave Overture." Writers, poets, and artists have also visited the cave to be inspired.

SEALED UP

Every fall, hundreds of gray seal pups are born on England's Farne Islands. For more than 70 years, rangers have been counting the seals in the colony. Nowadays, new pups are recorded in part using drone technology, which helps count and track the population.

NORTHERN LIGHTS

Who needs fireworks when you can watch the northern lights? This spectacular nighttime display can be seen in Canada, Greenland, Sweden, and numerous other locations in the Northern Hemisphere. Tromsø, Norway, has perfect viewing conditions—long, dark nights between September and March and little light pollution. Also called the aurora borealis, the spectacular colors are created when tiny particles called electrons come from the sun and mix with gases in Earth's atmosphere, making them glow.

Europe's Longest Rivers

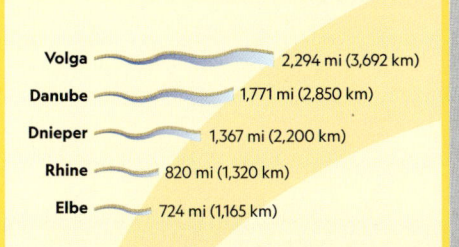

Volga	2,294 mi (3,692 km)
Danube	1,771 mi (2,850 km)
Dnieper	1,367 mi (2,200 km)
Rhine	820 mi (1,320 km)
Elbe	724 mi (1,165 km)

CONTINENTS

PHYSICAL

LAND AREA
3,841,000 sq mi
(9,947,000 sq km)

HIGHEST POINT
El'brus, Russia
18,510 ft (5,642 m)

LOWEST POINT
Caspian Sea
-92 ft (-28 m)

LONGEST RIVER
Volga, Russia
2,294 mi
(3,692 km)

LARGEST LAKE ENTIRELY IN EUROPE
Ladoga, Russia
6,800 sq mi
(17,700 sq km)

POLITICAL

POPULATION
743,424,000

LARGEST METROPOLITAN AREA
Moscow, Russia
Pop. 12,712,000

LARGEST COUNTRY ENTIRELY IN EUROPE
France
248,573 sq mi
(643,801 sq km)

MOST DENSELY POPULATED COUNTRY
Monaco
31,813 people per sq mi
(15,907 per sq km)

Map Key
- ⊛ National capital
- ⊛ Capital of Northern Ireland, Scotland, or Wales
- ○ Other capital
- · Other city
- ☐ Small country
- ▲ Highest point (above sea level)
- ▼ Lowest point (below sea level)

400 Miles
400 Kilometers
Azimuthal Equidistant Projection

296

GEOGRAPHY ROCKS

Europe-Asia Boundary
A commonly accepted division between Asia and Europe — marked here by a maroon dashed line — is formed by the Ural Mountains, Ural River, Caspian Sea, Caucasus Mountains and the Black Sea with its outlets to the Bosporus and Dardanelles.

EUROPE

CONTINENTS

NORTH AMERICA

There are 160 active volcanoes in the United States.

In mariachi bands, there are no lead singers.

Two people dance at a mariachi festival in Guadalajara, Mexico.

298

GEOGRAPHY ROCKS

From the Great Plains of Canada and the United States to the rainforests of Panama, North America stretches 5,500 miles (8,850 km) from north to south. The third largest continent, North America can be divided into five regions: the mountainous west (including parts of Mexico and Central America's western coast), the Great Plains, the Canadian Shield, the varied eastern region (including Central America's lowlands and coastal plains), and the Caribbean.

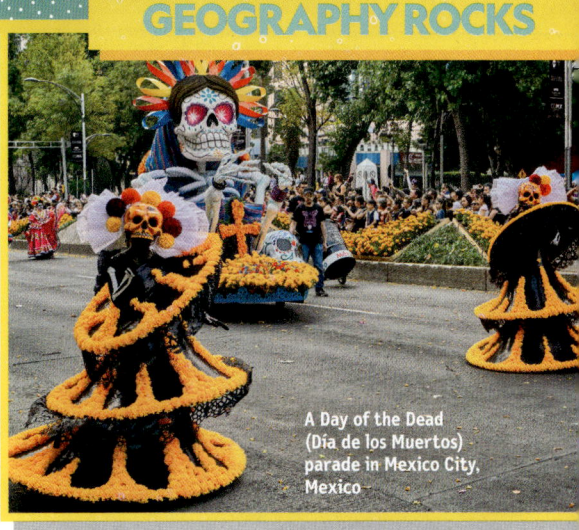

A Day of the Dead (Día de los Muertos) parade in Mexico City, Mexico

WEIRDLY CUTE

A cute salamander? You bet! Axolotls (pronounced ACK-suh-LAH-tuhls) spend their whole lives in water and are found only in Mexico, in the Xochimilco (pronounced SO-chee-MILL-koh) lake complex. Axolotls have captured the hearts of many, and scientists are working to save them through education and conservation programs.

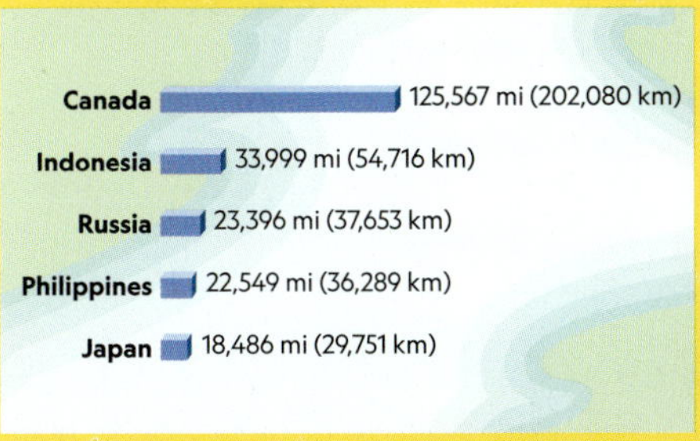

FANTASTIC FOSSILS

Fossils abound near the Bay of Fundy, located between Canada's Nova Scotia and New Brunswick Provinces. Rising up from the bay are the Joggins Fossil Cliffs, which contain fossils from the Coal Age, 50 million years before dinosaurs lived! Some of the ancient creatures encased in the rock: plants, spiders, and a giant millipede that is thought to be one of the largest prehistoric invertebrates.

LONG TRAIL

Imagine walking from Washington State to Washington, D.C.—without ever having to share the road with a car. That may be reality soon, thanks to the 3,700-mile (5,955-km) Great American Rail-Trail. With this extensive project, what were once abandoned railways crossing the United States will soon be safe places for people to walk, bike, and run.

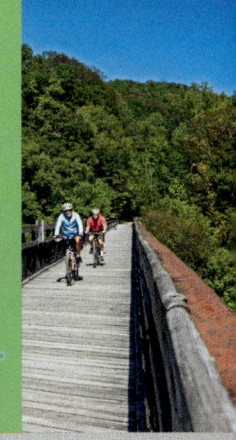

World's Longest Coastlines

Canada	125,567 mi (202,080 km)
Indonesia	33,999 mi (54,716 km)
Russia	23,396 mi (37,653 km)
Philippines	22,549 mi (36,289 km)
Japan	18,486 mi (29,751 km)

CONTINENTS

POLITICAL

POPULATION
605,655,000

LARGEST COUNTRY
Canada
3,855,101 sq mi
(9,984,670 sq km)

LARGEST METROPOLITAN AREA
Mexico City, Mexico
Pop. 22,505,000

MOST DENSELY POPULATED COUNTRY
Barbados / 1,832 people per sq mi (707 per sq km)

PHYSICAL

LAND AREA
9,449,000 sq mi
(24,474,000 sq km)

HIGHEST POINT
Denali, Alaska, U.S.A.
20,310 ft (6,190 m)

LOWEST POINT
Death Valley, California, U.S.A.
-282 ft (-86 m)

LONGEST RIVER
Mississippi–Missouri, U.S.A.
3,710 mi (5,971 km)

LARGEST LAKE
Lake Superior, U.S.A.–Canada / 31,700 sq mi
(82,100 sq km)

Map Key
- ⊛ National capital
- • Other city
- ▲ Highest point (above sea level)
- ▼ Lowest point (below sea level)

300

GEOGRAPHY ROCKS

NORTH AMERICA

CONTINENTS

SOUTH AMERICA

A woman in Ecuador sells produce from a market stall.

The *arazá*, also known as an Amazonian pear, is a super-sour fruit.

Capoeira, a sport combining martial arts and dance, was invented in Brazil.

GEOGRAPHY ROCKS

South America is bordered by three major bodies of water: the Caribbean Sea, Atlantic Ocean, and Pacific Ocean. The world's fourth largest continent extends over a range of climates, from tropical in the north to subarctic in the south. South America produces a rich diversity of natural resources, including nuts, fruits, sugar, grains, coffee, and chocolate.

Santiago Cathedral in Santiago, Chile

CUYABA DWARF FROG

Bottoms up! Instead of facing off against an opponent or making a run for it, this unusual amphibian turns around and presents its backside! This two-inch (5-cm)-long frog has two black glands with outer white rings on its rear end. When the frog feels threatened, it puffs up its body, making the glands look like big eyes! If that doesn't scare away its predators, the glands also squirt poison!

LARGEST LILY PADS

These leaves are unbelievable! Bolivia's La Rinconada ecological park boasts both the world's largest and strongest lily pads. Growing to be as wide as a garage door, the aquatic pads are sturdy enough to support the weight of a small child without sinking—but it's probably better to view these floating leaves from land!

Vast Watershed

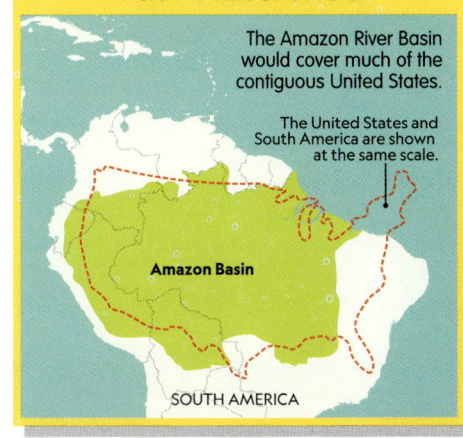

The Amazon River Basin would cover much of the contiguous United States.

The United States and South America are shown at the same scale.

Amazon Basin

SOUTH AMERICA

LENÇÓIS MARANHENSES NATIONAL PARK

Lençóis Maranhenses National Park is a surreal but natural mix of rolling sand dunes and stunning blue-green freshwater lagoons that stretch as far as the eye can see. The park is almost the size of London, England. Hundreds of temporary lakes in the park fill up during the rainy season (between January and June). The water can't drain through the impermeable rock below, so the lagoons remain full for many months.

CONTINENTS

PHYSICAL

LAND AREA
6,880,000 sq mi
(17,819,000 sq km)

HIGHEST POINT
Cerro Aconcagua, Argentina
22,831 ft (6,959 m)

LOWEST POINT
Laguna del Carbón, Argentina
-344 ft (-105 m)

LONGEST RIVER
Amazon / 4,150 mi (6,679 km)

LARGEST LAKE
Lake Titicaca, Bolivia–Peru
3,200 sq mi (8,300 sq km)

POLITICAL

POPULATION
442,164,000

LARGEST COUNTRY
Brazil
3,287,956 sq mi (8,515,770 sq km)

LARGEST METROPOLITAN AREA
São Paulo, Brazil
Pop. 22,807,000

MOST DENSELY POPULATED COUNTRY
Ecuador / 167 people per sq mi (65 per sq km)

Map Key
- ⊛ National capital
- • Other city
- ▲ Highest point (above sea level)
- ▼ Lowest point (below sea level)

304

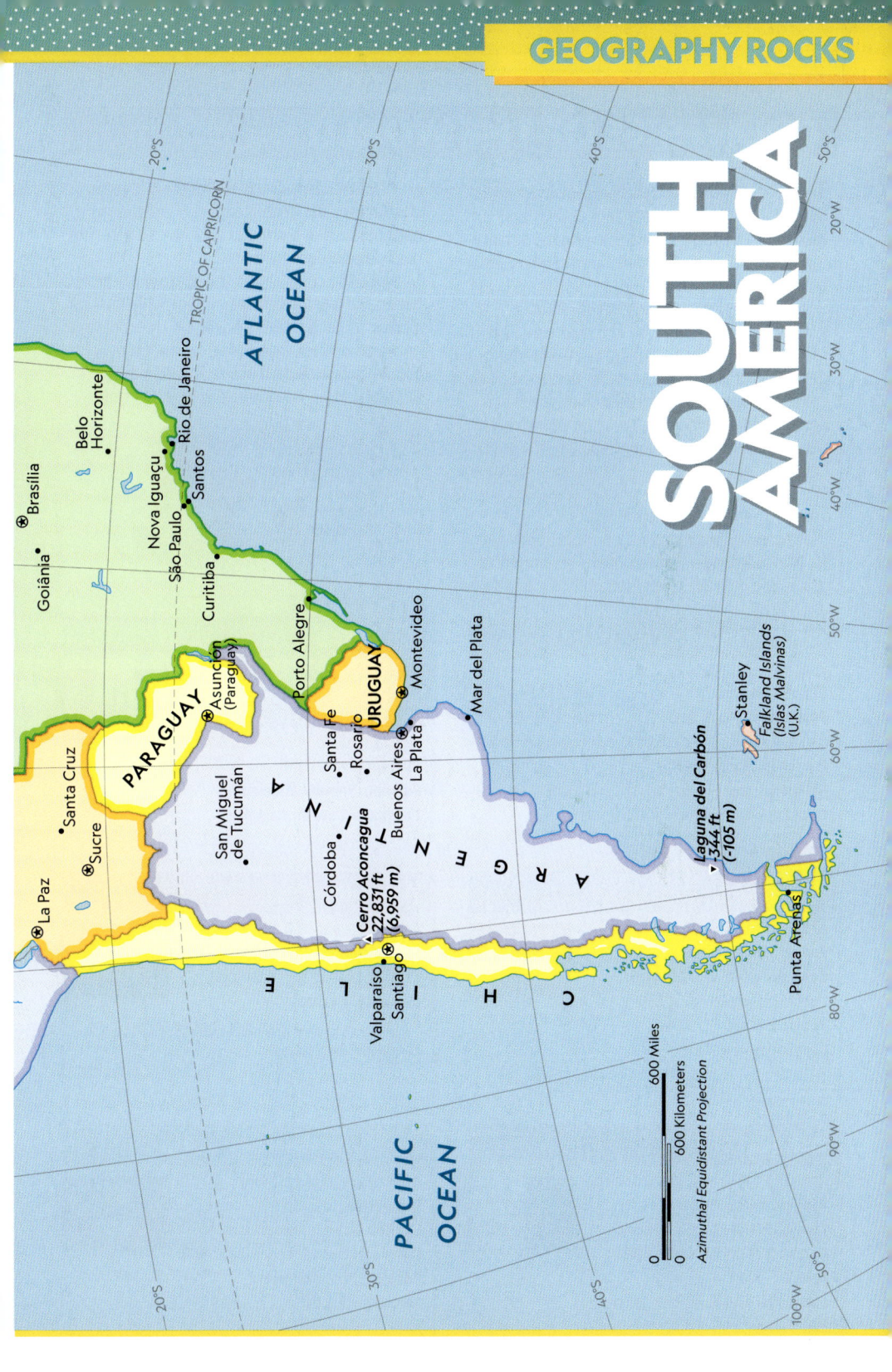

GEOGRAPHY ROCKS

SOUTH AMERICA

COUNTRIES OF THE WORLD

The following pages present a general overview of all 195 independent countries recognized by the National Geographic Society, including the newest nation, South Sudan, which gained independence in 2011.

The flags of each independent country symbolize diverse cultures and histories. The statistical data cover highlights of geography and demography and provide a brief overview of each country. They present general characteristics and are not intended to be comprehensive. For example, not every language spoken in a specific country can be listed. Thus, languages shown are the most representative of that area. This is also true of the religions mentioned.

A country is defined as a political body with its own independent government, geographical space, and, in most cases, laws, military, and taxes.

Disputed areas such as Northern Cyprus and Taiwan, and dependencies of independent nations, such as Bermuda and Puerto Rico, are not included in this listing.

Note the color key at the bottom of the pages and the locator map below, which assign a color to each country based on the continent on which it is located. Some capital city populations include that city's metro area. All information is accurate as of press time.

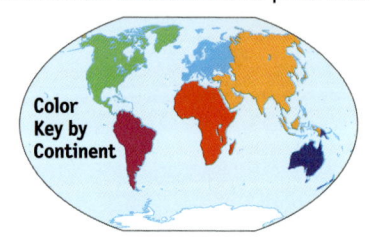

Color Key by Continent

Afghanistan
Area: 251,827 sq mi (652,230 sq km)
Population: 40,122,000
Capital: Kabul, pop. 4,728,000
Currency: afghani (AFN)
Religion: Islam
Language: Afghan Persian (Dari), Pashto

Albania
Area: 11,100 sq mi (28,748 sq km)
Population: 3,107,000
Capital: Tirana, pop. 528,000
Currency: lek (ALL)
Religion: Islam
Language: Albanian

Algeria
Area: 919,595 sq mi (2,381,740 sq km)
Population: 47,022,000
Capital: Algiers, pop. 2,952,000
Currency: Algerian dinar (DZD)
Religion: Islam
Language: Arabic, Berber (Tamazight)

Andorra
Area: 181 sq mi (468 sq km)
Population: 85,000
Capital: Andorra la Vella, pop. 23,000
Currency: euro (EUR)
Religion: Roman Catholicism
Language: Catalan, Castilian

Angola
Area: 481,353 sq mi (1,246,700 sq km)
Population: 37,202,000
Capital: Luanda, pop. 9,651,000
Currency: kwanza (AOA)
Religion: Roman Catholicism, Protestantism
Language: Portuguese

Antigua and Barbuda
Area: 171 sq mi (443 sq km)
Population: 103,000
Capital: St. John's, pop. 21,000
Currency: East Caribbean dollar (XCD)
Religion: Protestantism
Language: English

COLOR KEY ● Africa ● Australia, New Zealand, and Oceania

GEOGRAPHY ROCKS

Argentina
Area: 1,073,518 sq mi (2,780,400 sq km)
Population: 46,994,000
Capital: Buenos Aires, pop. 15,618,000
Currency: Argentine peso (ARS)
Religion: Roman Catholicism
Language: Spanish

Armenia
Area: 11,484 sq mi (29,743 sq km)
Population: 2,977,000
Capital: Yerevan, pop. 1,098,000
Currency: dram (AMD)
Religion: Oriental Orthodoxy
Language: Armenian, Russian

3 cool things about ARMENIA

1. Dating back to the fourth century, Armenia's Etchmiadzin Cathedral is one of the oldest Christian churches in the world.

2. A 5,500-year-old leather shoe preserved in sheep dung was found in an Armenian cave.

3. The Armenian language has its own unique written alphabet. It was created in A.D. 405 and has 38 letters.

Australia
Area: 2,988,901 sq mi (7,741,220 sq km)
Population: 26,769,000
Capital: Canberra, A.C.T., pop. 478,000
Currency: Australian dollar (AUD)
Religion: Roman Catholicism, Protestantism
Language: English

Austria
Area: 32,383 sq mi (83,871 sq km)
Population: 8,968,000
Capital: Vienna, pop. 1,990,000
Currency: euro (EUR)
Religion: Roman Catholicism
Language: German

Azerbaijan
Area: 33,436 sq mi (86,600 sq km)
Population: 10,650,000
Capital: Baku, pop. 2,464,000
Currency: Azerbaijani manat (AZN)
Religion: Islam
Language: Azerbaijani (Azeri)

Bahamas, The
Area: 5,359 sq mi (13,880 sq km)
Population: 411,000
Capital: Nassau, pop. 280,000
Currency: Bahamian dollar (BSD)
Religion: Protestantism
Language: English

Bahrain
Area: 293 sq mi (760 sq km)
Population: 1,567,000
Capital: Manama, pop. 727,000
Currency: Bahraini dinar (BHD)
Religion: Islam
Language: Arabic

Bangladesh
Area: 57,321 sq mi (148,460 sq km)
Population: 168,697,000
Capital: Dhaka, pop. 23,936,000
Currency: taka (BDT)
Religion: Islam
Language: Bangla (Bengali)

● Asia ● Europe ● North America ● South America

COUNTRIES

Barbados
Area: 166 sq mi (430 sq km)
Population: 304,000
Capital: Bridgetown, pop. 89,000
Currency: Barbadian dollar (BBD)
Religion: Protestantism
Language: English, Bajan

Belgium
Area: 11,787 sq mi (30,528 sq km)
Population: 11,978,000
Capital: Brussels, pop. 2,132,000
Currency: euro (EUR)
Religion: Roman Catholicism
Language: Dutch, French, German

Belarus
Area: 80,155 sq mi (207,600 sq km)
Population: 9,501,000
Capital: Minsk, pop. 2,065,000
Currency: Belarusian ruble (BYN)
Religion: Eastern Orthodoxy
Language: Russian, Belarusian

Belize
Area: 8,867 sq mi (22,966 sq km)
Population: 416,000
Capital: Belmopan, pop. 23,000
Currency: Belizean dollar (BZD)
Religion: Roman Catholicism, Protestantism
Language: English, Spanish, Creole

SNAPSHOT Barbados

A sea turtle swims in the Caribbean Sea off the coast of Barbados.

COLOR KEY ● Africa ● Australia, New Zealand, and Oceania

GEOGRAPHY ROCKS

Benin
Area: 43,484 sq mi (112,622 sq km)
Population: 14,697,000
Capitals: Porto-Novo, pop. 285,000; Cotonou, pop. 738,000
Currency: CFA franc BCEAO (XOF)
Religion: Islam, Roman Catholicism
Language: French, Indigenous languages

Bhutan
Area: 14,824 sq mi (38,394 sq km)
Population: 885,000
Capital: Thimphu, pop. 203,000
Currency: ngultrum (BTN)
Religion: Buddhism
Language: Sharchhopka, Dzongkha, Lhotshamkha

Bolivia
Area: 424,164 sq mi (1,098,581 sq km)
Population: 12,312,000
Capitals: La Paz, pop. 1,966,000; Sucre, pop. 278,000
Currency: boliviano (BOB)
Religion: Roman Catholicism
Language: Spanish, Quechua, Aymara, Guaraní

Bosnia and Herzegovina
Area: 19,767 sq mi (51,197 sq km)
Population: 3,799,000
Capital: Sarajevo, pop. 347,000
Currency: convertible mark (BAM)
Religion: Islam, Eastern Orthodoxy
Language: Bosnian, Serbian, Croatian

Botswana
Area: 224,607 sq mi (581,730 sq km)
Population: 2,451,000
Capital: Gaborone, pop. 269,000
Currency: pula (BWP)
Religion: Christianity
Language: Setswana, English

Brazil
Area: 3,287,956 sq mi (8,515,770 sq km)
Population: 220,052,000
Capital: Brasília, pop. 4,935,000
Currency: real (BRL)
Religion: Roman Catholicism
Language: Portuguese

Brunei
Area: 2,226 sq mi (5,765 sq km)
Population: 492,000
Capital: Bandar Seri Begawan, pop. 267,000
Currency: Bruneian dollar (BND)
Religion: Islam
Language: Malay

Bulgaria
Area: 42,811 sq mi (110,879 sq km)
Population: 6,783,000
Capital: Sofia, pop. 1,288,000
Currency: lev (BGN)
Religion: Christianity
Language: Bulgarian

Burkina Faso
Area: 105,869 sq mi (274,200 sq km)
Population: 23,042,000
Capital: Ouagadougou, pop. 3,359,000
Currency: CFA franc BCEAO (XOF)
Religion: Islam
Language: Mossi, French

Burundi
Area: 10,745 sq mi (27,830 sq km)
Population: 13,590,000
Capitals: Bujumbura, pop. 1,277,000; Gitega, pop. 135,000
Currency: Burundi franc (BIF)
Religion: Roman Catholicism, Protestantism
Language: Kirundi, French, English

● Asia ● Europe ● North America ● South America

COUNTRIES

Cabo Verde
Area: 1,557 sq mi (4,033 sq km)
Population: 611,000
Capital: Praia, pop. 168,000
Currency: Cabo Verdean escudo (CVE)
Religion: Roman Catholicism
Language: Portuguese

Cambodia
Area: 69,898 sq mi (181,035 sq km)
Population: 17,064,000
Capital: Phnom Penh, pop. 2,353,000
Currency: riel (KHR)
Religion: Buddhism
Language: Khmer

Cameroon
Area: 183,568 sq mi (475,440 sq km)
Population: 30,966,000
Capital: Yaoundé, pop. 4,682,000
Currency: CFA franc BEAC (XAF)
Religion: Roman Catholicism, Islam, Protestantism
Language: Indigenous languages, English, French

Canada
Area: 3,855,101 sq mi (9,984,670 sq km)
Population: 38,795,000
Capital: Ottawa, pop. 1,452,000
Currency: Canadian dollar (CAD)
Religion: Christianity
Language: English, French

Central African Republic
Area: 240,535 sq mi (622,984 sq km)
Population: 5,651,000
Capital: Bangui, pop. 986,000
Currency: CFA franc BEAC (XAF)
Religion: Roman Catholicism
Language: French, Sangho

Chad
Area: 495,755 sq mi (1,284,000 sq km)
Population: 19,094,000
Capital: N'Djamena, pop. 1,656,000
Currency: CFA franc BEAC (XAF)
Religion: Islam
Language: French, Arabic

Chile
Area: 291,932 sq mi (756,102 sq km)
Population: 18,665,000
Capital: Santiago, pop. 6,951,000
Currency: Chilean peso (CLP)
Religion: Roman Catholicism
Language: Spanish

China
Area: 3,705,405 sq mi (9,596,960 sq km)
Population: 1,416,043,000
Capital: Beijing, pop. 22,189,000
Currency: Renminbi yuan (RMB)
Religion: Unspecified
Language: Standard Chinese (Mandarin, Putonghua)

Colombia
Area: 439,735 sq mi (1,138,910 sq km)
Population: 49,588,000
Capital: Bogotá, pop. 11,658,000
Currency: Colombian peso (COP)
Religion: Roman Catholicism, Islam
Language: Spanish

Comoros
Area: 863 sq mi (2,235 sq km)
Population: 900,000
Capital: Moroni, pop. 62,000
Currency: Comoran franc (KMF)
Religion: Islam
Language: Arabic, French, Shikomoro (Comorian)

COLOR KEY ● Africa ● Australia, New Zealand, and Oceania

GEOGRAPHY ROCKS

Congo
Area: 132,047 sq mi (342,000 sq km)
Population: 6,098,000
Capital: Brazzaville, pop. 2,725,000
Currency: CFA franc BEAC (XAF)
Religion: Roman Catholicism, other Christianity, Protestantism
Language: French

Côte d'Ivoire (Ivory Coast)
Area: 124,504 sq mi (322,463 sq km)
Population: 29,982,000
Capitals: Abidjan, pop. 5,867,000; Yamoussoukro, pop. 231,000
Currency: CFA franc BCEAO (XOF)
Religion: Islam
Language: French

Costa Rica
Area: 19,730 sq mi (51,100 sq km)
Population: 5,266,000
Capital: San José, pop. 1,482,000
Currency: Costa Rican colón (CRC)
Religion: Roman Catholicism
Language: Spanish

Croatia
Area: 21,851 sq mi (56,594 sq km)
Population: 4,150,000
Capital: Zagreb, pop. 684,000
Currency: kuna (HRK)
Religion: Roman Catholicism
Language: Croatian

SNAPSHOT
Costa Rica

A keel-billed toucan perches on a branch in Costa Rica.

● Asia ● Europe ● North America ● South America

COUNTRIES

Cuba
Area: 42,803 sq mi (110,860 sq km)
Population: 10,966,000
Capital: Havana, pop. 2,153,000
Currency: Cuban peso (CUP)
Religion: Christianity
Language: Spanish

Cyprus
Area: 3,572 sq mi (9,251 sq km)
Population: 1,321,000
Capital: Nicosia, pop. 269,000
Currency: euro (EUR)
Religion: Eastern Orthodoxy
Language: Greek, Turkish

Czechia (Czech Republic)
Area: 30,451 sq mi (78,867 sq km)
Population: 10,838,000
Capital: Prague, pop. 1,328,000
Currency: koruna (CZK)
Religion: None
Language: Czech

Democratic Republic of the Congo
Area: 905,354 sq mi (2,344,858 sq km)
Population: 115,403,000
Capital: Kinshasa, pop. 17,032,000
Currency: Congolese franc (CDF)
Religion: Other Christianity, Roman Catholicism, Protestantism
Language: French

Denmark
Area: 16,639 sq mi (43,094 sq km)
Population: 5,973,000
Capital: Copenhagen, pop. 1,391,000
Currency: Danish krone (DKK)
Religion: Protestantism
Language: Danish, English

Djibouti
Area: 8,958 sq mi (23,200 sq km)
Population: 995,000
Capital: Djibouti, pop. 608,000
Currency: Djiboutian franc (DJF)
Religion: Islam
Language: French, Arabic

Dominica
Area: 290 sq mi (751 sq km)
Population: 75,000
Capital: Roseau, pop. 15,000
Currency: East Caribbean dollar (XCD)
Religion: Roman Catholicism
Language: English

Dominican Republic
Area: 18,792 sq mi (48,670 sq km)
Population: 10,816,000
Capital: Santo Domingo, pop. 3,587,000
Currency: Dominican peso (DOP)
Religion: Protestantism
Language: Spanish

3 cool things about the DOMINICAN REPUBLIC

1. Larimar, a very rare blue gemstone, is found only in the Dominican Republic.

2. Measuring about the size of a pencil eraser (about 0.4 inch [10 mm]), one of the world's smallest scorpions is native to the Dominican Republic.

3. The Dominican Republic is one of the largest producers of organic cocoa in the world.

312

COLOR KEY • Africa • Australia, New Zealand, and Oceania

GEOGRAPHY ROCKS

Ecuador
Area: 109,483 sq mi (283,561 sq km)
Population: 18,310,000
Capital: Quito, pop. 1,987,000
Currency: U.S. dollar (USD)
Religion: Roman Catholicism
Language: Spanish

Egypt
Area: 386,662 sq mi (1,001,450 sq km)
Population: 111,247,000
Capital: Cairo, pop. 22,624,000
Currency: Egyptian pound (EGP)
Religion: Islam
Language: Arabic, English, French

El Salvador
Area: 8,124 sq mi (21,041 sq km)
Population: 6,629,000
Capital: San Salvador, pop. 1,123,000
Currency: U.S. dollar (USD)
Religion: Roman Catholicism, Protestantism
Language: Spanish

Equatorial Guinea
Area: 10,831 sq mi (28,051 sq km)
Population: 1,796,000
Capital: Malabo, pop. 297,000
Currency: CFA franc BEAC (XAF)
Religion: Roman Catholicism
Language: Spanish, Portuguese, French

Eritrea
Area: 45,406 sq mi (117,600 sq km)
Population: 6,344,000
Capital: Asmara, pop. 1,112,000
Currency: nakfa (ERN)
Religion: Christianity, Islam
Language: Tigrinya, Arabic, English

Estonia
Area: 17,463 sq mi (45,228 sq km)
Population: 1,194,000
Capital: Tallinn, pop. 456,000
Currency: euro (EUR)
Religion: None
Language: Estonian, Russian

Eswatini (Swaziland)
Area: 6,704 sq mi (17,364 sq km)
Population: 1,138,000
Capitals: Mbabane, pop. 68,000; Lobamba, pop. 90,000
Currency: lilangeni (SZL)
Religion: Christianity
Language: English, siSwati

Ethiopia
Area: 426,372 sq mi (1,104,300 sq km)
Population: 118,550,000
Capital: Addis Ababa, pop. 5,704,000
Currency: birr (ETB)
Religion: Oriental Orthodoxy, Islam
Language: Oromo, Amharic

Fiji
Area: 7,056 sq mi (18,274 sq km)
Population: 952,000
Capital: Suva, pop. 178,000
Currency: Fijian dollar (FJD)
Religion: Protestantism, Hinduism
Language: English, Fijian, Fiji Hindi

The DANAKIL DEPRESSION in Ethiopia and Eritrea is one of the HOTTEST PLACES on Earth.

● Asia ● Europe ● North America ● South America

COUNTRIES

Finland
Area: 130,558 sq mi (338,145 sq km)
Population: 5,626,000
Capital: Helsinki, pop. 1,347,000
Currency: euro (EUR)
Religion: Protestantism
Language: Finnish, Swedish

France
Area: 248,573 sq mi (643,801 sq km)
Population: 68,375,000
Capital: Paris, pop. 11,277,000
Currency: euro (EUR)
Religion: Roman Catholicism
Language: French

Gabon
Area: 103,347 sq mi (267,667 sq km)
Population: 2,455,000
Capital: Libreville, pop. 884,000
Currency: CFA franc BEAC (XAF)
Religion: Protestantism, Roman Catholicism
Language: French

Gambia, The
Area: 4,363 sq mi (11,300 sq km)
Population: 2,523,000
Capital: Banjul, pop. 495,000
Currency: dalasi (GMD)
Religion: Islam
Language: English

Georgia
Area: 26,911 sq mi (69,700 sq km)
Population: 4,901,000
Capital: Tbilisi, pop. 1,084,000
Currency: lari (GEL)
Religion: Eastern Orthodoxy
Language: Georgian

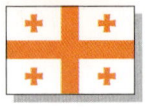

Germany
Area: 137,847 sq mi (357,022 sq km)
Population: 84,119,000
Capital: Berlin, pop. 3,577,000
Currency: euro (EUR)
Religion: Roman Catholicism, Protestantism
Language: German

Ghana
Area: 92,098 sq mi (238,533 sq km)
Population: 34,589,000
Capital: Accra, pop. 2,721,000
Currency: cedi (GHC)
Religion: Protestantism
Language: Indigenous languages, English

Greece
Area: 50,949 sq mi (131,957 sq km)
Population: 10,461,000
Capital: Athens, pop. 3,155,000
Currency: euro (EUR)
Religion: Eastern Orthodoxy
Language: Greek

Grenada
Area: 133 sq mi (344 sq km)
Population: 115,000
Capital: St. George's, pop. 39,000
Currency: East Caribbean dollar (XCD)
Religion: Protestantism, Roman Catholicism
Language: English

Guatemala
Area: 42,042 sq mi (108,889 sq km)
Population: 18,255,000
Capital: Guatemala City, pop. 3,160,000
Currency: quetzal (GTQ)
Religion: Protestantism, Roman Catholicism
Language: Spanish, Indigenous languages

COLOR KEY ● Africa ● Australia, New Zealand, and Oceania

GEOGRAPHY ROCKS

Guinea
Area: 94,926 sq mi (245,857 sq km)
Population: 13,986,000
Capital: Conakry, pop. 2,179,000
Currency: Guinean franc (GNF)
Religion: Islam
Language: French

Guyana
Area: 83,000 sq mi (214,969 sq km)
Population: 794,000
Capital: Georgetown, pop. 110,000
Currency: Guyanese dollar (GYD)
Religion: Protestantism, Hinduism, other Christianity
Language: English

Guinea-Bissau
Area: 13,948 sq mi (36,125 sq km)
Population: 2,132,000
Capital: Bissau, pop. 687,000
Currency: CFA franc BCEAO (XOF)
Religion: Islam, folk religion
Language: Crioulu, Portuguese

Haiti
Area: 10,714 sq mi (27,750 sq km)
Population: 11,754,000
Capital: Port-au-Prince, pop. 3,060,000
Currency: gourde (HTG)
Religion: Roman Catholicism
Language: French, Creole

SNAPSHOT Germany

In the Middle Ages, townspeople built the old town hall in Bamberg, a city in southern Germany, on an artificial island in the middle of the Regnitz River.

● Asia ● Europe ● North America ● South America

COUNTRIES

Honduras
Area: 43,278 sq mi (112,090 sq km)
Population: 9,529,000
Capital: Tegucigalpa, pop. 1,609,000
Currency: lempira (HNL)
Religion: Protestantism
Language: Spanish

Iceland
Area: 39,769 sq mi (103,000 sq km)
Population: 364,000
Capital: Reykjavík, pop. 216,000
Currency: Icelandic krona (ISK)
Religion: Protestantism
Language: Icelandic

Hungary
Area: 35,918 sq mi (93,028 sq km)
Population: 9,856,000
Capital: Budapest, pop. 1,780,000
Currency: forint (HUF)
Religion: Roman Catholicism
Language: Hungarian, English

India
Area: 1,269,219 sq mi (3,287,263 sq km)
Population: 1,409,128,000
Capital: New Delhi, pop. 33,807,000
Currency: Indian rupee (INR)
Religion: Hinduism
Language: Hindi

SNAPSHOT India

More than 8,000 volunteers spent more than 300 million hours helping build Akshardham Temple in Delhi, India.

COLOR KEY ● Africa ● Australia, New Zealand, and Oceania

GEOGRAPHY ROCKS

Indonesia
Area: 735,358 sq mi
(1,904,569 sq km)
Population: 281,562,000
Capital: Jakarta, pop. 11,436,000
Currency: Indonesian rupiah (IDR)
Religion: Islam
Language: Bahasa Indonesia

Iran
Area: 636,371 sq mi
(1,648,195 sq km)
Population: 88,387,000
Capital: Tehran, pop. 9,616,000
Currency: Iranian rial (IRR)
Religion: Islam
Language: Persian (Farsi)

Iraq
Area: 169,235 sq mi
(438,317 sq km)
Population: 42,083,000
Capital: Baghdad, pop. 7,921,000
Currency: Iraqi dinar (IQD)
Religion: Islam
Language: Arabic, Kurdish

Ireland (Éire)
Area: 27,133 sq mi
(70,273 sq km)
Population: 5,233,000
Capital: Dublin
(Baile Átha Cliath), pop. 1,285,000
Currency: euro (EUR)
Religion: Roman Catholicism
Language: English, Irish (Gaelic)

Israel
Area: 8,970 sq mi (23,232 sq km)
Population: 9,403,000
Capital: Jerusalem, pop. 983,000
Currency: new Israeli shekel (ILS)
Religion: Judaism
Language: Hebrew, Arabic

Italy
Area: 116,348 sq mi
(301,340 sq km)
Population: 60,965,000
Capital: Rome, pop. 4,332,000
Currency: euro (EUR)
Religion: Roman Catholicism
Language: Italian

Jamaica
Area: 4,244 sq mi
(10,991 sq km)
Population: 2,824,000
Capital: Kingston, pop. 600,000
Currency: Jamaican dollar (JMD)
Religion: Protestantism
Language: English, Jamaican patois

Japan
Area: 145,914 sq mi (377,915 sq km)
Population: 123,202,000
Capital: Tokyo, pop. 37,115,000
Currency: yen (JPY)
Religion: Shinto, Buddhism
Language: Japanese

Jordan
Area: 34,495 sq mi
(89,342 sq km)
Population: 11,174,000
Capital: Amman, pop. 2,253,000
Currency: Jordanian dinar (JOD)
Religion: Islam
Language: Arabic, English

Kazakhstan
Area: 1,052,089 sq mi
(2,724,900 sq km)
Population: 20,260,000
Capital: Astana, pop. 1,324,000
Currency: tenge (KZT)
Religion: Islam
Language: Kazakh (Qazaq), Russian, English

● Asia ● Europe ● North America ● South America

COUNTRIES

Kenya
Area: 224,081 sq mi (580,367 sq km)
Population: 58,246,000
Capital: Nairobi, pop. 5,541,000
Currency: Kenyan shilling (KES)
Religion: Protestantism
Language: English, Kiswahili (Swahili)

Kiribati
Area: 313 sq mi (811 sq km)
Population: 117,000
Capital: Tarawa, pop. 64,000
Currency: Australian dollar (AUD)
Religion: Roman Catholicism
Language: Gilbertese, English

Kosovo
Area: 4,203 sq mi (10,887 sq km)
Population: 1,977,000
Capital: Pristina, pop. 219,000
Currency: euro (EUR)
Religion: Islam
Language: Albanian, Serbian

Kuwait
Area: 6,880 sq mi (17,818 sq km)
Population: 3,138,000
Capital: Kuwait City, pop. 3,104,000
Currency: Kuwaiti dinar (KWD)
Religion: Islam
Language: Arabic, English

Kyrgyzstan
Area: 77,201 sq mi (199,951 sq km)
Population: 6,172,000
Capital: Bishkek, pop. 1,128,000
Currency: Som (KGS)
Religion: Islam
Language: Kyrgyz, Uzbek, Russian

Laos
Area: 91,429 sq mi (236,800 sq km)
Population: 7,954,000
Capital: Vientiane, pop. 738,000
Currency: kip (LAK)
Religion: Buddhism
Language: Lao

Latvia
Area: 24,938 sq mi (64,589 sq km)
Population: 1,801,000
Capital: Riga, pop. 619,000
Currency: euro (EUR)
Religion: Protestantism, unspecified or none
Language: Latvian, Russian

Lebanon
Area: 4,015 sq mi (10,400 sq km)
Population: 5,364,000
Capital: Beirut, pop. 2,402,000
Currency: Lebanese pound (LBP)
Religion: Islam
Language: Arabic

Lesotho
Area: 11,720 sq mi (30,355 sq km)
Population: 2,228,000
Capital: Maseru, pop. 202,000
Currency: loti (LSL)
Religion: Protestantism, Roman Catholicism
Language: Sesotho, English

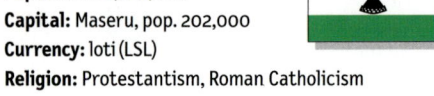

Liberia
Area: 43,000 sq mi (111,369 sq km)
Population: 5,437,000
Capital: Monrovia, pop. 1,735,000
Currency: Liberian dollar (LRD)
Religion: Christianity
Language: English

COLOR KEY ● Africa ● Australia, New Zealand, and Oceania

GEOGRAPHY ROCKS

Libya
Area: 679,362 sq mi (1,759,540 sq km)
Population: 7,361,000
Capital: Tripoli, pop. 1,192,000
Currency: Libyan dinar (LYD)
Religion: Islam
Language: Arabic, Italian, English

Lithuania
Area: 25,212 sq mi (65,300 sq km)
Population: 2,628,000
Capital: Vilnius, pop. 542,000
Currency: euro (EUR)
Religion: Roman Catholicism
Language: Lithuanian

Liechtenstein
Area: 62 sq mi (160 sq km)
Population: 40,000
Capital: Vaduz, pop. 5,000
Currency: Swiss franc (CHF)
Religion: Roman Catholicism
Language: German

Luxembourg
Area: 998 sq mi (2,586 sq km)
Population: 671,000
Capital: Luxembourg, pop. 120,000
Currency: euro (EUR)
Religion: Roman Catholicism
Language: Luxembourgish, French, German

SNAPSHOT Kyrgyzstan

Tombstones known as *balbas* stand at the ancient site of Burana, Kyrgyzstan.

● Asia ● Europe ● North America ● South America

COUNTRIES

Madagascar
Area: 226,658 sq mi (587,041 sq km)
Population: 29,453,000
Capital: Antananarivo, pop. 4,049,000
Currency: Malagasy ariary (MGA)
Religion: Protestantism, Roman Catholicism
Language: Malagasy, French

Maldives
Area: 115 sq mi (298 sq km)
Population: 389,000
Capital: Male, pop. 177,000
Currency: rufiyaa (MVR)
Religion: Islam
Language: Dhivehi

Malawi
Area: 45,747 sq mi (118,484 sq km)
Population: 21,763,000
Capital: Lilongwe, pop. 1,333,000
Currency: Malawian kwacha (MWK)
Religion: Protestantism, other Christianity
Language: English

Mali
Area: 478,841 sq mi (1,240,192 sq km)
Population: 21,991,000
Capital: Bamako, pop. 3,051,000
Currency: CFA franc BCEAO (XOF)
Religion: Islam
Language: Bambara, French

3 cool things about MALAWI

1. Lake Malawi is home to the largest number of fish species of any lake in the world. The majority of the lake's fish are brightly colored cichlids.

2. Lake Malawi National Park is the world's first freshwater national park.

3. Malawi's Mount Mulanje, soaring some 10,000 feet (3,000 m), is one of the tallest peaks in Africa.

Malta
Area: 122 sq mi (316 sq km)
Population: 470,000
Capital: Valletta, pop. 213,000
Currency: euro (EUR)
Religion: Roman Catholicism
Language: Maltese, English

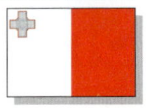

Marshall Islands
Area: 70 sq mi (181 sq km)
Population: 82,000
Capital: Majuro, pop. 31,000
Currency: U.S. dollar (USD)
Religion: Protestantism
Language: Marshallese

Malaysia
Area: 127,355 sq mi (329,847 sq km)
Population: 34,565,000
Capital: Kuala Lumpur, pop. 8,816,000
Currency: ringgit (MYR)
Religion: Islam
Language: Bahasa Malaysia

Mauritania
Area: 397,955 sq mi (1,030,700 sq km)
Population: 4,328,000
Capital: Nouakchott, pop. 1,552,000
Currency: ouguiya (MRU)
Religion: Islam
Language: Arabic

COLOR KEY ● Africa ● Australia, New Zealand, and Oceania

GEOGRAPHY ROCKS

Mauritius
Area: 788 sq mi (2,040 sq km)
Population: 1,311,000
Capital: Port Louis, pop. 149,000
Currency: Mauritian rupee (MUR)
Religion: Hinduism
Language: Creole

Mexico
Area: 758,449 sq mi (1,964,375 sq km)
Population: 130,740,000
Capital: Mexico City, pop. 22,505,000
Currency: Mexican peso (MXN)
Religion: Roman Catholicism
Language: Spanish

Micronesia, Federated States of
Area: 271 sq mi (702 sq km)
Population: 100,000
Capital: Palikir, pop. 7,000
Currency: U.S. dollar (USD)
Religion: Roman Catholicism, Protestantism
Language: English

Moldova
Area: 13,070 sq mi (33,851 sq km)
Population: 3,600,000
Capital: Chișinău, pop. 486,000
Currency: Moldovan leu (MDL)
Religion: Eastern Orthodoxy
Language: Romanian

Monaco
Area: 1 sq mi (2 sq km)
Population: 32,000
Capital: Monaco, pop. 32,000
Currency: euro (EUR)
Religion: Roman Catholicism
Language: French

Mongolia
Area: 603,908 sq mi (1,564,116 sq km)
Population: 3,282,000
Capital: Ulan Bator, pop. 1,699,000
Currency: tugrik (MNT)
Religion: Buddhism
Language: Mongolian

SHUVUUIA, a small, birdlike dinosaur, once roamed what is now Mongolia some 75 MILLION YEARS AGO.

Montenegro
Area: 5,333 sq mi (13,812 sq km)
Population: 600,000
Capital: Podgorica, pop. 177,000
Currency: euro (EUR)
Religion: Eastern Orthodoxy
Language: Serbian, Montenegrin

Morocco
Area: 276,662 sq mi (716,550 sq km)
Population: 37,388,000
Capital: Rabat, pop. 1,989,000
Currency: Moroccan dirham (MAD)
Religion: Islam
Language: Arabic, Berber (Tamazight)

Mozambique
Area: 308,642 sq mi (799,380 sq km)
Population: 33,351,000
Capital: Maputo, pop. 1,193,000
Currency: metical (MZN)
Religion: Roman Catholicism
Language: Makhuwa, Portuguese

● Asia ● Europe ● North America ● South America

COUNTRIES

Myanmar (Burma)
Area: 261,228 sq mi (676,578 sq km)
Population: 57,527,000
Capital: Nay Pyi Taw, pop. 723,000
Currency: kyat (MMK)
Religion: Buddhism
Language: Burmese

Nauru
Area: 8 sq mi (21 sq km)
Population: 10,000
Capital: Yaren, pop. 700
Currency: Australian dollar (AUD)
Religion: Protestantism
Language: Nauruan

Namibia
Area: 318,261 sq mi (824,292 sq km)
Population: 2,804,000
Capital: Windhoek, pop. 494,000
Currency: Namibian dollar (NAD)
Religion: Christianity
Language: Indigenous languages, English

Nepal
Area: 56,827 sq mi (147,181 sq km)
Population: 31,122,000
Capital: Kathmandu, pop. 1,622,000
Currency: Nepalese rupee (NPR)
Religion: Hinduism
Language: Nepali

SNAPSHOT Nepal

Living in the high elevations of the Himalaya of Nepal, these wild goats grow a soft undercoat to keep them warm in the harsh winters.

COLOR KEY ● Africa ● Australia, New Zealand, and Oceania

GEOGRAPHY ROCKS

Netherlands
Area: 16,040 sq mi (41,543 sq km)
Population: 17,772,000
Capitals: Amsterdam, pop. 1,182,000; The Hague, pop. 715,000
Currency: euro (EUR)
Religion: None
Language: Dutch

New Zealand
Area: 103,799 sq mi (268,838 sq km)
Population: 5,161,000
Capital: Wellington, pop. 424,000
Currency: New Zealand dollar (NZD)
Religion: None
Language: English, Maori

Nicaragua
Area: 50,336 sq mi (130,370 sq km)
Population: 6,677,000
Capital: Managua, pop. 1,107,000
Currency: cordoba oro (NIO)
Religion: Roman Catholicism, Protestantism
Language: Spanish

Niger
Area: 489,191 sq mi (1,267,000 sq km)
Population: 26,343,000
Capital: Niamey, pop. 1,496,000
Currency: CFA franc BCEAO (XOF)
Religion: Islam
Language: Indigenous languages, French

Nigeria
Area: 356,669 sq mi (923,768 sq km)
Population: 236,747,000
Capital: Abuja, pop. 4,026,000
Currency: naira (NGN)
Religion: Islam
Language: English

North Korea
Area: 46,540 sq mi (120,538 sq km)
Population: 26,299,000
Capital: Pyongyang, pop. 3,183,000
Currency: North Korean won (KPW)
Religion: Buddhism, Confucianism
Language: Korean

North Macedonia
Area: 9,928 sq mi (25,713 sq km)
Population: 2,136,000
Capital: Skopje, pop. 616,000
Currency: Macedonian denar (MKD)
Religion: Eastern Orthodoxy, Islam
Language: Macedonian, Albanian

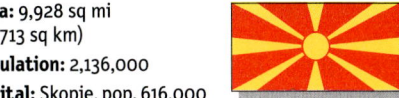

Norway
Area: 125,021 sq mi (323,802 sq km)
Population: 5,510,000
Capital: Oslo, pop. 1,101,000
Currency: Norwegian krone (NOK)
Religion: Protestantism
Language: Bokmal Norwegian, Nynorsk Norwegian

Oman
Area: 119,499 sq mi (309,500 sq km)
Population: 3,902,000
Capital: Muscat, pop. 1,676,000
Currency: Omani rial (OMR)
Religion: Islam
Language: Arabic

Pakistan
Area: 307,374 sq mi (796,095 sq km)
Population: 252,364,000
Capital: Islamabad, pop. 1,267,000
Currency: Pakistan rupee (PKR)
Religion: Islam
Language: Punjabi, Urdu

● Asia ● Europe ● North America ● South America

COUNTRIES

Palau
Area: 177 sq mi (459 sq km)
Population: 22,000
Capital: Ngerulmud, pop. 300
Currency: U.S. dollar (USD)
Religion: Roman Catholicism, Protestantism
Language: Palauan, English

Panama
Area: 29,120 sq mi (75,420 sq km)
Population: 4,470,000
Capital: Panama City, pop. 2,016,000
Currency: balboa (PAB)
Religion: Protestantism
Language: Spanish

Papua New Guinea
Area: 178,703 sq mi (462,840 sq km)
Population: 10,046,000
Capital: Port Moresby, pop. 420,000
Currency: kina (PGK)
Religion: Protestantism
Language: Tok Pisin, English, Hiri Motu

Paraguay
Area: 157,048 sq mi (406,752 sq km)
Population: 7,523,000
Capital: Asunción (Paraguay), pop. 3,569,000
Currency: Guaraní (PYG)
Religion: Roman Catholicism
Language: Spanish, Guaraní

Peru
Area: 496,224 sq mi (1,285,216 sq km)
Population: 32,600,000
Capital: Lima, pop. 11,362,000
Currency: nuevo sol (PEN)
Religion: Roman Catholicism
Language: Spanish, Quechua, Aymara

Philippines
Area: 115,831 sq mi (300,000 sq km)
Population: 118,277,000
Capital: Manila, pop. 14,942,000
Currency: Philippine peso (PHP)
Religion: Roman Catholicism
Language: Tagalog, Filipino, English

Poland
Area: 120,728 sq mi (312,685 sq km)
Population: 38,746,000
Capital: Warsaw, pop. 1,799,000
Currency: zloty (PLN)
Religion: Roman Catholicism
Language: Polish

Portugal
Area: 35,556 sq mi (92,090 sq km)
Population: 10,207,000
Capital: Lisbon, pop. 3,015,000
Currency: euro (EUR)
Religion: Roman Catholicism
Language: Portuguese, Mirandese

Qatar
Area: 4,473 sq mi (11,586 sq km)
Population: 2,552,000
Capital: Doha, pop. 666,000
Currency: Qatari rial (QAR)
Religion: Islam
Language: Arabic, English

Romania
Area: 92,043 sq mi (238,391 sq km)
Population: 18,148,000
Capital: Bucharest, pop. 1,768,000
Currency: leu (RON)
Religion: Eastern Orthodoxy
Language: Romanian

COLOR KEY ● Africa ● Australia, New Zealand, and Oceania

GEOGRAPHY ROCKS

Russia
Area: 6,601,665 sq mi (17,098,242 sq km)
Population: 140,821,000
Capital: Moscow, pop. 12,712,000
Currency: Russian ruble (RUB)
Religion: Eastern Orthodoxy, Islam
Language: Russian
Note: Russia is in both Europe and Asia, but its capital is in Europe, so it is classified here as a European country.

Samoa
Area: 1,093 sq mi (2,831 sq km)
Population: 209,000
Capital: Apia, pop. 36,000
Currency: tala (SAT)
Religion: Protestantism
Language: Samoan (Polynesian), English

Rwanda
Area: 10,169 sq mi (26,338 sq km)
Population: 13,623,000
Capital: Kigali, pop. 1,288,000
Currency: Rwandan franc (RWF)
Religion: Protestantism, Roman Catholicism
Language: Kinyarwanda, French, English, Kiswahili (Swahili)

San Marino
Area: 24 sq mi (61 sq km)
Population: 35,000
Capital: San Marino, pop. 4,000
Currency: euro (EUR)
Religion: Roman Catholicism
Language: Italian

SNAPSHOT Portugal

The National Palace of Pena sits high on a hill in Sintra, Portugal.

● Asia   ● Europe   ● North America   ● South America

325

COUNTRIES

Sao Tome and Principe
Area: 372 sq mi (964 sq km)
Population: 224,000
Capital: São Tomé, pop. 80,000
Currency: dobra (STN)
Religion: Roman Catholicism
Language: Portuguese, Forro

Saudi Arabia
Area: 830,000 sq mi (2,149,690 sq km)
Population: 36,544,000
Capital: Riyadh, pop. 7,821,000
Currency: Saudi riyal (SAR)
Religion: Islam
Language: Arabic

Senegal
Area: 75,955 sq mi (196,722 sq km)
Population: 18,848,000
Capital: Dakar, pop. 3,540,000
Currency: CFA franc BCEAO (XOF)
Religion: Islam
Language: French

Serbia
Area: 29,913 sq mi (77,474 sq km)
Population: 6,652,000
Capital: Belgrade, pop. 1,411,000
Currency: Serbian dinar (RSD)
Religion: Eastern Orthodoxy
Language: Serbian

Seychelles
Area: 176 sq mi (455 sq km)
Population: 98,000
Capital: Victoria, pop. 28,000
Currency: Seychelles rupee (SCR)
Religion: Roman Catholicism
Language: Seychellois Creole, English, French

Sierra Leone
Area: 27,699 sq mi (71,740 sq km)
Population: 9,121,000
Capital: Freetown, pop. 1,348,000
Currency: leone (SLL)
Religion: Islam
Language: English, Krio

Singapore
Area: 278 sq mi (719 sq km)
Population: 6,028,000
Capital: Singapore, pop. 6,028,000
Currency: Singapore dollar (SGD)
Religion: Buddhism, none
Language: English, Mandarin, Malay, Tamil

Slovakia
Area: 18,933 sq mi (49,035 sq km)
Population: 5,564,000
Capital: Bratislava, pop. 442,000
Currency: euro (EUR)
Religion: Roman Catholicism
Language: Slovak

Slovenia
Area: 7,827 sq mi (20,273 sq km)
Population: 2,098,000
Capital: Ljubljana, pop. 286,000
Currency: euro (EUR)
Religion: Roman Catholicism
Language: Slovene

Solomon Islands
Area: 11,157 sq mi (28,896 sq km)
Population: 727,000
Capital: Honiara, pop. 82,000
Currency: Solomon Islands dollar (SBD)
Religion: Protestantism
Language: Melanesian pidgin, English

COLOR KEY ● Africa ● Australia, New Zealand, and Oceania

GEOGRAPHY ROCKS

Somalia
Area: 246,201 sq mi (637,657 sq km)
Population: 13,017,000
Capital: Mogadishu, pop. 2,727,000
Currency: Somali shilling (SOS)
Religion: Islam
Language: Somali, Arabic

South Sudan
Area: 248,777 sq mi (644,329 sq km)
Population: 12,704,000
Capital: Juba, pop. 479,000
Currency: South Sudanese pound (SSP)
Religion: Christianity
Language: English

South Africa
Area: 470,693 sq mi (1,219,090 sq km)
Population: 60,443,000
Capitals: Pretoria (Tshwane), pop. 2,890,000; Cape Town, pop. 4,978,000; Bloemfontein, pop. 598,000
Currency: rand (ZAR)
Religion: Christianity
Language: isiZulu, isiXhosa, Afrikaans, Sepedi

Spain
Area: 195,124 sq mi (505,370 sq km)
Population: 47,280,000
Capital: Madrid, pop. 6,783,000
Currency: euro (EUR)
Religion: Roman Catholicism
Language: Castilian Spanish

3 cool things about SOUTH KOREA

1. K-pop music—which draws influence from other music styles including pop, rock, R & B, and hip-hop—originated in South Korea in the 1990s.

2. There are about 3,000 islands off the coast of South Korea. If you went to one island each day, it would take you more than nine years to visit them all.

3. More than 60 percent of South Korea is covered in forest.

Sri Lanka
Area: 25,332 sq mi (65,610 sq km)
Population: 21,983,000
Capitals: Colombo, pop. 640,000; Sri Jayewardenepura Kotte, pop. 103,000
Currency: Sri Lankan rupee (LKR)
Religion: Buddhism
Language: Sinhala, Tamil

St. Kitts and Nevis
Area: 101 sq mi (261 sq km)
Population: 55,000
Capital: Basseterre, pop. 14,000
Currency: East Caribbean dollar (XCD)
Religion: Protestantism
Language: English

South Korea
Area: 38,502 sq mi (99,720 sq km)
Population: 52,082,000
Capital: Seoul, pop. 10,005,000
Currency: South Korean won (KRW)
Religion: None
Language: Korean, English

St. Lucia
Area: 238 sq mi (616 sq km)
Population: 168,000
Capital: Castries, pop. 22,000
Currency: East Caribbean dollar (XCD)
Religion: Roman Catholicism
Language: English

● Asia ● Europe ● North America ● South America

COUNTRIES

St. Vincent and the Grenadines
Area: 150 sq mi (389 sq km)
Population: 101,000
Capital: Kingstown, pop. 27,000
Currency: East Caribbean dollar (XCD)
Religion: Protestantism
Language: English

Sudan
Area: 718,723 sq mi (1,861,484 sq km)
Population: 50,467,000
Capital: Khartoum, pop. 6,542,000
Currency: Sudanese pound (SDG)
Religion: Islam
Language: Arabic, English

Suriname
Area: 63,251 sq mi (163,820 sq km)
Population: 647,000
Capital: Paramaribo, pop. 239,000
Currency: Surinamese dollar (SRD)
Religion: Protestantism, Hinduism, Roman Catholicism
Language: Dutch, English, Sranan Tongo

Sweden
Area: 173,860 sq mi (450,295 sq km)
Population: 10,590,000
Capital: Stockholm, pop. 1,720,000
Currency: Swedish krona (SEK)
Religion: Protestantism, unspecified or none
Language: Swedish

A MONSTER with a dog's head and a long neck and tail is SAID TO HAUNT Sweden's LAKE STORSJÖN.

Switzerland
Area: 15,937 sq mi (41,277 sq km)
Population: 8,861,000
Capital: Bern, pop. 445,000
Currency: Swiss franc (CHF)
Religion: Roman Catholicism, unspecified, Protestantism
Language: German (Swiss German), French, Italian, Romansch

Syria
Area: 71,870 sq mi (186,142 sq km)
Population: 23,865,000
Capital: Damascus, pop. 2,685,000
Currency: Syrian pound (SYP)
Religion: Islam
Language: Arabic

Tajikistan
Area: 55,637 sq mi (144,100 sq km)
Population: 10,394,000
Capital: Dushanbe, pop. 1,013,000
Currency: Tajikistani somoni (TJS)
Religion: Islam
Language: Tajik

Tanzania
Area: 365,754 sq mi (947,300 sq km)
Population: 67,462,000
Capitals: Dodoma, pop. 262,000
Currency: Tanzanian shilling (TZS)
Religion: Christianity
Language: Kiswahili (Swahili), English

Thailand
Area: 198,117 sq mi (513,120 sq km)
Population: 69,921,000
Capital: Bangkok, pop. 11,234,000
Currency: baht (THB)
Religion: Buddhism
Language: Thai

COLOR KEY ● Africa ● Australia, New Zealand, and Oceania

GEOGRAPHY ROCKS

Timor-Leste (East Timor)
Area: 5,743 sq mi (14,874 sq km)
Population: 1,507,000
Capital: Dili, pop. 281,000
Currency: U.S. dollar (USD)
Religion: Roman Catholicism
Language: Tetun Prasa, Portuguese

Togo
Area: 21,925 sq mi (56,785 sq km)
Population: 8,918,000
Capital: Lomé, pop. 2,043,000
Currency: CFA franc BCEAO (XOF)
Religion: Christianity, folk religion
Language: French

Tonga
Area: 288 sq mi (747 sq km)
Population: 105,000
Capital: Nuku´alofa, pop. 23,000
Currency: pa'anga (TOP)
Religion: Protestantism
Language: Tongan, English

Trinidad and Tobago
Area: 1,980 sq mi (5,128 sq km)
Population: 1,409,000
Capital: Port of Spain, pop. 546,000
Currency: Trinidad and Tobago dollar (TTD)
Religion: Protestantism, Roman Catholicism
Language: English

Tunisia
Area: 63,170 sq mi (163,610 sq km)
Population: 12,049,000
Capital: Tunis, pop. 2,511,000
Currency: Tunisian dinar (TND)
Religion: Islam
Language: Arabic, French

Türkiye (Turkey)
Area: 302,535 sq mi (783,562 sq km)
Population: 84,120,000
Capital: Ankara, pop. 5,477,000
Currency: Turkish lira (TRY)
Religion: Islam
Language: Turkish

Türkiye is one of the MOST EARTHQUAKE-PRONE areas on Earth.

Turkmenistan
Area: 188,456 sq mi (488,100 sq km)
Population: 5,744,000
Capital: Ashgabat, pop. 922,000
Currency: Turkmenistani manat (TMT)
Religion: Islam
Language: Turkmen

Tuvalu
Area: 10 sq mi (26 sq km)
Population: 12,000
Capital: Funafuti, pop. 7,000
Currency: Australian dollar (AUD)
Religion: Protestantism
Language: Tuvaluan, English

Uganda
Area: 93,065 sq mi (241,038 sq km)
Population: 49,283,000
Capital: Kampala, pop. 4,051,000
Currency: Ugandan shilling (UGX)
Religion: Protestantism, Roman Catholicism
Language: English, Ganda (Luganda), Swahili

● Asia   ● Europe   ● North America   ● South America

COUNTRIES

Ukraine
Area: 233,032 sq mi (603,550 sq km)
Population: 35,662,000
Capital: Kyiv, pop. 3,020,000
Currency: hryvnia (UAH)
Religion: Eastern Orthodoxy
Language: Ukrainian, Russian

United Kingdom
Area: 94,058 sq mi (243,610 sq km)
Population: 68,459,000
Capital: London, pop. 9,748,000
Currency: pound sterling (GBP)
Religion: Christianity
Language: English

United Arab Emirates
Area: 32,278 sq mi (83,600 sq km)
Population: 10,032,000
Capital: Abu Dhabi, pop. 1,593,000
Currency: UAE dirham (AED)
Religion: Islam
Language: Arabic

United States
Area: 3,796,741 sq mi (9,833,517 sq km)
Population: 341,963,000
Capital: Washington, D.C., pop. 679,000
Currency: U.S. dollar (USD)
Religion: Protestantism
Language: English

SNAPSHOT
Vatican City

St. Peter's Basilica, at the center of Vatican City, is one of the largest religious buildings in the world.

COLOR KEY ● Africa ● Australia, New Zealand, and Oceania

GEOGRAPHY ROCKS

Uruguay
Area: 68,037 sq mi (176,215 sq km)
Population: 3,425,000
Capital: Montevideo, pop. 1,781,000
Currency: Uruguayan peso (UYU)
Religion: None, Roman Catholicism
Language: Spanish

Uzbekistan
Area: 172,742 sq mi (447,400 sq km)
Population: 36,521,000
Capital: Tashkent, pop. 2,634,000
Currency: Uzbekistan sum (UZS)
Religion: Islam
Language: Uzbek

Vanuatu
Area: 4,706 sq mi (12,189 sq km)
Population: 318,000
Capital: Port-Vila, pop. 53,000
Currency: Vatu (VUV)
Religion: Protestantism
Language: Indigenous languages, Bislama, English, French

Vatican City
Area: 0.2 sq mi (0.4 sq km)
Population: 1,000
Capital: Vatican City, pop. 1,000
Currency: euro (EUR)
Religion: Roman Catholicism
Language: Italian

Venezuela
Area: 352,144 sq mi (912,050 sq km)
Population: 31,250,000
Capital: Caracas, pop. 2,992,000
Currency: bolivar soberano (VES)
Religion: Roman Catholicism
Language: Spanish

Vietnam
Area: 127,881 sq mi (331,210 sq km)
Population: 105,759,000
Capital: Hanoi, pop. 5,432,000
Currency: dong (VND)
Religion: None
Language: Vietnamese, English

Yemen
Area: 203,850 sq mi (527,968 sq km)
Population: 32,140,000
Capital: Sanaa, pop. 3,408,000
Currency: Yemeni rial (YER)
Religion: Islam
Language: Arabic

Zambia
Area: 290,587 sq mi (752,618 sq km)
Population: 20,799,000
Capital: Lusaka, pop. 3,324,000
Currency: Zambian kwacha (ZMW)
Religion: Protestantism
Language: Indigenous languages, English

Zimbabwe
Area: 150,872 sq mi (390,757 sq km)
Population: 17,150,000
Capital: Harare, pop. 1,603,000
Currency: Zimbabwean dollar (ZWL)
Religion: Protestantism
Language: Shona, Ndebele, English

Taller than two Empire State Buildings stacked on top of each other, ANGEL FALLS in Venezuela is the WORLD'S TALLEST uninterrupted WATERFALL.

● Asia ● Europe ● North America ● South America

TRAVEL

awes8me

THESE EIGHT ARCHITECTURAL WONDERS STRETCH ENGINEERING.

Brilliant Bridges

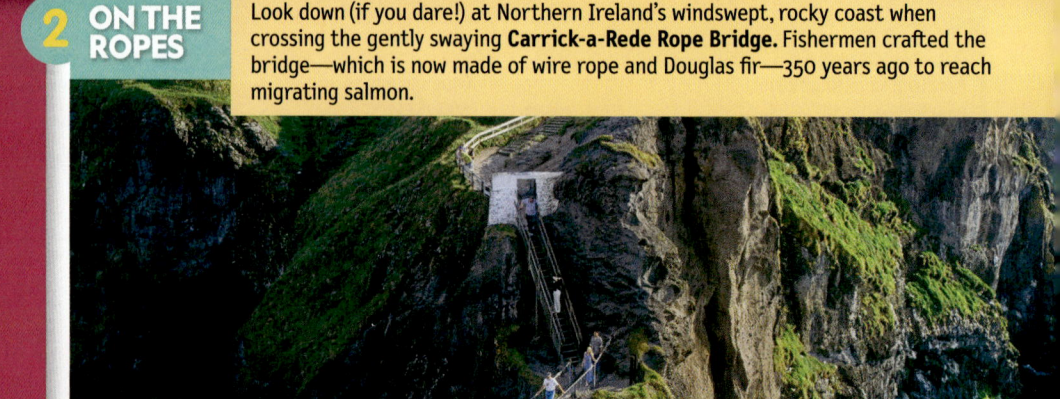

1 RECORD BREAKER

Glass panels built into the deck of this bridge add a heart-pounding thrill. Located in central China, the **Zhangjiajie Grand Canyon Glass Bridge** is the longest, at 1,410 feet (430 m), and highest, at 985 feet (300 m), glass-bottomed suspension bridge in the world.

2 ON THE ROPES

Look down (if you dare!) at Northern Ireland's windswept, rocky coast when crossing the gently swaying **Carrick-a-Rede Rope Bridge.** Fishermen crafted the bridge—which is now made of wire rope and Douglas fir—350 years ago to reach migrating salmon.

GEOGRAPHY ROCKS

4 FLOATING WALKWAY

For about two weeks in the summer of 2016, an artist named Christo created a saffron-colored floating bridge to connect two islands in northern Italy's Lake Iseo to the mainland. The fabric of **"The Floating Piers"** changed colors depending on the temperature and weather.

5 RENAISSANCE MARVEL

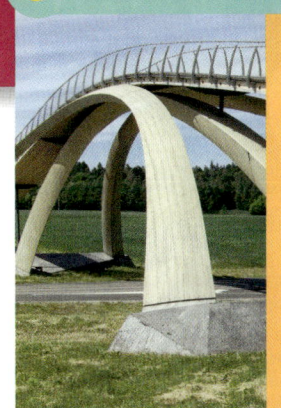

This bridge took almost 500 years to build—sort of. Renaissance artist **Leonardo da Vinci** designed the bridge for a sultan, but it was never built. When completed in 2001 near Oslo, Norway, the wooden pedestrian bridge brought Leonardo da Vinci's design to life.

3 FLYING FOOTBRIDGE

When completed in 2000, the **Millennium Footbridge** became the first walkway built over the Thames River in central London, England, in more than a hundred years. This 1,210-foot (370-m)-long steel bridge was destroyed in the movie *Harry Potter and the Half-Blood Prince*—but don't worry, that was all done by special effects.

6 WAVY WONDER

This bridge knows how to make a splash! The **Henderson Waves** bridge in Singapore is made from balau wood, found only in Southeast Asia. The wavy bridge, which glows at dusk, extends 900 feet (274 m) and offers walkers places to rest and spots to hide.

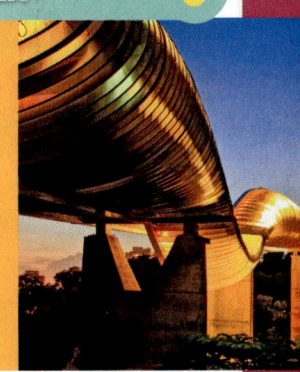

7 TREETOP TRANSFER

Stretching for 450 feet (137 m) through a lush rainforest, the **Capilano Suspension Bridge** looks remote, but it's located just 10 minutes from downtown Vancouver, Canada. Visitors can see 230 feet (70 m) down to the Capilano River below or gaze out through the trees.

8 STEEL SAILS

Peeking above low clouds, the **Øresund Bridge** soars more than 1,600 feet (490 m) over the Flint Channel to connect Malmö, Sweden, to Copenhagen, Denmark. The cable-stayed bridge carries cars on the upper level and trains on the lower.

TRAVEL

15 AMAZING FACTS ABOUT CITIES

RHESUS MACAQUES IN NEW DELHI, INDIA, CAN **SNATCH EYEGLASSES** AND **PURSES** FROM PEDESTRIANS.

MEXICO CITY, MEXICO, has more than 150 **MUSEUMS.**

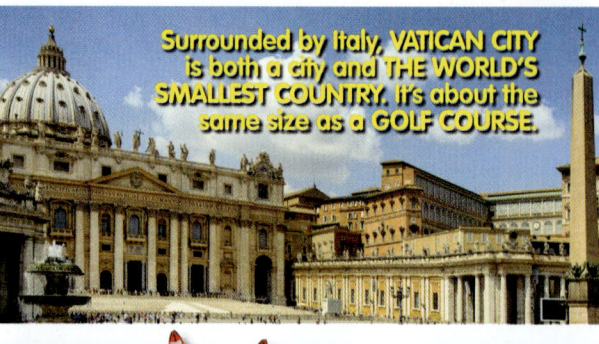

Surrounded by Italy, **VATICAN CITY** is both a city and **THE WORLD'S SMALLEST COUNTRY.** It's about the same size as a **GOLF COURSE.**

About one-third of the 5.4 million people living in Dar es Salaam, Tanzania, **ARE 14 YEARS OLD OR YOUNGER.**

A mall in the desert city of Dubai, United Arab Emirates, **HAS AN INDOOR SKI RESORT.**

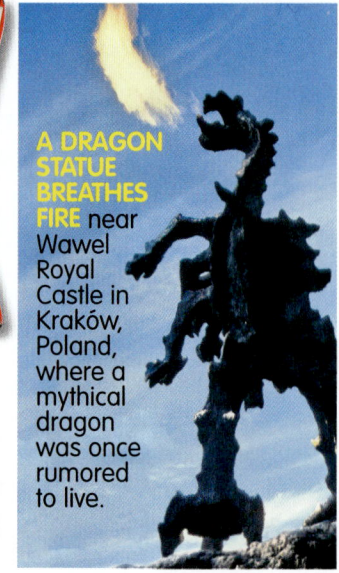

A DRAGON STATUE BREATHES FIRE near Wawel Royal Castle in Kraków, Poland, where a mythical dragon was once rumored to live.

EVERY SUMMER NIGHT IN AUSTIN, TEXAS, U.S.A., MORE THAN **A MILLION BATS** fly out from under a bridge to eat insects.

GEOGRAPHY ROCKS

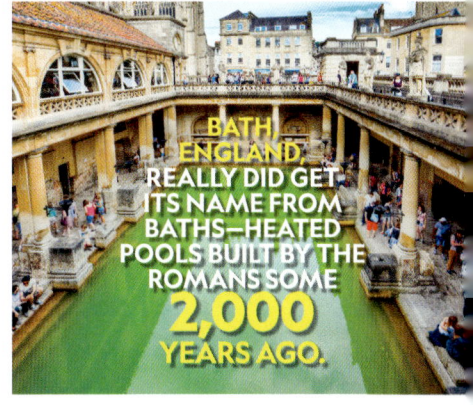

In Canberra, Australia, thousands of **eastern gray kangaroos** often invade the city **to drink water and munch grass.**

In Curitiba, Brazil, the local government has used **30 sheep** to "mow" the parks.

LIMA, PERU, averages about **A HALF INCH** (1.3 cm) of rain a year.

In the Philippines, **FLIGHTS AT THE AIRPORT** in Manila have been canceled on New Year's Eve because of smoke from the **MILLIONS OF FIREWORKS AND FIRECRACKERS** people shoot off.

City Hall in San Francisco, California, U.S.A., sits on 530 shock absorbers the size of washing machines that help protect the building during earthquakes.

ISTANBUL, TÜRKİYE, is the only major city to stand on two continents: **ASIA AND EUROPE.**

THE TUK-TUK— A THREE-WHEELED, MOTORIZED RICKSHAW— IS A COMMON FORM OF PUBLIC TRANSPORTATION IN BANGKOK, THAILAND.

BATH, ENGLAND, REALLY DID GET ITS NAME FROM BATHS—HEATED POOLS BUILT BY THE ROMANS SOME 2,000 YEARS AGO.

TRAVEL

COOLEST DIVE

SILFRA FISSURE
ÞINGVELLIR (THINGVELLIR) NATIONAL PARK, ICELAND

Did you know you could actually witness continents spreading apart? It's true, but you would have to be pretty patient! The underwater Silfra fissure offers a prime spot for a firsthand look at the dynamics of the tectonic plates that make up the crust of our planet. The fissure, or crack between two tectonic plates, is located off the coast of western Iceland and is along the divide between Europe and North America. While the water is so clear that scuba divers can see for more than 300 feet (100 m), watching the continents spreading apart takes more than clear water: The deep fissure widens by only about .75 inch (2 cm) a year.

The three colors in Iceland's flag represent the elements that make up the island country: red for volcanic fires, white for snow and ice fields, and blue for the surrounding ocean.

Iceland's coastline is marked by fjords, which are deep inlets formed by glaciers.

GEOGRAPHY ROCKS

8 COOL THINGS ABOUT RAINFOREST CULTURES

Groups of people have been living in rainforests around the world for tens of thousands of years. Check out amazing facts about the history, art, and contributions of these cultures.

THE KAYAPO OF BRAZIL MAKE HUNTING SPEAR TIPS WITH SHARP STINGRAY SPINES.

The Olmec, which thrived some 3,000 years ago in Central America, carved 11-foot (3.4 m)-high stone heads.

By spraying bee-repelling sap onto hives, India's Jarawa people draw away the insects so they can extract honey.

Some 2,000 years ago, voyagers canoed 1,500 miles (2,400 km) from the rainforest-covered Solomon Islands to other Pacific islands.

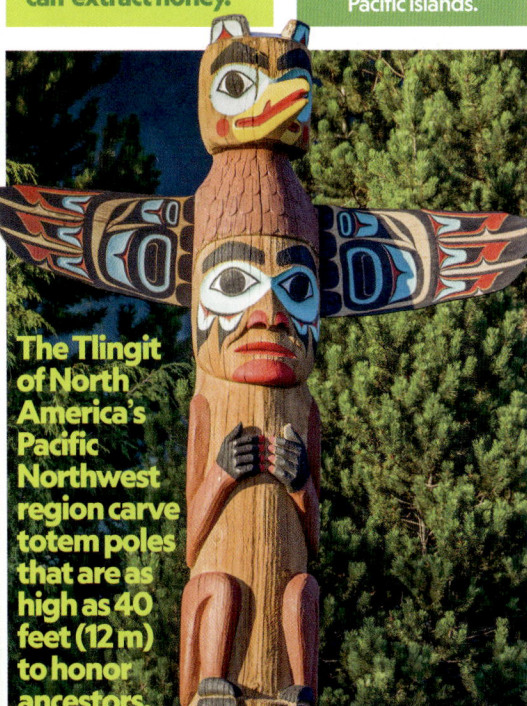

Indonesia's Korowai people dwell in tree houses often built over a hundred feet (30 m) aboveground.

The Tlingit of North America's Pacific Northwest region carve totem poles that are as high as 40 feet (12 m) to honor ancestors.

Ecuador's Waorani people capture anacondas with bare hands as a test of strength.

The Tzeltal, a Maya people in Mexico, use beetle wings as jewelry.

337

TRAVEL

WILD VACATIONS

Cave Hotel
YUNAK EVLERI HOTEL

WHERE: Cappadocia region, Türkiye (Turkey)
WHY IT'S COOL: Here's a hotel that really rocks. The Yunak Evleri is built into caves left by volcanic activity 10 million years ago. Follow narrow passageways and stone stairs to rooms that are a cool 57°F (14°C). Spend the day hiking rocky terrain, exploring caverns, or riding hot-air balloons over "fairy chimneys"—tall rock formations that dot the skyline. At night you won't have to worry about being awakened by eruptions because the Cappadocia volcanoes are now dormant. So they're "sleeping," too!

SLEEP HERE!

COOL THINGS ABOUT TÜRKIYE

Dating from A.D. 537, the famous Hagia Sophia was built as a church, turned into a mosque, then a museum, and then back into a mosque.

Early Turkish settlers once lived in the caves of the Cappadocia region.

King Midas may not have turned everything he touched into gold. But he did rule over the kingdom of Phrygia, in what is now Türkiye, in the eighth century B.C.

THINGS TO DO IN TÜRKIYE

Take a boat ride across the Bosporus and get from Asia to Europe in 15 minutes.

Wander the ruins of the Temple of Artemis, built more than 2,500 years ago for the Greek goddess of hunting.

Haggle with shopkeepers in the bustling market of Istanbul's Grand Bazaar.

GEOGRAPHY ROCKS

EAT ON TABLES AND CHAIRS MADE OF SALT!

Salt Hotel
TAYKA HOTEL DE SAL

COOL THINGS ABOUT BOLIVIA

During rainy summer months, Bolivia's Salar de Uyuni salt flat looks like a giant mirror.

The bus station in La Paz was designed by Gustav Eiffel, the same architect who built the Eiffel Tower and the Statue of Liberty.

Every August in Bolivia, dogs are honored during the Feast of St. Roch.

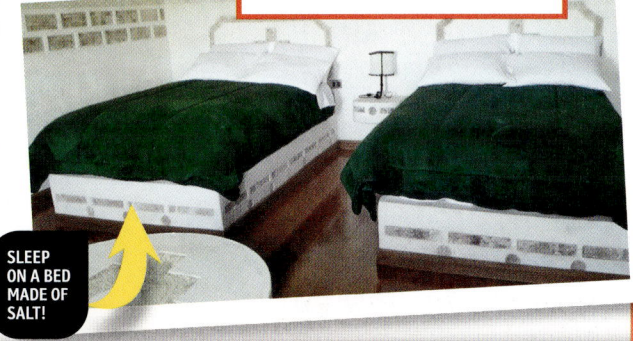

WHERE: Tahua, Bolivia

WHY IT'S COOL: You've stayed at hotels made of brick or wood. But salt? Tayka Hotel de Sal is made mostly of salt (*sal* means "salt" in Spanish), including some beds—though you'll sleep with regular mattresses and blankets. The hotel sits on the border of Salar de Uyuni, a prehistoric dried-up lake that's the world's biggest salt flat. Builders use the salt from the over 4,000-square-mile (10,000-sq-km) flat to make the bricks and glue them together with a paste of wet salt that hardens when it dries. When rain starts to dissolve the hotel, it's no problem: The owners just mix up more salt paste to strengthen the bricks.

SLEEP ON A BED MADE OF SALT!

THINGS TO DO IN BOLIVIA

Take a boat to Isla del Sol, an island in Lake Titicaca, where motorized vehicles aren't allowed.

Walk up to the Gate of the Sun, a huge stone doorway built by the ancient Tiwanaku culture.

Dance with thousands of masked and costumed performers at the Carnival de Oruro.

339

TRAVEL

Bet You Didn't Know!
6 rad facts about the beach

1 According to legend, **wild horses** roaming a beach shared by Maryland and Virginia, U.S.A., descend from **survivors** of a 17th-century **shipwreck.**

2 At **Hot Water Beach** in New Zealand, underground **volcanic water** creates natural **hot springs** during low tide.

3 Tourists at a Hawaiian beach discovered **rock carvings** more than **400** years old.

WILD HORSES REST ON ASSATEAGUE ISLAND IN MARYLAND.

4 Glass Beach in California, U.S.A., is made up of multicolored pieces of **sea glass** that formed over the past 100 years from a nearby **trash site.**

5 A man once surfed an 80-foot (24-m)-tall **wave**—that's about as high as an **8-story building.**

6 People swim at the same speed in both **water** and **syrup.**

340

GEOGRAPHY ROCKS

BY THE NUMBERS

GREAT BARRIER REEF

"Great" is putting it mildly when it comes to the Great Barrier Reef, the world's largest coral reef system. And these numbers prove it!

STRETCHES 1,249 MILES (2,010 KM)

INCLUDES 3,000 CORAL REEFS AND 600 CONTINENTAL ISLANDS

COVERS 132,974 SQUARE MILES (344,400 SQ KM), ABOUT THE SAME SIZE AS JAPAN

1,625 TYPES OF **FISH**

136 VARIETIES OF **SHARKS** AND **RAYS**

30 SPECIES OF **WHALES, PORPOISES,** AND **DOLPHINS**

14 SPECIES OF **SEA SNAKES**

600 TYPES OF SOFT AND HARD **CORAL**

215 SPECIES OF **BIRDS** THAT **VISIT** OR **NEST** THERE

TRAVEL

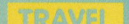

SUPERSIZE SITES

Check out some of the biggest wow-worthy spots on Earth.

SKY-HIGH BUILDING
BURJ KHALIFA

New York City's Empire State Building held the title of "world's tallest building" from the time it was completed in 1931 to 1970, when the World Trade Center's north tower was built. Since the 1970s, the race to build the tallest has been a series of one-uppings. For several years, Burj Khalifa—located in Dubai, United Arab Emirates—has kept a firm grasp on the title. The skyscraper stands more than 2,716.5 feet (828 m) tall and contains a whopping 163 stories. (It also boasts the highest elevator!)

GEOGRAPHY ROCKS

FANTASTIC FERRIS WHEEL
HIGH ROLLER

Talk about reinventing the wheel! Covered in more than 2,000 lights, the 550-foot (168-m) High Roller observation wheel, located in Las Vegas, Nevada, U.S.A., isn't the average Ferris wheel you find at a county fair. Passengers sit in one of the wheel's 28 "pods"—glass cabins that provide a 360-degree view. Adrenaline-seekers be warned: This is a leisurely ride. It takes 30 minutes for the wheel to complete one revolution—that's just one foot (0.3 m) a second!

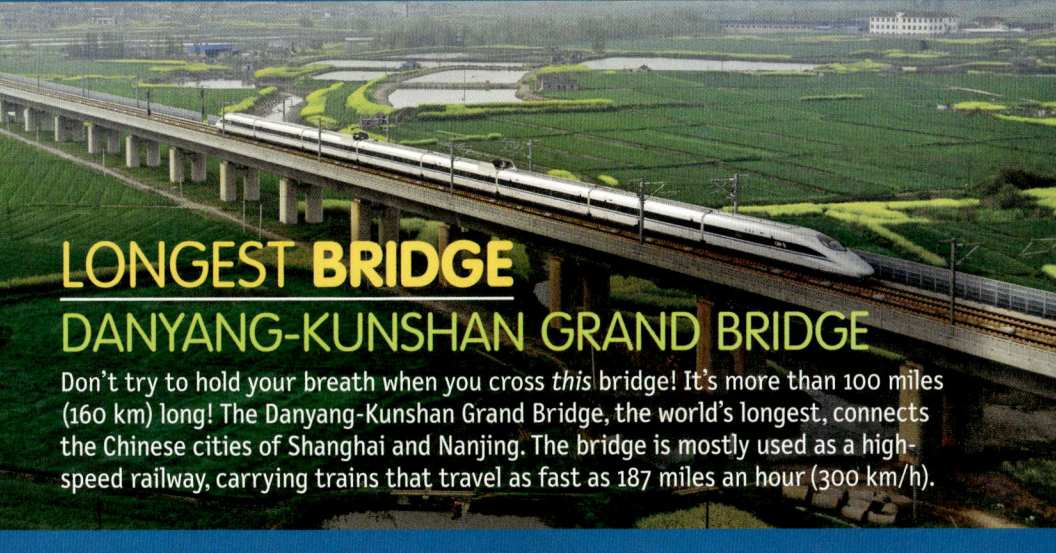

LONGEST BRIDGE
DANYANG-KUNSHAN GRAND BRIDGE

Don't try to hold your breath when you cross *this* bridge! It's more than 100 miles (160 km) long! The Danyang-Kunshan Grand Bridge, the world's longest, connects the Chinese cities of Shanghai and Nanjing. The bridge is mostly used as a high-speed railway, carrying trains that travel as fast as 187 miles an hour (300 km/h).

MASSIVE SWIMMING POOL
SAN ALFONSO DEL MAR

Want to hit the pool and swim a few laps? Put on your goggles and clear your afternoon! Just one lap in the San Alfonso del Mar seawater pool, located in Algarrobo, Chile, is the equivalent of 20 laps in an Olympic-size pool. It holds 66 million gallons (250 million L) of water and is so big that small sailboats can cruise on it!

TRAVEL

10 NEAT FACTS ABOUT NATIONAL PARKS

Ruins from Maya settlements more than 1,000 years old are found at **Tikal National Park** in Guatemala.

Bryce Canyon National Park in Utah, U.S.A., is filled with **hoodoos**—limestone spires created by weather and erosion.

SERENGETI NATIONAL PARK IN TANZANIA SEES THE ANNUAL MIGRATION OF HUNDREDS OF THOUSANDS OF WILDEBEESTS, ZEBRAS, AND GAZELLES. IT IS CONSIDERED TO HAVE ONE OF THE PLANET'S OLDEST ECOSYSTEMS.

Italy's Etna National Park holds one of the **MOST ACTIVE VOLCANOES** on Earth. Mount Etna has been in a state of near continuous eruption **FOR HALF A MILLION YEARS!**

Kaieteur Falls in **GUYANA'S Kaieteur National Park** is five times higher than Niagara Falls.

344

GEOGRAPHY ROCKS

Edelweiss is a protected flower that grows thousands of feet above sea level in **the Swiss National Park in Switzerland;** it is the subject of a song in the movie *The Sound of Music.*

You can take an elevator down 750 feet (229 m) into a cave at **Carlsbad Caverns National Park in New Mexico, U.S.A.**

Saguaro National Park in Arizona, U.S.A., has 25 species of cactus, including the teddy-bear cholla cactus and the pinkflower hedgehog cactus.

India's Kaziranga National Park is home to **2,000 one-horned rhinos;** rhinos can **run 25 miles an hour** (40 km/h).

THE PETIT TRAIN D'ARTOUSTE, THE LITTLE RAILWAY IN **FRANCE'S PYRÉNÉES NATIONAL PARK, TAKES TOURISTS TO AN ALTITUDE OF 6,562 FEET** (2,000 M). IT IS ONE OF EUROPE'S HIGHEST RAILWAYS.

TRAVEL

awes8me
UNIQUE JAW-DROPPING STRUCTURES FROM AROUND THE WORLD

1 BLAZING BUILDINGS

These towers in Baku, Azerbaijan, are hot! Not only are they the tallest buildings in the capital city, rising some 800 feet (244 m), they also contain living and office spaces. What makes the **Flame Towers** really sizzle? At night, they light up as if they're on fire.

BIZARRE BUILDINGS

2 FLOWING FACADE

The **Museum of Pop Culture** in Seattle, Washington, U.S.A., changes its look depending on the light and the viewer's location. Three thousand panels made of 21,000 aluminum and steel shingles give the building its fluid form.

ALL THE STEEL USED IN THE BUILDING, STRETCHED OUT TO BE AS THIN AS THE THINNEST BANJO STRING, WOULD REACH A QUARTER OF THE WAY TO VENUS.

GEOGRAPHY ROCKS

3 TEA TIME

This 10-story-tall building isn't designed to make an extremely large cup of morning brew. The **Wuxi Wanda Cultural Tourism City Exhibition Center** in Wuxi, China, pays homage to local teapot culture. A mini roller coaster, Ferris wheel, and movable sand table are located inside.

4 TRUNK TOWER

The **Chang Building** in Bangkok, Thailand, should be called the Pachyderm Palace. At 335 feet (102 m) high, the elephant-shaped building includes offices, apartments, and a shopping mall. And this building's "ears" are actually multilevel balconies.

5 ROUND WONDER

There's no bad view from the **headquarters of Aldar**, a real estate company in Abu Dhabi, United Arab Emirates. The 23-floor, spherical building also performs as well as it looks: An underground recycling facility reuses waste from the building.

6 DIAMOND DAZZLER

The diamond-shaped **National Library of Belarus**, located in the capital city of Minsk, uses natural light to shine during the day. But at night it performs its own light show, with more than 4,600 LED fixtures that can be controlled for different effects.

7 SHOWSTOPPER

The **Haines Shoe House** looks like it was made for hiking, but this vacation rental near York, Pennsylvania, U.S.A., has a sweet side: It once had an ice-cream shop inside. At nearly three stories tall and 48 feet (15 m) long, this is one *boot*-iful building.

8 FLOWER POWER

Thousands of people visit the Bahá'í **Lotus Temple** in New Delhi, India, every day. Nine is a mystical number for the followers of the Bahá'í Faith, and nine pools surround 27 marble "lotus" petals, which make the temple appear to float on water.

347

TRAVEL

WINTER OLYMPICS 2026

Milan and Cortina
February 6-22

IN 1956, THE WINTER OLYMPICS WERE HELD IN CORTINA, ITALY.

THE SKATING RINK IN THE ITALIAN ALPS AT THE 1956 WINTER GAMES

When the Olympics kick off in February 2026, it will mark the first time two cities have hosted the Winter Games. With the majority of the events taking place in either Milan or Cortina d'Ampezzo, Italy, the entire event will cover a total of 8,494 square miles (22,000 sq km), making it the most geographically widespread Winter Games ever.

ITALY'S OLYMPIC HISTORY

This isn't the first time Italy has hosted the Winter Games. In fact, Cortina, perched high in the Italian Alps, was the site of the 1956 Winter Olympics. The XX Olympic Winter Games in 2006 took place in Turin. Rome, Italy, also hosted the Summer Games in 1960. This time, events will be held in various areas throughout the country, from the slopes outside Cortina and Bormio for the skiing events to the arenas of Milan for events like hockey, figure skating, and short-track speed skating.

SHANI DAVIS (U.S.A.) SPEED SKATING AT THE 2006 WINTER GAMES IN TURIN, ITALY

IN 2006, THE WINTER OLYMPIC GAMES WERE HELD IN TURIN, ITALY.

In ancient Greece, Olympic athletes COVERED THEIR BODIES IN OLIVE OIL AND FINE SAND, in part to protect their skin from the sun.

348

GEOGRAPHY ROCKS

GENDER-BALANCED GAMES

These games are set to be the most balanced Winter Olympics in terms of gender. Out of approximately 2,900 athletes, about 47 percent of them are expected to be female, participating in 50 women's events. This is a jump up from 40 percent female participation in 2014, and quite a leap from the very first time the Winter Games were held as a stand-alone event in 1924, when women represented just 11 out of 258 athletes (that's 4 percent!).

WOMEN first took part in the 1900 OLYMPICS, held in Paris, France, competing in tennis, sailing, croquet, horseback riding, and golf.

AUSTRIAN LUGER ANDREA TAGWERKER AT THE 1994 OLYMPIC GAMES IN LILLEHAMMER, NORWAY

NEW EVENTS TO WATCH

Another stand-out stat from these games? The addition of eight new events. For the first time, we'll see a mixed-team event (one man and one woman) in the skeleton, women's doubles in luge, men's and women's dual moguls in freestyle skiing, and women's large hill ski jumping. Ski mountaineering—also known as skimo—is another new event to the Olympic lineup. In skimo, athletes race to see who's the fastest as they hike or ski up a mountain and then ski down it. Medals will be awarded in the men's sprint, women's sprint, and mixed-gender relay.

SKI MOUNTAINEERING (KNOWN AS SKIMO) WILL BE A NEW EVENT AT THE 2026 WINTER GAMES.

FASTER, HIGHER, STRONGER

The Olympic motto is "Citius, Altius, Fortius—Communiter" ("Faster, Higher, Stronger—Together") and there's no doubt that's exactly what the athletes will be focusing on during their competitions throughout the Winter Games. When it comes to the podium, all eyes will be on Norway, which is the all-time leader in the Winter Olympics medal count. Can the Norwegians top the 16 gold medals they earned in the Beijing games in 2022—the most by any country in one Winter Olympics? Only time, and a lot of amazing competition, will tell.

Olympic GOLD MEDALS are actually more than 90 PERCENT SILVER.

TRAVEL

Bizarre EVENTS

MEXICO CITY'S SUMMER CELEBRATION
WHAT: Kermit Salutes Statue
WHERE: Mexico City, Mexico
WHY IT'S BIZARRE: It's easy being green when you're the star of the parade. A giant Kermit the Frog balloon floated by the capital's famous Angel of Independence monument as part of a parade to welcome summer. The Muppet was joined by the likes of Mickey Mouse and Spider-Man. Who knew frogs could fly?

OUTHOUSE RACE
WHAT: Skiing Toilet
WHERE: Anchorage, Alaska, U.S.A.
WHY IT'S BIZARRE: This event brings new meaning to "potty training." Alaska's most populous city hosts a winter festival each year to celebrate the state's history. A crowd favorite is the outhouse race in which residents paint outhouses, or outdoor bathrooms, before pushing them through town on skis. Wonder if the prize is a golden plunger?

Aside from being the fastest, competitors can also pick up prizes for having the cleanest and most realistic-looking outhouses.

INTERNATIONAL PILLOW FIGHT DAY
WHAT: Attack of the Feathers
WHERE: Budapest, Hungary
WHY IT'S BIZARRE: Feathers fly as a massive crowd bops each other with pillows. Many cities participate in the April event, held to encourage people to get off their rumps and play.

Down pillows are discouraged in some cities because they make too much of a mess.

GEOGRAPHY ROCKS

THE ORIGINAL 7 WONDERS of the WORLD

More than 2,000 years ago, many travelers wrote about sights they had seen on their journeys. Over time, seven of those places made history as the "wonders of the ancient world." There are seven because the Greeks, who made the list, believed the number seven to be magical.

THE PYRAMIDS OF GIZA, EGYPT
BUILT: ABOUT 2600 B.C.
MASSIVE TOMBS OF EGYPTIAN PHARAOHS LIE INSIDE THIS ANCIENT WONDER—THE ONLY ONE STILL STANDING TODAY.

HANGING GARDENS OF BABYLON, IRAQ
BUILT: DATE UNKNOWN
LEGEND HAS IT THAT THIS GARDEN PARADISE WAS PLANTED ON AN ARTIFICIAL MOUNTAIN, BUT MANY EXPERTS SAY IT NEVER REALLY EXISTED.

TEMPLE OF ARTEMIS AT EPHESUS, TÜRKİYE
BUILT: SIXTH CENTURY B.C.
THIS TOWERING TEMPLE WAS BUILT TO HONOR ARTEMIS, THE GREEK GODDESS OF THE HUNT.

STATUE OF ZEUS, GREECE
BUILT: FIFTH CENTURY B.C.
THIS 40-FOOT (12-M) STATUE DEPICTED THE KING OF THE GREEK GODS.

MAUSOLEUM AT HALICARNASSUS, TÜRKİYE
BUILT: FOURTH CENTURY B.C.
THIS ELABORATE TOMB WAS BUILT FOR KING MAUSOLUS.

COLOSSUS OF RHODES, RHODES (AN ISLAND IN THE AEGEAN SEA)
BUILT: FOURTH CENTURY B.C.
THE 110-FOOT (34-M) STATUE HONORED THE GREEK SUN GOD HELIOS.

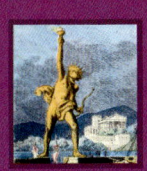

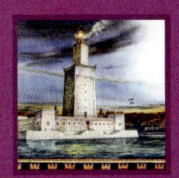

LIGHTHOUSE OF ALEXANDRIA, EGYPT
BUILT: THIRD CENTURY B.C.
THE WORLD'S FIRST LIGHTHOUSE, IT USED MIRRORS TO REFLECT SUNLIGHT FOR MILES OUT TO SEA.

THE NEW 7 WONDERS of the WORLD

Why name new wonders of the world? Most of the original ancient wonders no longer exist. To be eligible for the new list, the wonders had to be human-made before the year 2000 and in preservation. They were selected through a poll of more than 100 million voters!

TAJ MAHAL, INDIA
COMPLETED: 1648
THIS LAVISH TOMB WAS BUILT AS A FINAL RESTING PLACE FOR MUMTAZ MAHAL, THE BELOVED WIFE OF EMPEROR SHAH JAHAN.

PETRA, SOUTHWEST JORDAN
COMPLETED: ABOUT 200 B.C.
SOME 30,000 PEOPLE ONCE LIVED IN THIS ROCK CITY CARVED INTO CLIFF WALLS.

MACHU PICCHU, PERU
COMPLETED: ABOUT 1450
OFTEN CALLED THE "LOST CITY IN THE CLOUDS," MACHU PICCHU IS PERCHED 7,710 FEET (2,350 M) HIGH IN THE ANDES.

THE COLOSSEUM, ITALY
COMPLETED: A.D. 80
WILD ANIMALS—AND HUMANS—FOUGHT EACH OTHER TO THE DEATH BEFORE 50,000 SPECTATORS IN THIS ARENA.

CHRIST THE REDEEMER STATUE, BRAZIL
COMPLETED: 1931
TOWERING ATOP CORCOVADO MOUNTAIN, THIS STATUE IS TALLER THAN A 12-STORY BUILDING AND WEIGHS ABOUT 2.5 MILLION POUNDS (1.1 MILLION KG).

CHICHÉN ITZÁ, MEXICO
COMPLETED: 10TH CENTURY
ONCE THE CAPITAL CITY OF THE ANCIENT MAYA EMPIRE, CHICHÉN ITZÁ IS HOME TO THE FAMOUS PYRAMID OF KUKULCÁN.

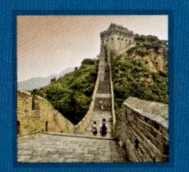

GREAT WALL OF CHINA, CHINA
COMPLETED: 1644
THE LONGEST HUMAN-MADE STRUCTURE EVER BUILT, IT WINDS OVER AN ESTIMATED 4,500 MILES (7,200 KM).

MORE FOR YOU

QUIZ WHIZ

Is your geography knowledge off the map? Quiz yourself to find out!

Write your answers on a piece of paper. Then check them below.

1 **True or false?** The world's deepest lake is in Russia.

2 Which country is host to the Winter Olympics in 2026?
a. the United States
b. Sweden
c. Italy
d. China

3 **True or false?** New Zealand has more people than sheep.

4 Fossils in the area around the Bay of Fundy are from _____.
a. the Coal Age
b. the Bronze Age
c. the New Age
d. the Old Age

5 Axolotls can be found in the wild _____.
a. on every continent
b. in tropical waters
c. only in South America
d. only in one lake in Mexico

Not **STUMPED** yet? Check out the *NATIONAL GEOGRAPHIC KIDS QUIZ WHIZ* collection for more fun **GEOGRAPHY** questions!

ANSWERS: 1. True; 2. c; 3. False; 4. a; 5. d

HOMEWORK HELP

GEOGRAPHY ROCKS

Finding Your Way Around

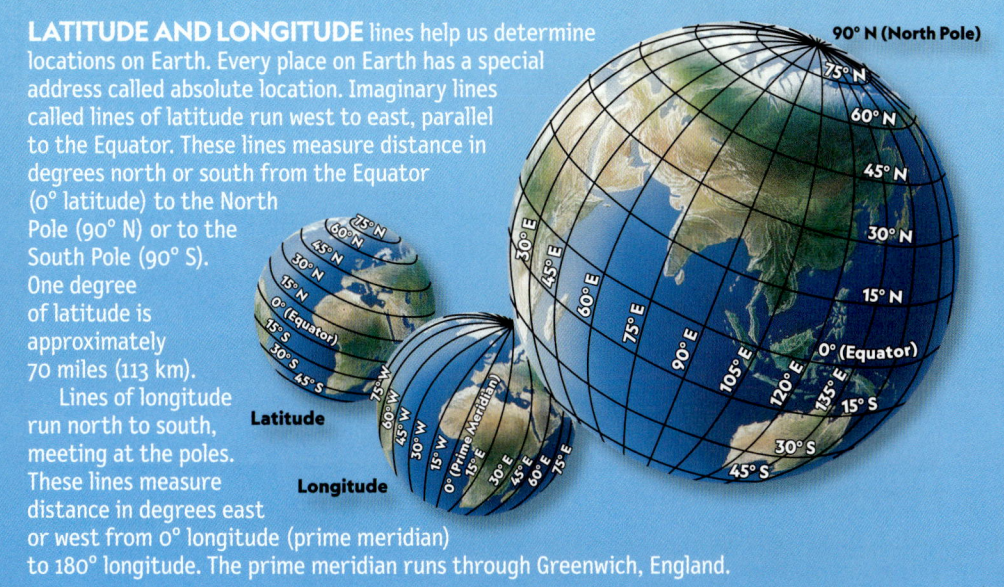

LATITUDE AND LONGITUDE lines help us determine locations on Earth. Every place on Earth has a special address called absolute location. Imaginary lines called lines of latitude run west to east, parallel to the Equator. These lines measure distance in degrees north or south from the Equator (0° latitude) to the North Pole (90° N) or to the South Pole (90° S). One degree of latitude is approximately 70 miles (113 km).

Lines of longitude run north to south, meeting at the poles. These lines measure distance in degrees east or west from 0° longitude (prime meridian) to 180° longitude. The prime meridian runs through Greenwich, England.

ABSOLUTE LOCATION: Suppose you are using latitude and longitude to play a game of global scavenger hunt. The clue says the prize is hidden at absolute location 30° S, 60° W. You know that the first number is south of the Equator, and the second is west of the prime meridian. On the map at right, find the line of latitude labeled 30° S. Now find the line of longitude labeled 60° W. Trace these lines with your fingers until they meet. Identify this spot. The prize must be located in northern Argentina (see arrow, right).

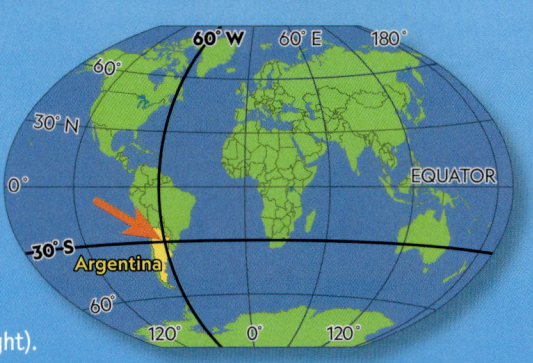

CHALLENGE!

1. Look at the map of Africa on pp. 280–281. Which country can you find at 10° S, 20° E?
2. Look at the map of Asia on pp. 288–289. Which country can you find at 20° N, 80° E?
3. On the map of Europe on pp. 296–297, which country is found at 50° N, 30° E?
4. Look at the map of North America on pp. 300–301. Which country can you find at 20° N, 100° W?

ANSWERS: 1. Angola; 2. India; 3. Ukraine; 4. Mexico

GAME ANSWERS

Shivering Shapes
page 130
1. giant panda
2. Japanese macaque
3. Amur leopard
4. northern cardinal

What in the World?
page 132
Top row: jelly bean, window, fish
Middle row: blimp, cat's eye, stadium
Bottom row: beetle, opal, kiwi fruit

Find the Hidden Animals
pages 134–135
1. F, 2. B, 3. A, 4. E, 5. G 6. D, 7. C

Stump Your Parents
page 137
1. C, 2. D, 3. C, 4. D, 5. C, 6. A, 7. A, 8. D, 9. B

Signs of the Times
page 138
Signs 2 and 4 are fake.

What in the World?
page 140
Top row: sunflowers, peas, cars
Middle row: bicycles, marching band, paint set
Bottom row: houses, dominoes, stadium seats

Stump Your Parents
page 141
1. D, 2. A, 3. B, 4. B, 5. C, 6. C, 7. B, 8. B, 9. A, 10. D

Surf's Up!
pages 144–145

GAME ANSWERS & MORE RESOURCES

Want to Learn More?
Find more information about topics in this book in these National Geographic Kids resources.

Weird But True! series

Just Joking series

5,000 Awesome Facts (About Everything!) series

1,000 Facts series

Ultimate Book of the Future
Stephanie Warren Drimmer
June 2022

Break Down
Mara Grunbaum
August 2022

Not-So-Common Cents
Sarah Wassner Flynn
January 2023

Critter Chat: World Wild Web
Jason Viola
August 2023

The Ultimate Book of Reptiles
Ruchira Somaweera and Stephanie Warren Drimmer
August 2023

How to Survive in the Age of Pirates
Crispin Boyer
June 2024

Yes! No? Maybe So...
National Geographic Kids
July 2024

Weird But True! World 2025
National Geographic Kids
August 2024

Your World 2026
(8–17)
All articles in section by Sarah Wassner Flynn

Greatest Breakthroughs
(18–33)
pp. 20–25 all articles by Sarah Wassner Flynn; pp. 26–27 "How to Find a Fossil" by Lee Berger; pp. 28–29 "Eye in the Sky" by Stephanie Warren Drimmer; pp. 30–31 "Make a Telescope" by Nancy Honovich and Julie Beer

Amazing Animals
(34–85)
pp. 36–37 "Dog Hangs Ten" by Aaron Sidder, "Goats 'Fight' Fires" by Chris Iovenko, "Pricey Pig Painting" by Kay Boatner; p. 38 "Big Question" by Julie Beer; p. 39 "Animal Myths Busted" by Paige Towler; pp. 40–43 "Cool Animal Superlatives" by Sarah Wassner Flynn; pp. 44–45 "What Is Taxonomy?" and "Vertebrates"/"Invertebrates" by Susan K. Donnelly; pp. 46–47 "Comeback Critter: Horseshoe Crab" by Amy McKeever; pp. 48–49 "Comeback Critter: Scarlet Macaw" by Allyson Shaw; pp. 50–51 "So. Many. Penguins!" by Jamie Kiffel-Alcheh; pp. 52–53 "10 Cool Facts About Penguins" by Leonie Joubert, Julie Beer, and Michelle Harris; pp. 54–55 "Clever Creatures" by Julie Beer and Michelle Harris; pp. 56–57 "Invisible Frogs" by Jason Bittel; pp. 58–59 "Incredible Animal Friends" by Kitson Jazynka; pp. 60–61 "10 Tips to Help Animals" by Allyson Shaw; p. 62 "Moment of Huh?" by Allyson Shaw; p. 63 "7 Terrific Facts About Tails" by Paige Towler; pp. 64–65 "Glowworm Cave" by Jamie Kiffel-Alcheh; pp. 66–67 "Bizarre Bugs" by Allyson Shaw; pp. 68–69 "Big Cats" by Elizabeth Carney; pp. 70–71 "10 Cool Facts About Big Cats" by Steve Winter and Sharon Guynup; pp. 72–73 "Cheetah Rescue" by Rachael Bale; p. 74 "Poo Powers Zoo" by Cheryl Maguire; p. 75 "Real Animal Heroes" by Kitson Jazynka (dolphins) and Aline Alexander Newman (dog); pp. 76–77 "Prehistoric Timeline" by Susan K. Donnelly; pp. 78–79 "Field Notes From a Paleontologist" by Sarah Wassner Flynn; p. 80 "Dino Classification" by Susan K. Donnelly; p. 81 "4 Newly Discovered Dinos" by Sarah Wassner Flynn; pp. 82–83 "Would You Survive in the Age of Dinosaurs?" by Stephanie Warren Drimmer and Kay Boatner

Space and Earth
(86–107)
p. 92 "Dwarf Planets" by Sarah Wassner Flynn; p. 93 "Black Hole Turns Star Into Doughnut and Eats It" by Sarah Wassner Flynn, "What if aliens came to Earth?" by Crispin Boyer; p. 95 "Sky Calendar 2026" by Sarah Wassner Flynn; p. 96 "A Look Inside" by Kathy Furgang; p. 97 "Rock Stars" by Steve Tomecek; pp. 98–99 "Minerals: The Inside Story" by Michael Burgan; pp. 100–101 "10 Cool Facts About Rocks and Minerals" by Michael Burgan; pp. 102–103 "A Hot Topic" by Kathy Furgang; pp. 104–105 "Supervolcanoes" by Ariana Soldati

Awesome Exploration
(108–127)
pp. 110–111 "Dare to Explore" by Chris Tomlin; pp. 112–113 "Science Bloopers" by Allyson Shaw; pp. 114–115 "Kids on a Mission" by Julie Beer and Michelle Harris; pp. 116–117 "10 Ways to Protect the Planet" by Allyson Shaw; pp. 118–119 "Photo Secrets Revealed" by Scott Elder; p. 120 "Gray Fox Photo Shoot" by Elizabeth Hilfrank; p. 121 "Ru Somaweera: The Reptile Man" by Sarah Wassner Flynn; pp. 122–123 "Trapped in Ice!" by Simon Worrall; p. 124 "What's the Buzz on Bugs?" by Sarah Wassner Flynn

Fun and Games
(128–147)
p. 131 "Critter Chat: *Tyrannosaurus rex*" by Allyson Shaw; p. 133 "Funny Fill-In: Farm Frenzy" by Margaret J. Krauss; p. 136 "Critter Chat: Orca" by Allyson Shaw; p. 139 "Funny Fill-In: Party Animals" by Kay Boatner; pp. 142–143 "Critter Chat: Animals Online" by Rosemary Mosco; pp. 146–147 "Unleashed" by Strika Entertainment

Laugh Out Loud
(148–163)
p. 151 "Animal Bloopers" by Allyson Shaw; pp. 152–153 "Say What?" by Kelley Miller; p. 154 "Riddle Me This" by Rosie Gowsell Pattison; p. 155 "Funny Bites" by Chris Ware; p. 156 "Just Joking" by Kelley Miller; p. 157 "Pun Fun" by Kelley Miller; p. 158 "Say What?" by Kelley Miller; p. 159 "Funny Bites" by Chris Ware; p. 160 "Just Joking" by Rosie Gowsell Pattison; p. 161 "It's a Long Story ..." by Kelley Miller; p. 163 "Tongue Twisters" by Kelley Miller

Culture Connection
(164–187)
pp. 166–167 "Celebrations Around the World" by Sarah Wassner Flynn; pp. 168–169 "Diwali" by Stephanie Warren Drimmer; p. 170 "6 Winter Feast Facts to Fill Up On" by Paige Towler; p. 171 "What's Your Chinese Horoscope?" by Geoff Williams; pp. 172–173 "The Secret History of Halloween" by Kay Boatner; pp. 174–175 "Uplifting Balloons" by Julie Beer and Michelle Harris; pp. 176–177 "10 Cool Things About Food" by Kay Boatner; pp. 178–179 "Money Around the World!" by Kristin Baird Rattini and Sarah Wassner Flynn; pp. 182–183 "Monster Mash" by Kenny Curtis and Jillian Hughes; pp. 184–185 "World Religions" by Mark Bockenhauer, "Holi" by Sarah Wassner Flynn

Science and Technology
(188–211)
pp. 192–193 "Eye-Popping Creations" by Julie Beer and Michelle Harris; p. 195 "The Three Domains of Life" by Susan K. Donnelly; p. 196 "Freaky Plants" by Alicia Klepeis; p. 197 "Weird and Wonderful Trees" by Julie Beer and Michelle Harris; p. 199 "What Are Genes?" by Paige Towler; p. 200 "Why Do Our ..." by Sarah Wassner Flynn; p. 201 "Why Do I Have 10 Fingers?" by Crispin Boyer; pp. 202–203 "How Viruses Spread" and "How Vaccines Work" by Sarah Wassner Flynn; pp. 204–205 "The Science of Cute" by Jamie Kiffel-Alcheh; pp. 206–207 "Future World: Clothing" by Stephanie Warren Drimmer; pp. 208–209 "Future World: Climate Tech" by Stephanie Warren Drimmer

Wonders of Nature
(212–235)
pp. 214–215 "Biomes" by Susan K. Donnelly; pp. 216–217 "Antarctica" by Jen Agresta; pp. 220–221 "Weird Wonders" by Julie Beer and Michelle Harris; p. 222 "Weather and Climate" by Mark Bockenhauer; p. 223 "Climate Change" by Sarah Wassner Flynn; pp. 224–225 "10 Facts About Freaky Forces of Nature" by Douglas E. Richards; p. 226 "Water on the Move" by Lisa M. Gerry; p. 227 "Types of Clouds" by Kathy Furgang; p. 230 "Hurricane Happenings" by Sarah Wassner Flynn; p. 231 "What Is a Tornado?" by Kathy Furgang; p. 232 "What Is a Bomb Cyclone?" by Sarah Wassner Flynn; p. 233 "Koala Rescue" by Cheryl Maguire

History Happens
(236–267)
pp. 238–240 "Tut's Tomb" and "Brainy Questions" by Allyson Shaw; p. 241 "Buried Treasure" by Jen Agresta; pp. 242–243 "History's Mysteries: The Ancient Maya" by Kitson Jazynka; pp. 244–245 "Ancient Mysteries" by Julie Beer and Michelle Harris; pp. 246–247 "Pirate Queen" by Leigh Lewis; pp. 248–249 "History's Mysteries: Easter Island/Rapa Nui" by Kitson Jazynka; pp. 250–251 "Going to War" by Susan K. Donnelly and Sarah Wassner Flynn; p. 251 "Wartime Inventions" by Sarah Wassner Flynn; p. 252 "The Constitution & the Bill of Rights" by Susan K. Donnelly; p. 253 "What the Constitution Created" by Michael Burgan; p. 254 "The Native American Experience" by Martha B. Sharma; pp. 255–259 Fun Facts by Brianna Dumont; pp. 260–261 "10 Wild Facts About Presidential Pets" by Sarah Wassner Flynn; p. 262 "Civil Rights" by Susan K. Donnelly; pp. 262–263 "Woolworth Counter Sit-in" and "Stone of Hope" and "John Lewis" by Sarah Wassner Flynn; pp. 264–265 "Women Fighting for Equality" by Sarah Wassner Flynn

Geography Rocks
(268–353)
pp. 270–274 and pp. 276–277 by Mark Bockenhauer; pp. 278–305 by Sarah Wassner Flynn, Mark Bockenhauer, and Susan K. Donnelly; pp. 332–333 "Brilliant Bridges" by Julie Beer and Michelle Harris; pp. 334–335 "15 Amazing Facts About Cities" by Sean McCollum; p. 336 "Coolest Dive" by Julie Beer and Michelle Harris; p. 337 "8 Cool Things About Rainforest Cultures" by Julie Beer; p. 338 "Wild Vacations: Cave Hotel" by C.M. Tomlin; p. 339 "Wild Vacations: Salt Hotel" by Jamie Kiffel-Alcheh; p. 340 "6 Rad Facts About the Beach" by Paige Towler; p. 341 "Great Barrier Reef" by Julie Beer and Michelle Harris; pp. 342–343 "Supersize Sites" by Julie Beer and Michelle Harris; pp. 346–347 "Bizarre Buildings" by Julie Beer and Michelle Harris; pp. 348–349 "Winter Olympics 2026" by Sarah Wassner Flynn; p. 351 "7 Wonders" by Elisabeth Deffner

All "Homework Help" by Vicki Ariyasu, except p. 211 "This Is How It's Done!" by Sarah Wassner Flynn

TEXT & ILLUSTRATION CREDITS

Abbreviations:
AS: Adobe Stock; ASP: Alamy Stock Photo; DR: Dreamstime; GI: Getty Images; MP: Minden Pictures; NGIC: National Geographic Image Collection; NGP: National Geographic Partners, LLC; SS: Shutterstock

All Maps
By National Geographic

Front Cover
(black leopard), Shaaz Jung; (Explorers), Renan Ozturk/NGIC; (James Webb Space Telescope), 24K-Production/AS

Spine
(black leopard), Shaaz Jung

Back Cover
(Earth), ixpert/SS; (kangaroo), Reinhard Dirscherl/Biosphoto; (Jupiter), NASA/ESA/Jupiter ERS Team/Judy Schmidt; (dinosaur), Franco Tempesta/NGP; (Easter Island), Volanthevist/GI; (beetle), alslutsky/SS; (butterfly), Steven Russell Smith/ASP

Front Matter (2–7)
2–3, Paul Nicklen/NGIC; 5 (UP), Ezra Shaw/GI; 5 (lemurs), Quentin Martinez/Biosphoto; 5 (robots), Imago/Liu Ying/ASP; 5 (phone), Kaspars Grinvalds/AS; 5 (James Webb Space Telescope), Best-Backgrounds/SS; 5 (LO RT), Kennedy News & Media; 6 (UP LE), Ru Somaweera; 6 (UP CTR LE), Sylvain Cordier/Biosphoto; 6 (UP RT), Steve Winter/NGIC; 6 (UP CTR RT), Dan Sipple; 6 (LO LE), Xinhua/SS; 6 (LO CTR RT), DLILLC/Corbis/VCG/GI; 6 (LO RT), diplomedia/SS; 6, Aram Williams/ASP; 7 (UP LE), Costfoto/NurPhoto/SS; 7 (UP CTR RT), Tomas Griger/Panther Media GmbH/ASP; 7 (UP RT), Mondolithic Studios; 7 (LO), Mariusz Prusawicz/DR; 7 (LO CTR LE), Andreas Hermannspann/SS; 7, Mike Mezeul II

Your World 2026 (8–17)
8–9, Ezra Shaw/GI; 10 (UP), besjunior/AS; 10 (LO), Joe McUbed/AS; 11 (UP), AP Photo/Cover Images/Brights Zoo; 11 (CTR & LO), HANNAH; 12 (UP), AP Photo/California Department of Fish and Wildlife; 12 (LO), Mohamad Haghani/ASP; 13 (dog eyes), Ivanova N/SS; 13 (dog apple), Bocskai Istvan/SS; 13 (human vision bird), Volker Steger/Science Source; 13 (bird vision), Volker Steger/Science Source; 13 (bee vision), Yon Marsh Science/ASP; 13 (bee eyes), stevenwellingson/AS; 13 (owl eyes), Ammit/AS; 13 (dog paint), Bocskai Istvan/SS; 14 (UP), Evgenia Terekhova/SS; 14 (CTR), Ekaterina Kolomeets/AS; 14 (LO LE), Liza/SS; 14 (LO CTR), Vyacheslav Dumchev/AS; 14 (LO RT), struvictory/AS; 15 (UP), ungvar/AS; 15 (LO), Kateryna Kon/SS; 16 (Olympics), Bruce Bennett/GI; 16 (Kindness), Svetlana/AS; 16 (Friendship), kegfire/AS; 16 (Friday the 13th), ronniechua/AS; 16 (Dance), JackF/AS; 16 (Braille), Mikhail Reshetnikov/AS; 16 (Art), AlexeyRyumin/SS; 16 (Wildlife), Jak Wonderly/NGIC; 16 (Vegetarian), Rawf8/AS; 17 (UP), Adam Makarenko/Science Source; 17 (LO), Sam Yue/ASP

Greatest Breakthroughs (18–33)
18–19, Imago/Liu Ying/ASP; 20, ktsdesign/AS; 21 (UP), Kaspars Grinvalds/AS; 21 (CTR), Victor de Schwanberg/Science Source; 21 (LO), Franco Tempesta/NGP; 22 (UP), Kaspars Grinvalds/AS; 22 (CTR), gadzius/AS; 22 (LO), Vera Kuttelvaserova/AS; 23 (UP), ArgitopIA/AS; 23 (CTR), Arshad Mohammed/Anadolu Agency/GI; 23 (LO), Robert Clark/NGIC; 24 (UP INSET), Mark Thiessen/NGP; 24 (UP), Robert Clark/NGIC; 24 (LO), Mathabela Tsikoane; 25 (UP & LO LE), Lee Berger; 25 (CTR), Mark Thiessen/NGIC; 25 (LO RT), Robert Clark/NGIC; 26–27 (BACKGROUND), Paul Bullen/GI; 26–27 (step 1–5), Lee Berger; 28–29 (BACKGROUND), NASA/ESA/CSA/STScI; 29 (Cartwheel galaxy), NASA/ESA/CSA/STScI; 29 (Neptune), NASA/ESA/CSA/STScI; 29 (James Webb Space Telescope), NASA; 29 (Jupiter), NASA/ESA/Jupiter ERS Team/Judy Schmidt; 30, Lori Epstein/NGP; 31 (UP), NASA; 31 (LO), ajbarr/iStockphoto; 32 (UP), Kaspars Grinvalds/AS; 32 (CTR), NASA/ESA/Jupiter ERS Team/Judy Schmidt; 32 (LO), NASA

Amazing Animals (34–85)
34–35, Quentin Martinez/Biosphoto; 36 (UP), Mark Ralston/AFP/GI; 36 (LO), Michael Uy; 36 (LO CTR), Chris M. Leung; 36 (LO RT), Christopher Briscoe; 37 (UP), Robyn Beck/AFP/GI; 37 (CTR), Robyn Beck/AFP/GI; 37 (LO), Farm Sanctuary SA/Caters News Agency; 38 (UP), Lisa Basile Ellwood/SS; 38 (CTR LE), Brian E Kushner/SS; 38 (CTR RT), David Maxwell/EPA-EFE/SS; 38 (LO), OceanFishing/GI; 39 (UP), JL Images/ASP; 39 (CTR), MriyaWildlife/GI; 39 (LO), Paul Bertner/MP; 40 (LE), Marcel Schauer/AS; 40 (RT), Martin Willis/MP; 40 (UP), Nick Hobgood/AS; 41 (UP LE), Suzi Eszterhas/MP; 41 (RT), Roberto/AS; 41 (CTR LE), sergiobocardo/GI; 41 (LO), Vitalii Kalutskyi/GI; 42 (UP), Michael Shake/AS; 42 (CTR), slowmotiongli/AS; 42 (LO LE), Joe Blossom/ASP; 42 (LO RT), Karel Zahradka/SS; 43 (UP), Petri/AS; 43 (CTR LE), Cloudtail/AS; 43 (CTR RT), Roland Seitre/MP; 43 (LO), creativenature.nl/AS; 44 (UP), Dani Vincek/SS; 44 (CTR), DioGen/SS; 44 (LO), Nick Garbutt; 45 (UP CTR), Kant Liang/EyeEm/GI; 45 (UP RT), reptiles4all/SS; 45 (CTR), Hiroya Minakuchi/MP; 45 (CTR RT), FP media/SS; 45 (LO), Ziva_K/iStockphoto/GI; 46 (UP & LO), Laurent Ballesta/NGIC; 47 (UP LE), Martin Garnham/DR; 47 (CTR LE), Don Johnston/GI; 47 (CTR RT), Georgette Douwma/Nature Picture Library; 47 (LO LE), Juergen Freund/Nature Picture Library; 47 (LO RT), Viter8/DR; 48–49, Clay Enos; 48 (UP), Howard Morris; 48 (LO), Guillermo Ordoñez; 50 (UP), Fred Olivier/NPL/MP; 51 (UP), Jay Dickman/GI; 51 (LO), Breck P. Kent/Animals Animals/Earth Scenes/NGIC; 52, iStock/Coldimages; 52 (UP), Juergen & Christine Sohns/MP; 53 (UP LE), Otto Plantema/MP; 53 (UP RT), Slew11/DR; 53 (CTR LE), Enrique/AS; 53 (CTR RT), Stefan Christmann/Nature Picture Library; 53 (LO), Kevin Schafer/Moment Mobile RF/GI; 54 (UP), Blue Planet Archive/Scubazoo/Jason Isley; 54 (LO LE), Niels van Gijn/GI; 54 (LO RT), talseN/SS; 55 (UP LE), Tom McHugh/Science Source; 55 (UP RT), Christian Ziegler/MP/NGIC; 55 (CTR LE), Helen E. Grose/DR; 55 (CTR RT), Auscape/GI; 55 (LO), Alex Mustard/Nature Picture Library; 56–57 (BACKGROUND), Phil Savoie/NPL/MP; 56 (UP), Jaime Culebras/NGIC; 56 (LO), Jesse Delia; 57 (UP), Alex Hyde/NPL/MP; 57 (A), Karl Van Ginderdeuren/Buiten-beeld/MP; 57 (B), © 2004 MBARI; 57 (C), J. Bedek; 57 (D), Solvin Zankl/NPL/MP; 57 (E), David Shale/NPL/MP; 57 (F), Ryan Hagerty/USFWS; 58 (LO), Stefanie Schweers/Zoo Krefeld; 59 (UP), Kildare Animal Foundation; 60 (1), James R.D. Scott/GI; 60 (2), Suzi Eszterhas/MP; 60 (3), JDzacovsky/SS; 60 (4), Lydia Sokor/GI; 61 (5), Yi-Fu Ke/500px/GI; 61 (6), Carlton Ward/NGIC; 61 (7), Atsuo Fujimaru/Nature Production/MP; 61 (8), Sylvain Cordier/NPL/MP; 61 (9), Norbert Wu/MP; 62 (UP LE), Mark Bowler/Nature Picture Library; 62 (UP RT), Michael Milicia/BIA/MP; 62 (CTR), Ayub Khan; 62 (LO), ZSSD/MP; 63, Ignacio Yufera/Biosphoto/MP; 64–65, Shaun Jeffers; 65 (UP), Brian Enting/Science Source; 65 (CTR), Julian Money-Kyrle/ASP; 65 (LO), Solvin Zankl/NPL/MP; 66 (UP & LO), Alejandro Mesa; 67 (UP & LO & CTR), Alejandro Mesa; 68, Krzysztof Wiktor/AS; 69 (lion fur), Eric Isselée/SS; 69 (jaguar), DLILLC/Corbis/GI; 69 (leopard), Eric Isselée/SS; 69 (tiger), Eric Isselée/SS; 69 (snow leopard), Eric Isselée/SS; 69 (jaguar fur), worldswildlifewonders/SS; 69 (lion), Eric Isselée/SS; 69 (snow leopard fur), Eric Isselée/SS; 69 (tiger fur), Kesu/SS; 69 (leopard fur), WitR/SS; 70 (UP), Ingo Arndt/MP; 70 (CTR), Carol Walker/NPL/MP; 70 (LO), Suzi Eszterhas/MP; 71 (UP), Anup Shah/NPL/MP; 71 (CTR LE), GP232/GI; 71 (CTR RT), Carol Walker/Nature Picture Library; 71 (LO), Winfried Wisniewski/GI; 72 (UP & LO), Nichole Sobecki/NGIC; 73 (UP & LO), Nichole Sobecki/NGIC; 74 (UP RT & LO RT), Paul Collins/Marwell Zoo; 74 (LE), Jason Brown/Marwell Zoo; 75 (UP), Ocean Walker; 75 (UP CTR), Ole Jorgen Liodden/Nature Picture Library; 75 (LO CTR), Rolf Kopfle/Ardea; 75 (LO RT), Falcon1708/DR; 76 (UP), Chris Butler/Science Source; 76 (CTR), Christian Jegou/Science Source; 76 (LO), Pixeldust Studios/NGIC; 77 (A), Christian Jegou/Science Source; 77 (B–D), Franco Tempesta/NGP; 77 (E), Chase Studio/Science Source; 78 (UP), Christian Ziegler; 78 (LO LE), John Flynn/Rodolfo Salas Gismondi; 78 (LO RT), Anjali Goswami/Rodolfo Salas Gismondi; 79 (UP LE), John Flynn/Rodolfo Salas Gismondi; 79 (UP RT, LO LE & LO RT), Rodolfo Salas Gismondi; 80 (UP & LO), Franco Tempesta, NGP; 81 (ALL), Franco Tempesta/NGP; 82–83 (eggs), Jaroslav Moravcik/AS; 82 (*Brachiosaurus*), Franco Tempesta/NGP; 82 (chocolate), baibaz/SS; 82 (plates), Sommai/SS; 82 (*T. rex*), DMX/SS; 82 (*Velociraptor*), Chris Clor/GI; 82 (tablecloth), Maor Glam/DR; 83 (*Titanosaurus*), Franco Tempesta/NGP; 83 (*Ankylosaurus*), Roger Harris/Science Source; 83 (*Allosaurus*), Joe Tucciarone/Science Source; 83 (tree), Maria Wachala/GI; 83 (cave), fotoVoyager/GI; 83 (fire), Liudmila Chernetska/GI; 84 (UP), JL Images/ASP; 84 (LE), Cloudtail/AS; 84 (LO), Shaun Jeffers; 85 (UP RT), GOLFX/SS

Space and Earth (86–107)
86–87, Best-Backgrounds/SS; 88–89, David Aguilar; 88, Kei Shooting/SS; 89, SSSCCC/SS; 90–91, David Aguilar; 92 (Haumea), David Aguilar; 92 (Pluto), NASA/JHUAPL/SwRI; 92 (Eris), David Aguilar; 93 (UP), Science History Images/ASP; 93 (LO), Joe Rocco; 94 (UP), Dima Zel/SS; 94 (LO), Transferred from the National Aeronautics and Space Administration/National Air and Space Museum; 94 (LO), NASA/AP; 94 (CTR RT), Maike Hildebrandt/iStock/GI; 95 (UP), Allexxandar/iStockphoto/GI; 96 (UP), NGP; 96 (LO), Joe Rocco; 97 (UP), Ralph Lee Hopkins/NGIC; 97 (granite), NASA/JPL/MP; 97 (gneiss), Dirk Wiersma/Science Source; 97 (halite), Theodore Clutter/Science Source; 97 (andesite), MarekPhotoDesign/AS; 97 (limestone), Charles D. Winters/Science Source; 97 (mica), Yes058 Montree Nanta/SS; 98 (UP), LVV/SS; 98 (LE), Art Collection 3/ASP; 99 (UP LE), Harry Taylor/Dorling Kindersley/Science Source; 99 (UP RT), vvoe/AS; 99 (CTR LE), Epitavi/SS; 99 (CTR RT), Ekaterina/AS; 99 (CTR RT), michal812/AS; 99 (LO LE), Björn Wylezich/AS; 99 (LO CTR), Amineah/AS; 99 (LO RT), vvoe/AS; 100 (UP), Photoworld/AS; 100 (CTR), Kennedy News & Media; 100 (LO), Ralf Lehmann/SS; 101 (UP LE), PhotoRoman/SS; 101 (UP RT), Dinodia Photos/

357

ASP; 101 (CTR LE), Björn Wylezich/AS; 101 (CTR RT), Sergey Chernyaev/AS; 101 (LO), suronin/SS; 102, Frank Ippolito; 103 (UP LE), Gary Fiegehen/All Canada Photos/Alamy; 103 (UP RT), Salvatore Gebbia/NGIC; 103 (CTR RT), Diane Cook & Len Jenshel/NGIC; 103 (CTR LE), NASA/JSC; 104 (CTR), Robbert Madden/NGIC; 105 (UP RT), Jorge Santos/age fotostock/ASP; 105 (UP LE), Peng Zhuang/DR; 105 (LO), Don C. Powell/Yellowstone National Park Ranger Naturalist Service/Library of Congress; 106 (UP), Charles D. Winters/Science Source; 106 (CTR), Science History Images/ASP; 106 (LO), Dima Zel/SS; 107 (UP RT), pixhook/E+/GI

Awesome Exploration (108-127)

108-109, Ru Somaweera; 110 (UP), A.J. Hardie; 110 (CTR LE), Bruno A. Buzatto; 110 (CTR RT), Emily Hoffmann; 110 (LO), Emily Hoffmann; 111 (UP), Rodrigo Chagas; 111 (LO LE), Veena Mushrif-Tripathy; 111 (LO RT), Veena Mushrif-Tripathy; 112 (UP), Tony Wu/Nature Picture Library; 112 (LO), Clarissa Teixeir; 113 (UP LE), Jordan Damyanov; 113 (UP CTR), imageBROKER/ASP; 113 (UP RT), Krum Sirakov; 113 (LE), Casie Zalud; 113 (LO), David Guttenfelder/NGIC; 114 (LE), Aurora Photos/ASP; 114 (LO RT), SWNS/Splash News/Newscom; 115 (UP LE), © Paul Hameister; 115 (UP RT), Library of Congress Prints and Photographs Division, Washington, DC; 115 (UP RT), North Wind Picture Archives/The Image Works; 115 (CTR LE), Johnny Green/Photoshot/Newscom; 115 (CTR RT), Brendon Thorne/GI; 115 (LO RT), © Arnaud Guerin; 116 (UP LE), Anna Sedneva/AS; 116 (UP RT), Allyson Shaw; 116 (CTR LE), khuruzero/AS; 116 (LO LE), Ursula Page/AS; 116 (LO RT), Monty Rakusen/GI; 117 (UP), kotijelly/GI; 117 (CTR), Alexander Raths/AS; 117 (LO), Skip Brown/NGIC; 118 (UP), Steve Winter/NGIC; 118 (LO), Jay Fleming; 119 (UP), Paul Nicklen/NGIC; 119 (LO), Birgitte Wilms/MP; 120 (UP), Mark Thiessen/NGIC; 120 (LO), Joel Sartore, National Geographic Photo Ark/NGIC; 121 (UP), Rolf Sjogren/National Geographic Society; 121 (CTR LE), Ruchira Somaweera/NGIC; 121 (CTR RT), Ru Somaweera; 121 (LO), Ru Somaweera; 122 (UP), Frank Hurley/Royal Geographical Society via GI; 122 (CTR), Frank Hurley/Scott Polar Research Institute, University of Cambridge/GI; 122 (LO), Frank Hurley/Scott Polar Research Institute, University of Cambridge/GI; 123 (UP LE & UP RT), Falklands Maritime Heritage Trust; 124 (UP, CTR & LO), Mark Thiessen/NGP; 125 (bumblebee), Ivaschenko Roman/SS; 125 (butterfly), Butterfly Hunter/SS; 125 (honeybee), vtupinamba/iStock; 125 (mantis), dwi/AS; 125 (stinkbug), Melinda Fawver/AS; 126 (UP RT), koosen/AS; 126 (CTR), Joel Sartore, National Geographic Photo Ark/NGIC; 127 (UP), Grady Reese/iStockphoto

Fun and Games (128-147)

128-129, Sylvain Cordier/Biosphoto; 130 (UP), Keren Su/GI; 130 (LO), Jeff Caverly/SS; 130 (LE), ZSSD/MP; 130 (RT), Dave Hansche/SS; 131 (UP), Herschel Hoffmeyer/SS; 131 (UP LE), Mark Garlick/Sceince Photo Library/GI; 131 (CTR LE), Daniel Eskridge/ASP; 131 (*Triceratops*), Vladimir Bolokh/SS; 131 (*Ankylosaurus*), Roger Harris/Science Source; 131 (LO), Franco Tempesta/NGP; 131 (*Edmontosaurus*), Franco Tempesta/NGP; 131 (*T. rex*), Franco Tempesta/NGP; 131 (emojis), Turgay Malikli/SS; 132 (UP LE), Andrew Burgess/SS; 132 (UP CTR), Ingram Publishing/

age fotostock; 132 (UP RT), Gaid Kornsilapa/SS; 132 (CTR LE), tonyz20/SS; 132 (CTR CTR), Purestock/Jupiter Images; 132 (CTR RT), Krysja/SS; 132 (LO LE), alslutsky/SS; 132 (LO CTR), Alexander Hoffmann/SS; 132 (LO RT), Simple Stock Shots; 133, Dan Sipple; 134 (A), Noorhussain/GI; 134 (B), Fred Bavendam/MP; 134 (C), David Laurent/EyeEm/GI; 135 (D), Todd Mintz/NPL/MP; 135 (E), James Christensen/MP; 135 (F), Michael and Patricia Fogden/MP; 135 (G), Rolf Nussbaumer Photography/ASP; 136 (UP), Christian Musat/SS; 136 (CTR), Flip Nicklin/MP; 136 (LO), TCYuen/GI; 136 (seal), Wolfgang Kaehler/LightRocket/GI; 136 (orca), Jens Kuhfs/GI; 136 (krill), Gerald and Buff Corsi/Visuals Unlimited, Inc./GI; 136 (penguin), Ingo Arndt/MP/GI; 137 (1), Ron Niebrugge/ASP; 137 (3), Emily Lai/ASP; 137 (5), Ross Anania/GI; 137 (6), Nick Garbutt/NPL/MP; 137 (7), Yulia Naumenko/GI; 137 (9), Karl Weatherly/GI; 138 (1), David Zaitz/GI; 138 (2), Jennifer Chen/ASP; 138 (3), Steve Lewis/GI; 138 (4), Angelo Cavalli/age fotostock/SuperStock; 138 (5), RS Smith Photography/SS; 138 (6), E.J. West/Photolibrary/GI; 138 (7), Gary Braasch/GI; 139, Dan Sipple; 140 (UP LE), R Rizvanov/SS; 140 (UP CTR), Laszlo Podor/GI; 140 (UP RT), GlowImages/ASP; 140 (CTR LE), Keith Erskine/ASP; 140 (CTR CTR), Brendan Mcdermid/Reuters; 140 (CTR RT), MaraZe/SS; 140 (LO LE), Glasshouse Images/SuperStock; 140 (LO CTR), Ingram Publishing/SuperStock; 140 (LO RT), Peter Alvey/ASP; 141 (1), Science Photo Library/SuperStock; 141 (3), Bayside–StockFood Munich/StockFood; 141 (5), © 2026 MARVEL; 141 (6), Marka/ASP; 141 (7), Tom Delme/DR; 141 (10), Kristoffer Tripplaar/ASP; 142 (UP LE), Cigdem Cooper/SS; 142 (UP RT), Przemyslaw Skibinski/SS; 142 (CTR RT), Robert Winslow/age fotostock; 142 (LO LE), Frhojdysz/DR; 142 (LO RT), prapass/SS; 143 (UP LE), Sylvain Cordier/GI; 143 (UP CTR), Adam Fletcher/MP; 143 (UP RT), Selyutina Olga/SS; 143 (CTR), Jurgen Otto/SS; 143 (LO LE), Juergen & Christine Sohns/MP; 143 (LO RT), Luca Santilli/SS; 144-145, James Yamasaki; 146-147, Strika Entertainment

Laugh Out Loud (148-163)

148-149, Aram Williams/ASP; 150 (UP LE), skip caplan/ASP; 150 (UP RT), Thomas Marent/ARDEA; 150 (CTR LE), Imagebroker RF/Photo-Library; 150 (LO LE), Mike Hill/SS; 150 (LO RT), Yann Hubert/Biosphoto/MP; 151 (UP LE), Carol Walker/Nature Picture Library; 151 (UP RT), Tui De Roy/MP; 151 (LO), Yukihiro Fukuda/NPL/MP; 152-153, DLILLC/Corbis/VCG/GI; 155, Chris Ware; 156 (UP LE & UP RT), Family Business/SS; 156 (UP CTR), Gudkov Andrey/SS; 156 (UP RT), Family Business/SS; 156 (CTR LE), Ljupco Smokovski/SS; 156 (CTR), Gerisima/SS; 156 (CTR RT), 9george/SS; 156 (LO LE), mekcar/SS; 156 (LO LE), Willyam Bradberry/SS; 157 (UP LE), M. Unal Ozmen/SS; 157 (UP RT), ESA and the Hubble Heritage Team(STScI/AURA)/NASA; 157 (CTR), Ivan_Nikulin/SS; 157 (sign), Andy Dean Photography/SS; 157 (CTR RT), Ninell/SS; 157 (LO LE), EpicStockMedia/SS; 157 (LO RT), yevgenly11/SS; 158, James.Pintar/SS; 159, Chris Ware; 160 (UP), Suzi Eszterhas/MP; 160 (CTR LE), Simon Reddy/ASP; 160 (CTR RT), Pavel Losevsky/DR; 160 (CTR RT INSET), Aaron Amat/SS; 160 (LO LE), Juniors Bildarchiv GmbH/ASP; 160 (LO CTR), light poet/SS; 160 (LO RT), Knostpix/DR; 161 (LO LE), Robynrg/SS; 161 (LO RT), Rebecca Hale/National Geographic Partners, LLC; 161 (BACKGROUND), B Brown/SS; 161 (UP), artjazz/SS; 162 (UP LE), M. Unal Ozmen/SS; 162 (UP RT), Arindom Chowdhury/DR; 162 (CTR LE),

Vilainecrevette/DR; 162 (LO LE), Neil Juggins/ASP; 162 (LO RT), William Mullins/ASP; 163 (UP LE), Africa Studio/AS; 163 (UP RT), petrrgoskov/AS; 163 (CTR LE), tarasov_vl/AS; 163 (CTR RT), BillionPhotos/AS; 163 (LO LE), zaharov43/AS; 163 (LO RT), GLandStudio/AS

Culture Connection (164-187)

164-165, Xinhua/SS; 166 (March Equinox), frans lemmens/ASP; 166 (Losar), Thomas Dutour/AS; 166 (Difference Day), addkm/SS; 166 (Yom Kippur), Hanna Kim/ASP; 166 (Songkran), Tong_stocker/SS; 166 (Ramadan), diplomedia/SS; 166 (Midsummer), Snowbelle/SS; 167 (Reconciliation Day), Stringer/EPA/SS; 167 (Hanukkah), blueeyes/SS; 167 (Christmas), Yellowj/SS; 168, phive/SS; 168 (banner), StockImageFactory.com/SS; 169, Subir Basak/GI; 170, Nalidsa/ASP; 171 (throughout), MaeW/SS; 172 (UP LE), Jean-Christophe Verhaegen/AFP/GI; 172 (LO RT), stepmorem/SS; 173 (LE), Justin Goff/UK Press via GI; 173 (UP RT), Ritu Manoj Jethani/SS; 173 (UP RT), Thomas Woodruff/DR; 173 (CTR LE), Marcos Delgado/Clasos/LatinContent/GI; 173 (CTR RT), Berbar Halim/SIPA/Newscom; 173 (LO RT), Patrick Lynch Photography/SS; 174 (UP LE), Preto Perola/SS; 174 (UP LE INSET), Subbotina Anna/SS; 174 (UP RT), mayakova/SS; 174 (CTR), Lightspring/SS; 174 (LO LE), Chutima Chaochaiya/SS; 174 (LO RT), Todd Taulman/DR; 175 (UP LE), Volosina/SS; 175 (UP RT), Elizabeth A. Cummings/SS; 175 (LE), Pani_Elena/SS; 175 (CTR), Diana Taliun/SS; 175 (LO RT), oksana2010/SS; 176-177, Joe Rocco; 178 (UP LE), Royal Canadian Mint; 179 (UP CTR LE), marino bocelli/SS; 178 (UP RT), John Lamb/GI; 178 (CTR RT), Milan/AS; 178 (LO LE), Yevgen Romanenko/GI; 178 (LO RT), Universal History Archive/Universal Images Group/GI; 179 (UP LE), hueberto/GI; 179 (UP CTR RT), © Bank of England; 179 (UP RT), pamela_d_mcadams/GI; 179 (LO LE), Darrell Gulin/GI; 179 (LO CTR RT), Nataly Studio/SS; 179 (LO CTR RT), elnavegante/GI; 179 (LO LE), Kelley Miller/NGS Staff; 182, Nevena Tsvetanova/ASP; 183 (UP), Lefteris_/GI; 183 (CTR), Bodor Tivadar/SS; 183 (LO), IanDagnall Computing/ASP; 184 (UP), Randy Olson; 184 (LO LE), Martin Gray/NGIC; 184 (LO RT), Sam Panthaky/AFP/GI; 185 (UP), Animesh Hazra/NGIC; 185 (LO LE), Reza/NGIC; 185 (LO RT), Richard Nowitz/NGIC; 186 (UP), Elizabeth A. Cummings/SS; 186 (CTR), Jennifer Barrow/DR; 186 (LO), Bodor Tivadar/SS; 187 (UP LE), spatule-tail/SS; 187 (UP RT), PictureLake/E+/GI; 187 (CTR), cifotart/SS; 187 (LO), zydesign/SS

Science and Technology (188-211)

188-189, Costfoto/NurPhoto/SS; 190 (UP), Mondolithic Studios; 191 (CTR), Inna/AS; 191 (LO), Mondolithic Studios; 192 (UP), Andrey Rudenko; 192 (LO), Andrew Harrer/Bloomberg via GI; 193 (UP LE), VCG/VCG via GI; 193 (UP RT), CB2/ZOB/Supplied by WENN/Newscom; 193 (CTR LE), Michael Appleton/The New York Times/Redux Pictures; 193 (CTR RT), Will Ragozzino/BFA/REX/SS; 193 (LO LE), Piero Cruciatti/ASP; 194 (LO CTR), Ted Kinsman/Science Source; 193 (LO RT), Tobias Schwarz/AFP/GI; 195 (protists), sgame/SS; 195 (animals), kwest/SS; 195 (plants), puwanai/SS; 195 (fungi), eurobanks/GI; 195 (1), Sebastian Kaulitzki/SS; 195 (2), Eye of Science/Science Source; 195 (3), Volker Steger/Christian Bardele/Photo Researchers Inc.; 196 (A), imageBROKER GmbH & Co. KG/NielsDK/ASP; 196 (B), Richard Gardner/SS;

358

ILLUSTRATION CREDITS

196 (C), Mark Moffett/MP; 196 (D), Katuhiko Motonaga; 196 (E), Ed Reschke/GI; 196 (F), Neil Lucas/MP; 196 (G), KPG-Payless2/SS; 197 (UP LE), Chris Mattison/age fotostock; 197 (UP RT), Michael Nichols/NGIC; 197 (LO LE), Buena Vista Images/GI; 197 (LO RT), Noradoa/SS; 198 (UP LE), SciePro/SS; 199, adimas/AS; 200 (UP), Eric Isselée/SS; 200 (CTR), Alessandro Grandini/AS; 200 (LO), radub85/AS; 201 (UP), andrewsafonov/iStockphoto; 201 (LO), cate_89/iStockphoto; 202 (UP), WavebreakMediaMicro/AS; 202 (UP CTR), Rost9/SS; 202 (CTR), Maxximmm/DR; 202 (CTR RT), alswart/AS; 203 (BACKGROUND), Siberian Art/AS; 203 (UP), Looker_Studio/AS; 203 (LO), Photo Sesaon/AS; 204 (UP), Patrick Endres/age fotostock; 204 (LO), allstars/SS; 205 (UP LE), Suzi Eszterhas/MP; 205 (UP RT), Chris Radburn/PA Images/ASP; 205 (LO), Stefan Christmann/MP; 206–207, Mondolithic Studios Inc; 208–209, Mondolithic Studios Inc; 210 (UP LE), Michael Nichols/NGIC; 210 (UP RT), Suzi Eszterhas/MP; 210 (LO), Looker_Studio/AS; 211 (LO LE), Klaus Vedfelt/GI

Wonders of Nature (212–235)

212–213, Mike Mezeul II; 214 (LE), AVTG/iStockphoto; 214 (RT), Brad Wynnyk/SS; 215 (UP LE), Rich Carey/SS; 215 (UP RT), Richard Walters/iStockphoto; 215 (LO LE), Karen Graham/iStockphoto; 215 (LO RT), Michio Hoshino/MP/NGIC; 216–217, Frank Krahmer/Corbis; 216 (INSET), Carsten Peter/NGIC; 217 (A–D), Carsten Peter/NGIC; 218–219 (globes), NG Maps; 218–219 (BACKGROUND), Chris Anderson/SS; 218 (LE), cbpix/SS; 218 (RT), Mike Hill/Photographer's Choice/GI; 219 (CTR LE), Wil Meinderts/Buiten-beeld/MP; 219 (CTR RT), Paul Nicklen/NGIC; 219 (LO RT), Jan Vermeer/MP; 220 (1), hugy/GI; 220 (2), Kent Kobersteen/NGIC; 221 (3), RogerTWong/GI; 221 (4), StephanHoerold/iStock; 221 (5), Vadim Petrakov/SS; 221 (6), Ockert le Roux; 221 (7), Mike Theiss/NGIC; 221 (8), Mario Carvajal; 222, Tomas Griger/Panther Media GmbH/ASP; 223 (UP), Chasing Light – Photography by James Stone/GI; 223 (RT), James Balog/NGIC; 224 (UP LE), Wead/AS; 224 (CTR RT), USFS Photo/ASP; 224 (A), Farinoza/DR; 224 (B), Valt Ahyppo/SS; 224 (C), reptiles4all/SS; 224 (D), Farinoza/DR; 224 (LO LE), Jim Reed/Science Source; 225 (UP LE), Nature and Science/ASP; 225 (UP RT), Ivan Kmit/AS; 225 (CTR LE), OAR/National Undersea Research Program/World History Archive/ASP; 225 (CTR RT), AP Photo/Norman Transcript/Mike Harmon; 226 (UP), Arctic-Images/Stone/GI; 226 (LO), Chris Philpot; 226 (LO), Franco Tempesta, NGP; 227 (1), Leonid Tit/SS; 227 (2), Frans Lanting/NGIC; 227 (3), Lars Christensen/SS; 227 (4), Daniel Loretto/SS; 227 (LO), Richard Peterson/SS; 228 (UP), STR/AFP/GI; 228 (CTR), Daniel L. Osborne/Detlev van Ravenswaay/Science Source; 228 (LO), Sven Hagolani/GI; 229 (UP), Ursula Sander/GI; 229 (CTR), Hady Khandani/ASP; 229 (LO), Karen Anderson Photography/GI; 230, 3dmotus/SS; 231 (UP LE), Lori Mehmen/Associated Press; 231 (EFo), Susan Law Cain/SS; 231 (EF1), Brian Nolan/iStockphoto; 231 (EF2), Susan Law Cain/SS; 231 (EF3), Judy Kennamer/SS; 231 (EF4), jam4travel/SS; 231 (EF5), jam4travel/SS; 231 (LO LE), Jim Reed; 232 (UP), ZUMA Press, Inc./ASP; 232 (LE), Justin Sullivan/GI; 232 (LO), Josh Edelson/AFP/GI; 233 (UP), Jouan Rius/MP; 233 (LO), Currumbin Wildlife Hospital; 234, Frank Krahmer/Corbis; 234 (RT), Ockert le Roux; 234 (LO), Jim Reed

History Happens (236–267)

236–237, Andreas Hermanspann/SS; 238–239, Clayton Hanmer; 240 (UP & LO), Alice Brereton; 241 (BACKGROUND), Israel Antiquities Authority/Xinhua News Agency/Newscom; 241 (UP LE), Victor R. Boswell, Jr/NGIC; 241 (UP CTR), Aristidis Vafeiadakis/ZUMA Press; 241 (UP RT), Brett Seymour/ARGO via Greek Culture Ministry/AP Photo; 241 (CTR LE), Derek McLennan & Martin McSweeney/Reuters/Newscom; 241 (CTR RT), Xinhua/eyevine/Redux; 241 (LO LE), Franck Goddio/Hilti Foundation, photo: Jérôme Delafosse; 241 (LO CTR), Baz Ratner/Reuters; 241 (LO RT), Anglia Press Agency Ltd./REX; 242–243 (UP CTR), Kenneth Garrett/NGIC; 242 (LO RT), RJ Lerich/SS; 243 (UP RT), Art of Life/SS; 243 (CTR RT), Michael DeFreitas/robertharding/ASP; 244 (UP), Zbiq/SS; 244 (LO), Vicky Jirayu/SS; 245 (UP LE), Science History Images/ASP; 245 (UP RT), AF archive/Alamy; 245 (CTR LE), Pius Lee/SS; 245 (CTR RT), Cesar Manso/AFP/GI; 245 (LO LE), Wojtek Buss/GI; 245 (LO RT), Regissercom/SS; 246 (UP LE & LO RT), Sara Woolley-Gomez; 247 (UP LE), Ian Dagnall Computing/ASP; 247 (UP RT), lunstream/ASP; 247 (LO RT), Sara Woolley-Gomez; 248, Volanthevist/GI; 249 (UP), Jim Richardson/NGIC; 249 (CTR), miralex/GI; 249 (LO), Fernando G. Baptista/National Geographic Creative; 250 (UP), Vera/AS; 251 (UP), bergamont/SS; 251 (CTR), Kimberly Reinick/AS; 251 (LO), Coprid/AS; 254 (LO), Mark Carwardine/Nature Picture Library; 257, photoff/AS; 258, PhotoSpirit/AS; 263 (LO), Paco Como/AS; 266 (UP), Jaroslav Moravcik/SS; 266 (CTR), RJ Lerich/SS; 266 (LO), Volanthevist/GI; 267 (UP), Christopher Furlong/GI

Geography Rocks (268–353)

268–269, Mariusz Prusaczyk/DR; 275, Mark Thiessen/NGP; 275 (LO), NASA; 277 (BACKGROUND), Fabiano Rebeque/Moment/GI; 277 (UP LE), Thomas J. Abercrombie/NGIC; 277 (UP CTR), Maria Stenzel/NGIC; 277 (UP RT), Gordon Wiltsie/NGIC; 277 (LO LE), James P. Blair/NGIC; 277 (LO CTR), Bill Hatcher/NGIC; 277 (LO RT), Carsten Peter/NGIC; 278, Michel & Christine Denis-Huot/Biosphoto; 279 (UP), Olena Zn/AS; 279 (CTR LE), Alamy/MP; 279 (CTR RT), Reuters/ASP; 279 (LO LE), Chris Philpot; 279 (LO RT), David Havel/SS; 282, Mike Theiss/NGIC; 283 (UP), Ryan Rossotto/Stocktrek Images/NGIC; 283 (CTR LE), Daniel P. Zitterbart/Woods Hole Oceanographic Institution; 283 (CTR RT), Michel Roggo/Nature Picture Library/Science Source; 283 (LO LE), Chris Philpot; 283 (LO RT), Antony Gilbert; 286, Antonio Ribeiro/Gamma-Rapho/GI; 287 (UP), Arsgera/AS; 287 (CTR LE), rudiernst/AS; 287 (CTR RT), Visual China Group/VCG/GI; 287 (LO LE), Chris Philpot; 287 (LO RT), R.M. Nunes/AS; 290, slowmotiongli/SS; 291 (UP), Andrew Watson/John Warburton-Lee Photography/ASP; 291 (CTR LE), Adwo/AS; 291 (CTR RT), imageBROKER/ASP; 291 (LO LE), Chris Philpot; 291 (LO RT), Stephen Belcher/MP; 294, Andy Trowbridge/Nature Picture Library; 295 (UP RT), Roy Pedersen/SS; 295 (CTR LE), drhfoto/AS; 295 (CTR RT), gmsphotography/Moment/GI; 295 (LO RT), Leonardo Papera/AWL Images; 298, Yaacov Dagan/ASP; 299 (UP), Dina Julayeva/SS; 299 (CTR LE), Life on white/ASP; 299 (CTR RT), Kitchin and Hurst/All Canada Photos/ASP; 299 (LO), Jim West/ASP; 302, Ecuadorpostales/SS; 303 (UP), Soberka Richard/hemis.fr/GI; 303 (CTR LE), Felipe Bittioli; 303 (CTR RT), Sarmat/AS; 303 (LO RT), Anderson Spinelli/iStock/GI; 308 (LO), Steven M Lang/SS; 311, Ondrej Prosicky/SS; 315 (LO), elxeneize/AS; 316, Sean Hsu/SS; 319, Mehmet0/SS; 322 (LO), bbtomas/AS; 325, DaLiu/SS; 330 (LO), TTstudio/AS; 332 (UP), VCG/GI; 332 (LO), Brian Lawrence/GI; 333 (UP LE), PoohFotoz/SS; 333 (UP RT), Anne-BrittSvinnset/GI; 333 (CTR LE), Claudia Beretta/age fotostock; 333 (CTR RT), vichie81/SS; 333 (LO LE), Songquan Deng/SS; 333 (LO RT), DeadDuck/GI; 334 (UP LE), blickwinkel/ASP; 334 (UP RT), Michele Falzone/ASP; 334 (CTR RT), George-hopkins/DR; 334 (LO LE), Pascal Franck/SS; 334 (LO CTR LE), Eric Nathan/ASP; 334 (LO CTR RT), Exactostock/SuperStock; 334 (LO RT), Kasia Nowak/ASP; 335 (UP LE), Arco Images GmbH/ASP; 335 (UP RT), Julia Mcclunie/DR; 335 (UP CTR LE), Andrzej Tokarski/DR; 335 (UP CTR RT), Igorkov/DR; 335 (LO LE), Tupungato/DR; 335 (LO CTR LE), Jpldesigns/DR; 335 (LO CTR RT), Mikael Damkier/DR; 335 (LO RT), Christian Mueller/SS; 336, Alex Mustard/Nature Picture Library; 336 (LO LE), Wild Wonders of Europe/Lundgre/Nature Picture Library; 337 (A), Keith Levit/GI; 337 (B), Design Pics Inc./NGIC; 337 (C), Manfred Gottschalk/GI; 337 (D), AndamanSE/GI; 337 (E), ToniFlap/GI; 337 (F), Claudio Contreras/NPL/MP; 338 (UP), Courtesy of Yunak Evleri Cave Hotel; 338 (LO RT), Courtesy of Yunak Evleri Cave Hotel; 339 (UP), Red De Hoteles Tayka; 339 (INSET), Red De Hoteles Tayka; 339 (LO), Red De Hoteles Tayka; 340, Aschen/GI; 341 (BACKGROUND), JC Photo/SS; 342–343 (BACKGROUND), dpa picture alliance archive/ASP; 342 (UP RT), stock_photo_world/SS; 342 (LO CTR), Zhang Bingtao/Xinhua Press/Corbis; 342 (LO CTR), Xinhua Press/Landov; 343 (RT), Jean-Christophe Godet/GI; 343 (LO RT), Mike Greenslade/Australia/Alamy; 344 (UP LE), Leonid Andronov/AS; 344 (UP RT), Jenifoto/AS; 344 (LO LE), Crea il tuo web/AS; 344 (LO RT), gudkovandrey/AS; 345 (UP LE), Stefan/AS; 345 (UP RT), AnKudi/AS; 345 (CTR LE), Jaahnlieb/DR; 345 (LE), KK/AS; 345 (LO), photlook/AS; 346 (UP), Alexmama/SS; 346 (LO), Zack Frank/SS; 347 (UP LE), Reuters/ASP; 347 (UP RT), Gabriela Maj/Bloomberg via GI; 347 (CTR LE), RIA Novosti/TopFoto/The Image Works; 347 (CTR RT), jirawatfoto/SS; 347 (LO LE), Wiskerke/ASP; 347 (LO RT), saiko3p/SS; 348 (UP), The Picture Art Collection/ASP; 348 (CTR), History and Art Collection/ASP; 348 (LO LE), PCN Black/PCN Photography/ASP; 348 (LO RT), Maria Grazia Casella/ASP; 349 (UP), APA-PictureDesk/ASP; 349 (CTR), Yohei Osada/AFLO/SS; 349 (LO), Thomas Dutour/AS; 350 (UP LE), Susana Gonzalez/Corbis; 350 (UP RT), Design Pics Inc/ASP; 350 (LO), Laszlo Balogh/Reuters; 351 (A), sculpies/GI; 351 (B), Archives Charmet/Bridgeman Images; 351 (C), Archives Charmet/Bridgeman Images; 351 (D), Archives Charmet/Bridgeman Images; 351 (E), Bridgeman Images; 351 (F), Archives Charmet/Bridgeman Images; 351 (G), Dea Picture Library/GI; 351 (H), Holger Mette/SS; 351 (I), Holger Mette/SS; 351 (J), Jarno Gonzalez Zarraonandia/SS; 351 (K), David Iliff/SS; 351 (L), ostill/SS; 351 (M), Hannamariah/SS; 351 (N), Jarno Gonzalez Zarraonandia/SS; 352 (UP LE), Thomas Dutour/AS; 352 (LO), Life on white/ASP; 352 (LO RT), Erik Lam/SS

359

Boldface indicates illustration; **boldface** page spans include text and illustrations.

A

Abu Dhabi, United Arab Emirates 347, **347**
Acacia trees 196, **196**
Activities and projects
    games and puzzles 128–147
    make a telescope 30–31, **30–31**
Adélie penguins 50–52
Adirondack Balloon Festival, Glens Falls, New York, U.S.A. 175, **175**
Afghanistan 251, 252, 306
Africa 215, **278–281**
African Americans 170
African gray parrots 54, **54**
African killifish 42, **42**
African lions 69, **69**
African penguins 52, **52**
Agama lizards 62, **62**
AI (artificial intelligence) 22, **22**
Air travel 335, **335**
Airbus (company) 193
Al Qaeda 251
Alaska, U.S.A. **137**, 160, 277, **277**, 350, **350**
Albania 252, 306
Alberta, Canada 12, **12**
Albuquerque International Balloon Fiesta, New Mexico, U.S.A. 175, **175**
Aldar (company) 347, **347**
Alexandria, Egypt 241, **241**, 351, **351**
Algarrobo, Chile 343, **343**
Algeria 252, 306
Aliens 93, **93**
All Saints' Day/All Hallows' Eve 172–173
Alligators 141, **141**
Allosaurus 83, **83**
Almonds 176, **176**
Alternative energy *see* Renewable energy
Amazon (company) 22, **22**
Amazon Basin, South America 78–79, **78–79**, 116, **268–269**, 303, **303**
American Civil War 115, **115**, 250
American Revolution 250
Amphibians
    classification 44, **44**, 45, **45**
    frogs 45, 56–57, **56–57**, 150, **150**, **155**, 224, **224**, 303, **303**
    jokes 155
    myths busted 39, **39**
    salamanders 44, **44**, 57, 299, **299**, 352, **352**
    toads 39, **39**, 42, **42**
    tongue twisters 150, **150**
    translucent 56–57, **56–57**
Amur leopards 130, **130**
Amusement parks and rides 343, **343**
Anacondas 337, **337**
Anchorage, Alaska, U.S.A. 350, **350**
Ancient world
    beliefs 182–183, **182–183**, 186, **186**
    China 178, **178**, 241, **241**
    Egypt 238–239, **238–239**, 241, **241**, 245, **245**, 266, **266**, 279, **279**, 351, **351**
    Greece 158, 182–183, **182–183**, 186, **186**, 241, **241**, 348, **348**, 351, **351**
    holidays 172, **172**
    Maya 242–243, **242–243**, 266, **266**, 344, **344**, 351, **351**
    money 178, **178**

Rome 172, **172**, 241, **241**, 335, **335**, 351, **351**
wonders of the world 338, 351, **351**
Andorra 252, 306
Anemones 119, **119**
Angel Falls, Venezuela 331
Angkor Wat, Cambodia 287, **287**
Angola 252, 306
Angry Birds 175, **175**
Animals **34–85**
    in action 74–75, **74–75**
    animal fun **36–43**
    careers with 110–113, 121, **121**
    classification 44–45, **44–45**, 195, **195**
    color vision 13, **13**
    cute animals 204–205, **204–205**, 210, **210**
    extinctions 76, **137**
    friendships 58–59, **58–59**
    fun and games 128–138, **141–147**
    homework help 85
    jokes 148–163
    losing teeth 200, **200**
    on money 178, **178**, 179, **179**
    myths 39, **39**
    oddities 47, **47**
    in peril 44, **46–49**
    photography of 118–120, **118–120**, 126, **126**
    quiz 84
    rescues by 75, **75**
    rescues of 72–73, **72–73**, 233, **233**
    standout species **54–57**
    tail facts 63, **63**
    tips to help them 60–61, **60–61**, 117, **117**
    in the water **50–53**
    in the wild **60–63**
    World Wildlife Day 16, **16**
    see also Dinosaurs; Pets; specific animals
Ankylosaurus 83, **83**, 131, **131**
Antarctic krill 136, **136**
Antarctica **282–285**
    deepest lake 287
    as desert 217, 234, **234**
    exploration 122–123, **122–123**, 216–217, **216–217**
    map 284–285
    overview 282–284
    Southern Ocean 219, **219**
    wildlife 2, **2–3**, 50–53, **50–53**, 119, **119**, 136, **136**, 205, **205**, 217, **217**, 219, **219**, 282, **282**, 283
    young explorer 114, **114**, 115, **115**
Antelope 27
Antigua and Barbuda 252, 306
Ants 55, **55**, 67, **67**, 113, 196, **196**
Apple (company) 21, **21**, 22
Apples 177, **177**
Apps 211
Aquariums 117
Arce Catacora, Luis Alberto 253
Archaea 195, **195**
Archaeological discoveries **23–27**, 32, 111, **111**, 241–245, 248–249, **248–249**
Arctic foxes 204, **204**
Arctic Ocean 151, **151**, 219, **219**
Argentina 81, **81**, 252, 277, 307
Arizona, U.S.A. 221, **221**, 345, **345**
Armenia 252, 307
Army ants 55, **55**
Art 16, **16**, 37, **37**, 140, 197, **197**
Artemis, Temple of, Ephesus, Türkiye 338, 351, **351**
Arthropods 45, **45**
Artificial intelligence (AI) 22, **22**

Asia 181, 186, **286–289**
Asparagus 176, **176**
Assateague Island, Maryland, U.S.A. 340
Asteroids 88
Astrology 171, **171**
Astronauts 94, **94**, 152
Astronomy *see* Space
Atlantic Ocean 218, **218**
Atlantis (legendary island) 245, **245**
Auroras 29, **29**, 32, **32**, 225, **225**, 295, **295**
Austin, Texas, U.S.A. 334, **334**
Australia
    geology 221, **221**
    government leaders 252
    Great Barrier Reef 341, **341**
    Indigenous dancers **291**
    Lake Hillier (pink lake) 221, **221**, 234, **234**
    map 292–293
    money 179, **179**
    overview (continent) **290–292**
    overview (country) 307
    travel 335, **335**, 341, **341**
    wars 251
    wildfires 233
    wildlife 42, **42**, 108–110, 205, **205**, 233, **233**, 290, **290**, 335, **335**
Austria 252, 307
Automobiles 17, **140**, 191, **191**, 192, **192**
Axolotls 299, **299**, 352, **352**
Azerbaijan 253, 307, 346, **346**
Aztec 179

B

Bacteria 194, 195, **195**, 202, 203
Bahá'í Faith 347, **347**
Bahamas 179, **179**, 253, 307
Bahrain 253, 307
Baikal, Lake, Russia 287
Baku, Azerbaijan 346, **346**
Balloons 174–175, **174–175**, 350, **350**
Bamberg, Germany 315, **315**
Bananas 176, **176**
Bangkok, Thailand 335, **335**, 347, **347**
Bangladesh 253, 307
Baobab trees 196
Barbados 253, 308, **308**
Barreleye fish **57**
Barringer Crater, Arizona, U.S.A. 221, **221**
Basalt rock 100, **100**
Baseball 163, **163**
Basega (festival) 170
Basketball 157, 163
Bath, England, U.K. 335, **335**
Bats 43, **43**, 113, **113**, 334, **334**
Beaches 117, **117**, 240, **240**, 340, **340**
Bearded seals 151, **151**
Bears 12, **12**, 160, **160**, 223, **223**, 254, **254**
Beavers **155**
Bees 13, **13**, 61, **61**, 67, **67**, 124, **124**, **334**
Beetles 66, **66**, 132, **132**, 337, **337**
Beijing, China 193, **193**, 206
Belarus 253, 308, 347, **347**
Belgium 253, 308
Belize 242, 253, 308
Bengal tigers 69, **69**
Benin 253, 309
Berger, Lee **23–27**
Berger, Matthew 26
Berger, Megan 24
Bezos, Jeff 209
Bhutan 253, 309
Bicycling 137, **137**, 140, 299, **299**

Big cats 68–73, 200, **200**; *see also* Cheetahs; Jaguars; Lions; Snow leopards; Tigers
Bikes and biking *see* Bicycling
Bin Laden, Osama 251
Biographies 267
Biology **194–205**
    biomes **214–217**
    domains of life 195, **195**, 210
    human body **198–205**
    plants 196–197, **196–197**, 210, **210**
    what is life? 194, **194**
Bioluminescence 64–65, **64–65**, 84, **84**
Biomes **214–217**
Birds
    animal friendships 59, **59**
    color vision 13, **13**
    definition and example 45, **45**
    digits 201
    endangered 44, 48–49, **48–49**
    fun and games 130, **130**, **134–135**, 136, **136**
    Great Barrier Reef, Australia 341
    intelligent 54, **54**, 55, **55**
    jokes 158, **158**
    photography of 118, **118**, 119, **119**
    superlatives 40, **40**, 41, **41**, 43, **43**
    tails 63
    tips to help them 60, **60**
    see also specific birds
Bjelland, Amanda 75
Black Americans 170
Black-backed jackals 278, **278**
Black bears 12, **12**
Black holes 93, **93**, 106, **106**
Black mustard 37, **37**
Blackbeard (pirate) 141
Blimp 132
Blue Hole, Jamaica 258, **258**
Bobcats 70, 71, **71**
Body *see* Human body; Medicine and health
Boko, Duma 253
Bolivia 221, **221**, 253, 303, **303**, 309, 339, **339**
Bomb cyclones 232, **232**
Bombardier beetles 66, **66**
Borate 99, **99**
Bosnia and Herzegovina 253, 309
Boston, Massachusetts, U.S.A. 232
Botswana 253, 309
Bottiglieri, Joe 73
Bottlenose dolphins 75, **75**, 218
Boudhanath Temple, Nepal 287
Bound, Mensun 123
Brachiosaurus 80, 82, **82**, 154
Braille 16, **16**
Braille, Louis 16
Brain, human 177, 191, 198, 204–205
Brain, robot 191, **191**
Brain, spider 47, **47**
Brazil
    Amazon rainforest **268–269**
    capoeira 302
    coins, flag, stamps 187
    geode rock 100, **100**
    Iguazú Falls 277
    Lençóis Maranhenses National Park 303, **303**
    overview 309
    president 253
    rainforest cultures 337
    travel 335, **335**, 351, **351**
    wildlife 110, 118, **118**
Breakthroughs **18–33**
    discoveries **20–25**
    homework help 33

360

INDEX

quiz 32
research 26–31
Bridges 332–334, 343, **343**
Brown howler monkeys 110, **111**
Brown-throated sloths 178, **178**
Brunei 253, 309
Bryce Canyon National Park, Utah, U.S.A. 344, **344**
Buckskin Gulch, Utah, U.S.A. 277, **277**
Budapest, Hungary 350, **350**
Buddhism 168, **168**, 184, **184**
Buffalo, New York, U.S.A. 283
Buildings
    bizarre buildings 346–347, **346–347**
    earthquake protection 335, **335**
    fun and games **140**
    future 190, 191
    supersize sites 342–343, **342–343**
    3D-printed 11, **11**, 192–193, **192–193**
Bulgaria 113, **113**, 253, 309
Bullhorn acacia trees 196, **196**
Burana, Kyrgyzstan 319
Burj Khalifa, Dubai, United Arab Emirates 342, **342**
Burkina Faso 170, 253, 309
Burma (Myanmar) 260, 322
Burundi 254, 309
Butter, as money 179, **179**
Butterflies 61, **61**, 62, **62**, 179, **179**
Buzatto, Bruno Alves 110, **110**

C

Cabo Verde 254, 310
Cactus 345, **345**
Caddisflies 67, **67**
Caesarea, Israel 241, **241**
Calendars 16, **16**, 95, 166–167, **166–167**
California, U.S.A.
    amazing animals 36–37, **36–37**
    bomb cyclone 232, **232**
    burgling bear 12, **12**
    earthquake protection 335, **335**
    Glass Beach 340
    world's tallest tree 197, **197**
Cambodia 254, **254**, 287, **287**, 310
Camels 277
Cameras *see* Photography
Cameroon 254, 310
Camouflage 43, **43**, 134–135, 279, **279**
Canada
    coastline 299
    Eve Cone (volcano) 103, **103**
    fossils 299, **299**, 352
    government leaders 254
    money 178, **178**
    northern lights 295, **295**
    overview 310
    paleontology 12, **12**, 178, **178**
    travel 333, **333**
Canary Islands 22, **22–23**
Canberra, Australia 335, **335**
Candlemas 38
Cane toads 42, **42**
Caño Cristales river, Colombia 221, **221**
Cantor, Mauricio 112, **112**
Canyons 277, **277**
Capilano Suspension Bridge, Vancouver, Canada 333, **333**
Capoeira 302
Cappadocia region, Türkiye 338, **338**
Carbon dioxide 208
Carbonates 99, **99**

Cardinals 130, **130**
Careers 110–113, 120–121, **120–121**, 275, **275**
Carlsbad Caverns National Park, New Mexico, U.S.A. 345
Carnarvon, Lord 239
Carrick-a-Rede Rope Bridge, Northern Ireland, U.K. 332, **332**
Cars 17, **140**, 191, **191**, 192, **192**
Carter, Howard 238–239
Cartography 274–276, 353, **353**
Cartwheel galaxy 29, **29**
Caspian Sea 287
Castles 192, **192**, 236, **236–237**
Caterpillars 22, **22**, 62, **62**
Cats, domestic
    barking 47, **47**
    cute cats 204, **204**
    facial expressions 14, **14**
    fun and games 132, 141, **141**, **146–147**
    myths about 39, **39**, 84, **84**
    rescued by dog 75, **75**
    teeth 200
Cats, wild 68–73, 200, **200**; *see also* Cheetahs; Florida panthers; Jaguars; Lions; Snow leopards; Tigers
Cattle 116, **133**, **133**, 265, 291, **291**
Caudipteryx 21
Caves
    archaeology 111, **111**
    Bulgaria 113, **113**
    Carlsbad Caverns National Park, New Mexico, U.S.A. 345
    Fingal's Cave, Scotland, U.K. 295, **295**
    glowworm cave, New Zealand 64–65, **64–65**, 84, **84**
    hotel in 338, **338**
    Rising Star cave, South Africa 23–25
    shoe preserved in sheep dung 307
    stalactites 101, **101**, 220, **220**
Cell phones 21, **21**, 32, **32**, 61, 206
Celts, ancient 172, **172**
Cenozoic era 76, 77, **77**
Central African Republic 254, 310
Ceres (dwarf planet) 90, **92**
Chad 254, 310
Chang Building, Bangkok, Thailand 347, **347**
Charles III, King (United Kingdom) 179, **179**, 265
Chatbots 22, **22**
Cheese 179, **179**
Cheetahs 63, 68, **71–73**
Chefchaouen, Morocco 279
Cheng I Sao *see* Ching Shih
Cherrapunji, India 222
Chesapeake Bay, U.S.A. 118, **118**
Cheung Po Tsai 246
Chichén Itzá, Mexico 351, **351**
Chickens 160, **160**
Chile
    Easter Island 245, **245**, 248–249, **248–249**, 266, **266**
    Licancábur volcano 103, **103**
    overview 310
    president 254
    Santiago Cathedral 303, **303**
    travel 343, **343**
Chimpanzees 55, **55**, 199
China
    ancient China 178, **178**, 241, **241**
    astrology 171, **171**
    bizarre building 347, **347**
    civil war 251

Dragon Boat Festival 164–165, 165
drones 188, **188–189**
government leaders 255
Great Wall 286, **286**, 351, **351**
languages 181, 186
Mount Everest 277, **277**
Olympics 206
overview 310
pirates 246–247, **246–247**, 266
Rainbow Mountains 101, **101**, 106, 287, **287**
robots **18–19**
3D-printed house 193, **193**
travel 332, **332**, 343, **343**, 351, **351**
wildlife 130, **130**
Ching Shih 246–247, **246–247**, 266, **266**
Chinnawat, Phaethongthan 264
Cho, Sookyung 204
Chocolate 176, **176**, 179, **179**, 251
Christ the Redeemer statue, Brazil 351, **351**
Christianity
    cathedrals **303**, 307, 330, **330**
    divisions 184
    holidays 167, **167**, 170, 172, 184, **184**
Christmas 167, **167**, 170
Christmas Island crabs 291, **291**
Christo (artist) 333
Chromosomes 199
Chucarosaurus diripienda 81, **81**
Ciezarek, Anna 73
Cinder cone volcanoes 103, **103**
Circulatory system 198, **198**
Cirrus clouds 227, **227**
Civil War, U.S.A. 115, **115**, 250
Clarke, Lewis 114, **114**
Classification 44–45, **44–45**, 80, 195, 210
Cleopatra VII, Pharaoh 241
Climate 222
Climate change
    about 223, **223**
    Alaska, U.S.A. 277
    Antarctica 283, **283**
    dinosaur extinction 76
    energy impacts 23
    future technology 208–209, **208–209**
    quiz 234
    sea level rise 137
Clothes 191, **193**, **193**, 206–207, **206–207**
Clouded leopards 143, **143**
Clouds 225, **225**, 227, **227**, 229, **229**, 231
Clover 61, **61**
Clownfish 119, **119**, 218
Cnidaria 45
Coastlines, world's longest 299
Cobras 121
Cockroaches 66, **66**, 190, **190**
Cocoa 312
Cold-blooded animals 45
Coins 178–179, **178–179**, 187, 241, **241**
Colombia 221, **221**, 255, 310
Color vision 13, **13**
Colosseum, Rome, Italy 351, **351**
Colossus of Rhodes, Greece 351, **351**
Comb jelly 57
Common pigeons 59, **59**
Communication 10, **10**, 21, **21**, 32, **32**, 111, 127
Comoros 255, 310
Composite volcanoes 103, **103**
Computers 61
Concrete 17, 193, **193**
Condensation 226

Congo 255, 311
Congo, Democratic Republic of the 255, 312
Constantine, Rochelle 75
Constellations 95
Continents 270–273, **278–305**
Cookie Monster 100, **100**
Cookies 141, **141**
Coover, Harry 251
Cope, Alissa 37
Coral reefs 215, **215**, 240, 341, **341**
Corn 137, **137**
Cortina d'Ampezzo, Italy 16, 348–349, **348–349**
Costa Rica 178, **178**, 255, 311, **311**
Côte d'Ivoire (Ivory Coast) 255, 311
Cougars 68
Countries **306–331**
    government leaders 252–265
    quiz 352
    reports about 187
    world map 270–271
Coupons 179
COVID-19 vaccines 203
Cows 116, **133**, **133**, 265, 291, **291**
Crab Nebula 88
Crabs 291, **291**
Cretaceous period 77, **77**, 81
Croatia 255, 311
Crocodiles 79, 279, **279**
Crows 55, **55**
Crusades 250
Cryptobiosis 15, **15**
Cuba 255, 312
Cucula (asteroid) 88
Cultures **164–187**
    food 141, 170, **170**, 173, **175–177**, 179, **179**, 186, **186**, 302, **302**
    homework help 187
    hot-air balloons 174–175, **174–175**
    money 178–179, **178–179**, 187
    quiz 186
    rainforest cultures 337, **337**
    see also Art; Holidays and festivals; Languages; Religions
Cumulonimbus clouds 227, **227**, 231
Cumulus clouds 227, **227**, 229, **229**, 231
Curitiba, Brazil 335, **335**
Currency 178–179, **178–179**, 187, 240
Cuteness 204–205, **204–205**, 210, **210**
Cuyaba dwarf frogs 303, **303**
Cycling 137, **137**, **140**, 299, **299**
Cyclones 230, **232**, **232**
Cyprus 255, 312
Czechia (Czech Republic) 255, 312

D

Da Vinci, Leonardo 333
Dale, Joshua Paul 205
Dallol volcano 220, **220**
Danakil Depression, Eritrea and Ethiopia 220, **220**, 313
Dance 16, **16**, 291, **295**, **298**, 302
Danube River, Europe 295
Danyang-Kunshan Grand Bridge, China 343, **343**
Dar es Salaam, Tanzania 334, **334**
Darth Vader 174, **174**, 196, **196**
Davey, Owen 111
Davidson, Lloyd 48–49
Davis, Shani 348
Day of Reconciliation 167, **167**
Day of the Dead 299
Deforestation 242, **242**, 243
Delhi, India 316, **316**
Delia, Jesse 56, 57

361

Democratic Republic of the Congo 255, 312
Denali National Park and Preserve, Alaska, U.S.A. **137**
Denmark 255, 312, 333, **333**
Deserts 215, **215**, 234, **234**, 277, **277**
Detroit, Michigan, U.S.A. 192, **192**
Día de los Muertos (Day of the Dead) **299**
Diamonds 101, **101**
Díaz, Porfirio 250
Digestive system 198
Dinosaurs **76–83**
　classification 80
　color 21, **21**
　early 77, **77**
　extinction 76
　fun and games 131, **131**
　jokes 154
　last meal 12, **12**
　on money 178, **178**
　Mongolia 321
　newly discovered 81, **81**
　survival in the age of 82–83, **82–83**
　water supply 226, **226**
Diseases *see* Medicine and health
Divers and diving 336, **336**
Diwali (festival) 168–169, **168–169**, 186
Djibouti 255, 312
Djojohadikusumo, Prabowo Subianto 257
DNA 20, **20**, 199, **199**
Dnieper River, Europe 295
Dogs, domestic
　color vision 13, **13**
　exploration 122, **122**
　fun and games 146–147
　holidays 339
　paws smelling like corn chips 177, **177**
　rescuing cat 75, **75**
　surfing 36, **36**
　teeth 200
Doll's eye plant 196, **196**
Dolphins 55, **55**, 61, 75, **75**, 79, 218, 341
Dome of the Rock, Jerusalem **185**
Dome volcanoes 103, **103**
Domed land snail **57**
Dominica 255, 312
Dominican Republic 255, 312
Dominoes **140**
Dongzhi (festival) 170
Donkeys 74, **74**
Donoher, Dan 59
Double rainbows 228, **228**
Doughnuts 170, **170**
Dragon statues 334, **334**
Dragons 101, **164–165**, 165, 188, **188–189**
Drones 188, **188–189**, 193, **193**
Drums, 3D-printed 193
Dubai, United Arab Emirates 334, **334**, 342, **342**
Ducks 175
Duct tape 251, **251**
Dust storms 228, **228**
Dwarf planets **90–92**
Dwarf reed snakes 17, **17**

E

Eaglehawk Neck, Tasmania, Australia 221, **221**
Early humans **23–27**
Earth **96–107**
　homework help 107
　if aliens visited 93, **93**
　interior 96, **96**
　quiz 106

rocks and minerals **97–101**, 106, **106**
in solar system 88, 90, **90**
see also Turbulent Earth; Volcanoes
Earthquakes 103, 105, 190, 329, 335
East, Duncan 74
East Timor (Timor-Leste) 264, 329
Easter 184, **184**
Easter Island 245, **245**, 248–249, **248–249**, 266, **266**
Eastern gray kangaroos 335, **335**
Echinoderms 45
Echoes 95
Eclipses 95
Ecosystems 117, **117**, **214–217**, 344, **344**
Ecuador 112, 151, **151**, 255, 302, **302**, 313, 337
Edelweiss 345, **345**
Edmontosaurus 131, **131**
Egrets 118, **118**
Egypt 251, 255, 313
Egypt, ancient 238–239, **238–239**, 241, **241**, 245, **245**, 266, **266**, 279, **279**, 351, **351**
Eid al-Fitr 166, **166**
Eiffel, Gustav 339
Einstein, Albert 21
Éire (Ireland) 258, 317
El Hierro, Canary Islands 22, **22–23**
El Salvador 242–243, 255, 313
Elbe River, Europe 295
Electric cars 17, 192, **192**
Elements 161
Elephants 42, **42**, 160, **160**, 176, 200, 227, **227**, 347, **347**
Elizabeth II, Queen (United Kingdom) 179
Emeralds 100, **100**
Emperor penguins 2, **2–3**, **50–53**, 119, **119**, 136, **136**, 205, **205**, **219**
Endangered species 44, 48–49, **48–49**, 61, 137, **137**
Endocrine system 198
Endurance (ship) 122–123, **122–123**
Energy
　electric cars 17, 192, **192**
　fun and games 137, **137**
　fusion ignition 23, **23**
　future 190–191
　from poop 74, **74**, 84
　solar energy 10, **10**, 15, **15**, 190, 197, **197**, 207, **207**
　stored in concrete 17
　water power 22
　wind energy 22, **22–23**
England, U.K.
　buried treasure 241, **241**
　gray seals 295, **295**
　holidays 172
　London jokes 156
　Millennium Footbridge, London 333, **333**
　Poison Garden 196, **196**
　Sherwood Forest 197, **197**
　Stonehenge 244, **244**
　travel 335, **335**
　wars 250
　zoo powered by poop 74, **74**
English (language) 181
Enhanced Fujita (EF) Scale 231, **231**, 234
Environments 277, **277**
Epidemic 202
Equatorial Guinea 255, 313
Equinoxes 95, 166, **166**
Eris (dwarf planet) **91**, 92, **92**
Eritrea 256, 313
Essays 127, 187
Estonia 256, 313
Eswatini (Swaziland) 256, 313
Ethiopia 220, **220**, 256, 313

Etna National Park, Italy 344, **344**
Eucalyptus trees 291, **291**
Eukarya 195, **195**
Europe **294–297**
　maps 296–297
　overview **294–296**
European rabbits 59, **59**
Evaporation 226
Eve Cone, Canada 103, **103**
Everest, Mount, China-Nepal 104, 277, **277**
Exoplanets 17, **17**
Experiment design 107
Exploration **108–127**
　bloopers 112–113, **112–113**
　explorers **110–115**, 216–217, **216–217**
　homework help 127
　in the know 124–125, **124–125**
　no limits 122–123, **122–123**
　photography 118–119, **118–119**
　quiz 126
　ways to protect the planet 116–117, **116–117**, 126, **126**
　young explorers 114–115, **114–115**
Extinctions 76, 137
Extraterrestrials 93, **93**
Eyelash vipers **134–135**
Eyes 13, **13**, 47, **47**, 207, **207**

F

Farms 133, **133**
Farne Islands, England, U.K. 295, **295**
Feldspar 98
Ferris wheels 343, **343**
Festivals *see* Holidays and festivals
Fiji 256, 313
Fingal's Cave, Scotland, U.K. 295, **295**
Fingers 201, **201**
Finland 256, 314
Fire salamanders 44, **44**
Fire whirls 224, **224**
Fireflies 61, **61**
Fires 37, 84, 233, **233**
Fish
　clownfish 119, **119**, 218
　definition 45
　endangered 44
　fun and games 132, **134–135**, 142, **142**
　Great Barrier Reef, Australia 341
　hot-air balloon 175, **175**
　jokes 150, **150**, 156, **156**, 159, **159**
　Lake Malawi 320
　rays 337, **337**, 341
　science bloopers 113, **113**
　sharks 75, 142, **142**, 200, 341
　superlatives 41, **41**, 42, **42**
　tips to help them 61
　tongue twisters 163, **163**
　translucent **57**
Flame Towers, Baku, Azerbaijan 346, **346**
Fleming, Jay 118
Florida, U.S.A. 241, **241**
Florida panthers 61, **61**
Flowers 163, **163**, 196, **196**, 345, **345**
Food
　chocolate 176, **176**, 179, **179**, 251
　cocoa 312
　cultural aspects 141, 170, **170**, 173, **175–177**, 179, **179**, 186, **186**, 302, **302**
　in Egyptian tombs 238, **239**
　fun and games 132, 140, **141**

from insects 177, **177**, 186, **186**
jokes 150, **150**, 156, **156**, 157, **157**, 160, **160**
microwave ovens 251, **251**
from minerals 101, **101**
as money 179, **179**
plant power 16, **16**, 116, **116**
potatoes 89
in space 89, 94, **94**
teapot-shaped building 347, **347**
tongue twisters 162, 163
Forests 214, **214**, 242, **242**, 243, 327
Fossils **23–27**, 32, 78–79, **78–79**, 299, **299**, 352; *see also* Dinosaurs
Foxes 120, **120**, 204, **204**
France 250, 256, 314, 345, **345**, 349
French and Indian War 250
Freshwater biomes 214, **214**
Friday the 13th 16, **16**
Frogs **45**, 56–57, **56–57**, 150, **150**, 155, 224, **224**, 303, **303**
Fujita, T. Theodore 231
Fun and games **128–147**, 354; *see also* Laugh out loud
Fundy, Bay of, Canada 218, 299, 352
Fungi 113, 195, **195**
Fungus pants 64–65, **64–65**
Fusion ignition 23, **23**
Future world 190–191, **190–191**, **206–209**

G

Gabon 256, 314
Galápagos Islands, Ecuador 112, 151, **151**
Galápagos tortoises 151, **151**
Galaxies 29, **29**
Gambia 256, 314
Games and puzzles **128–147**, 354
Garbage 116–117, **116–117**, 340
Gazelles 344, **344**
Geckos 43, **43**, 44, **44**, 110, 279, **279**
Gelato 176, **176**
Gemstones 238, 312
Genes 199
Genome 20, **20**
Gentoo penguins 53, **53**, 282
Geode rocks 100, **100**
Geographic Information System (GIS) 275
Geography **268–353**
　continents **278–305**
　countries **306–331**
　geographic features 277, **277**
　homework help 353
　maps 270–276
　quiz 352
　travel **342–351**, **344–352**
Georgia (country) 256, 314
Germany 38, 236, **236–237**, 256, 314, 315, **315**
Geysers **105**
Ghana 256, 314
Giant Pacific octopuses **134–135**
Giant pandas 16, 130, **130**, 201
Giant phantom jellyfish 283, **283**
Gibbons 287, **287**
Gilardi, James 48–49
Giraffes 11, **11**, 63, 74, 142, **142**, 162, **162**, 205, **205**
Girl Scouts 141
Girsu, Iraq 23, **23**
GIS (Geographic Information System) 275
Gismondi, Rodolfo M. Salas 78–79, **78–79**
Giza, Egypt 245, **245**, 279, **279**, 351, **351**
Glaciers 208, 277, **277**
Glass Beach, California, U.S.A. 340
Glass frogs 56–57, **56–57**

362

INDEX

Glass octopus **57**
Glass shrimp **57**
Glasswing butterflies 62, **62**
Glens Falls, New York, U.S.A. 175, **175**
Global warming *see* Climate change
Glowworm Grotto, New Zealand 64–65, **64–65**, 84, **84**
Gnats 64–65, **64–65**
Gnatusuchus 79
Goats 37, **37**, 84, 322, **322**
Goodall, Jane 111
Gorgosaurus 12, **12**
Gorillas 61
Grand Mosque, Mecca, Saudi Arabia 185, **185**
Grasslands 215, **215**
Gravitational waves 21, **21**
Gravity 93, 94
Gray foxes 120, **120**
Gray seals 295, **295**
Gray squirrels 55, **55**
Great American Rail-Trail, U.S.A. 299, **299**
Great Barrier Reef, Australia 341, **341**
Great egrets 118, **118**
Great Pyramid, Giza, Egypt 279, **279**, 351, **351**
Great Sphinx of Giza, Egypt 245, **245**, 266
Great Wall of China 286, **286**, 351, **351**
Great white sharks 75
Greece 256, **295**, 314
Greece, ancient 158, 182–183, **182–183**, 186, **186**, 241, **241**, 348, 351, **351**
Green iguanas 58, **58**
Greenland 295, **295**
Greenland ice sheet 223, **223**
Grenada 256, 314
Groundhogs 38, **38**
Guadalajara, Mexico 298, **298**
Guatemala 242, **242**, 256, 314, 344, **344**
Guerin, Kyllian 115, **115**
Guinea 256, 315
Guinea-Bissau 256, 315
Guitars 156, **156**, 193, **193**
Guyana 257, 315, 344
Gymnastics 264

H

Ha Long Bay, Vietnam 101, **101**
Haboobs 228, **228**
Hail 224, **224**
Haines Shoe House, Pennsylvania, U.S.A. 347, **347**
Hair 141, 198
Haiti 257, 315
Halicarnassus, Türkiye 351, **351**
Halides 99, **99**
Halloween 172–173, **172–173**, 186, **186**
Hameister, Jade 115, **115**
Hamsters 146–147, 159, **159**
Hanging Gardens of Babylon, Iraq 351, **351**
HANNAH (design studio) 11
Hanukkah 167, **167**, 170, **170**
Hardie, AJ 111, **111**
Harlequin ghost pipefish **134–135**
Harpies (mythical creatures) 183, **183**, 186, **186**
Harry Potter movies 333
Haumea (dwarf planet) **91**, 92, **92**
Hawaii, U.S.A. **103–105**, 340
Hawaiian monk seals 61
Hawk moth caterpillars 62, **62**
Hawking, Stephen 93
HD 63433 d (exoplanet) 17, **17**

Health *see* Human body; Medicine and health
Hedgehogs **44**
Hempleman-Adams, Amelia 115, **115**
Hempleman-Adams, David 115
Henderson Waves bridge, Singapore 333, **333**
Henri, Grand Duke (Luxembourg) 259
Hermit crabs 61
Hersi, Asma Bile 73
Hichilema, Hakainde 265
Hieroglyphic scripts 245, **245**, 249
High Roller observation wheel, Las Vegas, Nevada, U.S.A. 343, **343**
Hillier, Lake, Australia 221, **221**, 234, **234**
Himalaya, Asia 104, 224, 322, **322**
Hinduism 168–169, **168–169**, **184–186**
History **236–267**
  homework help 267
  life in the past **238–249**, 266, **266**
  mysteries 244–245, **244–245**, 248–249, **248–249**
  quiz 266
  wars 115, **115**, 250–251, **250–251**
  world leaders 252–265
Holi (festival) 185, **185**
Holidays and festivals **164–173**
  bizarre events 350, **350**
  Bolivia 339
  calendar 16, **16**, 166–167, **166–167**
  Chinese horoscope 171, **171**
  Día de los Muertos (Day of the Dead) **299**
  Diwali 168–169, **168–169**, 186
  Dragon Boat Festival **164–165**, 165
  Easter 184, **184**
  Groundhog Day 38, **38**
  Halloween 172–173, **172–173**, 186, **186**
  Holi 185, **185**
  hot-air balloons 174–175, **174–175**
  mariachi festival 298, **298**
  Navratri 184, **184**
  New Year celebrations 166, **166**, 335, **335**
  parades **299**, 350, **350**
  winter feast facts 170, **170**
Homer 245
Homework help
  maps and atlases 353
  presentations 235
  science fair 107
  writing animal reports 85
  writing biographies 267
  writing country reports 187
  writing essays 127
  writing letters 33
  writing process analysis essay 211
Homo naledi **23–25**
Honduras 48–49, **48–49**, 242, 257, 316
Honeybees 13, 67, **67**
Hoodoos 344, **344**
Horner, Michael **275**
Hornets 67, **67**
Horoscope, Chinese 171, **171**
Horses 150, **150**, 340, **340**
Horseshoe bats 113, **113**
Horseshoe crabs 46, **46**
Hot-air balloons 174–175, **174–175**
Hot Water Beach, New Zealand 340
Hotels 338–339, **338–339**
Houses 11, **11**, 140, 190, 191, 193, **193**
"How-to" instructions 211

Howler monkeys **110**, 111
Huaynaputina volcano, Peru 105
Hubbard Glacier, Alaska, U.S.A. 277, **277**
Hula-Hoop 141, **141**
Human ancestors **23–27**
Human body **198–205**
  brain 177, 191, 198, 204–205
  color vision 13, **13**
  fingers 201, **201**
  freezing temperatures 217
  genes 199, **199**
  genome 20, **20**
  hair 141, 198
  quiz 210
  systems 198, **198**, 203, 210
  teeth 200, **200**
  see also Medicine and health
Human rights activists 267, **267**
Humpback whales 156, **156**
Hundred Years' War 250
Hungary 257, 316, 350, **350**
Hunter, Rick **24**
Hurricanes 222, **222**, 230, **230**
Hurwitz, Jonty 193
Hydro energy 22
Hydrothermal vents 225, **225**
Hydroxides 99, **99**
Hyperion (tree) 197, **197**

I

Iani smithi 81, **81**
Ibarrola, Agustín 197
Ice 217, **217**, 223, **223**, 283, **283**
Ice skating 261
Iceland 257, 316, 336, **336**
Igbo-Ora, Nigeria 279, **279**
Igneous rocks 97, **97**
Iguanas 58, **58**
Iguazú Falls, Argentina-Brazil 277, **277**
The Iliad (Homer) 245
Immune system 198, 203
The Incredibles (movie) 141
India
  archaeology 111, **111**
  City Palace, Udaipur 257, **257**
  desserts 101, **101**
  environments 277, **277**
  festivals and holidays 168–169, **168–169**, 185, **185**
  government leaders 257
  Jarawa people 337
  overview 316
  Taj Mahal 351, **351**
  temples 316, **316**, 347, **347**
  weather 222
  wildlife **334**, **334**, 345, **345**
Indian jumping ants 67, **67**
Indian Ocean 219, **219**
Indonesia
  coastline 299
  Korowai people 337, **337**
  overview 317
  president 257
  trees 291, **291**
  volcanoes 105, **105**
  wildlife 287, **287**
Indri **34–35**, 35
Indus River Valley, India 277, **277**
Insects
  bizarre bugs 66–67, **66–67**
  breaking down plastic 22, **22**
  careers with 124, **124**
  eaten by plants 196, **196**
  endangered 44
  food coloring from 177, **177**, 186, **186**
  fun and games 132, **134–135**
  importance of 125, **125**
  as jewelry 337, **337**
  jokes 150

  remote-controlled 190, **190**
  tips to help them 61, **61**
  see also specific insects
Intelligence, animal 54–55, **54–55**
International Balloon Festival, León, Mexico 175, **175**
International holidays 16, **16**, 350, **350**
International Space Station (ISS) 94, **94**, 106, **106**
Inventions and technology
  artificial intelligence (AI) 22, **22**
  clothing 206–207, **206–207**
  future world 190–191, **190–191**, **206–209**
  homework help 211
  robots 191, **191**, 208, 283, **283**
  3D printing 11, **11**, 191–193
  wartime inventions 251, **251**
Invertebrates 45, **45**; *see also* specific invertebrates
iPhone 21, **21**
Iran 257, 317
Iraq 23, **23**, 251, 257, 317, 351, **351**
Ireland (Éire) 172, 173, 258, 317
Iron Man 141
Iseo, Lake, Italy 333, **333**
Islam 166, **166**, 184, 185, **185**
Israel 241, **241**, 251, 258, 317
ISS (International Space Station) 94, **94**, 106, **106**
Istanbul, Türkiye 335, **335**, 338
Italy
  ancient Rome 172, **172**, 241, **241**, 335, **335**, 351, **351**
  cheese as money 179, **179**
  gelato museum 176, **176**
  government leaders 258
  Middle Ages 179
  overview 317
  travel 333, **333**
  volcanoes 344, **344**
  Winter Olympics 16, **16**, 348–349, **348–349**, 352
Ivory Coast (Côte d'Ivoire) 255, 311

J

Jackals 278, **278**
Jaguars 68, **68**, 69, **69**, 71, 118, **118**, 137, **137**
Jamaica 258, **258**, 317
James Webb Space Telescope 28–29, **29**, 32, **32**, 86, **86–87**
Japan 151, **151**, 170, 258, 299, 317
Japanese honeybees 67, **67**
Japanese macaques 130, **130**
Jarawa people 337
Javan gibbons 287, **287**
Jelly beans 132, 177, **177**
Jellyfish **57**, 283, **283**
Jerusalem 185, **185**
Jewel wasps 66, **66**
Jewelry, beetles as 337, **337**
Jewish people *see* Judaism
Joggins Fossil Cliffs, Canada 299, **299**
Jokes **148–163**
Jordan 251, 258, 317, 351, **351**
Joya de Cerén, El Salvador 243
Judaism 166, **166**, 167, **167**, 170, **170**, 184, 185, **185**
Jupiter (planet) 29, **29**, 32, **32**, 90, 91, 95
Jurassic period 77, **77**

K

K-pop music 327
Kaieteur Falls, Guyana 344
Kalahari Desert, Africa 41, **41**
Kangaloo, Christine 264

363

Kangaroos 200, 335, **335**
Kayapo 337
Kayle, Charly 36
Kazakhstan 113, **113**, 258, 317
Kaziranga National Park, India 345, **345**
Keel-billed toucans 311, **311**
Kenworthy, Gus **8–9**, 9
Kenya 128–129, 259, 318
Kenyan rock agama 62, **62**
Kermit the Frog 350, **350**
Khmer Empire 287, **287**
Killifish 42, **42**
Kings and queens 260, 261
Kiribati 259, 318
Kiwi fruit **132**
Koalas 143, **143**, 205, **205**, 210, 233, **233**, 290, **290**
Kohe-Love, Hiria 65
Komodo dragons 121, **121**
Köppen system 222
Korean War 251
Kosovo 259, 318
Krakatau volcano, Indonesia 105
Kraków, Poland 334, **334**
Krause, Kurt 64
Krill 136, **136**
Kristersson, Ulf 264
Kruger National Park, South Africa **263**
Kuwait 259, 318
Kwanzaa 170
Kyrgyzstan 259, 318, **319**

L

La Paz, Bolivia 339
Lakes 221, **221**, 234, **234**, 287, **287**, 328, 352
Languages
  Armenian 307
  Easter Island 245, **245**, 249
  Maya 242, **243**
  quiz 186
  spoken by world leaders 259
  weird but true! 180–181
Laos 259, 318
Larimar (gemstone) 312
Las Vegas, Nevada, U.S.A. 343, **343**
Laser Interferometer Gravitational-Wave Observatory 21
Latitude 353, **353**
Latvia 259, 318
Laugh out loud **148–163**; *see also* Fun and games
Lava 100, **100**, 212, **217**
Lava dome volcanoes 103, **103**
Leaf-nosed lizards **121**
Leaf-tailed geckos 43, **43**
Leatherback sea turtles 47, **47**, 219
Lebanon 259, 318
Lemon sharks 142, **142**
Lemurs **34–35**, 35
Lençóis Maranhenses National Park, Brazil 303, **303**
León, Mexico 175, **175**
Leonardo da Vinci 333
Leopard seals **283**
Leopards **68–71**, 130, **130**, 143, **143**
Lesotho 259, 318
Letters, writing for results 33
Liberia 259, 318
Liburd, Marcella 263
Libya 259, 319
Licancábur, Chile 103, **103**
Liechtenstein 259, 319
Life zones **214–217**
Lighthouse of Alexandria, Egypt 351, **351**
Lightning 89
Lightning bugs (fireflies) 61, **61**
Lillehammer, Norway **349**
Lily pads 303, **303**

Lima, Peru 335
Limestone formations 220, **220**, 344, **344**
Limon giant glass frogs **57**
Lincoln, Abraham 160
Lions 63, **68–71**, **128–129**, 150, 200, **200**
Lithuania 259, 319
Lizards
  animal friendships 58, **58**
  careers with 121, **121**
  endangered 44, **44**
  fun and games **134–135**
  geckos 43, **43**, 44, **44**, 110, 279, **279**
  Kenyan rock agama 62, **62**
London, England, U.K. 156, 241, **241**, 333, **333**
Longitude 353, **353**
Lorenz, Konrad 204
Losar (Tibetan New Year) 166, **166**
Lotus Temple, New Delhi, India 347, **347**
Lunar eclipses 95
Luray Caverns, Virginia, U.S.A. 220, **220**
Luxembourg 259, 319
Lynch, Heather 50, 51

M

Macaques 130, **130**, 334, **334**
Macarenia clavigera 221, **221**
Macaws 48–49, **48–49**, **134–135**
Mace, Fred 64
Machu Picchu, Peru 351, **351**
Madagascar **34–35**, 35, 43, **43**, 259, 279, **279**, 320
Magee, Aideen 59
Magnificent chromodoris nudibranchs **45**
Maiasaura **82–83**, 83
Mail 33
Major Oak (tree) 197, **197**
Make a Difference Day 166, **166**
Makemake (dwarf planet) **91**, 92
Malawi 259, 320
Malawi, Lake, Africa 320
Malaysia 175, **175**, 259, 320
Maldives 259, 320
Mali (empire) 240, **240**
Mali (modern country) 260, 320
Malta 260, 320
Mammals 44–45; *see also* specific mammals
Mammatus clouds 225, **225**
Manatees 60, **60**, 200
Mandarin (language) 181, 186
Mangroves 46
Manila, Philippines 335, **335**
Mansa Musa 240, **240**
Mantises 43, **134–135**
Maori people 64, 65
Map facts and features **274–276**, 353, **353**
Maps
  Africa 280–281
  Amazon Basin 303
  Antarctica 284–285
  Asia 288–289
  Australia, New Zealand, and Oceania 292–293
  Europe 296–297
  global climate zones 222
  Glowworm Grotto, New Zealand 64
  North America 300–301
  Ring of Fire 103
  scarlet macaw range 49
  South America 304–305
  world physical 272–273
  world political 270–271
Marathons 286, **286**

Marcos, Ferdinand "Bongbong," Jr. 261
Mariachi festival 298, **298**
Marine biome 215, **215**
Mars (planet) 89, 90, **90**, 106, 157
Marshall Islands 260, 320
Martens 294, **294**
Maryland, U.S.A. 118, **118**, 173, 340, **340**
Massachusetts, U.S.A. 232
Mattarella, Sergio 258
Mauna Kea volcano, Hawaii, U.S.A. 104
Mauna Loa volcano, Hawaii, U.S.A. 103, **103**, 104, **104**
Mauritania 260, 320
Mauritius 260, 320
Mausoleum at Halicarnassus, Türkiye 351, **351**
Maya 242–243, **242–243**, 266, **266**, 337, 344, **344**, 351, **351**
McNey, Mike 275, **275**
Medicine and health
  bacteria 194, 195, **195**, 202, 203
  battlefield medicine 251, **251**
  human genome mapping 20, **20**
  vaccines 203, **203**, 210, **210**
  viruses 47, 194, 202, **202**, 203
  world leaders 264
  see also Human body
Medieval period (Middle Ages) 158, 179, **179**, 315, **315**
Meerkats 41, **41**
Memory 177
Mendelssohn, Felix 295
Mercury (planet) 90, **90**, 95
Mesozoic era 76, 77, **77**
Metamorphic rocks 97, **97**
Meteor showers 95
Meteorites 221, **221**, 282
Mexico
  Aztec 179
  holidays and festivals 175, **175**, 298, **298**, 299, 350, **350**
  hurricanes 222, **222**
  Maya 242, **242–243**, 351, **351**
  overview 320
  president 260
  Revolution 250
  travel 334, **334**
  wildlife 299, **299**, 352, **352**
Mexico City, Mexico 299, 334, **334**, 350, **350**
Mica 98
Mice 13, 156, **156**
Michal, Kristen 256
Michigan, U.S.A. 192, **192**
Micronesia 260, 321
Microwave ovens 251, **251**
Middle Ages (medieval period) 158, 179, **179**, 315, **315**
Midsummer (festival) 166, **166**
Migrations 344, **344**
Milan (Milano), Italy 16, 348–349, **348–349**
Milky Way galaxy **88**
Millard, Anne 111
Minerals **97–101**
Minnesota, U.S.A. 192, **192**
Minsk, Belarus 347, **347**
Moai 248–249, **248–249**, 266, **266**
Mobile phones 21, **21**, 32, **32**, 61, 206
Mohamed Siad Barre 251
Mohammed VI, King (Morocco) 260
Mohamoud, Shukri Haji Ismail 73
Mohs, Friedrich 98, **98**
Mohs Hardness Scale 98, **98**
Moldova 260, 321
Mollusks 45, **45**
Monaco 260, 321
Money 178–179, **178–179**, 187, 240

Mongolia 260, 321
Monkeys 58, **58**, 63, **63**, 110, 111, 130, **130**, 334, **334**
Monotheism 184
Monsters 328
Montenegro 260, 321
Moon 31, **31**, 88, **88**, 95, 152
Morocco 81, **81**, 260, **279**, 321
Mosquitoes 150
Mossi people 170
Moths 22
Mountains 277, **277**, 320
Movies 141, **141**, 174, **174**, 333, 345
Mozambique 260, 321
Mpete, Maropeng **24**
Mulanje, Mount, Malawi 320
Mummies 238–239, **239**, 266
Musa, Mansa 240, **240**
Muscular system 198
Museums 176, **334**, **334**, 346, **346**
Mushrif-Tripathy, Veena 111, **111**
Music
  "Cave of Melody" 295, **295**
  Civil War, U.S. 115, **115**
  fun and games **140**
  jokes 156, **156**
  K-pop 327
  mariachi 298, **298**
  played by world leaders 261
  3D-printed instruments 193, **193**
Muslims *see* Islam
Myanmar (Burma) 260, 322
Mythology 182–183, **182–183**, 186, **186**
Myths, about animals 39, **39**, 84, **84**

N

Namibia 260, 322
Nandi-Ndaitwah, Netumbo 260
Narwhals **219**
NASA 28–29, **29**, 32, **32**, 86, **86–87**, 94, **94**, 243
Nathusius' pipistrelle bats 43, **43**
National parks
  Denali National Park and Preserve, Alaska, U.S.A. **137**
  Lake Malawi National Park 320
  Lençóis Maranhenses National Park, Brazil 303, **303**
  neat facts 344–345, **344–345**
  South Africa **263**
  Þingvellir National Park, Iceland 336, **336**
  world's tallest tree 197, **197**
  Yellowstone National Park, U.S.A. 105, **105**
  Yosemite National Park, California, U.S.A. 212, **212–213**
Natural disasters *see* Turbulent Earth
Nature **212–235**
  biomes **214–217**
  bomb cyclones 232, **232**
  explorer 220–221, **220–221**
  homework help 235
  oceans 218–219, **218–219**
  quiz 234
  turbulent Earth **230–233**
  water cycle 226, **226**
  weather **222–232**, 234, **234**
Nauru 260, 322
Navratri (festival) 184, **184**
Nebulae 28, **28–29**, 88
Neogene period 77
Nepal 185, **185**, 260, 277, **277**, 287, 322, **322**
Neptune (planet) 29, **29**, 88, 89, 91, **91**
Nervous system 198
Netherlands 141, 261, 323

INDEX

New Caledonian crows 55, **55**
New Delhi, India 347, **347**
New Mexico, U.S.A. 175, **175**, 345
New Year celebrations 166, **166**, 335, **335**
New York (state), U.S.A. 175, **175**
New York City, U.S.A. 114, **114**, 342
New Zealand
  beaches 340
  dolphins protecting swimmer 75, **75**
  glowworm cave 64–65, **64–65**, 84, **84**
  government leaders 261
  map 292–293
  overview 323
  sheep 291, **291**, 352, **352**
Newnham, Zoe 74
Nicaragua 261, 323
Nicklen, Paul 119
Niger 261, 323
Nigeria 261, 279, **279**, 323
Nile River, Africa 279, **279**
Nittono, Hiroshi 205
Nobel Peace Prize 267
Noboa Azín, Daniel 255
Noon, Steve 111
Nordhaus, Hannah 113, **113**
North America **298–301**
North Carolina, U.S.A. 245, **245**
North Korea 251, 261, 323
North Macedonia 261, 323
North Pole 115, **115**
Northern cardinals 130, **130**
Northern giant hornets 67, **67**
Northern glass frogs **56**
Northern Ireland, U.K. 332, **332**
Northern lights *see* Auroras
Norway
  butter as currency 179, **179**
  government leaders 261
  Leonardo da Vinci bridge 333, **333**
  northern lights 295, **295**
  Olympics 349, **349**
  overview 323
  wildlife 151, **151**
Nudibranchs **45**
Nuestra Señora de Atocha (ship) 241, **241**
N|uu (language) 180

O

Oak trees 197, **197**
Oceania **290–293**
Oceans
  animals **50–53**, 60, 61, **61**
  future floating cities 190, **190**
  hydrothermal vents 225, **225**
  jokes 157, **157**
  marine biome 215, **215**
  overview 218–219, **218–219**
  pirates 141, 246–247, **246–247**, 266
  rogue waves 224
  sea level rise 137
Octopuses 54, **54**, 57, 61, **134–135**
O'Higgins/San Martin Lake, South America 287
Oklahoma, U.S.A. 225, **225**
Olmec people 244, **244**, 337, **337**
Olympics **8–9**, 9, 16, **16**, 206, 259, 348–**349**, **348–349**, 352, **352**
Oma Forest, Spain 197, **197**
Oman 261, 323
Opossums 39
Oral reports 235
Orangutans **152–153**
Orbán, Viktor 257
Orcas 136, **136**
Orchid mantises **134–135**
Oregon Trail 115, **115**

Øresund Bridge, Denmark-Sweden 333, **333**
Ornithischian dinosaurs 80, **80**, 81, **81**
Otters **60**, 155
Outhouse race 350, **350**
Owls 39, **39**, **134–135**, 158, **158**
Oxides 99, **99**

P

Pachyrhinosaurus 178, **178**
Pacific Ocean 218, **218**
Pacifica, California, U.S.A. 36, **36**
Pakistan 261, 267, 323
Palau 261, 324
Paleoanthropologists **23–27**
Paleogene period 77
Paleontologists 78–79, **78–79**
Paleontology *see* Dinosaurs; Early humans; Fossils
Paleozoic era 76, **76**
Pallid scops owls **134–135**
Panama 261, 324
Pandas, giant **16**, 130, **130**, 201
Pandemic 202
Pangaea 76, 77
Pangatalan Island Marine Protected Area, Philippines 46, **46**
Panthers 61, **61**
Papua New Guinea 119, **119**, 261, 290, 291, **291**, 324
Parades **299**, 350, **350**
Paraguay 261, 324
Paris, France 349
Parmesan cheese 179, **179**
Parrotfish 240, **240**
Parrots 48–**49**, **48–49**, 54, **54**, **134–135**
Peacock spiders 143, **143**
Peacocks 43, **43**, 84, **84**
Peas **140**
Pee 94
Peña Palacios, Santiago 261
Penguins
  Adélie penguins **50–52**
  adjusting blood flow to keep feet from freezing 282
  emperor penguins 2, **2–3**, **50–53**, 119, **119**, 136, **136**, 205, **205**, 219
  fun and games 136, **136**
  gentoo penguins 53, **53**, 282
  robot following 283, **283**
Pennsylvania, U.S.A. 38, **38**, 347, **347**
Permafrost 15, **15**
Peru
  Machu Picchu 351, **351**
  overview 324
  paleontologists 78–79, **78–79**
  president 261
  Rio Los Amigos 277, **277**
  travel 335, **335**
  volcanoes 105
Peter, Carsten 216–217
Petra, Jordan 351, **351**
Petrologists 100
Pets 75, **75**, **146–147**, 159, **159**; *see also* Cats, domestic; Dogs, domestic
Phaethongthan Chinnawat 264
Pharaohs 238–239, **238–239**, 266, **266**
Philippines 46, **46**, 261, 291, **291**, 299, 324, 335, **335**
Phones 21, **21**, 32, **32**, 61, 206
Photo Ark 120, **120**
Photography
  cameras in contact lenses 207, **207**
  fun and games 130, **130**, 132, **134–135**, 140

wildlife 118–120, **118–120**, 126, **126**
Phytoplankton 208
Pigeons 59, **59**
Pigs 37, **37**, 54, **54**, 157, **157**
Pine martens 294, **294**
Pineapples 179
Pipefish **134–135**
Piping plovers 62, **62**
Pirates 141, 246–247, **246–247**, 266
Planets 29, **29**, 31, **31**, **89–92**, 95
Plants
  biomes **214–217**
  cactus 345, **345**
  classification 195, **195**
  communication 10, **10**
  flowers 163, **163**, 196, **196**, 345, **345**
  freaky 196, **196**
  for insects 61, **61**
  invasive 37, **37**
  lily pads 303, **303**
  rainbow river 221, **221**
  trees 196–197, **196–197**, 210, **210**, 214, **214**, 291, **291**
  Voynich Manuscript 245, **245**
Plasma 229, **229**, 234
Plastic 22, **22**, 60, **60**
Plate tectonics 103, 336, **336**
Plato (Greek philosopher) 245
Platypus 43, **43**
Plovers 62, **62**
Pluto (dwarf planet) **91**, 92, **92**
Poetry 262
Poison frogs **45**, 303, **303**
Poison ivy 196, **196**
Poland 261, 324, 334, **334**
Polar bears **160**, 223
Polytheism 184
Poop 74, **74**, 84, 112, **112**, 240, **240**, 307
Popcorn 157, **157**
Porcupinefish 41, **41**
Porcupines 39
Porpoises 341
Portugal 262, 324, 325, **325**
Potatoes 89
Prabowo Subianto Djojohadikusumo 257
Prairie gray foxes 120, **120**
Pratt, Cynthia A. 253
Precambrian time 76, **76**
Precipitation 215, 222, **224–229**, 335; *see also* Snow
Presentations 235
Process analysis essay 211
Protists 195, **195**
Ptolemy XII, Pharaoh 241
Puns 157
Punxsutawney, Pennsylvania, U.S.A. 38, **38**
Putin, Vladimir 251
Putrajaya, Malaysia 175, **175**
Puzzles and games **128–147**, 354
Pyne, Michael 233
Pyramids 279, **279**, 351, **351**
Pyrénées National Park, France 345, **345**
Pyrite 100
Pyroclastic flow 224, **224**

Q

Qatar 262, 324
Quartz 98
Queens and kings 260, 261
Queensland, Australia **291**
Quiz Whiz
  amazing animals 84
  awesome exploration 126
  breakthroughs 32
  fun and games 137, 141
  geography 352

history happens 266
science and technology 210
space and Earth 106
wonders of nature 234

R

Rabbits 59, **59**, 151, **151**, 157, **157**, 159, **159**
Raccoons **148–149**
Rahmon, Emomali 264
Railways 345, **345**
Rain 215, 222, 224, **224**, 226, **226**, 335
Rainbow eucalyptus 291, **291**
Rainbow Mountains, China 101, **101**, 106, 287, **287**
Rainbows 228, **228**
Rainforests 214, 290, 337, **337**
Ramadan 166, **166**
Ramsey, Samuel 124, **124**
Rapa Nui *see* Easter Island
Rats 47, **47**
Rays 337, **337**, 341
Recycling 61, 116, **116**, 192, 347
Red-shouldered macaws **134–135**
Redwood National Park, California, U.S.A. 197, **197**
Reefs 215, **215**, 240, 341, **341**
Religions
  ancient beliefs 182–183, **182–183**, 186, **186**, 238
  crusades 250
  holidays 166–167, **166–167**, 184–185, **184–185**
  world religions 184–185, **184–185**, 186
  see also specific religions
Renewable energy
  electric cars 17, 192, **192**
  fusion ignition 23, **23**
  hydro energy 22
  poop 74, **74**, 84
  solar energy 10, **10**, 15, **15**, 190, 197, **197**, 207, **207**
  stored in concrete 17
  water power 22
  wind energy 22, **22–23**
Reproductive system 198
Reptiles 44, **44**, 45, 121, **121**, 141, **141**; *see also* Alligators; Crocodiles; Lizards; Snakes; Turtles
Research *see* Breakthroughs; Science and technology
Respiratory system 198
Reticulated glass frogs **57**
Revolutionary War, U.S. 250
Rhesus macaques 334, **334**
Rhine River, Europe 295
Rhinoceroses 345, **345**
Ring of Fire 103, **103**
Rio Los Amigos, Peru 277, **277**
Rising Star cave, South Africa **23–25**
Rivers 221, **221**, 277, **277**, 279, **279**, 295
Roanoke Island, North Carolina, U.S.A. 245, **245**
Robin Hood 197
Robots **18–19**, 191, **191**, 208, 283, **283**
Rock climbing 114, **114**
Rocks and minerals **97–101**, 106
Rogue waves 224
Romania 262, 324
Rome, ancient 172, **172**, 241, **241**, 335, **335**, 351, **351**
Rome, Italy 294
Rongorongo (hieroglyphic script) 245, **245**, 249
Roosters 175
Rosemary 177, **177**

365

Roses 163, **163**
Round Island day geckos 44, **44**
Roundworms 15, **15**
Rubbish 116–117, **116–117**, 340
Rudenko, Andrey 192
Russia
    cats 47, **47**
    coastline 299
    deepest lake 287, 352
    frozen worms 15, **15**
    government leaders 262
    overview 325
    wars 250, 251
    wildlife 130, **130**
    Winter Olympics **8–9,** 9
Rwanda 262, 325

S

Saguaro National Park, Arizona, U.S.A. 345, **345**
Sahara, Africa 215, **277,** 278, 279
Sailing 115, **115**
Sakellaropoulou, Katerina 256
Saki monkeys 58, **58**
Salamanders 44, **44, 57,** 299, **299,** 352, **352**
Salar de Uyuni, Bolivia 221, **221,** 339
Salas Gismondi, Rodolfo M. 78–79, **78–79**
Salt flats 221, **221,** 339
Salt hotel 339, **339**
Samhain (festival) 172
Samoa 262, 325
San Alfonso del Mar seawater pool, Algarrobo, Chile 343, **343**
San Francisco, California, U.S.A. 335, **335**
San Marino 262, 325
Sand 240, **240**
Sand dollars 61
Santiago, Chile **303**
Sao Tome and Principe 262, 326
Sapporo, Japan 283
Sartore, Joel 120, **120,** 126
Satanic leaf-tailed gecko 279, **279**
Satellites 275, **275**
Saturn (planet) 29, 89, **90–91,** 91
Saudi Arabia 185, **185,** 262, 326
Saurischian dinosaurs 80, **80,** 81, **81**
Scarlet macaws 48–49, **48–49**
School *see* Homework help
Schwerin Castle, Germany 236, **236–237**
Schwinn, Petra 58
Science and technology
    bloopers 112–113, **112–113**
    homework help 211
    jokes 161, **161**
    quiz 210
    see also Animals; Biology; Breakthroughs; Earth; Exploration; Human body; Inventions and technology; Nature; Plants; Space
Scientific method 107
Scorpions 312
Scotland, U.K. 172, 175, **175,** 241, **241,** 295, **295**
Screech owls 158, **158**
Scuba diving 336, **336**
Sea *see* Oceans
Sea glass 340
Sea snakes 121, 341
Sea sponges 45, **45**
Sea stars 61, **61,** 179, **179**
Sea turtles 47, **47,** 61, **219,** 308
Seahorses 85, **85**
Seals 61, **61,** 136, **136,** 151, **151,** 162, **217, 283,** 295, **295**
Seattle, Washington, U.S.A. 137, **137,** 346, **346**

Secret Jazz Band 193, **193**
Sedimentary rocks 97, **97,** 106, **106**
Senegal 262, 326
Serbia 224, 262, 326
Serengeti National Park, Tanzania 344, **344**
Seychelles 262, 326
Shackleton, Ernest **122,** 122–123
Shah Jahan (Mughal emperor) 351
Shanghai, China **18–19**
Shanmugaratnam, Tharman 262
Sharks 75, 142, **142,** 200, 341
Shaw, Allyson **116,** 116–117
Sheep
    dung 307
    as hot-air balloon passenger 175
    "mowing" grass 10, **10,** 335, **335**
    outnumbering people 65, 291, **291,** 352, **352**
Shells 61, 117, **117**
Sherwood Forest, England, U.K. 197, **197**
Shield volcanoes 103, **103,** 104
Shintoism 184
Shipwrecks 122–123, **122–123,** 241, **241,** 291, **291,** 340
Shiraishi, Ashima 114, **114**
Shoes 193, **193,** 307, 347, **347**
Shrimp 152
Shuvuuia 321
Siad Barre, Mohamed 251
Siberia, Russia 15, **15**
Sierra Leone 262, 326
Signs 138
Sikhs 168, **168**
Silfra fissure, Iceland 336, **336**
Silina, Evika 259
Simina, Wesley 260
Singapore 197, **197,** 262, 326, 333, **333**
Sintra, Portugal **325**
Sirens (mythical creatures) 183, **183**
Sisoulith, Thongloun 259
Six-Day War 251
Skateboarding 137, **137**
Skeletal system 198
Skeleton flowers 196, **196**
Ski mountaineering (skimo) 349, **349**
Skiing **8–9,** 9, 114, **114,** 115, 334, **334,** 349, **349**
Sloths 162, **162,** 178, **178**
Slovakia 262, 326
Slovenia 262, 326
Smart clothes 206, **206**
Smartphones 21, **21,** 32, **32,** 61, 206
Smith, Joshua Aaron 81
Snails **57,** 162
Snakes
    anacondas 337, **337**
    careers with 121, **121**
    cartwheeling 17, **17**
    fun and games **134–135**
    Great Barrier Reef, Australia 341
    tails 63
    viruses 47
Snow 225, **225,** 229, 232, 278, 283, **283**
Snow leopards 42, **42,** 68, 69, **69**
Sochi, Russia **8–9,** 9
Social media 131, 136, 142–143, **142–143**
Softball 253
Solar eclipses 95
Solar energy 10, **10,** 15, **15,** 190, 197, **197, 207**
Solar system **88–95**
Solomon Islands 263, 326, 337
Solstices 95, 166, **166**
Somalia 72–73, **72–73,** 251, 263, 327

Somaliland 72–73, **72–73**
Somaweera, Ru **108–109,** 109, 121, **121,** 126
Songkran (festival) 166, **166**
South Africa
    Day of Reconciliation 167, **167**
    early humans **23–27**
    emeralds 100, **100**
    languages 180
    overview 327
    painting by pig 37, **37**
    president 263
    wildlife **263**
South America **302–305**
South China Sea 246–247, **246–247**
South Korea 251, 263, 327
South Lake Tahoe, California, U.S.A. 12, **12**
South Pole 114, **114,** 115, **115,** 282
South Sudan 263, 327
Southern Ocean 219, **219**
Soviet Union 250, 251; *see also* Russia
Space **86–95**
    astronauts 94, **94,** 152
    black holes 93, **93,** 106, **106**
    dwarf planets **90–92**
    exoplanets 17, **17**
    facts 88–89, **88–89**
    homework help 107
    jokes 152–153, 157
    moons 31, **31,** 88, **88,** 95, 152
    nebulae 28, **28–29,** 88
    planets 29, **29,** 31, **31, 88–92,** 95
    quiz 106
    sky calendar 95
    stars 28, **28–29,** 31, **31**
    sun 94, 95
    telescopes **28–32,** 86, **86–87**
    tongue twisters 163, **163**
    weird but true! 94, **94**
Space shuttle 89
Space umbrella 208, **208–209**
Spain 197, **197,** 250, 251, 263, 327
Spalla, Timothy 72
Spencer, Percy 251
Sperm whales 112, **112**
Sphinx (mythical creature) 182, **182**
Sphinx (statue) 241, **241,** 245, **245,** 266
Spider monkeys 63, **63**
Spiders 47, **47,** 110, **110,** 126, 143, **143**
Spinosaurus 83
Sponges 45, **45**
Sports
    basketball 157, 163
    capoeira 302
    fun and games **132,** 140
    jokes 157, 163
    marathons 286, **286**
    skiing **8–9,** 9, 114, **114,** 115, 334, **334,** 349, **349**
    surfing 36, **36,** 115, **115,** 144, **144–145,** 340
    swimming 343, **343**
    tongue twisters 163, **163**
    Winter Olympics **8–9,** 9, 16, **16,** 348–**349,** 348–**349,** 352
    world leaders and 253, 259, 261, 264
Squirrels 55, **55**
Sri Lanka **112,** 121, 184, **184,** 263, 327
St. Elmo's Fire 229, **229,** 234
St. Helens, Mount, Washington, U.S.A. 103, **103**
St. Kitts and Nevis 263, 327
St. Lucia 263, 327
St. Peter's Basilica, Vatican City 330, **330**
St. Vincent and the Grenadines 264, 328

Stalactites 101, **101,** 220, **220**
Star Wars (movie series) 174, **174,** 196, **196**
Stars 28, **28–29,** 31, **31**
Steger, Will 217
Stegosaurus 80
Stelladens mysteriosus 81, **81**
Stingrays 337, **337**
Stonehenge, England, U.K. 244, **244**
Storsjön, Lake, Sweden 328
Stoudt, Vesta 251
Strati (3D-printed car) 192, **192**
Stratovolcanoes 103, **103**
Stratus clouds 227, **227**
Streptococcus bacteria 194
Sturgeon 113
Styracosaurus **80**
Subianto Djojohadikusumo, Prabowo 257
Sudan 264, 328
Sudan, South 263, 327
Sulfates 99, **99**
Sulfides 99, **99**
Sumerian civilization 23, **23**
Summer Olympics 348
Summer solstice *see* Solstices
Sun 94, 95
Sun bears 254, **254**
Sunflowers **140**
Super Glue 251, **251**
Superb lyrebirds 63
Superman 162, **162**
Supermoon 95
Supertree Grove, Singapore 197, **197**
Supervolcanoes 104–105, **104–105**
Surfing 36, **36,** 115, **115,** 144, **144–145,** 340
Suriname 264, 328
Survival 82–83, **82–83**
Swahili (language) 170
Swaziland (Eswatini) 256, 313
Sweden 264, 295, **295,** 328, 333, **333**
Swimming 340, 343, **343**
Switzerland 184, **184,** 264, 328, 345, **345**
Sydney funnel-web spider 110, **110,** 126
Syria 251, 264, 328

T

Tagwerker, Andrea **349**
Tahua, Bolivia 339, **339**
Taiga 214
Taiwan 174, **174**
Taj Mahal, India 351, **351**
Tajikistan 264, 328
Taliban 267
Tamu Massif 104–105
Tanganyika, Lake, Africa 287
Tanzania 264, 328, 334, **334,** 344, **344**
Tarantula Nebula 28, **28–29**
Tasmania, Australia 221, **221**
Tasmanian devils 160, **160**
Taxonomy 44–45, **44–45,** 195, 210
Tayka Hotel de Sal, Bolivia 339, **339**
Teapot culture 347, **347**
Technology *see* Inventions and technology; Science and technology
Tectonic plates 103, 336, **336**
Teeth 27, **27,** 200, **200**
Tel Aviv, Israel 241, **241**
Telephones 21, **21,** 32, **32,** 61, 206
Telescopes **28–32,** 86, **86–87**
Temperature 222, 223, 230
Tennessee, U.S.A. 11, **11**
Termites 47, **47**
Texas, U.S.A. 11, **11,** 334, **334**
Texas horned lizards **134–135**

INDEX

Thailand 124, 166, **166**, 264, 328, 335, **335**, 347, **347**
Thames River, London, England, U.K. 333, **333**
Tharman Shanmugaratnam 262
Þingvellir (Thingvellir) National Park, Iceland 336, **336**
Thongloun Sisoulith 259
Thor (drone) 193, **193**
3D printing 11, **11**, 191–193
Thunderstorms 225, **225**, 228, **228**, 229, **229**
Tibet 166, **166**, 286
Tibetan New Year 166, **166**
Tidal disruption 93, 106
Tigers 41, **41**, 68, 69, **69**
Tikal National Park, Guatemala 344, **344**
Timor-Leste (East Timor) 264, 329
Tinorau, Tane 64, 65
Titanosaurus 83, **83**
Tiwanaku culture 339
Tlingit 337, **337**
Toads 39, **39**, 42, **42**
Togo 264, 329
Toilet paper 116, **116**
Toilets 60, 116, 350, **350**
Toji (Japanese celebration) 170
Tokayev, Kasym-Zhomart 258
Tonga 264, 329
Tongue prints 198
Tongue twisters 150, 160, 162, 163
Tornadoes 224, **224**, 225, **225**, 231, **231**, 234, **234**
Tortoises 151, **151**
Totem poles 337, **337**
Toucans 311, **311**
Trains 345, **345**
Translucent animals 56–57, **56–57**
Transpiration 226
Transportation 17, 137, **137**, 140, 156, 191, **191**, 192, **192**
Trash 116–117, **116–117**, 340
Travel **332–351**
 beach facts 340, **340**
 bizarre buildings 346–347, **346–347**
 bizarre events 350, **350**
 brilliant bridges 332–333, **332–333**
 city facts 334–335, **334–335**
 coolest dive 336, **336**
 fun and games 133, **133**
 Great Wall of China 351, **351**
 hotels 338–339, **338–339**
 national parks 344–345, **344–345**
 quiz 352
 supersize sites 342–343, **342–343**
 Winter Olympics 348–349, **348–349**
 wonders of the world 351, **351**
Tree houses 337, **337**
Trees 196–197, **196–197**, 210, **210**, 214, **214**, 291, **291**
Triassic period 77, **77**
Triceratops 131, **131**
Trinidad and Tobago 264, 329
Trojan War 245
Tromsø, Norway 295
Tropical royal flycatcher 41, **41**
Troy (ancient city) 245, **245**
Trudeau, Justin 254
Trump, Donald J. 265
Tundra 215, **215**
Tunisia 264, 329
Turbulent Earth **230–233**
 earthquakes 103, 105, 190, 329
 hurricanes 222, **222**, 230, **230**
 tornadoes 224, **224**, 225, **225**, 231, **231**, 234, **234**

typhoons 230
 see also Volcanoes
Turin, Italy 348
Türkiye (Turkey) 245, **245**, 264, 329, 335, **335**, 338, **338**, 351, **351**
Turkmenistan 265, 329
Turtles 47, **47**, 61, **108–109**, 109, 151, **151**, 219, 308
Tutankhamun, Pharaoh 238–239, 266, **266**
Tuvalu 265, 329
Tweety balloon 175, **175**
Twins 279, **279**
Typhon (mythical creature) 183, **183**
Typhoons 230
Tyrannosaurs 12, **12**
Tyrannosaurus rex 80, **80**, 82, 82–83, 131, **131**
Tzeltal 337

U

Udaipur, India 257, **257**
Uganda 265, 329
Ukraine 251, 265, 330
Ultraviolet (UV) light 13
Umbrellas 206, **206**, 208, **208–209**
United Arab Emirates 265, 330, 334, **334**, 342, **342**, 347, **347**
United Kingdom
 dinosaurs 81, **81**
 government leaders 265
 money 178, **178**, 179, **179**
 overview 330
 travel 332–333, **332–333**, 335, **335**
 wars 250, 251
 see also England, U.K.; Scotland, U.K.
United States
 history 173, **173**
 holidays and festivals 38, **38**, 173, **173**, 175, **175**
 languages 180
 money 178, **178**
 number of active volcanoes 298
 overview 330
 president 265
 travel 299, **299**, 343–347, 350, **350**
 wars 250, 251
Up (movie) 174, **174**
Uranus (planet) 88, 89, 91, **91**
Urchins 61
Uruguay 265, 331
Utah, U.S.A. 81, **81**, 277, **277**, 344, **344**
UV (ultraviolet) light 13
Uy, Michael 36, **36**
Uzbekistan 265, 331

V

Vacations *see* Travel
Vaccines 203, **203**, 210, **210**
Valleys 277, **277**
Vancouver, Canada 333, **333**
Vanilla 176, **176**
Vanuatu 265, 331
Vatican City 265, 294, 330, **330**, 331, 334, **334**
Vectipelta barretti 81, **81**
Vegetation *see* Plants
Velociraptor 82, **82**
Venezuela 170, 265, 331
Venus (planet) 90, **90**
Venus flytraps 196, **196**
Vermilion sea stars 61
Vertebrates 45, **45**
Victoria Falls, Zambia-Zimbabwe 221, **221**
Video games 175, **175**

Vietnam 101, **101**, 251, 265, 331
Vietnam War 251
Vikings 241, **241**
Virginia, U.S.A. 173, 220, **220**, 340
Viruses 47, 194, 202, **202**, 203
Visually impaired people 16, **16**
Volcanoes
 active volcanoes 298
 climate impact 209
 colorful crater 220, **220**
 eruptions **102–105**, 344, **344**
 lava flows 100, **100**
 pyroclastic flow 224, **224**
 Ring of Fire 103, **103**
 supervolcanoes 104–105, **104–105**
 types 103, **103**
 underground 340
Volga River, Europe 295
Volunteering 166, **166**, 316
Vostok, Lake, Antarctica 287
Voynich, Wilfrid M. 245
Voynich Manuscript 245, **245**

W

Waitomo Caves, New Zealand 64–65, **64–65**, 84, **84**
Walker, Adam 75, **75**
Warm-blooded animals 45
Wars 115, **115**, 250–251, **250–251**
Warthogs **263**
Warts 39
Washington, George 160, **160**
Washington (state), U.S.A. 103, **103**, 137, **137**, 346, **346**
Wasps 66, **66**
Water 214, **214**, 226, **226**
Water power 22
Waterfalls 212, **212–213**, 221, **221**, 258, **258**, 277, **277**, 331, 344
Watershed 303
Waterspouts 229, **229**
Watson, Jessica 115, **115**
Waves, rogue 224
Wax worms 22, **22**
Weasels 294, **294**
Weather **222–232**
 Antarctica 216–217
 bomb cyclones 232, **232**
 climate zones 222
 clouds 225, **225**, 227, **227**, 229, **229**, 231
 cyclones 230, 232, **232**
 extremes 222, **222**
 freaky forces 224–225, **224–225**
 future reports 206, **206**
 groundhog predictions 38, **38**
 hurricanes 222, **222**, 230, **230**
 quiz 234
 rain 215, 222, 224, **224**, 226, **226**
 snow 225, **225**, 229, 232, 278, 283, **283**
 tornadoes 224, **224**, 225, **225**, 231, **231**, 234, **234**
 typhoons 230
 water cycle 226, **226**
 weird weather 228–229, **228–229**
 see also Climate change
Weddell seals 136, **136**
Wellington, New Zealand 64
West Indian manatees **60**
Western Wall, Jerusalem **185**
Wetlands 214
Whales 112, **112**, 136, **136**, 156, **156**, 219, 341
Whipps, Surangel, Jr. 261
Whistle pigs 38, **38**
White-faced saki monkeys 58, **58**
Whittier, California, U.S.A. 37, **37**

Wienecke, Barbara 51
Wight, Isle of, U.K. 81, **81**
Wildebeests 344, **344**
Wildfires 37, 84, 233, **233**
Wildlife *see* Animals
Willem-Alexander, King (Netherlands) 261
Wilms, Birgitte 119
Wind energy 22, **22–23**
Window **132**
Winds 225, 230, 231, 232
Winter, Steve 118
Winter feast facts 170, **170**
Winter Olympics **8–9**, 9, 16, **16**, 206, 348–349, **348–349**, 352
Wisdom teeth 200, **200**
Witches 39, 158
Women 253, 256, 259, 263, 264, 349
Wonders of the world 338, 351, **351**
Woodchucks 38, **38**
World holidays 16, **16**, 350, **350**
World leaders 252–265
World maps 222, 270–273
World War I 250
World War II 250, 251
World's Fairs 176
Worms 15, **15**, 45
Writing
 animal reports 85
 biographies 267
 country reports 187
 essays 127
 letters 33
 process analysis essay 211
 by world leaders 262, 265
Wuxi, China 347, **347**

Y

Yellowstone National Park, U.S.A. 105, **105**
Yemen 265, 331
Yoda balloon 174
Yom Kippur 166, **166**
Yosemite National Park, California, U.S.A. 212, **212–213**
Yousafzai, Malala 267, **267**
Yunak Evleri Hotel, Türkiye 338, **338**

Z

Zambia 221, **221**, 265, 331
Zebras 63, 74, 344, **344**
Zeus statue, Greece 351, **351**
Zhangjiajie Grand Canyon Glass Bridge, China 332, **332**
Zhangye National Geopark, China 101, **101**, 287, **287**
Zhelyazkova, Violeta 113, **113**
Zimbabwe 221, **221**, 265, 331
Zodiac 171, **171**
Zoos 11, **11**, 58, **58**, 74, **74**, 84, 117, **117**

Copyright © 2025 National Geographic Partners, LLC

All rights reserved. Reproduction of the whole or any part of the contents without written permission from the publisher is prohibited.

NATIONAL GEOGRAPHIC and Yellow Border Design are trademarks of the National Geographic Society, used under license.

Since 1888, the National Geographic Society has funded more than 14,000 research, conservation, education, and storytelling projects around the world. National Geographic Partners distributes a portion of the funds it receives from your purchase to National Geographic Society to support programs including the conservation of animals and their habitats. To learn more, visit natgeo.com/info.

For more information, visit nationalgeographic.com, call 1-877-873-6846, or write to the following address:

National Geographic Partners, LLC
1145 17th Street N.W.
Washington, DC 20036-4688 U.S.A.

More for kids from National Geographic: natgeokids.com

National Geographic Kids magazine inspires children to explore their world with fun yet educational articles on animals, science, nature, and more. Using fresh storytelling and amazing photography, *Nat Geo Kids* shows kids ages 6 to 14 the fascinating truth about the world—and why they should care.
natgeo.com/subscribe

For rights or permissions inquiries, please contact National Geographic Books Subsidiary Rights: bookrights@natgeo.com

Designed by Kathryn Robbins

Trade paperback ISBN: 978-1-4263-7784-6

The publisher would like to acknowledge the book team:
Maya Myers, project editor; Ariane Szu-Tu and Lisa M. Gerry, editors; Sarah Wassner Flynn, writer; Lori Epstein, photo manager; Colin Wheeler, photo editor; Michelle Harris, researcher; Mike McNey, map production; Michael J. Horner, map editor; Joan Gossett, senior manager, production editorial; Yogi Carroll, production manager; and Lauren Sciortino and David Marvin, associate designers.

Printed in the United States of America
25/WOR/1